SYNTAX and SEMANTICS

VOLUME 13

SYNTAX and SEMANTICS

VOLUME 13
Current Approaches to Syntax

Edited by

Edith A. Moravcsik

Jessica R. Wirth

Department of Linguistics
University of Wisconsin—Milwaukee
Milwaukee, Wisconsin

ACADEMIC PRESS

A Subsidiary of Harcourt Brace Jovanovich, Publishers

New York   London   Toronto   Sydney   San Francisco

ACADEMIC PRESS, INC.
111 Fifth Avenue, New York, New York 10003

United Kingdom Edition published by
ACADEMIC PRESS, INC. (LONDON) LTD.
24/28 Oval Road, London NW1 7DX

LIBRARY OF CONGRESS CATALOG CARD NUMBER: 72–9423

ISBN 0–12–613513–4

PRINTED IN THE UNITED STATES OF AMERICA

80 81 82 83   9 8 7 6 5 4 3 2 1

CONTENTS

Epilogue: An Assessment   383

JESSICA R. WIRTH

Appendix: Basic Issues and Sample Sentences

LIST OF CONTRIBUTORS

Numbers in parentheses indicate the pages on which the authors' contributions begin.

ROBIN COOPER (19), *Department of Linguistics, University of Wisconsin—Madison, Madison, Wisconsin 53706*

SIMON C. DIK (45), *Institute for General Linguistics, University of Amsterdam, Amsterdam, The Netherlands*

WILLIAM A. FOLEY (329), *Department of Linguistics, Australian National University, Canberra, Australia*

LINDA K. JONES (77), *7500 W Camp Wisdom Road, Dallas, Texas 75236*

MICHAEL B. KAC (97), *Department of Linguistics, University of Minnesota, Minneapolis, Minnesota 55455*

SUSUMU KUNO (117), *Department of Linguistics, Harvard University, Cambridge, Massachusetts 02138*

DAVID LIGHTFOOT (137), *Department of Linguistics, English Institute, Rijksuniversiteit te Utrecht, Utrecht, The Netherlands*

JAMES D. McCAWLEY (167), *Department of Linguistics, University of Chicago, Chicago, Illinois 60637*

EDITH A. MORAVCSIK (1), *Department of Linguistics, University of Wisconsin–Milwaukee, Milwaukee, Wisconsin 53201*

DAVID M. PERLMUTTER (195), *Department of Linguistics, University of California, San Diego, La Jolla, California 92093*

xi

GERALD A. SANDERS (231), *Department of Linguistics, University of Minnesota, Minneapolis, Minnesota 55455*

PAUL SCHACHTER (267), *Department of Linguistics, University of California, Los Angeles, Los Angeles, California 90024*

ROBERT P. STOCKWELL (353), *Department of Linguistics, University of California, Los Angeles, California 90024*

WILLIAM J. SULLIVAN (301), *Department of Linguistics, University of Florida, Gainesville, Florida 32611*

ROBERT D. VAN VALIN, JR.[1] (329), *Department of Anthropology, Temple University, Philadelphia, Pennsylvania 19122*

JESSICA R. WIRTH (383), *Department of Linguistics, University of Wisconsin—Milwaukee, Milwaukee, Wisconsin 53201*

[1] PRESENT ADDRESS: Department of Anthropology, Research School of Pacific Studies, Australian National University, Canberra, ACT 2600, Australia.

PREFACE

This book contains papers from the Conference on Current Approaches to Syntax held on March 15, 1979 on the campus of the University of Wisconsin—Milwaukee and sponsored by the Department of Linguistics and the College of Letters and Science of that institution.

The intended goal of the conference was to bring together representatives of 14 of the currently practiced approaches to syntax, to have them present their theories described according to a set of uniform parameters, and to probe into the nature and significance of the differences that obtain among them. The conference consisted of the presentation of 16 papers. Of these, 14 were descriptions of the syntactic theories chosen. Each of these was followed by comments by a designated discussant. The remaining 2 papers were an initial introductory presentation on comparing syntactic theories in general and a final summary paper comparing the theories presented. The 14 principal speakers had been given a set of questions before the conference and were asked to describe their theories according to these parameters. They had also been given a set of 17 English sentences and were asked to produce a sample grammar for them stated in terms of their theories.

The 14 syntactic approaches, their representatives, and the designated discussants were as follows:

1. *Cognitive grammar*—presented by John Ross, Massachusetts Institute of Technology (a last-minute replacement for George Lakoff), and discussed by John Lawler, University of Michigan (a last-minute replacement for John Ross)
2. *Corepresentational grammar*—presented by Michael Kac, University of Minnesota, Twin Cities, and discussed by C. L. Baker, University of Texas
3. *Daughter-dependency grammar*—presented by Paul Schachter, University of California, Los Angeles, and discussed by Josh Ard, University of Wisconsin—Milwaukee
4. *Epiphenomenal grammar*—presented by James McCawley, University of Chicago, and discussed by Lawrence Horn, University of Wisconsin—Madison
5. *Equational grammar*—presented by Gerald Sanders, University of Minnesota, Twin Cities, and discussed by Ashley Hastings, University of Wisconsin—Milwaukee
6. *Functional grammar*—presented by Simon Dik, University of Amsterdam (The Netherlands), and discussed by Bernard Comrie, University of Southern California
7. *Functional Grammar*—presented by Susumo Kuno, Harvard University, and discussed by Jeanette Gundel, University of Hawaii
8. *Functionally interpreted base generated grammar*—presented by Michael Brame, University of Washington, and discussed by Thomas Wasow, Stanford University
9. *Montague grammar*—presented by Robin Cooper, University of Wisconsin—Madison, and discussed by Ivan Sag, Stanford University
10. *Relational grammar*—presented by David Perlmutter, University of California, San Diego, and discussed by Kenneth Hale, Massachusetts Institute of Technology
11. *Role and reference grammar*—presented by Robert Van Valin, Temple University, and William Foley, Australian National University, and discussed by Jerrold Sadock, University of Chicago
12. *Stratificational grammar*—presented by William Sullivan, University of Florida, and discussed by Henry Gleason, University of Toronto
13. *Tagmemics*—presented by Linda Jones, Summer Institute of Linguistics, and discussed by Alton Becker, University of Michigan
14. *Trace theory*—presented by David Lightfoot, University of Utrecht (The Netherlands), and discussed by Norbert Hornstein, Harvard University.

The speaker for the introductory talk was Edith Moravcsik, University of Wisconsin—Milwaukee; the summary paper was given by Robert Stockwell, University of California, Los Angeles.

This book contains revised versions of 12 of the 14 principal papers presented at the conference, arranged in alphabetical order by author. In addition, the book includes the general introductory and summary papers from the conference in revised form, an epilogue assessing what the conference and this volume have achieved, and an appendix containing the set of issues and the sample English sentences that the authors were requested to consider when writing their papers. By their own request, neither Brame's contribution nor Ross's is included. The designated discussants' comments and discussion from the floor do not appear in the volume for lack of space. However, a companion collection of the discussants' contributions has been compiled by Michael Kac and is being disseminated through the Indiana University Linguistics Club.

The conference was conceived as a sequel to the Conference on the Differentiation of Current Phonological Theories held September 30–October 1, 1977 on the campus of Indiana University in Bloomington, Indiana. We are grateful for the guidance and encouragement that we received from the organizer of the phonology conference, Daniel Dinnsen. The proceedings of that conference were published by Indiana University Press in 1979 under the title *Current Approaches to Phonological Theory,* edited by Daniel Dinnsen. We also gratefully acknowledge the generous support of the National Science Foundation, which funded the conference in toto (Grant No. BNS 7817098) and in addition saw fit to subsidize the publication of this book (Grant No. BNS 7817098 AOI) in order to facilitate wider dissemination of the papers from the conference through a lower-cost publication than would otherwise have been possible.

We feel that the book should provide useful reading and reference material for intermediate and advanced linguistics students on the undergraduate and graduate level, as well as for any scholar interested in syntactic theory, general linguistic theory, or the philosophy of linguistics.

INTRODUCTION: ON SYNTACTIC APPROACHES

EDITH A. MORAVCSIK
University of Wisconsin—Milwaukee

1. INTRODUCTION[1]

In recent years, the field of syntactic research appears to have been characterized by an abundance of new theoretical proposals, especially within the broad framework of transformational generative grammar. The present scene, at least in this country, seems to consist of a number of syntacticians all following different approaches most of which have not been shown to be superior to, or even distinct from, the others; while others of us do syntax "atheoretically"—that is, without explicitly adopting any particular conceptual framework.

Is there anything wrong with this situation at all? Are we not simply living an age of healthy diversity in the field of syntactic research? My feeling is that there is, indeed, nothing wrong with there being many different approaches to syntax—but only so long as the nature of the differences among them is clearly understood.

[1] This paper owes much to extensive discussions with Ashley Hastings, Barbara Wheatley, and especially with Jessica Wirth. I would like to thank them for their insightful contributions, and also to express my sincere gratitude to Jon D. Ringen for his willingness to read a draft of this paper and for his enlightening comments.

1

What exactly is the problem with unanalyzed differences among different syntactic theories? The problem appears to be simply this. All of us who are professionally involved with the study of language structure frequently face choices in our work that require an assessment of the relative values of different theories of syntax. In the absence of a clear understanding of how exactly various syntactic theories differ from each other, the choices that we are forced to make will turn out to be either random, or, most likely, more negative than they would really need to be. In what follows, I would like to briefly elaborate on these points.

Everyday situations abound where a syntactician faces choices whose rational resolution necessarily involves a comparative evaluation of various syntactic theories. Such common choices involve questions about what to read, what to teach, and how to do research. Suppose you are an adherent of tagmemics and you receive the Summer 1978 issue of *Linguistic Inquiry*, with David Dowty's article in it entitled "Governed Transformations as Lexical Rules in a Montague Grammar." Should you read it? Should you spend time and energy making your way through 33 pages of heavy-going highly technical text? Could a Montague grammarian say anything at all that may contribute to the professional goals of a tagmemicist? Or suppose you teach linguistics on the college level and you are scheduled to offer an introductory syntax course. What should be the syntactic approach that you suggest to your students as a fruitful framework for describing and explaining syntactic phenomena? Clearly, what you would like to familiarize your students with is the "best approach" since what you do may make the difference between turning students on to syntax and driving them away for good from this field of inquiry; but which of the many approaches is the best? Or, again, suppose you are an active researcher of syntax. What are the general assumptions that you can reliably make about syntax? What should be the framework within which you should investigate syntactic phenomena and present your results? Who should you do research WITH and who should you do research FOR? The decisions you make in these matters will at least in part be determined by your views about different linguists' theories and their relationship to your own. In other words, the interactional structure of the field is crucially dependent on how linguists assess differences among available theories; and the interactional structure of the field in turn crucially influences the efficiency and fruitfulness of work within the field.

Whereas these examples indicate that there are many situations where we are forced to make choices among various syntactic approaches for practical reasons, there is also the deeper, "nonpractical" question that underlies the above quandaries, that of what to "believe in." In other words, if I simply want to "think about syntax" as one of the many phenomena that jointly constitute our world, how exactly should I think about it? Our goal as syntacticians is to learn the true nature of syntax. But when different syntacticians appear to claim so many different kinds of truth, whose truth should I accept as my own truth?

This much so far suggests that once you are in the field of syntax, you cannot avoid having to evaluate different approaches. Although this by itself would suggest the necessity of a systematic investigation of the nature of the differences that obtain among different approaches, there is also a further motivation for such an investigation. This is that if choices are made in the absence of a clear understanding of these differences, they may not only turn out to be random, but would also probably be more negative than they would need to be. This I think simply follows from a fairly general tendency of people to view differences among various ways of doing things—whether they involve personal traits, social conventions, religions, or scientific theories—as differences between "right" and "wrong," rather than as differences between "one way" and "another way." As far as two syntactic approaches are concerned, it is of course possible that they differ in that one of them is right and the other is wrong; but this is not necessarily the case. Two syntactic approaches may be different without one of them being right and the other wrong. One of the less extreme types of substantive differences that may hide behind superficial differences is that both approaches are wrong—with some third approach being the right one. In other words, the claims of the two theories may be in a contrary, rather than contradictory, relation. Second, it is also possible that, of two different theories, both are right. This may be the case if their difference lies in that they deal with different kinds of data; or if their difference lies in that they aim at different goals with respect to the same or a different set of data; or if the seeming difference between the two theories is entirely superficial and does not hide any sort of substantive distinction—in which case the two approaches are simply notational variants, or paraphrases, of each other. And, finally, it should also be noted that the relation between two approaches may be complex, rather than simple, in that they may be substantively different in some of their aspects but identical in others; or they may be contradictory in some of their assumptions but contrary in others; and so forth.

The important point to realize is that recognizing the true nature of a difference between two syntactic approaches is crucial in that different interpretations of apparent differences call for different modes of coexistence among their practitioners. Whereas the adoption of the most extreme mode of interpretation, according to which the differences involve all-inclusive contradiction—total rightness versus total wrongness—will tend to generate seclusion or even animosity—the recognition of any of the less extensive and less severe difference types will invite various degrees and forms of cooperation among proponents. Thus, if two metatheories can be shown to be only partially, rather than fully, distinct in, let us say, their goals, there is still some room left for proponents of the two theories to cooperate with respect to those goals that they do share. Or, if the difference between the two metatheories turns out to hide different assumptions about what are relevant data to be accounted for, rather than different claims about the same data, openness and mutual tolerance, rather than rigid separation, may be in order. Or even if the difference does lie in opposing claims about the same data, just in case it can be shown that the two metatheories are contrary, rather than contradictory, in their claims, joint search for a third, true metatheory may be called for which would supersede both, rather than forcing a choice between the two existing ones. And, finally, if the two metatheories can be shown to be only notational variants, there should of course be nothing to prevent their proponents from simply merging their theories and resuming research with joint forces.

What I have attempted to show so far is that, given the present multitude of syntactic approaches, it is highly desirable that a systematic investigation concerning the nature of their differences be undertaken. This conviction was the motivating force behind the organization of the Conference on Current Approaches to Syntax held March 15–17, 1979 on the campus of the University of Wisconsin—Milwaukee and this is also the conviction that motivates the publication of the proceedings of the conference. What you will find in the following pages are presentations of 13 of the currently practical syntactic metatheories, followed by a concluding paper which takes up the question of comparison and evaluation explicitly along selected parameters.

There are two questions that most naturally arise in connection with any major endeavor that requires time, effort, and money. One is whether the intended goal is important enough. The other is whether it is possible to achieve that which is being aimed at. Whereas in the preceding pages I have illustrated the necessity of our goal, I shall now show that the comparison and comparative evaluation of different syntactic metatheories is not only necessary but also possible. In other words, if we would like to be able to evaluate comparatively, let us say, the standard theory of transformational generative syntax and Montague syntax, the question is: Are these two systems at all comparable? The answer appears to me to be an unambiguous yes.

How can we be really sure that any two syntactic metatheories are fruitfully comparable? It would seem that only things that are fully identical or fully distinct cannot be profitably compared. Thus, it is not very interesting to compare two plastic salad bowls mass-produced on the same mold since, for practical purposes, they would turn out to be exactly the same. Similarly, it is also not very interesting to compare, let us say, an insect such as a ladybug, and a religion such as Catholicism, since these two are—except for some very general shared features such as existence and complexity—completely different. In order for comparison to be interesting, two objects must be partly similar and partly different: They must belong to the same kind and constitute distinct subkinds within that kind. They have to have different properties that nonetheless belong to the same type. Thus, while an animal and a religion are not profitably comparable, two animals can be profitably compared since, by definition, they will have common types of properties, such as digestive organs, sensory organs, and a life cycle of some duration; and two religions are similarly comparable since, by definition, they will both include some concept of a divine being, some specification of human virtues, *etc.*

Thus, in order to show that any two syntactic metatheories are profitably comparable, all we need to show is that all syntactic metatheories, by definition, do share a common set of property types which can then serve as common denominators in the process of comparison. In Section 2, which is entirely devoted to the question of the comparability of syntactic metatheories, I will first discuss these basic property types which all syntactic metatheories, by definition, share, thereby showing how all of them are partially similar (2.1). The remaining subsections of Section 2 (2.2, 2.3, 2.4) will in turn list some of the subtypes within each general property type, thus showing how objects that all belong to the class of syntactic metatheories can nonetheless differ from each other. Section 3 will take up the question of evaluating the differences.

2. DIMENSIONS OF DIFFERENCES AMONG SYNTACTIC METATHEORIES

2.1. Definitionally Shared Properties of Syntactic Metatheories

The first question is, then: What are the common features of syntactic metatheories[2] that unite all of them into a single kind, or genus? I will assume that all syntactic metatheories are (more-or-less explicit and more-or-less autonomous) sets of stipulations concerning individual syntactic

---

[2] Although the term "(syntactic) approach" as commonly used is of wider application, in this paper it will be used interchangeably with the terms "(syntactic) theory" and "(syntactic) metatheory."

accounts. In other words, they impose limitations on the ways in which individual syntactic descriptions can be. These limitations extend to three domains: (*a*) to the KINDS OF FACTS that individual syntactic descriptions are to account for; (*b*) to the RANGE OF GOALS that individual syntactic descriptions of these facts are to achieve; and (*c*) to the RANGE OF MEANS which individual syntactic accounts are to employ in the pursuit of these goals in relation to the relevant facts. Furthermore, I will assume that all syntactic metatheories agree in at least some of the FACTS that they define as of interest and that they also agree in at least some of the GOALS that they prescribe as significant. That the range of goals assumed by different syntactic metatheories must always in part overlap appears to follow from the fact that all syntactic metatheories are assumed here to be scientific metatheories. What follows from this are three desiderata for individual syntactic descriptions that all scientific metatheories share: (*a*) that they make assertions that are TRUE; (*b*) that they make assertions that COULD BE FALSE; (*c*) that they provide GENERALIZATIONS from which such individual assertions follow. That the range of facts that various syntactic metatheories prescribe for their derivative syntactic descriptions should also overlap follows from the more specific fact that syntactic metatheories are theories of syntax. Since the concept "syntax" is most commonly understood to involve reference to the co-occurrence and temporal order of elements, I will assume that all syntactic metatheories agree in imposing the following restrictions on the range of facts individual descriptions should account for: All syntactic accounts must minimally deal with (*a*) THE MEMBERSHIP of the set of meaningful units of sound form that linguistic utterances consist of and (*b*) the TEMPORAL ORDER of these units within utterances.

To illustrate these points, let us consider some examples of syntactic statements par excellence—that is, syntactic statements of the kind that ANY syntactic metatheory, by definition, must require of its derivative syntactic accounts to include in some form. The following such examples are statements formulated as part of a syntactic account of the 17 English sentences listed in the Appendix which served as the basis of the sample grammars included in some of the papers of this book.

1. Every sentence has at least one verb and one noun prase.
2. All common nouns occur with an article or quantifier.
3. All articles and quantifiers immediately precede their nouns.
4. All affixes are suffixed.

Each of these is a syntactic statement par excellence since, first of all, all of them pertain to meaningful units of sound form, such as articles or nouns. The first two pertain to the membership of the sets of such units that make up a sentence (in 1) or a phrase (in 2); and the second two pertain to the order of constituents. Thus, they all fulfill the requirements concerning facts. They also fulfill the goal-related desiderata in that they are all true, all possibly false, and all general to the extent that they hold true for more than one linguistic utterance.

By contrast, consider the following statements.

1. Every sentence consists of a semantic predicate and at least one argument.
2. No word-internal consonant cluster includes more than two consonants.
3. All nouns precede their articles.
4. All sentences consist of at least one meaningful unit of form.
5. The sentence *The woman walked* consists of an article followed by a noun followed by a verb stem followed by an affix.

Purported syntactic descriptions that include only statements of such kinds would be disqualified from being descriptions of syntax, by our definition, since each statement violates at least one of the fact- or goal-related requirements. Statement 1 is disqualified from being a syntactic statement par excellence in that it deals with meaning constituents, rather than with meaningful units of sound form. Statement 2, on the other hand, pertains to meaningless phonetic constituents and is not syntactic for this reason. What is wrong with Statement 3 is that it is false for our data; Statement 4 is true but it is true by definition, not by fact; and Statement 5 is true but it has no cross-utterance generality. Thus, none of these five statements could serve as the SOLE type of statement that occurs in a syntactic description regardless of which particular syntactic metatheory it is governed by.

This much thus establishes that all syntactic metatheories must, by necessity, be comparable. To summarize: Their comparability rests on the assumption that all syntactic metatheories agree in that they define some domains of facts, some goals, and some means for their derivative syntactic accounts. Each of these three parameters thus provides an anchor point for comparison.

Given that we have now formulated some limiting assumptions about syntactic metatheories that place boundaries around the set of objects to which the label "syntactic metatheory" will be assumed to be applicable, the next task is to fill in the "inner space." We now know what the NECESSARY SIMILARITIES are among syntactic metatheories; what are the POSSIBLE DIFFERENCES? In other words, what are the subparameters along which syntactic metatheories can differ within each of these three shared domains? In what follows, I will take up each domain in turn and attempt to delimit some dimensions of possible variation.

2.2. Differences in the Range of Facts
To Be Accounted For

First, let us consider how syntactic metatheories could differ regarding the types of facts that they prescribe as the ones to be accounted for by individual syntaxes. As we have already seen, the variation here is not unlimited: The syntactic constituent membership of utterances and the linear order of these constituents must be among the facts of interest for any individual syntactic description. There are, however, at least five ways in which syntactic metatheories can nonetheless differ from the point of view of the selection of facts.

First, the possibility of variation exists regarding the SIZE OF SYNTAC- TIC CONSTITUENTS with respect to which membership and order are to be defined. Thus, syntactic metatheories may prescribe interest only in the co-occurrence and order of clauses within sentences; or in the co- occurrence and order of phrases within clauses; or in the co-occurrence and order of words within phrases; or they may go as far as prescribing concern with the co-occurrence and order of morphemes within words as well, thus subsuming "morphology" under syntax.

Second, syntactic metatheories may also differ regarding the SIZE OF THE LINGUISTIC UTTERANCE within which co-occurrence and order are to be characterized. Thus, there may be metatheories of word-internal structure; or metatheories of phrase-internal structure; or of clause-in- ternal, or sentence-internal structure; or there may be metatheories that adopt the discourse as their domain.

Third, the definition of the UTTERANCE SETS that individual descrip- tions should syntactically describe may also vary. One syntactic metathe- ory may stipulate that its derivative syntactic accounts describe lan- guage-size sets; others may aim at describing subvarieties of languages— such as regional or age-related dialects—or styles—as in role and ref- erence grammar—or arbitrary "fragments" of a language—as in Mon- tague grammar. Yet others may attempt to characterize classes of lan- guages—such as sets of diachronically related language stages; or sets of typologically related languages, as is explicitly stipulated in Dik's func- tional approach; or, they may attempt to characterize the largest possible class: the class of all human languages.

The fourth parameter of possible variation within the domain of facts has to do with the NATURE OF LINGUISTIC UTTERANCES that are as- sumed as basic data. Metatheories may vary here in that one approach may take utterances "as they come"—as perhaps the role-and-reference approach does—while another may insist that utterances be considered in some "cleaned-up" version. In other words, some metatheories may aim at being theories of syntactic performance, whereas others may aim at being theories of syntactic competence.

Whereas all four of these subparameters of variation among linguistic metatheories in relation to the choice of facts to be accounted for in syntax have to do with the selection of the relevant linguistic utterances and of their relevant basic syntactic constituents, syntactic metatheories may also vary in whether they are concerned with PROPERTIES OF LINGUISTIC UTTERANCES other than those definitionally required—that is, other than the co-occurrence and temporal order of meaningful constituents. First of all, there is a fundamental watershed between syntactic metatheories that are interested only in the fact that syntactic utterances and their constituents are meaningful, but not in the details of their meanings; and metatheories that are also concerned with some specific aspects of their meanings. To use familiar terminology, some syntactic metatheories may be concerned with "surface syntax" only, while others may want to go "deeper" than that. Concern with meaning—as opposed to just meaningfulness—may consist simply of concern with sameness and difference of meaning, including concern with such non-one-to-one relationships between total utterance meaning and total syntactic form as utterance synonymy and utterance ambiguity. However, it may also extend to facts about semantic relatedness among sentences beyond simple identity and difference; as well as to more particular discrepancies between total utterance meaning and the sum of morpheme meanings. Such discrepancies may be (a) some parts of the utterance meaning not having any morphemic expression, (b) some morphemes not carrying any part of the total utterance meaning, (c) the semantic constituent structure of the utterance being different from the corresponding syntactic constituent structure, and (d) the semantic cohesion relations in meaning not being paralled by temporal adjacency in syntactic structure. The two basic types of syntax could perhaps be called "surface syntax" and "correspondence syntax." The question for "surface syntax" is: What are (surface) syntactic structures? The question for "correspondence syntax" is: What are the pairings of (surface) syntactic structures and utterance meanings?

Thus, turning to the sample of 17 English sentences for purposes of illustration, for metatheories of "surface syntax," the only thing that is important about the meaning of sentence 13, *The farmer gave John the axe,* is that it exists, that is, that the sentence is meaningful; the facts that it is ambiguous—between the literal and the idiomatic readings—and that on one reading it is synonymous with Sentence 12, *The farmer gave the axe to John,* are not relevant syntactic facts. Metatheories of "correspondence syntax," however, will consider it incumbent upon a description to account for such facts of synonymy and ambiguity as well. Or, again, given Sentence 15, *John killed the woman and Bill, the farmer,* it may be of relevance for one kind of syntactic description governed by a "correspondence syntax" approach that there is an "understood" element in the second clause, *killed,* but it will not be a significant fact for another syntactic description governed by a "surface syntax" approach.

The factual realm of syntax may similarly be extended in the direction of sound form, rather than meaning. Whereas all syntactic descriptions must, by definition, by concerned with the *presence* of sound form—just as they must be concerned with the presence of meaning—and with the details of one aspect of phonetic form, linear order as it holds among syntactic constituents, some syntactic descriptions may also prescribe some additional aspects of phonetic form as ones to be accounted for by individual descriptions. Whereas probably no syntactician has ever argued that all concern with pronunciation be included in syntactic descriptions, certain aspects of suprasegmental structure, such as phrasing, stress, or intonation, are sometimes included in syntax.

The third direction in which the set of properties of linguistic utterances prescribed as relevant for syntactic accounts may be extended is the direction of what might be called "psycholinguistic evidence"—that is, facts about the actual use of utterances, such as how they are produced, or misproduced; how they are understood or misunderstood; how they are learned or forgotten; and how they are classified, related, or judged by speakers.

In sum, syntactic metatheories may differ with respect to the range of facts that they prescribe for individual syntactic descriptions to account for in at least five ways. These are: the size of syntactic constituents prescribed; the size of utterances prescribed; the size and kind of utterance sets prescribed; the nature of utterances; and the set of properties of utterances assumed to be of syntactic interest.

2.3. Differences in Goals

Let us now take up the question of how syntactic metatheories can differ in relation to the goals that they define for their derivative syntactic accounts. Again, variation is not unlimited since some of these goals— such as the truth-to-fact requirement, the empirical vulnerability requirement, and the generality requirement—are definitionally given. Nonetheless, variation is possible. I can see four sources of such variation.

The first has to do with the precise interpretation of the "truth-to-fact" requirement, the most fundamental and most important of the desiderata that all scientific theories share. This requirement—that syntactic accounts make assertions that are in line with facts—may be interpreted in a more confining or in a less confining manner. The more rigorous interpretation would require that syntactic descriptions describe all and only the true facts and nothing that is known to be not a fact. In other words, the requirement would be that syntactic descriptions account for all and only the grammatical utterances but exclude ones that are ungrammatical; or that they account for all and only those languages that are actual human languages but exclude ones that are known not to be such. The less rigorous interpretation would also require completeness with respect to all known facts but it would not bar the possible prediction of some untrue facts as well. According to this more lenient interpretation, it would be acceptable for a syntactic description to generate ungrammatical structures as long as it generates all of the grammatical ones as well; and it would be acceptable for a universal grammar to generate any class of the logically possible human languages as long as the class includes—whether properly or improperly—the class of actual ones.

The second source of possible variation among syntactic metatheories regarding goals has to do with the generality requirement. Here, metatheories may differ in whether they require only some degree of generality or whether they require maximal generality possibly within the domain.

The third source of variation regarding goals has to do with whether the goal requirements are only enforced globally on syntactic descriptions as wholes, or whether they are also enforced on individual statements included in syntactic descriptions. Thus some metatheories may require that every single descriptive statement included in a syntactic account be true to fact; whereas other metatheories may not insist on this so long as the total account provides for factually true assertions. For instance, the standard theory of transformational generative grammar allows for factually untrue statements about constituent order—in other words, for "underlying constituent order" to be different from "surface order"—as long as things eventually come out right; whereas daughter-dependency grammar, or Dik's functional grammar, or equational grammar require surface truth for all of their constituent order statements. Similarly, Standard Theory allows for syntactic statements that say that some constituent is "there" at some point in the derivation when in fact it does not end up being present in surface structure, whereas other metatheories, such as Dik's, do not allow for this.

Fourth, syntactic metatheories can differ regarding goals not only in their interpretations of the definitionally given goals but also in whether they assume any goals in addition to those definitionally given. Possible such additional goals may be aesthetic requirements such as simplicity, or pedagogical usefulness, or applicability of individual syntactic descriptions to translation procedures; and so forth.

In sum, then, there are at least four ways in which syntactic metatheories may differ from the point of view of the goals they stipulate for individual syntactic accounts. These are: in their interpretation of the truth-to-fact requirement; in their interpretation of the generality requirement; in whether they enforce the goal requirements globally or individually on statements that constitute syntactic accounts; and in whether they assume goals in addition to the ones definitionally given.

2.4. Differences in Means

Differences among syntactic metatheories regarding "means"—the ways in which the stipulated goals are supposed to be attained with respect to the stipulated facts by syntactic descriptions—are the most significant kind—more important than differences in facts and goals. There are two reasons for this. First, whereas the definition that we initially adopted for syntactic metatheories places a priori constraints on the kinds of facts and goals that such theories prescribe for their derivative descriptions, the area of means was left definitionally unconstrained. This is thus the area where the greatest variation may be expected and where it may be the most difficult to determine a limited number of parameters along which variations can pattern. The second reason for the significance of differences among syntactic metatheories regarding means is that this is where the true empirical substance of syntactic metatheories may lie. Metatheoretic restrictions on both goals and facts of syntactic descriptions basically have to do with the distribution of labor between syntax and other areas of linguistics and neighboring sciences. Thus, when two syntactic metatheories differ in whether syntactic descriptions should or should not account for facts of synonymy and ambiguity, what is at stake is simply the location of the borderline between syntax and semantics. Or, when two syntactic metatheories differ in whether syntactic descriptions ought to account for "psycholinguistic facts" such as processing or recall, what is at issue is not whether such facts are to be accounted for at all, but, rather, whether the subdiscipline of linguistics that should concern itself with these facts should be the same as the one that deals with facts about the syntactic structure of utterances. Or, again, if two metatheories differ in whether pedagogical purposes should concern a "theoretical syntactician," the difference is, once again, a matter of division of labor. Whatever choices are made such issues of facts and goals, the decisions cannot therefore be labeled "true" or "false" but can be rated only on scales such as naturalness or fruitfulness. However, when it comes to the choice of means that syntactic metatheories prescribe for their derivative descriptions, the choices *can* be labeled "true" or "false," since it is possible that metatheoretically prescribed means of syntactic accounts are capable of accounting for the facts and it is also possible that they are not. A simple example indicates this. Suppose that somebody advances a syntactic metatheory that stipulates that all syntactic statements stating the temporal order of syntactic constituents must specify these constituents only by reference to their phonetic properties, such as what consonant or vowel they start with. Although it is easy to conceive of languages where such a metatheoretical stipulation would be necessary, it is also clear that no human language currently known operates in this manner. Thus, such a metatheory would clearly be an emprically false one.

After this introduction highlighting the significance of the endeavor that we are about to launch on, let us attempt to delimit some dimensions along which syntactic metatheories can differ regarding the means, or descriptive devices, they prescribe for their derivative descriptions. Let us assume that any individual syntactic account can be logically analyzed into a set of descriptive statements and a set of instructions about how to apply these statements in the process of accounting for facts. Thus, for example, the rule S → NP + VP can be analyzed into a statement which says: "An S consists of an NP followed by a VP" and into the associated instruction: "Expand the term on the left of the arrow into the term on the right." Given this twofold structure of syntactic accounts, there must be two fundamental parameters of metatheoretical stipulations concerning means of accounting. One of these is the nature of the syntactic statements and the other one is the nature of the associated "instructions for use." I will consider each of these in turn.

As we consider possible variation among syntactic metatheories regarding the nature of syntactic statements that they permit, the question we are considering is really this: What do syntactic metatheories claim syntactic facts, such as constituent co-occurrence and order, are related to? In particular, what are such facts predictable from? What exactly are the properties of syntactic constituents and their relations that permit general statements about their empirically true co-occurrences and orderings? There are actually two logically possible ways in which syntactic metatheories can regulate the empirical contents of their derivative syntactic descriptions: by regulating the empirical contents of individual syntactic statements; and by placing constraints on the set of syntactic statements that can or must co-occur in individual syntactic descriptions.

What are the possible bases on which the co-occurrence and order relations of syntactic constituents could possibly be predicted? There are only three logically available property and relation types that could serve as proper bases on which the requisite co-occurrence and order classes of syntactic constituents could be defined. These are: semantic/pragmatic properties and relations; phonetic properties and relations; and "abstract" properties and relations—that is, ones that do not directly relate either to meaning or to sound form. Some of the metatheories that will be presented in this book do differ I think exactly along this parameter: in the kinds of bases in terms of which they assume the constituent membership and constituent order of utterances can be defined. For instance, role and reference grammar asserts that it is case roles and pragmatic properties that participate in providing the correct classification of syntactic constituents in terms of which generalizations about surface syntactic properties can be made. Relational grammar, on the other hand, posits an "abstract" classification of noun phrases—into classes such as "terms" and "non-terms," "subject," "object"—which are not represented as having any direct semantic or pragmatic correlates. Or, again, daughter-dependency grammar posits an abstract relation for syntactic constituents—that of "being dependent on"—for predicting temporal ordering. Some metatheories maintain that in order to predict all the facts assumed to be of interest to syntax, syntactic constituents must be multiply classified—that is, assigned to different kinds of classes. Thus, both in role and reference grammar and in tagmemics, syntactic constituents are represented in terms of both case roles and syntactic classes; and in corepresentational grammar, too, constituents are both categorically and functionally represented.

The other fundamental way in which syntactic metatheories can vary regarding the instrumental apparatus they define for their derivative descriptions has to do with the use of syntactic rules; or, more precisely, with the manner in which the validity of a syntactic description can be tested against reality. As far as the global use of syntactic descriptions are concerned, there appear to be essentially two basic kinds of metatheories. Some metatheories provide for the construction of syntactic structures; and the way to test the account is by searching for a matching structure in reality. The other type of account is the recognizing kind. This type of account does not construct random structures; rather, it needs to be presented with a putative fact—a hypothetical structure—of which the account is then capable of making a judgment; such as that it is well-formed or ill-formed; frequent or marginal. In the former kind, the product of the grammar is to be matched against reality; whereas in the latter kind, a piece of putative reality is to be checked against a description. The former kind constructs a hypothesis; the latter proves or disproves one. An example of the former kind is the standard theory of transformational generative grammar. Whereas this theory provides for the constructing of structures, equational grammar, for instance, is designed to work either way; other metatheories such as role and reference grammar, make no commitment.

The distinction between "constructing" and "recognizing" grammar involves only one aspect of the use of syntaxes: It has to do with the use of descriptions as wholes. Another aspect of grammar use is the application of individual syntactic statements included in a description: Given a particular statement, what exactly are the conditions under which it should be resorted to as an instrument of accounting for syntactic facts; and, once it is resorted to, exactly how is it to be used? Questions of obligatory–optional rule application, rule ordering, and—where applicable—the directionality of rule use belong here.

As mentioned above, instrumental stipulations included in syntactic metatheories may restrict individual syntactic accounts either globally or at the level of individual statements. There is also a third shared common variable to both metatheoretical content–restrictions of syntactic accounts and to metatheoretically given use–restrictions of such accounts. This is whether such stipulations are metatheoretically fully unconditioned (i.e., they pertain, to all syntactic statements included in descriptions of all languages) or whether they are restricted to subtypes of syntactic statements and/or to subclasses of languages. Thus, for instance, role and reference grammar appears to metatheoretically stipulate that syntactic statements can refer only to case role features and pragmatic noun phrase properties—but whether syntactic statements pertaining to a particular language will refer to one kind, or to the other, or both, is said to be a language-specific matter, a fact that serves to sort out languages into significant typological classes. In relational grammar, however, the kinds of terms that syntactic statements can refer to are claimed to be the same in all languages. Similar differences among metatheories also exist regarding the universality versus nonuniversality of rule-applicational principles. In the standard theory of transformational generative grammar, for instance, the obligatoriness and the optionality of syntactic rules are both metatheoretically unrestricted choices and thus they can vary with both rules and languages; whereas in equational grammar, all aspects of rule application are metatheoretically predictable for all rules and all languages.

In sum, syntactic metatheories may vary regarding the descriptive apparatus they stipulate for their derivative descriptions along two basic dimensions: the contents of syntactic statements and the use of syntactic statements. In both respects, stipulations may pertain to individual rules or to entire descriptions; and they may be stipulations that are fully un-restricted as well as ones that are limited to particular rules or to particular languages.

3. WAYS OF RATING THE DIFFERENCES

Considerations presented in Section 2 were meant to suggest that syntactic metatheories are fruitfully comparable. I attempted to make this point first by showing (see Section 2.1) that all syntactic metatheories, by definition, include identical types of properties—that is, that they all MUST be SIMILAR in some ways—and then by showing (see Sections 2.2, 2.3, and 2.4) some of the possible variations within the definitionally given limits—that is, how syntactic metatheories MAY be nonetheless DIFFERENT. However, in order to have shown that the total endeavor of which this book is intended to be an instrument, is feasible, one more thing needs to be shown. What we want to do is not only compare metatheories. The second, and ultimate, goal is, given the differences established, to assess their significance. In other words, we do not only want to compare theories but, provided that at least some of them indeed turn out to be different, we also want to evaluate them in relation to each other.

As was alluded to in Section 1, not all perceived differences between syntactic metatheories call for a choice, or evaluative judgment. There are at least two conditions under which two syntactic metatheories can appear different and nonetheless no choice is called for in the sense that their joint acceptance does not lead to conflict. One of these is if two syntactic metatheories are different in language only—in other words, are merely notational variants. The other condition is if they do make sub-stantively distinct claims but these are nonetheless compatible—for ex-ample, if the metatheories assume different but complementary types of data; or different but complementary kinds of goals, such as aiming at restricting different aspects of syntactic accounts in compatible ways. Thus, for example—as pointed out in Sanders' conference paper—the metatheory of equational grammar and that of role and reference grammar or of relational grammar, are distinct but compatible since the former makes distinctive claims about rule application, whereas the latter two make distinctive claims about syntactically significant noun phrase classes.

A choice, or some sort of rating, of metatheories is called for only if the two are substantively different and incompatible. Under such con-ditions there appear to be two significant types of criteria in terms of which metatheories can be rated. The first, which I assume takes prec-edence over all others, pertains to evaluating the contents of syntactic accounts: The criterion is truth, or empirical adequacy. Of two syntactic metatheories, the one that is sufficiently and appropriately constrained so as to allow for syntactic descriptions that provide for all and only true facts about natural language syntax is preferable to one that falls short of this.

Provided that two metatheories appear to be equally adequate from an empirical point of view, there is also a further criterion in terms of which they can be rated. This criterion could be termed fruitfulness, or instrumentality, or external validity. What this is is simply the extent to which different metatheories prove to be instrumental in intellectual and practical endeavors outside the domain of syntax itself. Just as it is the task of a syntactic metatheory to provide for the characterization of those kinds of syntactic phenomena as similar that are in fact known to be similar, and for the characterization of those kinds of syntactic phenomena as different that are known to be different, it is also to the advantage of a syntactic metatheory if it turns out to be instrumental in the characterization of syntax as a whole as being similar to other things in language and in the world in general that it is known to be similar to. Thus, first, it is appropriate to ask how a metatheory of syntax fits in with metatheories of other (nonsyntactic) aspects of language structure, such as phonology or lexicology or semantics or phonetics. Second, it is appropriate to ask how a syntactic metatheory fits in with metatheories of other (nonstructural) aspects of language such as language function. Third, it is again appropriate to ask how a metatheory of syntax fits in with theories of other (nonlinguistic) symbolic systems such as body language; or, fourth, how it fits in with theories of other (nonsymbolic) social institutions such as religions; or, fifth, how it fits in with theories of other (nonlinguistic) instruments such as hammers and cars and nuclear reactors; or, sixth, how it fits in with theories of other (noncommunicative) goal-directed human activities such as various types of problem-solving; or, seventh, how it fits in with theories of any other phenomena in the world. A syntactic metatheory that characterizes syntax as similar to phonology in some ways is better than one that does not do this, if syntax is independently known to be similar to phonology in those ways. A syntactic metatheory that represents human language syntax as sharing common features with the "syntax" of body language or of other symbolic systems is better than one that does not achieve this, if it is independently natural and fruitful to subsume natural human languages and other symbolic systems under the same genus. And a syntactic metatheory that provides a view of syntax that contributes to the characterization of human language as an instrument, or as a kind of goal-directed behavior is better than one that does not achieve this, provided that language is indeed an instrument, or a piece of goal-directed behavior.

In addition to gauging the contribution that a syntactic metatheory makes to various intellectual enterprises outside the domain of syntax proper and thus the extent to which it contributes to our comprehensive understanding of the phenomena of the world, there is also another way in which the fruitfulness, or instrumentality, or external validity of a syntactic metatheory can be gauged. This is by considering its usefulness in solving practical problems of individual humans and human societies. A syntactic metatheory that determines syntactic accounts that turn out to be instrumental in practical endeavors such as language teaching or translation or language planning, is to be valued more highly in this respect that another syntactic metatheory that does not do that.

4. CONCLUSIONS

This paper has argued that the comparison and evaluation of syntactic metatheories is both desirable and possible. It is my sincere hope that this volume will make some contribution toward achieving these goals, and that it will thus help channel syntactic research in fruitful directions, as well as help lessen seclusion and increase collaboration among scholars in the field.

MONTAGUE'S SYNTAX

ROBIN COOPER
University of Wisconsin—Madison

1. INTRODUCTION

I shall present general features of Montague's style of syntactic description [approximately as it is to be found in "The Proper Treatment of Quantification in Ordinary English" (PTQ), Montague, 1974]. I shall use examples from the sample syntax at the end of this paper to illustrate the discussion.

2. FRAGMENTS

One of the main problems in studying natural languages is that one can quickly become overwhelmed by the data. In contrast to formal languages, the complexity of natural languages cannot be arbitrarily regulated so that we have a complete system which we can account for entirely by a reasonably small well-defined set of rules. One way of attacking this problem, which I think is well-exemplified in much of the linguistic literature, is to argue in general for the nature of certain linguistic rules, drawing on any examples which the competent native speaker may be persuaded to have intuitions about. On such an approach, for example,

19

Syntax and Semantics, Volume 13:
Current Approaches to Syntax

it becomes meaningless to argue about the precise formulation of a rule of Raising-to-Object before we have harvested all the important data that will bear on the existence or nature of this rule. Thus this approach essentially gives up the idea of writing rigorous formal grammars in favor of trying to penetrate the general nature of certain constructions in the language at large. This is presumably to be viewed as an interim solution until such time as our knowledge advances to the stage where we may write completely formalized grammars.

Montague's interim solution takes the opposite strategy. He does not sacrifice the idea of writing fully specified and rigorous grammars but the rules that he writes are designed to generate a precisely defined sublanguage of the natural language, that is, a fragment of the language. He artificially regulates the fragment under study in a manner that is reminiscent of the logician's construction of a formal language which can be kept neat and tidy. The logician studies propositional logic and then finds that important properties of this logic carry over to the stronger logic of first order predicate calculus. Similarly first order logic may be embedded in even stronger second order logics of various kinds. It is possible to carry over the rigorous formalizations of the weaker languages into the stronger ones. Similarly by restricting one's study to a limited fragment of English and getting a grammar for it to work precisely and neatly one hopes to be able to carry over this formalization, or perhaps certain important aspects of it, into larger and larger superfragments.

I think there is an important advantage to Montague's fragment idea as a research strategy for linguists. If one pursues the program of constructing ever richer fragments of English, rigorously defined in all detail, then, in principle, one will end up with what many linguists would regard as a desideratum, namely a grammar of English. If one pursues the alternative strategy of first collecting the data and making arguments for the general nature of the rules needed, then what comes out at the end is a set of examples and arguments but not a grammar of English. And yet I think most linguists would agree that examples and arguments are mainly useful in that they should help us to construct grammars. If we collect a huge set of examples without trying to formalize grammars to account for them, I think we might be preparing more headaches than anything else for future generations of linguists.

I think Montague's idea of constructing fragments is an important contribution to linguistic research. This is not to say, however, that it should be used blindly. There is an important difference between the study of restricted formal languages and the study of restricted fragments of a natural language. The logician is creating a mathematical object of some interest in its own right. If it should turn out that some kind of logic is not embeddable in any interesting larger logic, the mathematician is not obliged to go back to the drawing board and reformulate the first logic. However, if it should turn out that some formulation of a fragment of English cannot be enlarged or adjusted easily to fit in the formulation of a larger fragment of English, then the linguist is obliged to go back and rethink the earlier analysis. The linguist, in formulating a fragment, has to keep an eye open for analyses that will obviously cause problems later on.

An example of the kind of progress that has been made by applying Montague's strategy is illustrated by the sample grammar. Given the task of providing a consistent grammar for a fairly wide range of data, I have borrowed analyses presented in a number of papers by various researchers working in Montague's framework. Yet, aside from details, I have taken the analyses as they were originally presented. While there are various competing analyses for different constructions in Montague grammar, I think they can be plugged into a grand grammar formalizable in one of the more recent variants of the PTQ style of description.

3. RECURSIVE DEFINITIONS AND THE WELL-FORMEDNESS CONSTRAINT

Montague's syntaxes are expressed in a way more familiar to logicians than linguists. In PTQ, he gives a recursive definition of the set of sentences in the fragment under study. A recursive definition of a set normally consists of three parts: a base, a recursive clause, and an exclusion clause. Thus, for example, if we wish to define the set of all strings consisting of a's and b's and containing at least either a or b, that is $\{a, b, aa, ab, ba, bb, aaa, \ldots\}$ we could use the recursive definition given in (1).

(1)   BASE: $a \in X$ and $b \in X$.
        RECURSION CLAUSE: If $\alpha \in X$ and $\beta \in X$, then $\alpha\beta \in X$.
        EXCLUSION CLAUSE: Nothing is a member of X except as required by the base and recursion clause.

Montague's version of syntax in PTQ may be seen as an elaboration of the kind of definition given in (1). Instead of defining just one set, as is normally the case for a recursive definition, Montague's syntax defines many sets, one set for each category of the language. Thus the definition not only tells you what is an expression of the language but also what category the expressions belong to. The base of the definition is taken to be the lexicon of the language. It tells you what basic elements (or lexical items) there are in the language and what category they belong to.

Rather than having just one recursion clause as in (1), Montague has
several. These are the rules of the language. They are of varying kinds.
The operation involved in the rule need not be simple concatenation as
in (1). A typical recursion clause or rule in Montague's syntax might be
of the form (2).

(2)   If $\alpha \in P_C$ and $\beta \in P_D$, then $F_i(\alpha,\beta) \in P_E$, where $F_i(\alpha,\beta)$ is . . . .

This is to be read as (3).

(3)   If α is a phrase of category C and β is a phrase of category D, then
        the result of applying the syntactic operation F_i to α and β is
        a phrase of category E, where the result of applying F_i to these
        arguments is . . . .

That the grammar must be in the form of a recursive definition is not
something that is required by the very general definitions given by Montague (1974) in his earlier paper "Universal Grammar" which gives a
general theory of grammar. However, he seems to have been aware that
the statement of the grammar in PTQ was consistent with a more restricted
theory that does make this requirement. Most of the subsequent work in
Montague Grammar has taken the kind of syntax used in PTQ as a model.
I would like to point out some things that follow immediately from viewing
the grammar of a language as a recursive definition. They distinguish it
in important ways from traditional transformational grammar.

3.1. Well-Formedness Constraint

A recursive definition may be regarded as generating the members of
a set by applying the recursion clauses. If the set you are characterizing
is a subset of the expressions of a natural langauge, then each recursion
clause must yield well-formed expressions of the language. It cannot be
the case that some recursion clauses generate intermediate forms which
are not members of the set in question but which could be turned into
bona fide members by future applications of other recursion clauses. This
feature of Montague's syntax has been called by Partee (1979a and 1979b)
the well-formedness constraint. As she has shown (Partee, 1979a) it rules
out a number of analyses that might be suggested in a transformational
framework. Closely associated with this property of Montague's syntax
is the fact that there are no obligatory rules. The recursion clauses are
simply if–then statements about membership in a set. They would simply
be false if some obligatory rule were required to change something consistent with the recursion clauses into a real member of the set.

3.2. No Extrinsic Rule-Ordering

Since the recursion clauses are simply if–then statements about the membership of a set there is no concept of applying the rules in any order specified by the grammar. Of course, if the only way you can discover whether something is of category *C* is to check whether it is consistent with some recursion clause which tells you the membership of category *C*, then any clause which mentions *C* in its antecedent will depend on the clause which produces things of category *C*. This dependency might be regarded as some kind of intrinsic ordering. It seems that this intrinsic ordering might be sufficient to account for the kind of phenomena accounted for by extrinsic ordering in transformational grammars of a traditional nature. In the grammar presented in the Sample Syntax, for example, Subject–Aux Inversion must apply after *wh*-Question Formation because of intrinsic ordering (see Rules S12 and S13).

3.3. No Abstract Levels in Syntax

In all traditional transformational grammars syntactic transformations are regarded as relating two or more levels of syntactic description. This notion of level is absent in Montague's syntax. The grammar may be regarded as generating trees which show a record of how one could construct a proof that some expression is a member of the set. This derivation or analysis tree is essentially similar to a phrase structure tree, except that complex expressions rather than category symbols are written at the higher nodes. This is necessary because, in putting phrases together, one may not only concatenate them but also perform transformation-like operations. An example of such a tree generated by the sample syntax is given in (4).

(4)

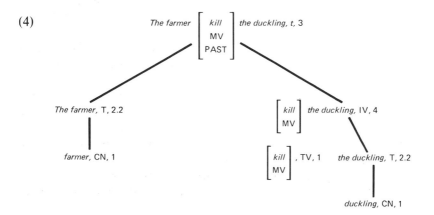

(The letters to the right of the phrases indicate the syntactic category of the phrase and the number indicates the syntactic operation which has been applied.)

These features of Montague's syntax mean that, at least in overall organization, it is a good deal simpler than a transformational grammar. The complexity of the grammar goes not into the overall organization but the typology of operations that may be employed in deriving larger phrases from smaller ones. [Some suggestions for what this typology might be are made by Bach (1979a) and Partee (1979b).]

Despite these apparent radical differences between Montague's syntax and transformational syntax, it can be shown that certain examples of Montague's syntax are equivalent to transformational syntaxes (Cooper and Parsons, 1976). I also believe that the features discussed here can be incorporated into a transformational grammar of a nonstandard kind and that one can therefore take advantage of a formal theory of transformations together with the overall simplicity of Montague's system (see Bach, 1979b, forthcoming, a; Cooper, 1977, 1978).

4. IMPORTANCE OF SEMANTICS

I believe that Montague's most important contribution to linguistic theory will eventually turn out to be that he has given us the tools to formulate a precise semantic theory of natural language. This is not the place to go into detail about what I have in mind. An example might be his unified semantic treatment of all noun phrases—both proper names and those which include determiners—as denoting sets of properties. One claim that might be made is that all languages have NPs, that is, phrases that denote sets of properties. It seems that such a universal could be stated much more simply in terms of semantics rather than trying to isolate syntactic properties that all noun phrases share. In addition NPs are normally the vehicle of quantification in natural languages. This might be seen as related to the fact that the denotation that Montague assigns to NPs—that is, a set of properties—is in fact essentially the denotation that a mathematical logician working in generalized quantification theory would assign to a QUANTIFIER (see Barwise and Cooper, in preparation, for discussion). This association of NPs rather than determiners with semantic quantifiers may help to explain why in natural language it seems to be the whole NP that is involved in moving around or receiving wide scope interpretation rather than just the determiner part of it. Indeed, the interpretation of NPs semantically as quantifiers and the association of what are traditionally considered to be movement rules with wide scope quantification may help to explain why it is the case that if anything undergoes movement in a language, NPs do.

Of major importance for the syntax, however, is that the introduction of an explicit semantics allows us to see exactly what kind of work the semantics might be able to do for us. Some regularities that in the early transformational framework would have had to be accounted for in the syntax, can now be accounted for precisely in the semantics, thus potentially allowing us to restrict the kinds of syntactic rules that we need. For example, we are not required to relate active and passive sentences by a transformation in order to show that they are related in meaning. The analysis of passives presented in the Sample Syntax (adapted from Bach, forthcoming b, which in turn represents a development from Thomason, 1976) uses the transitive verb in both the active and passive structures but combines it with its noun-phrase arguments in different orders. Thus the passive corresponding to (4) is given in (5).

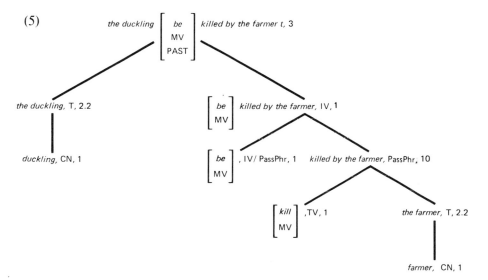

The rule that puts the transitive verb together with the agent phrase *the farmer* has a corresponding semantic rule which indicates that the interpretation of *the farmer* takes up the first argument place in the interpretation of the verb *kill* and at the same time indicates that the rule that will combine the passive phrase with a subject will fill the second argument place with the interpretation of the subject. Thus the interpretation derived from (5) will be the same as the interpretation derived from (4). It is not necessary that the sentences be more closely syntactically related in order for the semantics to achieve this. [This kind of analysis is similar in important ways to the analysis of passive proposed in Bresnan (1978) although Bach argues that passive should not be a lexical rule.]

Similar remarks can be made about the raising phenomena analyzed in the Sample Syntax. The analysis of raising-to-object phenomena makes use of having the verb *believe* in two lexical categories and related by a redundancy rule. The two categories are IV/*t* and IV//*t*, where IV stands for intransitive verb(phrase), corresponding to VP in transformational grammar, and *t* stands for truth-value denoting expression or sentence. The notation means that words in these categories combine with a sentence to make a verb phrase. The categories are held distinct by using a different number of slashes. If the verb is in category IV/*t* then it combines with a tensed sentence. If it is in the category IV//*t* then the sentence is changed into an infinitival form at the point where the combination takes place. The two derivations are given in (6).

(6)

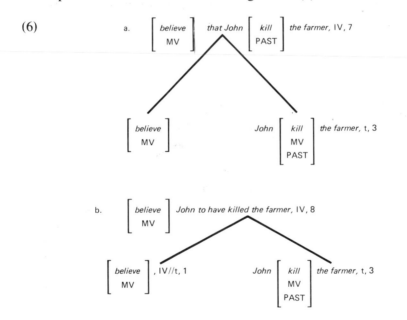

Since the interpretation of the two words *believe* can be the same, a transformational rule of Raising-to-Object is not necessary to show that the two verb-phrases receive the same interpretation. The particular treatment that I have proposed is not the only one available in a Montague framework, however. One could still maintain that there is a transformation of Raising-to-Object in the kind of Montague Grammar proposed by Partee (1975). Alternatively we may think of raising verbs as being in the category TV/INF, that is, they combine with an infinitive phrase to make a transitive verb. This has been proposed by Thomason (1976) and Dowty (1978b).

The treatment of Dative Movement (adapted from Dowty, 1979) illustrates the same point. The word *give* belongs to two lexical categories related by a lexical rule which may be thought of as playing a similar role as a redundancy rule in transformational grammar although Dowty does not use the term "redundancy rule." The verbs in one category combine with a direct object and a *to*-phrase. The verbs in the other category take two objects. This gives us a simple way of stating in the lexicon that some verbs may only occur with two objects and others may only occur with an object and a *to*-phrase. This is illustrated in (7).

(7)   a.   *Harriet denied her husband the opportunity to go to Australia*
      b.   **Harriet denied the opportunity to her husband*
      c.   **I donated the library the book*
      d.   *I donated the book to the library*

It is no accident that *give* has essentially the same meanings in both categories since the semantic rule associated with the redundancy rule indicates that the only difference in meaning is that the order in which the verb takes its arguments differs for the two categories.

As a last example of the work that an explicit semantics does for us I cite Montague's treatment of conjunction reduction phenomena. It is clear that semantically a sentence such as (8) involves the same kind of conjunction as one finds between sentences.

(8)   *John loved the woman and killed the farmer*

We would clearly be missing a generalization if we were to claim that the *and* of (8) had an essentially different meaning from the *and* of sentence conjunction. The generalization is captured in some transformational literature by deriving (8) from a deep structure corresponding to (9) and then applying a transformation of Conjunction Reduction.

(9)   *John loved the woman and John killed the farmer*

This transformation is, however, awkward to define and would not be allowed by some of the more restricted views of what a possible transformation is. Montague allows us to generate (8) directly, using a rule of Verb Phrase Conjunction, and yet he also captures the fact that the conjunction is semantically the same as the one involved in sentence conjunction. The conjoined verb phrase (10a) corresponds to the property represented in (10b).

(10)   a. *love the woman and kill the farmer*
         b. *the property of being an x such that x love the woman and x
            kill the farmer*

The verb phrase (10a) corresponds to a complex property, the definition
of which uses the familiar sentential connective *and*. (There is a problem
in the Sample Syntax in getting the right interpretation for the tenses in
sentences like (8). This is inherited from Montague's treatment in PTQ.
However, I believe that it is a problem of detail rather than a general
problem for the framework.)

5. CONCLUSION

In conclusion I should like to point out two ways in which Montague's syntax compares with current research in transformational syntax. The first comparison shows something on which the two differ and
the second, I think, reveals an important convergence between the two.

The difference has to do with the fact that a Montague syntax is a
recursive definition of the set of well-formed expressions of the language,
as discussed in Section 2. This means that the phrase-structure and transformation-like operations are not strictly separated as they are in a transformational grammar. Transformational operations apply as larger and
larger phrases are being built up; for each syntactic rule there is a corresponding semantic rule which operates on the meanings of the syntactic
constituents being put together. This gives us the opportunity to have a
semantic rule linked with a rule involving a transformational operation.
Thus, for example, there is a semantic rule indicated in the Sample Syntax
that is linked to the rule which achieves the same effect as *wh*-Movement
(the rule of Indirect Question Formation, S12). In a normal transformational grammar one has to interpret either a structure that occurs in the
derivation previous to *wh*-Movement or one that occurs after the application of *wh*-Movement. Attempts to fix the semantic interpretation at
one level have required the introduction of certain kinds of globality such
as derivational constraints or traces left behind to mark the deep structure
position of moved elements. I think it is an interesting and important task
to explore whether the possibility of interpreting the rules themselves may
provide us with an alternative to these devices. Another important question to be explored is whether phonological interpretation also may be
linked to the application of syntactic rules as the tree is being constructed
rather than applying to a completely derived surface structure as is nor-

mally assumed. For example, one can imagine that it might be possible
to formulate an account of the *to*-contraction facts (as in *I wanna go, who
do you wanna succeed*) without having to refer to traces to block the
contraction in the cases where it is not allowed. If the phonology interprets
the tree as it is being built up, then it may be possible to show that an
intervening NP is present at the stage of the derivation where the rule of
To-Contraction has to be blocked.

The point of convergence between Montague's syntax and transformational grammar has to do with the movement towards less abstract
syntax. We can make the semantics and the lexicon do work for us which
in earlier transformational frameworks had to be done in the syntax. The
examples discussed in Section 3 illustrate this. The treatment of Passive
as a rule which essentially changes an active verb into a passive verb
phrase is extremely closely related to the recent work done by Bresnan.
The lexical treatment which has been proposed by Dowty for rules such
as Dative Movement is again essentially the same kind of treatment that
Bresnan suggests. Montague was originally interested in nonabstract syntax because he wanted to show that you could define a semantics directly
on English without representing it as some artificial logical form. Linguists
wish to develop nonabstract syntaxes because they are concerned about
the psychological reality of syntax. I think it is encouraging that the two
points of view should be leading to such similar proposals.

6. SAMPLE SYNTAX

In the following syntax I have borrowed heavily from the work of other
researchers, although, naturally, none of them are responsible for inadequacies that I have introduced. The main debt is, of course, to Montague
(1974), PTQ, from whom the form of grammar as well as several specific
rules (S2, S3, S4, S14, S15, S26) have been adapted. The treatment of
lexical redundancy is based on Dowty (1978a, 1978b, 1979) [although
Redundancy Rule 2 is not the analysis that Dowty proposes: see discussion of Example (6) in the text]. The same work by Dowty also provides
the analysis embodied in Rules S5 and S6. Rules S9, S10, and S11 represent an analysis of Passive and Raising-to-Subject proposed in Bach
(forthcoming b). Rules S12 and S13 are adapted from Karttunen's (1977)
analysis of questions. With each rule I have included an impressionistic
account of the semantics in the hope that this will offer some insight into
the possibilities offered in this framework, without requiring any familiarity with the technicalities involved in a precise definition.

6.1. Categories

    i. *e,t* are category labels
    ii. for any two category labels *a*, *b* there are other category labels
       (*a*)/(*b*), (*a*)//(*b*), (*a*)///(*b*), (*a*)/
    iii. There are no category labels except as required by (i) and (ii)

EXAMPLES: *t*/(*t*/*e*), *t*/*e*, *t*//*e*. (We omit unnecessary parentheses.)

NOTES

    a. Expressions of category *e* denote entities. (According to Montague, there are no English phrases which belong to this category.)
    b. Expressions of category *t* denote truth-values (i.e., are declarative sentences).
    c. Expressions of category (*a*)/(*b*), (*a*)//(*b*), and (*a*)///(*b*) denote functions from things of the type corresponding to expressions of category *b* to things of the type denoted by expressions of category *a*. Correspondingly, in the syntax, expressions of category (*a*)/(*b*), (*a*)//(*b*), or (*a*)///(*b*) will often combine with expressions of category *b* to form an expression of category *a*. This corresponds to a rule of functional application in the semantics.
    d. Single and double slashes are used to distinguish different syntactic categories which have the same kind of denotation. The notation (*a*)/ is an innovation not used by Montague.

ABBREVIATIONS

    CN—"common noun"—*t*//*e*, e.g., **woman**
    IV—"intransitive verb (phrase)"—*t*/*e*, e.g., **walk, kill the duckling**
    T—"term phrase"—*t*/IV, e.g., **the woman, John**
    TV—"transitive verb (phrase)"—IV/T, e.g., **kill, give to John, give the axe**
    DQ—"direct question"—*t*/, e.g., **who did the farmer kill**?
    Q—"subordinate (indirect) question"—*t*//*t*, e.g., **who the farmer killed**
    WH—"*wh*-term phrase"—*t*///IV, e.g., **who**
    PassPhr—"passive phrase"—*t*///*e*, e.g., **killed by the farmer**
    PropPassPhr—"propositional passive phrase"—*t*////*t*, e.g., **believed by the woman**
    TTV—"double object verb"—TV/T, e.g., **give**
    DTV—"dative object verb"—TV//T, e.g., **give**

6.2. Lexicon

If A is some category, we represent the set of basic expressions (lexical items) of A as B_A. For many A, B_A is the nullset, for example, B_t (the set of basic sentences) is the nullset in this fragment.

B_{IV} = {**walk**}
B_{CN} = {**woman, farmer, duckling, axe**}
B_{TV} = {**kill, love**}
B_{WH} = {**who**}
$B_{IV/t}$ = {**believe, assert**}
$B_{IV//t}$ = {**believe**}
$B_{PropPassPhr}$ = {**rumored, said**}
$B_{t/t}$ = {**seem**}
B_T = {**John, Bill, he$_0$, he$_1$, . . .**}
$B_{IV/PassPlu}$ = {**be**}
B_{TTV} = {**give, deny**}
B_{DTV} = {**give, donate**}

Lexical Redundancy

1. *If $\alpha \in B_{DTV}$ then the lexicon may be extended by adding α to B_{TTV}*

If this is a SEMANTICALLY TRANSPARENT extension then the meaning of α will be the same in both categories EXCEPT THAT the order of functional application for the second and third arguments will be reversed.

Note

English has undergone a semantically transparent extension in respect of **give** but no extension in respect to **donate**.

I gave the library the book
*****I donated the library the book**

2. *If $\alpha \in B_{IV/t}$ then the lexicon may be extended by adding α to $B_{IV//t}$.*

If this is a SEMANTICALLY TRANSPARENT extension then the meaning of the IV-phrases using these verbs will be guaranteed to be the same.

6.3. Syntactic Rules

The syntactic rules tell us how to construct the set of phrases of any category A, which we shall represent as P_A.

BASIC RULES

S1. *Phrases Consisting of Single Lexical Items*
If $\alpha \in B_A$, then $F_1(\alpha) \in P_A$,

where

$$F_1(\alpha) = \begin{bmatrix} \alpha \\ MV \end{bmatrix} \quad \text{if } \alpha \in B_{IV}, B_{TV}, B_{IV/t}, B_{IV///t}, B_{t/t}, B_{IV/PassPhr}, B_{TTV},$$

or B_{DTV};

$F_1(\alpha) = \alpha \quad$ otherwise.

EXAMPLES

$$F_1(\textbf{walk}) = \begin{bmatrix} \textbf{walk} \\ \textbf{MV} \end{bmatrix}$$

$$F_1(\textbf{man}) = \textbf{man}$$

SEMANTICS: The phrases have the same meanings as the basic expressions.

NOTE
The notation MV for "main verb" is not used by Montague.

S2. *Term Phrase Formation*
If $\alpha \in P_{CN}$, then $F_{2.1}(\alpha)$, $F_{2.2}(\alpha)$, $F_{2.3}(\alpha) \in P_T$,

where

$$F_{2.1}(\alpha) = \textbf{every } \alpha$$

$$F_{2.2}(\alpha) = \textbf{the } \alpha$$

$$F_{2.3}(\alpha) = \begin{cases} \textbf{a } \alpha \text{ if } \alpha \text{ begins with a consonant} \\ \textbf{an } \alpha \text{ if } \alpha \text{ begins with a vowel} \end{cases}$$

EXAMPLE: $F_{2.2}(\textbf{woman}) = \textbf{the woman}$

SEMANTICS: $F_{2.1}(\alpha)$ or **every** α corresponds to the "set of properties which every α possesses." Thus **every woman** denotes the set of properties which all women have in common, for example, the property of being female, the property of being discriminated against (in an imperfect possible world).

$F_{2.2}(\alpha)$ or **the** α corresponds to the "set of properties which the unique α possesses."

$F_{2.3}(\alpha)$ or **a(n)** α corresponds to the "set of properties possessed by at least one α." Thus **a woman** denotes the set of properties which at least one woman possesses, for example, the property of running will be in this set if at least one woman runs.

RULES OF FUNCTIONAL APPLICATION

S3. *Subject + Intransitive Verb Phrase Is a Sentence*
If $\alpha \in P_T$ and $\delta \in P_{IV}$, then $F_3(\alpha, \delta) \in P_t$,

where $F_3(\alpha, \delta)$ is $\alpha\delta'$, and δ' is the result of replacing each item of the form

$$\begin{bmatrix} \zeta \\ MV \end{bmatrix}$$

in δ (i.e., "main verb" of δ) by

$$\begin{bmatrix} \zeta \\ MV \\ PAST \end{bmatrix}$$

EXAMPLES

$$F_3 \left(\text{the woman,} \begin{bmatrix} \textbf{walk} \\ MV \end{bmatrix} \right)$$

$$= \text{the woman} \begin{bmatrix} \textbf{walk} \\ MV \\ PAST \end{bmatrix}$$

$$F_3\left(\text{the farmer,} \begin{bmatrix} \textbf{kill} \\ MV \end{bmatrix} \text{the duckling}\right)$$

$$= \text{the farmer} \begin{bmatrix} \textbf{kill} \\ MV \\ PAST \end{bmatrix} \text{the duckling}$$

SEMANTICS: $F_3(\alpha, \delta)$ has the truth-conditions represented by "it was the case that the set of properties corresponding to α included the property corresponding to δ." Thus

$$F_3\left(\text{the woman,} \begin{bmatrix} \textbf{walk} \\ MV \end{bmatrix}\right) \text{or the woman} \begin{bmatrix} \textbf{walk} \\ MV \\ PAST \end{bmatrix}$$

corresponds to "it was the case that the set of properties of the unique woman included the property of walking."

NOTE
The notation PAST is not used by Montague.

S4.   *Transitive Verb (Phrase) + Term Phrase Is an Intransitive Verb Phrase*
If $\alpha \in P_{TV}$ and $\delta \in P_T$, then $F_4(\alpha, \delta) \in P_{IV}$,

where

i. if $\alpha \in B_{TV}$, $F_4(\alpha, \delta)$ is $\alpha\delta$ if δ is not of the form **he**$_n$ and $F_4(\alpha,$ **he**$_n)$ is α **him**$_n$
ii. if α is of the form

$$\begin{bmatrix} \zeta \\ MV \end{bmatrix} \xi,$$

$F_4(\alpha, \delta)$ is

$$\begin{bmatrix} \zeta \\ MV \end{bmatrix} \delta\xi$$

if δ is not of the form **he**$_n$ and

$$\begin{bmatrix} \zeta \\ MV \end{bmatrix} \textbf{him}_n \; \xi \text{ if } \delta \text{ is } \textbf{he}_n.$$

EXAMPLES

$$F_4(\begin{bmatrix} \textbf{kill} \\ MV \end{bmatrix}, \textbf{the duckling}) = \begin{bmatrix} \textbf{kill} \\ MV \end{bmatrix} \textbf{the duckling}$$

$$F_4(\begin{bmatrix} \textbf{love} \\ MV \end{bmatrix}, \textbf{he}_0) = \begin{bmatrix} \textbf{love} \\ MV \end{bmatrix} \textbf{him}_0$$

$$F_4(\begin{bmatrix} \textbf{give} \\ MV \end{bmatrix} \textbf{the axe}, \textbf{John}) = \begin{bmatrix} \textbf{give} \\ MV \end{bmatrix} \textbf{John the axe}$$

SEMANTICS: $F_4(\alpha, \delta)$ corresponds to the property obtained by applying the function represented by α to the intension of δ, the property of α-ing δ. Thus

$$F_4(\begin{bmatrix} \textbf{kill} \\ MV \end{bmatrix}, \textbf{the duckling})$$

or

$$\begin{bmatrix} \textbf{kill} \\ \text{MV} \end{bmatrix} \textbf{the duckling}$$

corresponds to the property of killing the duckling.

S5. *Dative Verb + **to** + Term Phrase Is a Transitive Verb Phrase*
If $\alpha \in P_{\text{DTV}}$ and $\delta \in P_{\text{T}}$, then $F_5(\alpha, \delta) \in P_{\text{TV}}$,

where $F_5(\alpha, \delta)$ is α **to** δ' and δ' is **him**$_n$ if δ is **he**$_n$ and δ' is δ otherwise.

EXAMPLE

$$F_5(\begin{bmatrix} \textbf{give} \\ \text{MV} \end{bmatrix}, \textbf{he}_0) = \begin{bmatrix} \textbf{give} \\ \text{MV} \end{bmatrix} \textbf{to him}_0$$

SEMANTICS: $F_5(\alpha, \delta)$ repesents the relation which any A and B stand in if A α's B to δ. Thus

$$\begin{bmatrix} \textbf{give} \\ \text{MV} \end{bmatrix} \textbf{to the farmer}$$

represents the relation which holds between A and B just in case A gives B to the farmer.

S6. *Double Object Verb + Term Phrase Is a Transitive Verb Phrase*
If $\alpha \in P_{\text{TTV}}$ and $\delta \in P_{\text{T}}$, then $F_6(\alpha, \delta) \in P_{\text{TV}}$,

where $F_6(\alpha, \delta) = F_4(\alpha, \delta)$

EXAMPLE:

$$F_6(\begin{bmatrix} \textbf{give} \\ \text{MV} \end{bmatrix}, \textbf{the axe}) = \begin{bmatrix} \textbf{give} \\ \text{MV} \end{bmatrix} \textbf{the axe}$$

SEMANTICS: $F_6(\alpha, \delta)$ represents the relation which any A and B stand in if A α's δ to B. Thus

$$\begin{bmatrix} \textbf{give} \\ \text{MV} \end{bmatrix} \textbf{the axe}$$

represents the relation which holds between A and B just in case A gives the axe to B.

S7. *Proposition Level Verb + Sentence Is an Intransitive Verb Phrase*
If $\alpha \in P_{\text{IV/}t}$ and $\delta \in P_t$, then $F_7(\alpha, \delta) \in P_{\text{IV}}$,

where $F_7(\alpha, \delta)$ is α **that** δ' where δ' is obtained from δ by removing every occurrence of the feature MV.

EXAMPLE

$$F_7(\begin{bmatrix} \textbf{believe} \\ \text{MV} \end{bmatrix}, \textbf{John} \begin{bmatrix} \textbf{kill} \\ \text{MV} \\ \text{PAST} \end{bmatrix} \textbf{the farmer})$$

$$= \begin{bmatrix} \textbf{believe} \\ \text{MV} \end{bmatrix} \textbf{that John} \begin{bmatrix} \textbf{kill} \\ \text{PAST} \end{bmatrix} \textbf{the farmer}$$

SEMANTICS: $F_7(\alpha, \delta)$ corresponds to the property of standing in the relation expressed by α to the proposition expressed by δ. Thus

$$F_7(\begin{bmatrix} \textbf{believe} \\ \text{MV} \end{bmatrix}, \textbf{John} \begin{bmatrix} \textbf{kill} \\ \text{MV} \\ \text{PAST} \end{bmatrix} \textbf{the farmer})$$

or

$$\begin{bmatrix} \textbf{believe} \\ \text{MV} \end{bmatrix} \textbf{that John} \begin{bmatrix} \textbf{kill} \\ \text{PAST} \end{bmatrix} \textbf{the farmer}$$

corresponds to the property of standing in the believe–relation to the proposition that John killed the farmer.

S8.   *Object-Raising Verb + Sentence Is an Intransitive Verb Phrase*

If $\alpha \in P_{\text{IV}/\!/t}$ and $\delta \in P_t$ of the form $\zeta \begin{bmatrix} \beta \\ \text{MV} \\ \text{PAST} \end{bmatrix} \xi$, then $F_8(\alpha, \delta) \in P_{\text{IV}}$

where $F_8(\alpha, \delta)$ is $\alpha\zeta$ **to have** $\beta'\xi$ and β' is the past participle of β.

EXAMPLE

$$F_8(\begin{bmatrix} \textbf{believe} \\ \text{MV} \end{bmatrix}, \textbf{John} \begin{bmatrix} \textbf{kill} \\ \text{MV} \\ \text{PAST} \end{bmatrix} \textbf{the farmer})$$

$$= \begin{bmatrix} \textbf{believe} \\ \text{MV} \end{bmatrix} \textbf{John to have killed the farmer}$$

SEMANTICS: Same as for S7.

S9.   *Subject-Raising Verb + Sentence Is a Sentence*

If $\alpha \in P_{t/t}$ of the form $\begin{bmatrix} \gamma \\ \text{MV} \end{bmatrix} \eta$ and $\varphi \in P_t$ of the form $\zeta \begin{bmatrix} \beta \\ \text{MV} \\ \text{PAST} \end{bmatrix} \xi$, then $F_9(\alpha, \varphi) \in P_t$,

where $F_9(\alpha, \varphi)$ is $\zeta \begin{bmatrix} \gamma \\ MV \\ PAST \end{bmatrix} \eta$ **to have** $\beta'\xi$ and β' is the past participle

of β.

EXAMPLES

$F_9(\begin{bmatrix} \text{seem} \\ MV \end{bmatrix}$, **the farmer** $\begin{bmatrix} \text{kill} \\ MV \\ PAST \end{bmatrix}$ **the duckling**)

$= $ **the farmer** $\begin{bmatrix} \text{seem} \\ MV \\ PAST \end{bmatrix}$ **to have killed the duckling**

$F_9(\begin{bmatrix} \text{be} \\ MV \end{bmatrix}$ **rumored, the farmer** $\begin{bmatrix} \text{kill} \\ MV \\ PAST \end{bmatrix}$ **the duckling**)

$= $ **the farmer** $\begin{bmatrix} \text{be} \\ MV \\ PAST \end{bmatrix}$ **rumored to have killed the duckling**

$F_9(\begin{bmatrix} \text{be} \\ MV \end{bmatrix}$ **believed by the woman, the farmer** $\begin{bmatrix} \text{kill} \\ MV \\ PAST \end{bmatrix}$ **the duckling**)

$= $ **the farmer** $\begin{bmatrix} \text{be} \\ MV \\ PAST \end{bmatrix}$ **believed by the woman to have killed**

the duckling

SEMANTICS: $F_9(\alpha, \varphi)$ is true just in case the proposition expressed by φ has the property expressed by α. Thus

$F_9(\begin{bmatrix} \text{seem} \\ MV \end{bmatrix}$, **the farmer** $\begin{bmatrix} \text{kill} \\ MV \\ PAST \end{bmatrix}$ **the duckling**)

or

The farmer $\begin{bmatrix} \text{seem} \\ MV \\ PAST \end{bmatrix}$ **to have killed the duckling**

is true just in case the proposition 'the farmer killed the duckling' seemed (to be true).

RULES OF PASSIVIZATION

S10. *Transitive Verb (Phrase)* **or** *Object-Raising Verb + Agent Is a (Propositional) Passive Phrase*

If $\alpha \in P_{TV}$ $(P_{IV//t})$ and $\delta \in P_{T}$, then $F_{10}(\alpha, \delta) \in P_{PassPhr}$ $(P_{PropPassPhr})$, where $F_{10}(\alpha, \delta)$ is α' **by** δ' and α ' is the result of replacing anything of the form

$$\begin{bmatrix} \zeta \\ MV \end{bmatrix}$$

in α by the past participle of ζ and δ' is δ or **him**$_n$, if δ is **he**$_n$.

EXAMPLES

$F_{10}(\begin{bmatrix} kill \\ MV \end{bmatrix}$, **the farmer)** = **killed by the farmer**

$F_{10}(\begin{bmatrix} give \\ MV \end{bmatrix}$ **to John, the farmer)** = **given to John by the farmer**

$F_{10}(\begin{bmatrix} give \\ MV \end{bmatrix}$ **the axe, the farmer)** = **given the axe by the farmer**

$F_{10}(\begin{bmatrix} believe, \\ MV \end{bmatrix}$ **the woman)** = **believed by the woman**

SEMANTICS: $F_{10}(\alpha, \delta)$ corresponds to the property of being an x such that δ α's x (i.e., the set of properties represented by δ includes the property of bearing relation α to x). Thus

$F_{10}(\begin{bmatrix} kill \\ MV \end{bmatrix}$, **the farmer)** or **killed by the farmer**

corresponds to the property of being an x such that the farmer kills x.

S11. ***Be + Passive Phrase Is an Intransitive Verb Phrase***

If $\alpha \in P_{IV/PassPhr}$ and $\delta \in P_{PassPhr}$ $(P_{PropPassPhr})$, then $F_{11}(\alpha, \delta) \in P_{IV}(P_{t/t})$ where $F_{11}(\alpha, \delta)$ is $\alpha\delta$.

EXAMPLES

$F_{11}(\begin{bmatrix} \textbf{be} \\ \text{MV} \end{bmatrix}$, **killed by the farmer**)$\quad = \begin{bmatrix} \textbf{be} \\ \text{MV} \end{bmatrix}$ **killed by the farmer**

$F_{11}(\begin{bmatrix} \textbf{be} \\ \text{MV} \end{bmatrix}$, **believed by the woman**)$= \begin{bmatrix} \textbf{be} \\ \text{MV} \end{bmatrix}$ **believed by the woman**

SEMANTICS: $F_{11}(\alpha, \delta)$ corresponds to the property represented by δ. Thus

$$F_{11}(\begin{bmatrix} \textbf{be} \\ \text{MV} \end{bmatrix}, \textbf{killed by the farmer})$$

or

$$\begin{bmatrix} \textbf{be} \\ \text{MV} \end{bmatrix} \textbf{killed by the farmer}$$

corresponds to the same property as **killed by the farmer**.

RULES OF QUANTIFICATION

S12. *Wh-Phrase + Sentence Is an Indirect Question*
If $\alpha \in P_{\text{WH}}$ and $\varphi \in P_t$ of the form ζ **he**$_n$ ξ or ζ **him**$_n$ ξ, then $F_{12,n}(\alpha, \varphi) \in P_Q$,

where $F_{12,n}(\alpha, \varphi)$ is $\alpha\varphi'$ and φ' is obtained from φ by deleting the first occurrence of **he**$_n$ or **him**$_n$ and replacing each remaining occurrence of **he**$_n$ or **him**$_n$ with **he** or **him** (or **she** or **her**) respectively.

EXAMPLE

$F_{12,0}(\textbf{who}, \textbf{he}_0 \begin{bmatrix} \textbf{kill} \\ \text{MV} \\ \text{PAST} \end{bmatrix}$ **the duckling**)$= \textbf{who} \begin{bmatrix} \textbf{kill} \\ \text{MV} \\ \text{PAST} \end{bmatrix}$ **the duckling**

SEMANTICS: $F_{12,n}(\alpha, \varphi)$ corresponds to the set of true propositions expressed by φ for some he$_n$. Thus

$F_{12,0}(\textbf{who}, \textbf{he}_0 \begin{bmatrix} \textbf{kill} \\ \text{MV} \\ \text{PAST} \end{bmatrix}$ **the duckling**)$\text{ or } \textbf{who} \begin{bmatrix} \textbf{kill} \\ \text{MV} \\ \text{PAST} \end{bmatrix}$ **the duckling**

corresponds to the set of true propositions 'he$_0$ killed the duckling' for some he$_0$; for example, if John killed the duckling, the proposition that John killed the duckling is a member of the set. If Mary did not kill the duckling then the proposition that Mary killed the duckling is not a member of the set.

S13. *Indirect Question + "Subject-Aux-Inversion" Is a Direct Question*

If $\alpha \in P_Q$, then $F_{13}(\alpha) \in P_{DQ}$

where

  i. if α is of the form **who** $\zeta \begin{bmatrix} \textbf{be} \\ \text{MV} \\ \text{PAST} \end{bmatrix} \xi$, then $F_{13}(a)$ is **who** $\begin{bmatrix} \textbf{be} \\ \text{PAST} \end{bmatrix} \zeta\xi$

  ii. if α is of the form **who** $\zeta \begin{bmatrix} \beta \\ \text{MV} \\ \text{PAST} \end{bmatrix} \xi$, $\beta \neq$ **be** and $\zeta \neq \emptyset$,

      then $F_{13}(\alpha)$ is **who did** $\zeta\beta\xi$

  iii. otherwise $F_{13}(\alpha)$ is α.

EXAMPLES

$$F_{13}(\textbf{who the farmer} \begin{bmatrix} \textbf{be} \\ \text{MV} \\ \text{PAST} \end{bmatrix} \textbf{loved by})$$

$$= \textbf{who} \begin{bmatrix} \textbf{be} \\ \text{PAST} \end{bmatrix} \textbf{the farmer loved by}$$

$$F_{13}(\textbf{who the farmer} \begin{bmatrix} \textbf{kill} \\ \text{MV} \\ \text{PAST} \end{bmatrix}) = \textbf{who did the farmer kill}$$

$$F_{13}(\textbf{who} \begin{bmatrix} \textbf{kill} \\ \text{MV} \\ \text{PAST} \end{bmatrix} \textbf{the duckling}) = \textbf{who} \begin{bmatrix} \textbf{kill} \\ \text{MV} \\ \text{PAST} \end{bmatrix} \textbf{the duckling}$$

SEMANTICS: $F_{13}(\alpha)$ corresponds to 'I ask you to tell me α' (i.e., 'I ask you to tell me what propositions are in the set denoted by α'). Thus

$$F_{13}(\textbf{who} \begin{bmatrix} \textbf{kill} \\ \text{MV} \\ \text{PAST} \end{bmatrix} \textbf{the duckling})$$

or

$$
\text{who} \begin{bmatrix} \text{kill} \\ \text{MV} \\ \text{PAST} \end{bmatrix} \text{the duckling}
$$

corresponds to 'I ask you to tell me who killed the duckling.'

S14. *Sentence/Direct Question Scope Quantification*

If $\alpha \in P_{\text{T}}$ not of the form $\textbf{he}_k$ and $\varphi \in P_t$ (or P_{DQ}) of the form $\zeta \, \textbf{he}_n \, \xi$ or $\zeta \, \textbf{him}_n \, \xi$, then $F_{14,n}(\alpha, \varphi) \in P_t$ (or P_{DQ})

where $F_{14,n}(\alpha, \varphi)$ comes from φ by replacing the first occurrence of $\textbf{he}_n$ or $\textbf{him}_n$ with α and all other occurrences of $\textbf{he}_n$ or $\textbf{him}_n$ by he/she/it or him/her/it according as the gender of the first B_{CN} or B_{T} in α is masculine/feminine/neuter.

EXAMPLES

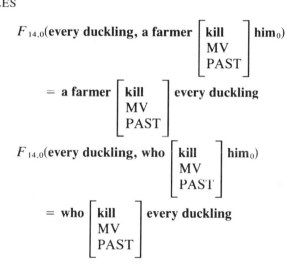

SEMANTICS: $F_{14,n}(\alpha, \varphi)$ corresponds to the proposition that the set of properties denoted by α includes the property of being a $\textbf{he}_n$ such that φ. Thus

$$
F_{14,0}(\textbf{every duckling, a farmer} \begin{bmatrix} \text{kill} \\ \text{MV} \\ \text{PAST} \end{bmatrix} \textbf{him}_0)
$$

or

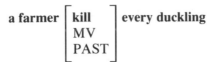

$$\text{a farmer} \begin{bmatrix} \text{kill} \\ \text{MV} \\ \text{PAST} \end{bmatrix} \text{every duckling}$$

corresponds to the proposition that the set of properties belonging to every duckling includes the property of being a he_0 such that a farmer killed him_0, that is, the property of being killed by a farmer is a property that every duckling has.

RULES OF CONJUNCTION

S15.   *Sentence **and** Sentence Is a Sentence*
If $\varphi, \psi \in P_t$, then $F_{15}(\varphi, \psi) \in P_t$

where $F_{15}(\varphi, \psi)$ is φ **and** ψ.

EXAMPLE

$$F_{15}(he_0 \begin{bmatrix} \text{love} \\ \text{MV} \\ \text{PAST} \end{bmatrix} \text{the woman}, he_0 \begin{bmatrix} \text{kill} \\ \text{MV} \\ \text{PAST} \end{bmatrix} \text{the farmer})$$

$$= he_0 \begin{bmatrix} \text{love} \\ \text{MV} \\ \text{PAST} \end{bmatrix} \text{the woman and } he_0 \begin{bmatrix} \text{kill} \\ \text{MV} \\ \text{PAST} \end{bmatrix} \text{the farmer}$$

SEMANTICS: $F_{15}(\varphi, \psi)$ is true just in case both φ and ψ are true.

S16.   *Intransitive Verb Phrase **and** Intransitive Verb Phrase Is an Intransitive Verb Phrase*
If $\alpha, \delta \in P_{IV}$, then $F_{16}(\alpha, \delta) \in P_{IV}$

where $F_{16}(\alpha, \delta)$ is α **and** δ.

EXAMPLE

$$F_{16}(\begin{bmatrix} \text{love} \\ \text{MV} \end{bmatrix} \text{the woman}, \begin{bmatrix} \text{kill} \\ \text{MV} \end{bmatrix} \text{the farmer})$$

$$= \begin{bmatrix} \text{love} \\ \text{MV} \end{bmatrix} \text{the woman and } \begin{bmatrix} \text{kill} \\ \text{MV} \end{bmatrix} \text{the farmer}$$

SEMANTICS: $F_{16}(\alpha, \delta)$ corresponds to the property of having the property associated with α as well as the property associated with δ. Thus

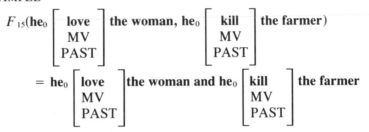

$$F_{16}(\begin{bmatrix} \text{love} \\ \text{MV} \end{bmatrix} \text{the woman}, \begin{bmatrix} \text{kill} \\ \text{MV} \end{bmatrix} \text{the farmer})$$

or

$$\begin{bmatrix} \text{love} \\ \text{MV} \end{bmatrix} \text{the woman and} \begin{bmatrix} \text{kill} \\ \text{MV} \end{bmatrix} \text{the farmer}$$

corresponds to the property of loving the woman and killing the farmer.

ACKNOWLEDGMENT

I should like to thank David Dowty, Barbara Partee, and Ivan Sag (the discussant of this paper at the conference) for invaluable comments on an earlier version of this paper. None of these people are responsible for any of its inadequacies.

REFERENCES

Bach, E. (1979a). Control in Montague Grammar. *Linguistic Inquiry, 10*, 515–531.

Bach, E. (1979b). Montague Grammar and classical transformational grammar. In M. Mithun and S. Davis (Eds.), *Linguistics, philosophy and Montague Grammar*. Austin: University of Texas Press.

Bach, E. (forthcoming a). A framework for syntax and semantics.

Bach, E. (forthcoming b). In defense of passive. *Linguistics and Philosophy*.

Barwise, J. and Cooper, R. (in preparation). Generalized quantifiers and natural languages.

Bresnan, J. (1978). A realistic transformational grammar. In M. Halle, J. Bresnan and G. A. Miller (Eds.), *Linguistic theory and psychological reality*. Cambridge, Mass.: MIT Press.

Cooper, R. (1977). Towards a semantic account of constraints on movement rules. Paper presented at the Montague Grammar Symposium, Winter LSA, Chicago.

Cooper, R. (1978). A fragment of English with questions and relative clauses. University of Wisconsin. Manuscript.

Cooper, R. and Parsons, T. (1976). Montague Grammar, generative semantics, and interpretative semantics. In B. Partee (Ed.), *Montague Grammar*. New York: Academic Press.

Dowty, D. (1978a). Applying Montague's views on linguistic metatheory to the structure of the lexicon. In *Parasession on the Lexicon*, Chicago Linguistic Society, 14, University of Chicago, Department of Linguistics.

Dowty, D. (1978b). Lexically governed transformations as lexical rules in a Montague Grammar. *Linguistic Inquiry, 9*, 393–426.

Dowty, D. (1979). Dative 'Movement' and Thomason's extensions of Montague Grammar. In M. Mithun and S. Davis (Eds.), *Linguistics, philosophy and Montague Grammar*. Austin: University of Texas Press.

Karttunen, L. (1977). Syntax and semantics of questions. *Linguistics and Philosophy, 1*, 3–44.

Montague, R. (1974). *Formal Philosophy*. Edited and with an introduction by R. H. Thomason. New Haven: Yale University Press.

Partee, B. (1975). Montague Grammar and transformational grammar. *Linguistic Inquiry, 6*, 202–300.

Partee, B. (1979a). Montague Grammar and the well-formedness constraint. In F. Heny and H. Schnelle (Eds.), *Syntax and Semantics, 10: Proceedings of the Third Groningen Round Table*. New York: Academic Press.

Partee, B. (1979b). Constraining transformational Montague Grammar: A framework and a fragment. In M. Mithun and S. Davis (Eds.), *Linguistics, philosophy and Montague Grammar*. Austin: University of Texas Press.

Thomason, R. (1976). Some extensions of Montague Grammar. In B. Partee (Ed.), *Montague Grammar*. New York: Academic Press

SEVENTEEN SENTENCES: BASIC PRINCIPLES AND APPLICATION OF FUNCTIONAL GRAMMAR[1]

SIMON C. DIK

Institute for General Linguisitcs, University of Amsterdam

1. INTRODUCTION

This paper discusses the basic principles of the theory of functional grammar (FG) as developed in Dik (1978a, henceforth referred to as *FG*), and applies these principles to a fragment of English grammar designed to account for the properties of Sentences (1)–(17). The paper is organized as follows: Section 1 discusses some general principles concerning the goals and methods of FG. Section 2 gives an outline of the structure of this theory. Each subsection of this outline contains the corresponding subpart of the grammar covering the 17 sentences. The various subparts add up to a complete and operational description of the sentences according to the principles of FG. The description is complete in the sense that if one starts with the information given in the lexicon, and applies all the procedures specified, a set of sentences is produced that includes

[1] This is the revised version of a paper read at the Conference on Current Approaches to Syntax, held at the University of Wisconsin—Milwaukee, March 15–17, 1979. The structure and content of the paper were in part determined by the questions which the organizers of the conference presented to the participants. The organizing committee also provided the sample sentences (1)–(17). The present version of this paper profited greatly from the discussions I had with Kwee Tjoe Liong, in connection with his attempt to write a computer program incorporating the functional grammar developed here (see Section 3).

45

Syntax and Semantics, Volume 13:
Current Approaches to Syntax

the 17 sentences as a proper subset. Where it seemed useful for arriving at a descriptively adequate account, elements of structure that do not occur in the sample sentences have nonetheless been included. The grammar has recursive properties and thus generates an infinite set of sentences. Obviously, an infinite complement set of English sentences remains outside the scope of the sample grammar. The description is operational in the sense that its rules and procedures have either been completely formalized, or have been made explicit to such a degree that formalization can in principle be achieved.

Functional grammar contains a number of principles that are not directly relevant for this sample grammar. These principles have nevertheless been summarized, in order to give a reasonably full picture of the theory. On the other hand, the sample sentences provide a number of problems for which no principled solutions have yet been developed in FG. For these problems this paper suggests solutions which seem compatible with the FG framework, but which may require modification if the problems involved are studied within a less ad hoc context.

2. ON THE GOALS AND METHODS OF FUNCTIONAL GRAMMAR

2.1. The Functional View

Functional grammar is based on a functional view of natural language: A language is regarded in the first place as an instrument by means of which people can enter into communicative relations with one other. From this point of view language is primarily a pragmatic phenomenon— a symbolic instrument used for communicative purposes. According to the functional view, the structure of a language cannot be adequately understood if these pragmatic purposes are left out of consideration.

In this view there is no room for such a thing as an "autonomous" syntax. On the contrary, to the extent that a clear division can be made between syntax and semantics, syntax is there for people to be able to form complex expressions by means of which complex meanings can be expressed, and such meanings are there for people to be able to communicate in differentiated ways. The study of syntax and semantics should be carried out against the background of the pragmatic conventions which determine the use of language in verbal interaction. Syntax is subservient to semantics, and semantics is subservient to pragmatics.

Natural language is not only a social, but also a psychological, phenomenon. The psychological correlate to a natural language is COMMU-

NICATIVE COMPETENCE in the sense of Hymes (1970), that is, the ability that enables people to communicate by verbal means. Communicative competence consists of grammatical competence (the ability to form and interpret linguistic expressions) intertwined with pragmatic competence (the ability to use these expressions in ways appropriate for arriving at the desired communicative effect). FG can thus also be regarded as a theory of the grammatical component of communicative competence.

2.2. Data and Scope

The rules and principles that constitute the system of a language are not observable as such, but must be "reconstructed" on the basis of various sorts of indirect and circumstantial evidence. By this I mean such evidence as the following:

1. Judgments of (in)correctness by the linguist or by native speakers. This data source is easily available and reliable for the clear cases; but it is notoriously unreliable for borderline cases: native speakers are not accustomed to judging isolated sentences, and linguists are naturally biased by the predictions derivable from their theories.
2. Where there is no unanimity as to correctness, a spectrum of acceptability judgments over a group of native speakers may provide comparative evidence about the status of different construction types.
3. Observed utterances in a corpus of spoken or written texts, though no doubt containing mistakes and idiosyncracies, nevertheless provide the best picture of how people actually use their language.
4. The frequency distribution of different construction types over a corpus of texts may provide information about the degree of markedness of these construction types.
5. Idiolectal, sociolectal, and dialectal differences may inform us about which parts of the system are relatively more stable and which are relatively less stable from speaker to speaker and from group to group.
6. Data on historical change may likewise give information about what belongs to the nuclear, and what to the more peripheral, parts of the system.
7. The results of psycholinguistic experiments concerning aspects of language processing may give clues about the psychological status of rules and principles of grammar.
8. The emergence of construction types in language acquisition may have similar relevance.

defining a system of prominence relations among the constituents of a predication. For example, at the semantic level, an Agent term is more prominent than a non-Agent term; at the syntactic level, a subject is more prominent than an Object; and at the pragmatic level, a Topic or Focus is more prominent than a non-Topic or non-Focus. Very often the three sorts of prominence will coincide, as when some Agent term is also assigned Subject and Topic function. In other cases, prominence at one level will not coincide with prominence at some other level (indeed, this is the main argument for distinguishing the three different levels of function in the first place). Semantic functions are for the most part coded in the lexicon.[3] Syntactic and pragmatic functions are added by later assignments, defined in such a way as to capture the partial independence of the three functional levels.

3.2. Constraints on the Descriptive Apparatus

For methodological and empirical reasons FG has been constrained rather heavily with respect to the power of the descriptive apparatus allowed:

1. NO TRANSFORMATIONS. FG does not allow transformations in the sense of structure-changing operations. This means that the structures in terms of which linguistic expressions are described are built up through gradual expansion, and that there are no possibilities for deleting, permuting, or substituting specified elements of those structures.
2. NO FILTERS. Functional grammar aims at defining construction rules which directly generate the target set of correct expressions, avoiding the use of filters.
3. NO ABSTRACT LEXICAL DECOMPOSITION. FG avoids the decomposition of lexical items in terms of any sort of metalanguage. Even at the deepest level of analysis, constructions in FG are built up from predicates which occur as lexical items of the object language.

Together, these constraints have the effect of tying FG rather firmly onto the language described: They restrict the possible degree of abstractness of the description considerably. The interesting task for FG is

---

[3] Except for "satellite" semantic functions, which are introduced by later rules (see Section 3.9).

to show that even within these constraints a satisfactory degree of descriptive and explanatory adequacy can be achieved.

3.3. The Seventeen Sentences

The grammar developed in this paper is meant to account for the following sentences:

(1)   *The woman walked*
(2)   *Every woman walked*
(3)   *The farmer killed the duckling*
(4)   *The duckling was killed by the farmer*
(5)   *Who killed the duckling?*
(6)   *A farmer killed every duckling*
(7)   *John killed a duckling with an axe*
(8)   *The woman believed that John killed the farmer*
(9)   *The woman believed John to have killed the farmer*
(10) *The woman believed the farmer to have been killed by John*
(11) *The farmer was believed by the woman to have been killed by John*
(12) *The farmer gave the axe to John*
(13) *The farmer gave John the axe*
(14) *The axe killed the duckling that John loved*
(15) *John killed the woman and Bill, the farmer*
(16) *John loved the woman and he killed the farmer*
(17) *John loved the woman and killed the farmer*

3.4. The Fund and the Lexicon

The description of a linguistic expression according to FG starts with the construction of an UNDERLYING PREDICATION, which is then mapped onto the form of the expression by means of rules which determine the form and the order in which the constituents of the underlying predication are realized. The underlying predication itself is basically formed through the insertion of TERMS (i.e., expressions that can be used to refer to entities in some world) into PREDICATE FRAMES, schemata specifying a predicate together with a skeleton of the structures in which it can appear. For the construction of underlying predications we thus need at least a set of predicate frames and a set of terms. These two sets together I call the FUND of the language. The fund and the lexicon relate to each other as indicated in the following diagram:

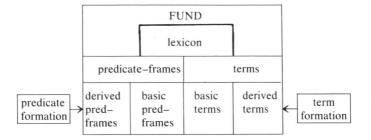

The lexicon contains the basic expressions of the language, that is, those that cannot be formed by means of synchronically productive rules. This includes basic terms and basic predicates. Each of these subsets can be extended by means of synchronically productive rules: Predicate formation rules produce derived predicates, and term formation rules produce derived terms. The former will not be discussed in the present paper. For the latter, see Section 3.5. Each predicate, whether basic or derived, is contained in a predicate frame, which specifies the following syntactic and semantic properties of the predicate: (*a*) its lexical form, (*b*) the (sub)category to which it belongs, (*c*) its number of arguments, (*d*) the semantic functions of these arguments, (*e*) the selection restrictions imposed on these arguments.[4]

The following is an example of a (basic) predicate frame:

(18) $walk_V (x_1 : \text{animate}(x_1))_{Ag}$

This predicate frame specifies that *walk* is a verbal (V) predicate taking one argument (x_1) with Agent function, and imposing on that argument the restriction that it be animate. The latter information is given in the form of an embedded predicate frame "animate(x_1)," which is added to the argument variable through the relation ":", to be read as "such that."

Each predicate frame can be thought of as designating a set of states of affairs, namely the set of states of affairs in which the property or relation specified by the predicate holds of or between an appropriate argument *n*-tuple. States of affairs are divided into four basic types, according to the values they have for two fundamental parameters, namely DYNAMISM (whether or not any change is involved) and CONTROL (whether or not the occurrence of the state of affairs is determined by one

---

[4] Each predicate–frame in the lexicon would further have to be associated with a meaning definition. How this could be done is discussed in Dik (1978b).

of the entities involved in it).[5] We thus get ACTIONS ($+$D, $+$C), POSITIONS ($-$D, $+$C), PROCESSES ($+$D, $-$C), and STATES ($-$D, $-$C). Semantic functions are assigned in such a way that the type of state of affairs designated by a predicate frame can be determined from the semantic function of the first argument:[6]

(19)   *Semantic function*   *State of Affairs*
        Agent (Ag)   Action
        Positioner (Po)   Position
        Processed (Proc) or Force (Fo)   Process
        Zero (Ø)   State

Some examples:

(20)   Action: *John* (Ag) *ran away.*
(21)   Position: *John* (Po) *stayed in the hotel* (Loc).
(22)   Process: a. *John* (Proc) *fell down.*
                   b. *The wind* (Fo) *opened the door* (Go).
(23)   State: *The roses* (Ø) *are beautiful.*

We are now in a position to give the lexicon for the sample grammar. Notice the following points: Basic terms are given in a standard format which will be clarified in Section 3.5. They include the personal pronoun *he*, the interrogative *who* and the relative *who*. Later sections will show how these basic terms are used. Selectional predicates are added to nominal predicates between angled brackets.

The predicate frame for *kill* combines two possibilities, one with an Agent as first argument and one with a Force. The predicate *believe* is given as belonging to a verbal subcategory Vs and as taking a Goal argument marked by an operator Sub and specifiable by an arbitrary predication Φ. The first argument of *love* is given as ambivalent between presence or absence of Control (i.e., *to love* is presented as either a Position or a State).

---

[5] These distinctions were first proposed in Dik (1975). For similar distinctions cf. Lyons (1977).

[6] Abbreviations used in this paper: Φ = some arbitrary (open) predication, $\varphi_i(x_i)$ = some arbitrary open predication in x_i, p = some arbitrary predicate. Categories: V = verbal, A = adjectival, N = nominal, PRO = pronominal, prop = proper, NP = Noun Phrase, PNP = prepositional phrase, NPP = postpositional phrase. Selectional predicates: anim = animate, inanim = inanimate, hum = human, fem = female. Semantic functions: Ag = Agent, Po = Positioner, Proc = Processed, Fo = Force, Go = Goal, Rec = Recipient, Ben = Beneficiary, Instr = Instrument, Loc = Location, Ø = Zero semantic function. Term operators: ω = arbitrary term operator(s), d = definite, i = indefinite, 1 = singular, m = plural.

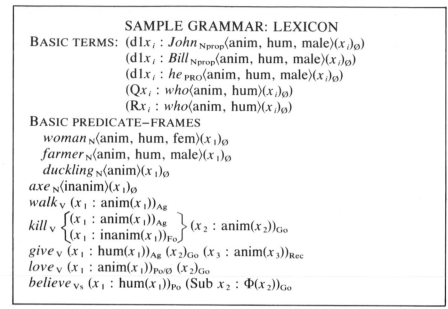

SAMPLE GRAMMAR: LEXICON

BASIC TERMS: $(d1x_i : John_{Nprop}\langle anim, hum, male\rangle(x_i)_\emptyset)$
$(d1x_i : Bill_{Nprop}\langle anim, hum, male\rangle(x_i)_\emptyset)$
$(d1x_i : he_{PRO}\langle anim, hum, male\rangle(x_i)_\emptyset)$
$(Qx_i : who\langle anim, hum\rangle(x_i)_\emptyset)$
$(Rx_i : who\langle anim, hum\rangle(x_i)_\emptyset)$

BASIC PREDICATE–FRAMES
$woman_N\langle anim, hum, fem\rangle(x_1)_\emptyset$
$farmer_N\langle anim, hum, male\rangle(x_1)_\emptyset$
$duckling_N\langle anim\rangle(x_1)_\emptyset$
$axe_N\langle inanim\rangle(x_1)_\emptyset$
$walk_V (x_1 : anim(x_1))_{Ag}$
$kill_V \begin{Bmatrix}(x_1 : anim(x_1))_{Ag}\\(x_1 : inanim(x_1))_{Fo}\end{Bmatrix} (x_2 : anim(x_2))_{Go}$
$give_V (x_1 : hum(x_1))_{Ag} (x_2)_{Go} (x_3 : anim(x_3))_{Rec}$
$love_V (x_1 : anim(x_1))_{Po/\emptyset} (x_2)_{Go}$
$believe_{Vs} (x_1 : hum(x_1))_{Po} (Sub\ x_2 : \Phi(x_2))_{Go}$

3.5. Term Formation

In order for a predicate frame to result in a predication, the free variables marking its argument positions must be bound in some way or other. One way of binding them is to insert appropriate terms into the argument slots. These terms may be basic ones, drawn from the lexicon; but most terms (in fact, an infinite set of them) will be formed via procedures of TERM FORMATION by means of the following general schema:

(24) $(\omega x_i : \varphi_1(x_i) : \varphi_2(x_i) : \cdots : \varphi_n(x_i))$

In this schema each $\varphi_i(x_i)$ stands for some "open predication in x_i," that is, a predicate frame all of whose argument positions have been bound except for x_i (where x_i indicates an arbitrary argument variable of the predicate frame in question). Each open predication in x_i can be regarded as a RESTRICTOR specifying some property which x_i must have in order to qualify as a potential referent of the term. Restrictors are stacked onto each other through the relation indicated by ":" ("such that"). Restrictors may have various degrees of internal complexity, including internal conjunction. The symbol ω represents one or more TERM OPERATORS. Term operators specify properties of the whole referent set of the term, whereas restrictors impose conditions on each of the referents taken separately.

Term operators include such categories as Definiteness, Number, Quantifiers, Demonstratives, Ordinators, and Classifiers.

Restrictors will finally get different types of formal expression. Usually the first restrictor of a term will contain a nominal predicate, and be realized as the head of the term phrase. Later restrictors will be realized as attributive modifiers or relative clauses. Thus, the derived term

(25)   *the old farmer*

would get the following underlying representation:

(26) $(d1x_i : farmer_N \langle anim, hum, male \rangle (x_i)_\emptyset : old_A (x_i)_\emptyset)$

where "d" indicates "definite" and "1" indicates "singular."

Term formation possibilities in the sample grammar can be restricted to the following:

SAMPLE GRAMMAR: TERM FORMATION

Term formation schema: $(\omega x_i : \varphi_1(x_i) : \cdots : \varphi_n(x_i))$ for $n \leq 2$

Conditions: φ_1 must contain a p_N; φ_2 must contain a p_V.

Expansion rules for ω:

$$\omega \rightarrow \left\{ \begin{array}{c} every \\ D \end{array} \right\} Num$$

$$D \rightarrow d, i$$

$$Num \rightarrow \left\{ \begin{array}{l} 1 / every \underline{\quad} \\ 1, m \end{array} \right\}$$

Notice that the universal quantifier *every* is treated as a term operator. It thus originates as part of the term to which it belongs, just as it will finally be realized as part of the term phrase in question.

3.6. Relativization

The term formation procedures sketched so far allow us to construct the underlying representation (27b) for the derived term (27a):

(27)   a. *the farmer who killed the duckling*
         b. $(d1x_i : farmer_N \langle anim, hum, male \rangle (x_i)_\emptyset : kill_V (x_i : anim(x_i))_{Ag}$
            $(d1x_j : duckling_N \langle anim \rangle (x_j)_\emptyset)_{Go})$

We now want to account for the fact that the second restrictor of (27b) will be realized as a relative clause. For this, two different strategies can be followed in English, which I have formalized in the following way. In the first strategy, the appropriate relative pronoun (in this case, the basic term marked by R) is selected from the lexicon and inserted into the Agent slot of *kill* in (27b). This strategy will finally lead to the realization (27a). The insertion of the R-term is subject to certain "accessibility" conditions,[7] for which the functional specification of the relativized variable and its hierarchical position in the predicate frame may be relevant. Since we need only limited relativization possibilities in the sample grammar, I shall not attempt to further specify these conditions here. In the second strategy, the operator Sub is simply preposed to the second restrictor of (27b). This strategy will finally lead to the realization (28a), to be derived from (28b):

(28)   a. *the farmer that killed the duckling*
          b. $(d1x_i : farmer_N \langle anim, hum, male \rangle (x_i)_\emptyset : Sub\ kill_V$
             $(x_i : anim(x_i))_{Ag} (d1x_j : duckling_N \langle anim \rangle (x_j)_\emptyset)_{Go})$

Again, I will not attempt to specify the conditions to be imposed on this second relativization strategy in a full grammar of English.

SAMPLE GRAMMAR: RELATIVIZATION
Given a restrictor taking the position of $\varphi_2(x_i)$ in underlying term structure, follow one of the following strategies.

(i) insert an appropriate R-term into the (x_i) position;
(ii) prepose Sub to the restrictor so as to result in: Sub $\varphi_2(x_i)$

Later some measures will be taken with respect to Subject and Object assignment in order to avoid incorrect results. Notice that the sample grammar overspecifies the set of sample sentences in allowing relative clauses introduced by *who*. This has been done in order to demonstrate the effects of the two different relativization strategies.

This ends our summary of term formation. For further discussion see *FG*, Chapter 4. Notice that we need "open predications in x_i" for the construction of underlying term representations. Obviously, all one-place predicate frames in the lexicon qualify as such immediately. But in the case of many-place predicate frames some term positions must have been filled before the predicate frame can be used as a restrictor. This pre-

---

[7] See Keenan and Comrie (1977).

supposes the development of a predicate frame into a predication. To this we turn now.

3.7. Deriving Underlying Predications

Given a fund of predicate frames and terms, the question is then how to arrive, from a given predicate frame, at a fully specified underlying predication which can form the input of the expression rules. Even within the limited scope of this sample grammar, this requires quite a few distinct operations, which will now be discussed one by one.

3.8. Conjunction

Since FG does not allow structure-changing operations, conjunction of constituents below the level of the sentence cannot be described in terms of some sort of reduction rule operating on the corresponding conjunction of full sentences. In particular, there can be no rules analogous to such rules as Conjunction Reduction or Gapping as formulated in transformational grammar. Therefore, FG will have to follow a different strategy for arriving at such conjunctions. This strategy will involve expansion of constituents into conjunctions of constituents rather than reduction from conjoined full sentences.[8] For this purpose we need a quite general conjunction schema of the following form:

(29) $\alpha \rightarrow \alpha(\text{and})\alpha^1(\text{and})\alpha^2(\text{and}) \cdots \text{and } \alpha^n$ $(n \geqslant 1)$

which, operating on some element α, will produce conjoined strings of the forms (30a) or (30b):

(30)   a. $\alpha, \alpha, \alpha, \alpha, \alpha, \cdots,$ and α
        b. α and α and α and α and α and $\cdots$ and α

In order to account for the different sorts of conjunction found in natural languages, we assume that α may take different values. When α is given the value Φ (the variable for arbitrary predications), schema (29) results in conjunctions of predications. Schema (29) can also be used to expand terms within some predication into conjunctions of terms. Here we distinguish two possibilities: Either full term positions, including the accompanying semantic function, are taken as the value for α, so that we get a conjunction of Agents, Goals, or other semantic functions; or the argument variable WITHIN the domain of the term is conjunctively expanded, so that we get one compound Agent, etc. The effects of these

---

[8] This is in line with the treatment of coordination first proposed in Dik (1968).

two procedures can be roughly represented as follows:

(31) $(John)_{Ag}$ and $(Bill)_{Ag}$ each killed a rabbit
(32) $(John$ and $Bill)_{Ag}$ together killed a rabbit

This procedure for conjunction would thus account for the difference between so-called "phrasal" and "nonphrasal" conjunction.

There are two cases of conjunction in our sample sentences, neither of which can be handled by the applications of the conjunction schema mentioned so far. Sentences of type (15) can be accounted for rather easily when we assume that α in (29) may take as possible value some n-tuple of term positions of a given predicate frame. Thus, the structure of (15) can be arrived at by taking the pair (Ag, Go) as a possible value for α.

Conjunction schema (29) cannot be used, however, for describing sentences of type (17). The reason for this is that, given the present framework of FG, there are no predicate variables which could be taken as a value for α in the conjunction schema: Predicates are lexically specified from the very start. For this reason the structure of (17) will be handled in terms of zero anaphora later on in this paper; that is, (17) is regarded as based on conjunction of full predicate frames in which the Agent of the second frame is treated as an anaphorical element which is given zero expression. For the sample grammar we need only some of the conjunction possibilities outlined above. For simplicity's sake we restrict conjunction to the following:

SAMPLE GRAMMAR: CONJUNCTION
Conjunction schema: $\alpha \rightarrow \alpha$ and α
Values for α: a. $\alpha = \Phi$
               b. $\alpha = (\ )_{Ag}(\ )_{Go}$

3.9. Extension with Satellites

So far we have restricted our attention to nuclear predicate frames, consisting of some predicate and the argument positions connected with it. Such nuclear predicate frames can be extended with "satellite" positions for terms which specify further properties of the state of affairs taken as a whole. Satellites will carry such semantic functions as Instrument, Beneficiary, Location, Reason, Cause, Manner, and Purpose. The introduction of such satellites will be sensitive to the basic properties of the sorts of states of affairs designated by the nuclear predicate frame (see Section 3.4), for example, the introduction of a Reason satellite will be restricted to states of affairs with the property Control (i.e., to Actions and Positions). Satellites are given the same internal structure and the same functional status as argument positions; that is, they consist of variables labeled for semantic functions.[9]

For the sample grammar we only need an Instrument satellite for capturing the phrase *with an axe* in (7). I have, however, added a position for Reason satellites to be expressed through a predication, in order to show how recursion through satellite positions is possible.

SAMPLE GRAMMAR: SATELLITE INTRODUCTION

Condition: Predicate frame contains:	May be extended with:
(i) Ag	$(x_i : \text{inanim}(x_i))_{\text{Instr}}$
(ii) Ag, Po	$(\text{Sub } x_i : \Phi(x_i))_{\text{Reason}}$

3.10. Anaphora

The general principle for the treatment of anaphoric relations in FG is as follows: Anaphoric elements are regarded as expressing term variables that have not been specified by term insertion or otherwise, but are co-indexed with another term variable in the context which has been so specified (the antecedent). The anaphoric variable can then be said to be bound by the antecedent.

Although this is not strictly necessary, I shall use a term operator A to mark the anaphoric variable. We can then say that the general schema for the introduction of anaphoric elements is:

(33)   antecedent   anaphoric variable
       $(\omega x_i : \varphi(x_i)) \cdots (\text{A} x_i)$

where the antecedent is some specified term. A number of structural and functional conditions will have to be imposed on the circumstances under which a given term variable can be anaphorically specified with respect to some given antecedent. Lack of space prevents me from going into these conditions in any detail. Let us simply say that the variable must be accessible to A, given these conditions.

Within a full grammar of English, A must be allowed to operate within

---

[9] For the in some respects problematic relationship between satellites and arguments, see *FG*, Chapter 3.

the domain of relative clauses, and to relate variables within that domain to antecedents both within and outside the relative clause. Again, I will disregard the complexities involved in this, and concentrate on the cases of anaphora which we find in the sample sentences. There is, in fact, only one case of overt anaphora in these sample sentences:

(16)   *John loved the woman and he killed the farmer*

As usual, this sentence can also be interpreted with a nonanaphoric (deictic) use of *he*. Our grammar accounts for this in the following way: In the anaphoric case, *he* represents an anaphoric variable co-indexed with *John*; in the deictic case, *he* represents an independent variable that has been filled with the basic term representing *he* from the lexicon. The relationships will thus be as indicated in:

(34) $(d1x_i : John_{Nprop}\langle anim, hum, male\rangle(x_i)_\emptyset) \cdots (Ax_i)$
(35) $(d1x_i : John_{Nprop}\langle anim, hum, male\rangle(x_i)_\emptyset) \cdots (d1x_j : he_{PRO}\langle anim, hum, male\rangle(x_j)_\emptyset)$

As announced above, Sentence (17) will be treated as a case of zero anaphora. It will thus be given the same underlying representation as (16) on its anaphoric reading, and the expression rules for anaphoric elements will then specify that in the given conditions the anaphoric variable may be either expressed by a personal pronoun, or get zero expression.

One of the conditions imposed on the application of A is that the selectional properties of its antecedent should be compatible with the selection restrictions imposed on the target variable. This condition has been added to the sample grammar, which allows for the appearance of anaphoric variables in the second member of a conjoined predication pair

---

SAMPLE GRAMMAR: ANAPHORA

The operator A may be applied to some term variable x_i so as to result in one of the following configurations:

$$\cdots (\omega x_i : \varphi(x_i)) \cdots \begin{cases} \text{and} \cdots (Ax_i) \cdots \\ (Sub\ x_j : \cdots (Ax_i) \cdots(x_j)) \end{cases}$$

Condition: The selectional properties of the antecedent should be compatible with the selection restrictions imposed on the (Ax_i) position.

[as in (16) and (17)], and also in subordinate clauses, although this does not occur in the sample sentences.

3.11. Question Formation

Term-questions (*wh*-questions) are formed by inserting some questioned term marked by an operator Q into some term position. Questioned terms may again be basic (*who, what*) or derived through term formation (*which man, what axe, what kind of farmer*). For reasons of space and in order to avoid a number of complexities, the sample grammar has been restricted to producing term-questions with *who* in Subject function, as required by Sentence (5), and Q-term insertion has been barred from subordinate clauses. It is evident that the present statement greatly underspecifies the questioning possibilities of English.

SAMPLE GRAMMAR: QUESTION FORMATION
Insert Q-term from lexicon into appropriate term position.
Constraint: do not apply in the context (Sub ···__···).

3.12. The Formation of Closed Predications

A closed predication is a predicate frame all of whose term variables have been bound. Term variables can be bound through (*a*) term insertion (including Q- and R-term insertion), (*b*) application of A. There are a number of complexities involved in the interaction of these various sorts of binding:

1. In principle more than one Q-term may occur in the same predicate frame, as in *Who saw what?*
2. Q-terms may occur within the domain of a relative clause, as in *the man who saw what?*
3. More than one A-term may occur within the same predicate frame, as in *John loved Mary and she loved him.*
4. A-terms may occur within the domain of relative clauses, as in *John saw the woman who loved him.*

All these complexities have been left out of account in the sample grammar, because they would require much more discussion than is possible in the present context. For practical purposes, therefore, I shall assume the following ordering of procedures for the sample grammar:

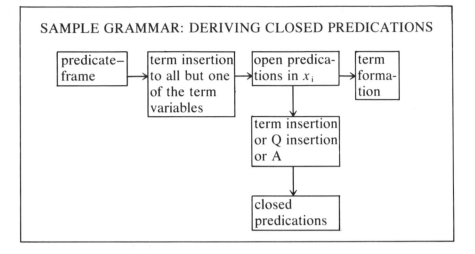

SAMPLE GRAMMAR: DERIVING CLOSED PREDICATIONS

Note: Term insertion should be handled in such a way that for each new term to be inserted, a new index $i, j, k, \ldots$ is chosen, in order to symbolize nonidentity of referents.

3.13. Subject and Object Assignment

Closed predications as developed so far cannot differentiate between alternative constructions such as:

(36)   *The farmer killed the duckling*
(37)   *The duckling was killed by the farmer*

In order to account for such differences FG makes use of differential assignments of Subject and Object function to the terms of the underlying predication. These assignments are semantically interpreted as defining alternative "perspectives" on the state of affairs designated by the predication: The Subj function characterizes that term which is the primary vantage point from which the state of affairs is "presented," and the Obj function the secondary vantage point. Thus, (36–37) differ in that the same state of affairs is presented from the point of view of the farmer in (36), and from the point of view of the duckling in (37). The differential effect of Obj function can be seen in the sample sentences (12) and (13). These are interpreted as expressing the same underlying predication, but with Obj assigned to Go in (12), and to Rec in (13). Correspondingly, *the axe* provides the secondary vantage point in (12), and *John* provides the secondary vantage point in (13). In the formalization of these facts in FG, Subj and Obj function are simply added to the terms of the predication as so far developed, with no further changes being made in this predication. Thus, when the predication underlying (12) and (13) is represented (in simplified form) as in (38), the output of Subj and Obj assignment, which will finally lead to (12) and (13), respectively, will look as indicated in (39a)–(39b):

(38) $give_V$ $(the\ farmer)_{Ag}$ $(the\ axe)_{Go}$ $(John)_{Rec}$
(39)   a. $give_V$ $(the\ farmer)_{AgSubj}$ $(the\ axe)_{GoObj}$ $(John)_{Rec}$
         b. $give_V$ $(the\ farmer)_{AgSubj}$ $(the\ axe)_{Go}$ $(John)_{RecObj}$

Subj and Obj assignment will later have a number of consequences for the form and the order in which the constituents of the predication will be realized. These consequences are not identical across languages; but they are quite similar. For English they involve the following aspects of sentence structure:

1. The voice of the verb will be passive when Subj is assigned to some non-Agent term.
2. Constituent ordering rules will give specific positions to Subj and Obj terms, while constituents with only a semantic function may be positioned more freely.
3. The form of the term in question will be influenced by Subj and Obj assignment. Formal differences connected with underlying semantic functions will typically be neutralized.
4. Agreement will obtain between the verb and the Subj term.

In FG the hypothesis is developed that Subj and Obj assignment possibilities are sensitive to a language-independent hierarchy of semantic functions in the following way:

(40)   SEMANTIC FUNCTION HIERARCHY (SFH)

	Ag		Go		Rec		Ben		Instr		Loc		Time
Subj	+	>	+	>	+	>	+	>	+	>	+	>	+
Obj			+	>	+	>	+	>	+	>	+	>	+

That is, the first candidate for receiving Subj function is the Agent, and the possibilities decrease from left to right through the hierarchy; similarly for Obj assignment. Each language has its own "cutoff points" for Subj and Obj assignment in the SFH. This theory is compatible with the possibility that some language may have no Obj or even no Subj assignment possibilities at all. The possibilities for Subj and Obj assignment in English are as predicted by this theory. The cutoff point for Obj assignment is after Ben, and for Subj assignment just before or just after Ben, depending on the grammaticalness of such sentences as:

(41)   *Mary was bought a dress by Peter*

For our sample grammer we need almost all the possibilities as they occur in English (except for Ben). We even need some special assignment possibilities for capturing the special properties of sentences (9–11), containing the verb *believe*. In Dik (1979) I have considered several possible solutions for these constructions within FG, and have concluded that they can best be handled by allowing Subj and Obj function at the level of the matrix verb *believe* to be exceptionally assigned to the Subj of the embedded Goal–predication of *believe*. This solution has been built into the sample grammar, with the condition that if one of these special assignments is applied, the embedded verbal predicate is specified as an infinitive. Finally, some special provisos have been made for the assignment of Subj and Obj to conjoined *n*-tuples of terms, and to Q- or R-terms. In the former case, this is systematically required; in the latter, it is an ad hoc measure to avoid the complications involved in the questioning and relativization of non-Subj terms.

SAMPLE GRAMMAR: SUBJ AND OBJ ASSIGNMENT
The following assignments are allowed:

		Ag/Fo/Po	Go	Rec	Ben	(Sub . . .$_{Subj}$)
for all p_V	(i)	Subj	Obj			
	(ii)	Subj		Obj		
	(iii)	Subj			Obj	
	(iv)		Subj			
	(v)			Subj		
	(vi)				Subj	
only for p_{Vs}	(vii)	Subj				Obj
	(viii)					Subj

Special requirements:
1. Start Subj and Obj assignment within the domain of (Sub . . .), if present.
2. When there are conjoined *n*-tuples of terms in the input predication, apply the same assignment to each *n*-tuple.
3. When there is a Q- or R-term in the predication, assign Subj to this term.
4. When Subj is assigned to Go or some later function, apply p_V → p_{VPass}
5. When (vii) or (viii) has been applied, then: Sub ... $p_{V(Pass)}$ → Sub ... $p_{V(Pass)Inf}$.

3.14. Tense and Aspect

Within FG no detailed theory has been developed so far about the treatment of tense and aspect, and it is obviously impossible to develop such a theory in the present paper. Therefore, the treatment of tense and aspect as included in the sample grammar should be regarded as anything but definitive. This treatment is descriptively adequate, however, in that it accounts for the following facts:

1. Both finite and infinite verbal predicates may be specified for the perfect and progressive aspects. The former is freely applicable to any state of affairs, the latter is excluded with certain states of affairs. Where each of them may occur, they may also occur together.
2. Only finite verbal predicates may be specified for the present and past tenses. In embedded predications the tense specification may be sensitive to the tense of the matrix predication. In our grammar tense specification will freely operate in matrix predications. This would of course have to be modified if the domain of the grammar were extended beyond the sentence.
3. Tense and aspect, though semantically relevant for the predication as a whole, are expressed through the different forms that predicates may take. For this reason tense and aspect are formalized by means of predicate operators. The introduction of these operators has been ordered after Subj and Obj assignment. This means that until then the predication remains tense- and aspect-less. This is by no means the only possible ordering solution, but for the purposes of the sample grammar it seemed the most practical one.

SAMPLE GRAMMAR: INTRODUCTION OF TENSE AND ASPECT

(i) $p_V \rightarrow \alpha p_V$

(ii) $\alpha p_V \rightarrow \tau \alpha p_V$ (unless $p_V = p_{VInf}$)

(iii) $\alpha \rightarrow \begin{Bmatrix} \text{(Perf)(Progr)} / \_\_ \text{ Ag} \\ \text{(Perf)} \end{Bmatrix}$

(iv) $\tau \rightarrow$ Pres, Past (blocked in the context Sub __)

$\tau \rightarrow \begin{Bmatrix} \text{Past / Past } \ldots \text{ (Sub__)} \\ \text{Pres, Past} \end{Bmatrix}$

3.15. The Assignment of Pragmatic Functions

Even the differentiation achieved through Subj and Obj assignment is insufficient to account for the different forms in which a given underlying predication can be realized. That is, even with a given distribution of syntactic functions, the resulting predication can usually be expressed in various forms, differentiated by constituent order and/or accent and intonation. These differences are not random, but correspond to differences in the informational status of the different parts of the predication within the wider pragmatic setting in which it is used. Such differences are accounted for by assigning different PRAGMATIC FUNCTIONS to the various parts of the underlying predication. This assignment of pragmatic functions has not been integrated into the sample grammar because, given that Sentences (1)–(17) are presented in isolation and without intonational characteristics, there is no way of determining their informational properties. For this reason I shall only briefly summarize the treatment of pragmatic functions in FG. For more extensive discussion see *FG*, Chapter 6.

I distinguish four pragmatic functions, two of which characterize material external to the predication proper, and the other two material internal to the predication. The external pragmatic functions, which I call Theme and Tail, mark those constituents preceding and following the predication which are commonly known as left- and right-dislocated constituents. Theme and Tail can be defined as follows:

THEME: The Theme specifies the universe of discourse with respect to which the subsequent predication is presented as relevant.

TAIL: The Tail presents, as an "afterthought" to the predication, information meant to specify, clarify, or modify it in various ways.

The introduction of Theme and Tail presupposes an initial schema of the form:

(42)   Theme, Predication, Tail

Thus, the Theme and the Tail will be outside the predication proper from the very start. In particular, they are not regarded as constituents extracted from the predication in any way.

Within the domain of the predication proper I recognize the two pragmatic functions Topic and Focus, defined as follows:

TOPIC: The Topic presents the entity about which the predication predicates something in the given setting.

FOCUS: The Focus presents what is relatively the most important or salient information in the given setting.

The assignment of pragmatic functions is dependent upon the development of the "pragmatic information" of speaker and addressee in the course of verbal interaction, and for that reason it is difficult to specify these functions for isolated sentences. On the other hand, these functions, once assigned, have their influence on the form in which the predication is going to be realized. Therefore, pragmatic functions must be assignable to the constituents of individual linguistic expressions, but their full significance can only be assessed within some wider setting. After the assignment of Topic and Focus function, the underlying predication will have a form such as that illustrated in:[10]

(43)   Past *kill*$_{VPass}$ (*the farmer*)$_{AgFoc}$ (*the duckling*)$_{GoSubjTop}$

which would finally be realized as:

(44)   *The duckling was killed by the farmer*

as used in a setting in which *the duckling* represents the topic of discourse and *the farmer* provides the most salient information.

Pragmatic functions will thus codetermine the form in which linguistic expressions are realized. On the other hand, they indicate how the information contained in the expression is structured in relation to the setting in which it is used, and they are important for determining the different presuppositions which are connected with the expression.

3.16. Expression Rules

The assignment of pragmatic functions is the last step in the construction of underlying predications. The output of the procedures discussed so far will thus be an infinite set of such underlying predications. We now need a mapping from these abstract representations to the form of the actual linguistic expressions by means of which they are realized. This mapping will consist of a system of EXPRESSION RULES determining the form and the order in which the constituents will appear, given their status in the underlying predication. In general, the expression rules will account for the following aspects of linguistic structure: (*a*) the form in which terms are realized, in particular with respect to case marking and adpositions; (*b*) the form in which the predicate is realized, in particular with respect to voice differences, auxiliary elements, agreement, and cross-reference; (*c*) the order of constituents; (*d*) stress and intonation patterns. The prosodic features mentioned under (*d*) will be disregarded here. For the expression features (*a*)–(*c*) I restrict myself to what is needed for the

---

[10] Again, the internal structure of the terms is left unspecified here.

SAMPLE GRAMMAR: EXPRESSION RULES DETERMINING THE FORM OF CONSTITUENTS

A. EXPRESSION RULES FOR VERBAL PREDICATES p_V

(i) $p_{VPass(Inf)} \rightarrow be_{V(Inf)}\ p_{Vpap}$

(ii)   Progr $p_{V(Inf)} \rightarrow be_{V(Inf)}\ p_{Vprp}$

(iii)   Perf $p_{V(Inf)} \rightarrow have_{V(Inf)}\ p_{Vpap}$

(iv) $p \rightarrow p\text{-ing}\ /\ \_\_{Vprp}$

(v) $be \rightarrow been\ /\ \_\_{Vpap}$

       $give \rightarrow given\ /\ \_\_{Vpap}$

       $p \rightarrow p\text{-ed}\ /\ \_\_{Vpap}$

(vi) $p \rightarrow to\ p\ /\ \_\_{VInf}$

(vii) Pres $be_V \rightarrow \begin{Bmatrix} is_V\ /\ \_\_(1)_{Subj} \\ are_V \end{Bmatrix}$

       Pres $have_V \rightarrow \begin{Bmatrix} has_V\ /\ \_\_(1)_{Subj} \\ have_V \end{Bmatrix}$

       Pres $p_V \rightarrow \begin{Bmatrix} p\text{-}s_V\ /\ \_\_(1)_{Subj} \\ p_V \end{Bmatrix}$

(viii) Past $be_V \rightarrow \begin{Bmatrix} was_V\ /\ \_\_(1)_{Subj} \\ were_V \end{Bmatrix}$

       Past $give_V \rightarrow gave_V$

       Past $have_V \rightarrow had_V$

       Past $p_V \rightarrow p\text{-ed}_V$

B. EXPRESSION RULES FOR ANAPHORICAL ELEMENTS (Ax_i)

Note: I assume here that the notion "antecedent" (ANT) has been defined in such a way that the antecedent of a given (Ax_i) can be effectively retrieved for the application of these rules.

(i) $(Ax_i)_{SubjObj} \rightarrow (\text{PRO-SELF})_{SubjObj}$

(ii) $\text{SELF} \rightarrow \begin{Bmatrix} self\ /\ (ANT1)\_\_ \\ selves \end{Bmatrix}$

(iii) $(Ax_i)_{Subj} \rightarrow \begin{Bmatrix} (\emptyset)_{Subj}\ /\ (ANT)_{Subj}\_\_ \\ (PRO)_{Subj} \end{Bmatrix}$

       $(Ax_i) \rightarrow (PRO)$

(iv) $(\_\_)_{Subj}$ Otherwise

     $\text{PRO} \rightarrow \begin{cases} he & him & /\ (ANT1\ \text{male})\_\_ \\ she & her & /\ (ANT1\ \text{female})\_\_ \\ it & it & /\ (ANT1)\_\_ \\ they & them \end{cases}$

sample grammar. I will assume, as I have done in *FG*, that the form of constituents is determined before their order is established, although alternatives to this ordering convention would be feasible, especially within the restricted domain of the sample grammar.

A number of expression rules are given in context-sensitive form. These rules account for the various sorts of dependencies operative in the formal expression of the constituents of a predication. Where different options are given for developing a single element, these options should be applied in the order given, with the last option as an "elsewhere" rule.

Some comments: Rules B (i) and (ii) are needed to get the correct output for such constructions as

(45)   *John believed himself to have killed the duckling*

in which, according to Subj/Obj assignment (vii) in Section 3.13, Obj has been assigned to the Subj of the embedded predication. The rules of anaphora given in Section 3.10 would allow this embedded Subj to be specified as an anaphorical element. Rule B (iii) allows for either zero or PRO expression of the anaphorical elements in the case of such sentences as (16) and (17). Rule B (iv) is an unorthodox two-dimensional rule in which the contextual conditions given in the top line specify the entry conditions for the columns, and selection within each column is determined by further context conditions in the usual way.

These expression rules are rather more complicated than the sample sentences strictly require. The sample grammar, however, goes far beyond the set of sample sentences. For example, the following sentence will be generated by the sample grammar as it stands:

(46)   *The women believed themselves to have been loved by John because the farmer who believed that he had killed the duckling had given the axe to them.*

3.17. Expression Rules: The Order of Constituents

FG incorporates a general theory of constituent ordering based on the following principles. The actual constituent orderings of individual languages are supposed to be the outcome of three main tendencies, which may partially counteract each other:

1. The preference for giving designated positions to constituents with specified syntactic functions
2. The tendency to give "special" positions to certain specific categories of constituents and to constituents with specified pragmatic functions

C. Expression Rules for Terms and Term Operators

(i) $d \rightarrow \left\{ \begin{array}{l} \emptyset \: / \: \text{—} \: p_{\text{Nprop}} \\ the \end{array} \right\}$

        $i \rightarrow \left\{ \begin{array}{l} a \: / \: \text{—} \: 1 \\ \emptyset \end{array} \right\}$

(ii) $m \ldots woman \rightarrow women$

        $m \ldots p_N \rightarrow p_N\text{-}s$

        $1 \rightarrow \emptyset$

D. Expression Rules for Sub

(i) $\text{Sub} \rightarrow \left\{ \begin{array}{l} because_{\text{Sub}} \: / \: (\text{—})_{\text{Reason}} \\ \emptyset \: / \: \text{—} p_{\text{VInf}} \\ that_{\text{Sub}} \: / \: \text{—} \: \cdots \: (x_i)_{\text{Subj}} \\ that, \: \emptyset \end{array} \right\}$

Comment: The third option here specifies that Sub must be expressed as *that* in a case such as *the farmer that killed the duckling*; the last option specifies that Sub may be either *that* or zero in other cases in which it occurs in relative clauses, as well as in subordinate clauses.

E. Expression Rules for Functions

If the outer function of a given term is:

$$\begin{bmatrix} \text{Subj/Obj/Go} \\ \text{Ag/Po/Fo} \\ \text{Rec} \\ \text{Instr} \end{bmatrix}$$

then prepose to that term:

$$\begin{bmatrix} \emptyset \\ by \\ to \\ with \end{bmatrix}$$

3. The preference for linearizing constituents in order of increasing internal complexity

The first two tendencies are captured by assuming that each language has one or more ordering patterns built on the following general schema:[11]

(47)   P2, P1 (V) S (V) O (V), P3

where P2 and P3 indicate the positions for Theme and Tail constituents, respectively; P1 indicates a special clause-initial position; S and O indicate the unmarked "pattern positions" for Subj and Obj; and the Vs mark possible positions for the predicate, sometimes to be divided into finite verb Vf and infinite verb Vi. The special position P1 is thought to be universally relevant as a position used for special purposes in the following way:

(i) Most languages have some categories of constituents which, if present in a predication, must go to P1 (in English this holds for question-words, relative pronouns, and subordinators).
(ii) If there is no such constituent in the predication, then P1 can be used for constituents having Topic or Focus function.

Preference (3) above is accounted for in terms of a "Language-independent preferred order of constituents" (LIPOC) which says that, other things being equal, constituents prefer to be ordered from left to right in order of increasing complexity, as follows:

(48)   CLITIC – PRO – NP – NPP – V – NP – PNP – SUB

A detailed argumentation for this theory can be found in *FG*, Chapter 9. The idea is thus that for each language we have the basic ordering pattern(s) based on schema (47), rules for the uses that can be made of P1, and particular applications of LIPOC. The outcome of these three principles, which may operate with varying strength in different languages, is a "compromise" solution for each language, embodied in the particular array of possible ordering patterns in that language.

Almost all clause types of English can be described in terms of two basic ordering patterns, one for declarative main clauses and subordinate clauses, and one for interrogative main clauses:

(49)   P1   S   Vf   Vi   O   X
(50)   P1   Vf   S   Vi   O   X

where X indicates constituents other than the predicate, the Subj, and the Obj.

For the sample grammar we only need pattern (49), since we have so heavily constrained the questioning operation that constructions requiring

---

[11] This schema does not account for VOS and OVS languages. For a discussion of the problem, see *FG*, pp. 176–177.

pattern (50) do not arise. Another point on which the sample grammar does not do justice to the full theory of constituent ordering of FG is the impact of pragmatic functions on constituent ordering. For this, see *FG*, Chapter 8.

SAMPLE GRAMMAR: CONSTITUENT ORDERING
ORDERING PATTERN: P1   S   Vf   Vi   O   X

Note: In the output of the expression rules A given in Section 3.16, any element marked with just V is a Vf; all other V-marked elements (VInf, Vprp, Vpap) are or belong to Vi.

P1 RULES: Q-terms, R-terms, and the elements marked Sub must go to P1.

LIPOC: The following rule should be applied obligatorily in subordinate clauses, and optionally in main clauses:

If the Subj is a subordinate predication (Sub ...), then place it in X and insert *it* into the position S.

All constituents not positioned so far go to their pattern position.

LIPOC: If there are more constituents to be positioned in X, their mutual ordering should be in accordance with LIPOC.

Some comments: the first LIPOC–based rule serves to avoid constructions with embedded sentential Subjects, such as:

(51)   * *That that John walked was believed by the woman was believed by the farmer.*

Obligatory application of the rule within the subordinate clause will produce:

(52)   *That it was believed by the woman that John walked was believed by the farmer*

And optional application of the same rule in the main clause will lead to:

(53)   *It was believed by the farmer that it was believed by the woman that John walked*

The explanation in terms of LIPOC is as follows: In the main clause, the sentential Subject, when having Topic or Focus function, can go to P1 and is there shielded off from the influence of LIPOC. In the subordinate clause, however, P1 is taken by the subordinator, and thus the sentential Subj could only go to S. This position, however, is within the domain of application of LIPOC, and therefore the sentential Subject must go to the very end of the clause.

The second LIPOC–based rule given above correctly predicts the following differences:

(54) a. *Bill was given **the axe by the farmer***   (NP – PNP)
    b. **Bill was given **by the farmer the axe***   (*PNP – NP)
(55) a. *Bill was given **her by the farmer***   (PRO – PNP)
    b. **John was given **by the farmer her***   (*PNP – PRO)
(56) a. *It was believed **by the woman that John walked***   (PNP – SUB)
    b. **It was believed **that John walked by the woman***
    (*SUB – PNP)
(57) a. *John killed the farmer **with an axe because he walked***
    (PNP – SUB)
    b. **John killed the farmer **because he walked with an axe***
    (*SUB – PNP)

4. COMPUTER IMPLEMENTATION

In the introduction to this paper I claimed that the Functional Grammar to be developed should be a complete and operational description of an infinite set of English sentences containing the 17 sample sentences as a proper subset. This claim has been put to the test in an interesting way by Kwee Tjoe Liong, who wrote a computer program in Algol 68 incorporating an earlier version of this grammar. Although this computer program is not yet finished, it is operational in the sense that it produces English sentences which closely approximate the target set of the grammar. A preliminary version of this program and its output are described in detail in Kwee (1979). Through this program, a number of mistakes and flaws were detected in the earlier version of the grammar. These have been remedied in the present version, to the extent that they have come to light so far. I expect that at a further stage the problems encountered in developing the computer program will provide suggestions for improving the grammar in even more fundamental ways. In order to illustrate the performance of Kwee's program as it stands now (December 1979), I end this paper with the first 10 output sentences of a set of 100 sentences randomly generated by the computer:

1. HE HAS BELIEVED THAT (A) WALKS WITH AN AXE
2. BILL BELIEVES THAT JOHN HAS BEEN GIVEN BY BILL TO A DUCKLING, AND THAT HE LOVED A DUCKLING

3. THE DUCKLING IS BELIEVED BY BILL TO HAVE BEEN BEING GIVEN BY JOHN TO EVERY FARMER
4. HE AND JOHN BELIEVED (A) TO BELIEVE BILL TO BE KILLING THE DUCKLING AND A DUCKLING
5. IT HAS BEEN BELIEVED BY JOHN AND A FARMER THAT (A) WALKS
6. THE FARMER HAS BELIEVED THAT (A) HAS BEEN KILLED BY THE AXE THAT KILLS JOHN, AND THAT HE GIVES EVERY WOMAN BILL WITH
7. IT IS BELIEVED BY BILL THAT THE AXE IS BEING GIVEN BY THE DUCKLING TO A WOMAN WHO LOVES JOHN, AND THAT (A) WALKS, AND THAT THE FARMER WAS LOVED BY EVERY FARMER, AND AN AXE, BY HIM
8. A WOMAN HAD BELIEVED THAT BILL LOVES THE FARMER, AND THAT AN AXE KILLED HIM, AND BILL, THAT BILL BELIEVES (A) TO BE WALKING
9. IT IS BELIEVED BY A WOMAN THAT BILL HAS BEEN KILLED BY HIM, AND THE DUCKLING, BY EVERY WOMAN THAT WAS BEING GIVEN BY (A) TO JOHN
10. WHO BELIEVED THAT HE AND JOHN ARE GIVEN EVERY DUCK-LING BY THE WOMAN?

Comment: (A) indicates anaphorical elements; the rules for retrieving their antecedent and giving them their proper form have not yet been captured in the program.

5. CONCLUSION

I hope that this paper has given a reasonable impression of the feasibility of grammatical description according to the theory of Functional Grammar. The reader who is interested in a more detailed discussion of the properties of this model is invited to consult the relevant items listed in the References.

REFERENCES

Dik, S. C. (1968). *Coordination: Its Implications for the Theory of General Linguistics.* Amsterdam: North-Holland.
Dik, S. C. (1975). The semantic representation of manner adverbials. In A. Kraak (Ed.), *Linguistics in the Netherlands 1972–73.* Assen: Van Gorcum. Pp. 96–121.

Dik, S. C. (1978a). *Functional Grammar*. North-Holland Linguistic Series 37. Amsterdam: North-Holland.

Dik, S. C. (1978b). *Stepwise Lexical Decomposition*. Amsterdam: Huis aan de Drie Grachten.

Dik, S. C. (1979). Raising in a functional grammar. *Lingua 47*, 119–140.

Dik, S. C. (1980). *Studies in Functional Grammar*. London: Academic Press.

Hymes, Dell (1970). On communicative competence. In J. J. Gumperz and D. Hymes (Eds.), *Directions in Sociolinguistics*. New York: Holt.

Keenan, E. L., and Comrie, B. (1977). Noun phrase accessibility and universal grammar. *Linguistic Inquiry 8*, 63–99.

Kwee, T.-L. (1979). A68-FG(3): *Simon Dik's funktionele grammatika geschreven in algol 68 versie nr 03*. Publications of the Institute for General Linguistics, University of Amsterdam, No. 23. (In Dutch.)

Lyons, J. (1977). *Semantics*. 2 vols. Cambridge: Cambridge University Press.

Vachek, J. (1966). *The linguistic school of Prague*. Bloomington: Indiana University Press.

A SYNOPSIS OF TAGMEMICS

LINDA K. JONES
Summer Institute of Linguistics

1. INTRODUCTION TO TAGMEMICS

The purpose of this paper[1] is to sketch the basic framework of tagmemic theory, especially with regard to some of its distinctive emphases.[2] The intention is to provide a broad overview of the theory. Some attention is given to how the theory may be applied to analyzing particular linguistic utterances, but this is primarily for the purpose of illustrating theoretical statements, as opposed to arguing the merits of a given analysis.

[1] I am grateful to the following linguists, including some nontagmemicists, who made helpful comments on earlier drafts of this paper: Kenneth Pike, Evelyn Pike, Robert Longacre, Alton Becker, Ruth Brend, Donald Burquest, Larry Jones, and Stephen Wallace. Of course, I take full responsibility for this final version.

[2] In general, this paper represents tagmemic theory as accepted by most tagmemicists. As in all theories, individual practitioners differ on some points. Where the leading theoreticians in tagmemics, Kenneth Pike and Robert Longacre, have differed, I normally follow Pike. See Longacre 1976a, especially Chapter 7, for his perspective on some of these matters. In particular, Longacre posits a lexical mode as the third mode of language (in place of Pike's referential hierarchy); employs a two-cell tagmeme (versus Pike's four-cell tagmeme); and distinguishes SURFACE and NOTIONAL structure in grammar at all hierarchical levels (his notional categories generally correspond to Pike's roles in the four-cell grammatical tagmeme).

77

Syntax and Semantics, Volume 13:
Current Approaches to Syntax

1.1. Language as Human Behavior

At the heart of tagmemic theory is the assertion that language is an integral part of human behavior. That is, language is best analyzed and understood as one aspect—closely related to other aspects—of human behavior. Tagmemics is rather unique in that its most basic principles, or axioms, are claimed to hold for all human behavior including, but not limited to, language (these axioms will be examined shortly). Consequently, tagmemics rejects any strictly mentalistic view of language. Although language shares with math and other formal codes various symbolic functions, language is different from these in that it is THE code used in normal interaction between human beings. Language has more than a symbolic, or representational, function; it has a very important communicational function. I believe these assumptions about language distinguish tagmemics in fundmental ways from various other current linguistic theories.

Viewing language as part of human behavior has several important implications. One of these is that tagmemics does not view linguistics as a tight, self-contained discipline. In order to fully account for facts of language, it is necessary to have input from other disciplines that study man and his behavior: psychology, sociology, anthropology, *etc.*

Another important implication of viewing language as part of human behavior touches on the place of formalism in linguistic theory. Whereas rigorous formalism is an important goal for some linguistic theories, this is not the case for tagmemics. Kenneth L. Pike, the founder of tagmemics, calls this stress on rigorous formalism an "abstractionist illusion" (see his 1978 paper). Tagmemics maintains that it is not possible to formalize all the relevant facts of language in as strict fashion as can be done for, say, matter with the laws of physics. It must be recognized that there are limits to formalizing language, such that no one uniform representational system can hope to accommodate all the relevant facts of language. Language is an extraordinarily complex system that has more variables interacting—and with constantly changing degrees of importance—than can possibly be captured in one particular formalism.

This does not, however, obviate the need for some formalism, since there are certainly very useful results of formalism—for example, capturing generalizations, forcing explicitness, exposing inadequacies of analysis, and revealing new patterns and parallel structures that might otherwise have remained obscure. Tagmemics seeks a balance here, recognizing the need for generalizations about language (the norm, the idealization), but at the same time insisting that room be left in the theory for handling the particularities, variations, and vagaries of real language used by real people. As Pike wrote, "Tagmemics is set up as part of a theory of the structure of behavior, not merely as a formal algebraic system [1967, p. 501]."

Consequently, tagmemics is willing and ready to embrace various representational devices for different purposes, and does not assign any empirical significance to the ones it normally uses, including the ones that will be used in this paper. Further, there is no insistence that there is only one correct grammar, or one correct theory.

1.2. Theoretical Postulates

The axioms or postulates of tagmemic theory are statements of universals claimed to hold for all human behavior, including language. Thus, they are very high-level generalizations. There are four postulates.

One postulate is that all purposive behavior, including language, comes in "chunks" or UNITS. A unit may be determined by the distinctive features which contrast it with other units, and by its relationship to other units in a class, sequence, or system. It may vary, within limits, in its physical form.

A second postulate concerns the significance of CONTEXT. Units do not occur in isolation; they occur in context. This means that conditioning factors for variation may often be found in the context. This postulate also means that in grammar, sentences should be analyzed not in isolation, but rather in context (e.g., in discourse), since choice of a particular discourse type—for example, narrative—affects linguistic units both large and small. This is in opposition to certain current views that claim that linguistic theory can be successfully formulated on the basis of analysis of only isolated sentences, presuming that a theoretical apparatus formulated in this way can be eventually extended to other levels of linguistic structure without substantial changes. To have as the goal of a syntactic theory an accounting of the set of sentences is inadequate. Not just sentences are to be accounted for, but entire discourses. Theory formulation must, from the very beginning, have ALL levels of linguistic structure in view; analysis of sentences only is an insufficient basis.

A third postulate concerns HIERARCHY, a cornerstone of tagmemic theory. Hierarchy here refers to a PART–WHOLE HIERARCHY, rather than a taxonomic or an accessibility-type hierarchy: that is, small units generally occur as parts of larger units, which may in turn be parts of still larger units. With regard to language, the claim is that languages have structurally significant levels, whereby units on one level are composed of units of the same or different levels. In particular, linguistic utterances (i.e., the stream of speech) are regarded as being structured with three

simultaneous, interlocking hierarchies: the PHONOLOGICAL, GRAMMAT-
ICAL,[3] and REFERENTIAL HIERARCHIES.

The phonological hierarchy includes the phoneme and syllable at lower
levels; then stress groups, rhythm groups, and on up. The referential
hierarchy[4] includes content structure, speaker–hearer interplay of attitudes, emotions, and performatives, presuppositions, truth and falsity,
purpose, encyclopedic references, paraphrases, *etc*. Thus pragmatics and
speech-act theory are part of the referential hierarchy.

With regard to grammar, tagmemics claims hierarchical structuring as
well. Although there is some variation in the world's languages with regard
to the structurally significant levels, they generally include (from lowest
to highest): morpheme (root), morpheme cluster (stem), word, phrase,
clause, sentence, paragraph, monologue discourse, dialogue exchange,
and dialogue conversation. These levels are near-universals, since very
few languages have either fewer or more structurally significant levels.
Morphology and syntax[5] are not treated distinctively as in other theories.
Rather, tagmemics claims parallel structuring in terms of hierarchical relations for words, sentences, AND discourses.

The fourth postulate overlaps somewhat with the other three. By this
postulate, tagmemic theory formally recognizes a varying observer PER-
SPECTIVE. At least three different, but complementary, perspectives may
be used to view the same items. In a STATIC view, items as individual,
discrete things are in focus. A DYNAMIC view focuses on the dynamics
of items overlapping, blending, and merging with each other. Finally, in
a RELATIONAL perspective, focus is on the relationships between units,
noting networks, fields, or matrices. Any one of the three perspectives
may underlie a particular linguistic description. A description from one
perspective complements, and adds to, a description from one of the other
perspectives, but does not replace it. Here also tagmemics leaves room
for more than one correct description or grammar.

1.3. Terms and Relations

At this point, I turn to some terms and relations that frequently figure
in tagmemic descriptions, in particular, those of grammar. Traditionally,

---

[3] Here, and in many other places in this paper, "grammatical" simply means "pertaining
to the grammar," and is not to be confused with "grammatical" in the sense of "grammatically well-formed." Context will disambiguate the two senses.

[4] The levels of the referential hierarchy have not as yet been definitively established. In
narratives, it appears that the referential levels are identity, event, story, and performative
interaction.

[5] The term "syntax" is used very little in tagmemics since it generally refers only to
sentential structure. As a broader term, "grammar" is preferred in tagmemics, and refers
to structures at all hierarchical levels (including "syntax" as just one level).

a TAGMEME is a grammatical unit consisting of at least two simultaneously occurring features—its SLOT and its CLASS. The slot represents the grammatical relation of that unit to other units in a construction, at the same level of constituent structure; the slot may be subject, predicate (on the clause level), head, modifier (on the phrase level), or one of the more generic terms nucleus and margin (on any level). The class may be noun, verb, noun phrase, verb phrase, adjective, adverb, transitive clause, contrafactual sentence, *etc*. In a tagmeme, BOTH slot and class must be represented. This is not notational redundancy, as some have suggested. Slot and class represent different types of information, and neither one can be derived from the other (as Pike (1967, p. 496) has pointed out). Thus in the noun phrase *the student employees*, the word *student* is simultaneously a modifier in terms of its functional slot, and a noun in terms of its formal class.

This simple two-cell tagmeme is the type used by Robert Longacre in his tagmemic writings. In recent years Pike, however, has used a tagmeme of four simultaneous features, with slot and class as above, and in addition, ROLE and COHESION. These features may be symbolized as a four-cell array, as in (1).

(1)

slot	class
role	cohesion

For Pike, a unit is a bundle of these four features. Note that both form and meaning are involved in this complex of features. This reflects Pike's view that, since linguistic units are composites of form and meaning, both analysis and representational notations should express this integration.

Role encodes various situational, or semantic case, features, such as actor, undergoer (which is roughly equivalent to patient), scope (which includes inner locative, goal, and some experiencer), benefactee, *etc*. Cohesion encodes certain agreement features such as number between subject and predicate in English, and number and gender in noun phrases in many Romance languages. The terms GOVERNS and GOVERNED BY are frequently used in connection with cohesion. In English subject–predicate number agreement, the number of the subject governs the number of the predicate, and in turn, the predicate is governed by the number of the subject. If a semantic category (number, gender, animateness, *etc*.) has a grammatical reflex such that two or more grammatical units are marked for this category, then this is grammatical cohesion. More generally, when the form or occurrence of one grammatical unit is affected by another grammatical unit in the language, then this is grammatical cohesion.

Tagmemes are constituents of SYNTAGMEMES, also called CONSTRUC-
TIONS. The relationship of tagmeme to construction may be illustrated
by means of the example sentence *The farmer walks*. This example will
also illustrate slot, class, role, and cohesion. In tagmemic notation
(Pikean–style), the constituent structure of the sentence may be represented
as in (2) below [see (1) for the basic four-cell notation].

(2)

Intransitive Clause =	Subject	Noun Phrase
+	Actor	Subject Number >

+	Predicate	Verb
	Statement	> Subject Number > Intransitive >

This construction is composed of two tagmemes. The first tagmeme
represents *the farmer*:

Subject	Noun Phrase
Actor	Subject Number >

The second tagmeme represents the word *walks*:

Predicate	Verb
Statement	> Subject Number > Intransitive >

The noun phrase *the farmer* is itself a construction composed of two
tagmemes, as shown in (3).

(3)

Noun Phrase =	Margin	Article
+	Specificity	> Noun Number > Singular Noun

+	Nucleus	Noun
	Item	> Noun Number > Singular Noun >

Further, the verb *walks* (and probably also the noun *farmer*) is a construction of two tagmemes. However, formulas are not given here for
these, as a full analysis is not intended. Instead, I would like to explain
more fully the notation used here for cohesion.

In the cohesion cell of each tagmeme [the lower right cell; see (1)],
there are words with arrowlike symbols on one or both sides. These are
indices to cohesion rules which generally appear elsewhere in the de-

scription. The arrows are to be interpreted as follows: when the arrow is to the right, it indicates that this tagmeme is the governing source; to the left, it indicates the governed target.

Note that there are indices to several cohesion rules in these formulas. First, the words "Subject Number" index to a subject–predicate number agreement rule, which might be stated as in (4).

(4)   SUBJECT NUMBER: The number of the subject governs the number of the predicate[6]

The word "Intransitive" indexes to a rule specifying co-occurrence requirements of transitivity, which might read as follows:

(5)   INTRANSITIVE: Mutual requirement of subject (as actor) and predicate tagmeme

In formula (3) above, the words "Noun Number" refer to a cohesion rule that governs the number of the article. This rule accounts for the grammatical well-formedness of *this farmer* and the lack of well-formedness of *these farmer*. The arrows on both sides of the words "Noun Number" in the second tagmeme of formula (3) indicate the mutual agreement of this tagmeme with a "number tagmeme" (such as *one* or *two*), which is implicit in some sentences—for example, *Farmers walk*—and explicit in others—for example, *Two farmers walk*. The rule might be formulated as in (6):

(6)   NOUN NUMBER: Mutual agreement of number of noun in nucleus of NP and number tagmeme in margin of NP (if present); these together govern number of article in NP margin and also number of anaphoric references to the noun

Note that this rule also governs the number of any anaphoric references; for example, to refer to *the farmer*, the pronoun *he* is appropriate, but the pronoun *they* is not.

Finally, "Singular Noun" in (3) refers to a cohesion rule requiring the occurrence of an article when there is a singular count noun:

(7)   SINGULAR NOUN: A singular count noun in the nucleus of NP requires the occurrence of an article in the margin of the NP

Thus, *the farmer walks* is grammatically well-formed, while *farmer walks* is not, unless *farmer* is construed as a proper, instead of a common, noun.

---

[6] Subject, predicate, and object are slot labels. Sometimes, if ambiguity does not result, slot labels are used as shorthand labels for tagmemes in place of a two-cell or four-cell notation.

1.4. Summary

Thus far, some basic assumptions of tagmemics, along with some basic terminology, have been set forth. The next section presents the tagmemic posture towards certain issues in current linguistic theory, particularly with regard to grammar.

2. TAGMEMICS WITH RESPECT TO CERTAIN ISSUES IN GRAMMAR

In this section, an attempt is made to address the list of issues prepared for this conference (listed in the Appendix to this volume). However, since the issues are not all equally relevant to tagmemics, discussion is fuller on some issues than on others. In this section, I deal with the goal of grammar and the organization of grammar, roughly following the order of the issues in the conference list (each issue is cued by a word or phrase heading the paragraph(s) that deal with that issue).

2.1. The Goal of Grammar

a. DATA

1. PRIMARY DATA. In tagmemics the primary data consists of elicited and unelicited materials, such as written texts and recorded conversations. Native speaker reactions and intuitions are considered important in the interpretation and analysis of these materials. Neither data from introspection or experimentation are highly valued as primary data, although they may provide supplementary data. Exclusive use of data from experimentation and/or introspection may lead to an unbalanced analysis (for example, by overlooking or ignoring crucial bits of data). Data gained from introspection, in particular, must be used with caution.

2. COMPETENCE VERSUS PERFORMANCE. Tagmemics does not make a theoretical distinction between competence and performance. However, it might be added that tagmemic analysis deals with both. To a very rough degree, matters of competence are the domain of the grammatical hierarchy, while matters of performance are dealt with in the referential hierarchy.

3. DOMAINS. In tagmemics, the linguistic analysis of a language includes analyzing its phonology, grammar, and reference. Since our focus

here is on grammar, let me recall my earlier statement that the domain
of grammar encompasses all hierarchical levels: morpheme (root), morpheme cluster (stem), word, phrase, clause, sentence, paragraph, monologue discourse, dialogue exchange, and dialogue conversation. Data
from any or all of these levels are used in analysis. In tagmemic analysis,
the sentence level is not favored over any other level; this is in contrast
to the practice of most current theories of grammar. As stressed earlier,
tagmemics maintains that analysis of just sentences (and their constituent
units) is an insufficient and inadequate starting point for theory articulation, particularly if one wishes to account for language in general and
not simply sets of isolated sentences.

4. CONSTANCY AND VARIABILITY. That both constancy and variation characterize data receives formal theoretical recognition in statements subsumed under the postulate concerning units (see Section 1.2).
These statements hold that (*a*) constancy is possible due to the contrastive–identificational features of a unit (which distinguish it from other
units and identify particular manifestations as instances of that unit); and
(*b*) variation is normal, each unit having a range of variability in which
differences between particular manifestations are ETIC, that is, not structurally significant.

Idiolectic variation may be handled in phonology, grammar, or reference, depending on the type of variation. Variation according to style,
register, age, sex, and other sociolinguistic factors is primarily the domain
of reference (context of situation), although there are grammatical implications as well. Variation due to historical change has been studied in
tagmemics thus far mainly with respect to phonology. Thus, variability—
idiolectic, sociolinguistic, and historical—is easily accommodated in the
theory. However, in terms of actual detailed analysis (as, for example,
in the Labov tradition), little has been done thus far with respect to these
areas of variability.

5. UNIVERSALS. The four postulates described in Section 1.2 are
claimed to be universals of human behavior (including language). In addition, Longacre has suggested a universal set of case frames. Also Pike's
referential hierarchy points towards universals, and his etic versus emic
distinction is similar to the distinction of universal grammar versus language-specific grammar made in many other theories. Hence, Pike's etic
lists (or conflated matrices of all observed contrasts) of construction
types, roles, grammatical relations at various hierarchical levels, *etc.*, are
statements of universals. And I believe that much recent tagmemic discourse analysis will relate to universals as well, as a universal set of

discourse functions is specified and then related to the grammatical means for encoding them.

b. ACCOUNTS

1. GOALS OF LINGUISTIC ACCOUNTS. Linguistic tagmemics is concerned with discovering the patterns and regularities of language, and with stating these as consistently, systematically, and elegantly as possible. Tagmemics does not distinguish between description and explanation, and I am skeptical that any substantive difference between description and explanation can be maintained. It seems to me more a matter of different degrees of adequacy along a single scale.

2. EMPIRICAL INTERPRETATIONS. Tagmemics is for the most part more concerned with the actually occurring languages than with the logically possible ones. To make the goal of one's linguistic theory the delimitation of the class of logically possible languages seems to me to stress formal characteristics. But in tagmemics, both formal and functional (i.e., language as human behavior and communication) characteristics are important. The emphasis on actually occurring languages respects the uniqueness of particular languages as parts of particular cultures of particular groups of peoples. Tagmemics is a theory which encourages the analyst to appreciate the individuality of each language, at the same time recognizing those features it shares with other, perhaps all, languages.

(Perhaps one further comment on empirical interpretations of tagmemic statements should be added. It is not a concern of these statements to explicate the psychological/cognitive mechanisms which underlie language production and comprehension.)

3. THE SOUND–MEANING RELATION. In tagmemics, linguistic pattern is seen in the interplay of three interlocking modes—phonology, grammar, and reference—in which form and meaning are present in all three. The theory makes no statements of directionality from meaning to sound, or vice versa. Furthermore, grammar is "not merely the interface of meaning and sound [Longacre, 1976a, p. 12]." Rather, like each of the other modes, it is semiautonomous.

c. PRACTICAL APPLICATIONS

A primary task of a linguistic theory is to account for the empirical data. As an important corollary, the theory ought to have practical uses in dealing with language. There have been numerous practical applications of tagmemic theory, and I believe that the great applicability of tagmemics is a significant strength in its favor. One application has been as a heuristic for helping students to understand the nature of language. But this is not all. There have been numerous successful applications of the theory to translation, language learning, literacy, and linguistic analysis—particularly in the study of unwritten and "exotic" languages. In addition, there have been many applications in other disciplines, including most notably, anthropology (since tagmemics is a theory not only of language, but also of human behavior).

For the analysis of unwritten languages, discovery procedures have evolved, perhaps better called ANALYTICAL TECHNIQUES. These do NOT, however, constitute a mechanical algorithm that automatically outputs an analysis. Practical goals of a theory hold pure theory–building in check, since "fruitful theory must to some extent be limited by analytical techniques for processing or evaluating data. Tagmemics has oscillation between theory and method rather than a one-way priority [Pike, 1967, p. 509]."

d. Evaluation, Argumentation, and Falsifiability

1. FALSIFIABILITY. The practical applications of tagmemics cited in the previous section provide a check on the theory. Claims of the theory might also be falsified by psycholinguistic tests on native speakers, or by finding additional texts where the claims do not hold. Tagmemic formulas are potentially falsifiable by the utterances they generate.[7] The claim that all three modes—phonology, grammar, and reference—have both form and meaning might be falsified, for example, by showing that grammar has no meaning [but cf. experiments that show the reverse by Koen, Becker, and Young (1968)]. But regarding the postulates of the theory (unit, hierarchy, context, and multiple perspectives), Pike has commented, "In spite of their demonstrated heuristic value, the principles are so sufficiently general that I do not know how to test them by ordinary methods [1976, p. 92]." Science fiction has been attempted as a means to falsify various of the postulates, but has not succeeded in falsifying any (Pike, 1973, 1978).

2. ARGUMENTATION AND EVALUATION. Various types of argumentation figure in tagmemics. Substantive arguments include arguing from context (as, for example, in discourse analysis), meaning, and questions

---

[7] In present-day tagmemics it is NOT true, as some have claimed, that tagmemic formulas are judged adequate if they generate ungrammatical strings so long as they also generate all the grammatical ones.

of sameness or difference of type. Results of experimental syntax (e.g., psychological tests) may occasionally be useful. However, "ungrammatical" (starred) utterances are seldom used in argumentation as it is difficult to be sure of the reason for their ungrammaticality (lack of proper context? collocational clashes? *etc.*).

Methodological arguments include consistency, general fit of hypotheses to data, and an occasional appeal to simplicity or economy. "Axiomatic argumentation" is an important type of argumentation in tagmemics; that is, arguing from the basic axioms or postulates of the theory (unit, hierarchy, context, and multiple perspectives). Various pragmatic and heuristic arguments may figure as well.

However, in all honesty, it must be said that tagmemics seldom uses the type of argumentation familiar in transformational generative writings. This is hardly a weakness, however. Botha (1973) has conducted a thorough, well-documented analysis of the types of arguments used in the generative tradition. He concluded that, for the most part, they are methodological arguments of the nondemonstrative type. He also found that they are all flawed in lacking evidential conditions and acceptability of standards (p. 328). Furthermore, criteria for evaluating hypotheses (or theories, for that matter) sorely lack specificity, making it impossible to apply them.

Therefore, although there is certainly a need in tagmemics to give more priority to the whole matter of argumentation, it is evident that a wholesale adaptation of generative methods of argumentation is not the solution. Indeed, there appears to be nowhere to look in current linguistics for adequate criteria for argumentation and evaluation. This much is certain, however: No mechanical evaluation procedure will be found, just as there can be no mechanical discovery procedure (see Pike, 1967, p. 494).

Part of the reason that no mechanical evaluation procedure is possible is that there is no way to evaluate various value judgments that lie at the heart of any theory: judgments of purpose, range of data to be included in the theory, and general worldview. Botha (1973, p. 18) has pointed out the great difficulty of comparing two theories that disagree as to the range of known facts to be accounted for. Kuhn (1970) has pointed out that each theory defines its own problems that need solving, as well as what counts as solutions, and admissible procedures and techniques. When theories disagree in these areas, they are incommensurable. Each falls short of the criteria established by the other. Although various tests for "verifying" a theory may be suggested, it usually proves impossible to conclude between competing theories on the basis of tests alone. The theories remain incommensurable. Ultimately choice of theories is a question of values, of choice of axioms. At best, one theory can hope to win through "conversion," but never by "proof" (Kuhn, 1970, p. 148).

Ultimately, then, each theory must be evaluated for its own merits, and NOT by comparison with other theories. In particular, how successfully a theory meets its stated purposes and goals, and the general usefulness or applicability of the theory, are what is to be evaluated.

3. ATTITUDE TOWARD OTHER THEORIES. Since different approaches are most useful for different purposes, perhaps we should be satisfied with accepting several complementary theories. Pike has said, "I, for one, welcome such a diversity of approaches, since it is a conviction of tagmemic theory that no one logically coherent perspective can ever expect to exhaust the total range of relevant characteristics of language or of the descriptions of language [1974, p. 163]." Hence, tagmemics assumes neither that there is only one correct linguistic theory nor that there is only one correct grammar for each set of data.

2.2. The Organization of Grammar

a. THE NATURE OF GRAMMATICAL STATEMENTS

Much has already been said regarding the organization of grammar in tagmemics. In Section 1.2, the grammar was described as having hierarchical organization from morpheme up to conversation. In Section 1.3, a description was given of the tagmeme, the basic grammatical unit.

b. THE PLACE OF GRAMMAR WITHIN A TOTAL LINGUISTIC ANALYSIS

In Section 1.2, the relationship of grammar to other linguistic components was discussed. Language is viewed as having trimodal structuring—grammar, phonology, and reference. There are no other distinct modes. Grammar includes morphology (at the lowest levels of the grammatical hierarchy). Reference includes pragmatics and much of speech-act theory. Semantics does not comprise a distinct mode in tagmemics. What others call semantics is found, in tagmemics, among the meaning features of phonology, grammar (particularly, in role), and in various aspects of reference. This entails, among other things, that the question of the division between syntax and semantics is not an issue in tagmemics.

In Pikean tagmemics, the lexicon is found at the interface of the three modes—grammar, phonology, and reference—and shares features of all three. The meaning of an utterance, however, is not accounted for solely in terms of lexicon, but rather in terms of meaning features in all the hierarchies. That is, the meaning of an utterance is not simply the sum of meanings of its lexical parts as entered in the lexicon, since grammatical role and referential context, among other things, also affect the meaning.

c. Levels of Syntactic Representation

Tagmemics holds that adequate descriptions can be stated in terms of surface structures alone. Thus, the theory deals only with surface structures. (Although Longacre speaks of "deep" or "notional" structure, this is very different from transformational generative deep structure.)

d. On Generativeness of Tagmemic Statements

Tagmemics is not a transformational theory. At no point are there representations of ungrammatical ("pre-surface") strings. All representations in tagmemics are of actually occurring utterances. There are no derivations and no transformations in the sense of a deep structure representation undergoing various structure-changing operations to ultimately produce a grammatical utterance. A possible exception is certain permutation rules in tagmemics, but these are stated only in terms of surface structures.

There is a sense, however, in which tagmemics is generative. A complete set of tagmemic formulas [such as those in (2) and (3)] is intended to be generative. "Formulas of a tagmemic construction are designed to be a set of obligatory and optional choices which, when followed out successively through descending layers (or levels) of structure, result in the producing of ALL—and ONLY—the specific clauses, phrases, or other constructions of the languages implied by the formula [Pike and Pike, 1977, p. 75]."

e. The Form of Grammatical Statements

Tagmemic formulas are one form of grammatical statements. They are perhaps the most frequent form—especially for basic grammatical analysis—but they are not the exclusive form. Other forms of grammatical statements include principles, matrices, rules, *etc*, and of course ordinary language. For example, most recent tagmemic discourse analysis has been couched in ordinary language. Rigorous formalism is not a valued goal in the theory, and the formalisms employed have no significant empirical status. As stated earlier, in our view no single formalism can accommodate all the relevant facts and generalizations of languages.

3. SAMPLE ANALYSES

The list of conference issues (which I addressed in Section 2) was accompanied by a list of 17 English sentences (see list in the Appendix of this volume). These were isolated sentences and no whole discourse was given. Thus, the data given appears to be already biased towards sentence grammars. I did not find any referential cohesion among the sentences in the list, except for some repetition of lexical items. In one sentence the farmer killed the duckling; while in another, John was the killer. In many sentences, the duckling was killed, but in others it is the farmer who was killed. It thus proved impossible to form these sentences into a coherent discourse, which was my original hope.

However, a few of the sentences—Sentences 13, 7, and 8 in the original conference list—can be formed into a small discourse, if the articles are modified:

(8)   a. *The farmer gave John* **an** *axe*
       b. *John killed* **a** *duckling with* **the** *axe*
       c. *The woman believed that John killed the farmer*

Note that *an axe* in (8a) becomes *the axe* in (8b). The indefinite article *an* introduces *axe* as new information, whereas the definite article *the* presumes *axe* is old information by the second sentence. Similarly, the indefinite article *a* introduces *duckling* in (8b). In addition, note the use of past tense in all these sentences, which gives cohesion. (If these sentences were part of a larger text, it might be seen that the past tense marks these sentences as part of the "backbone" of the narrative, that is, as carrying significant plot information. "Background" information might be marked by other tenses or by verbs of the *be* class [see Jones and Jones 1979].)

Let us now compare the discourse in (8) with the one in (9).

(9)   a. *The woman believed that John* **had** *killed the farmer*
       b. **And** *in fact the farmer* **had** *given John the axe*
       c. **But** *John killed a duckling with the axe*

Note that (8) and (9) convey the same referential content or information. However, (8) appears to represent the chronological sequence of events, while (9) seems to be out of chronological order. The telling order—which in tagmemics is an aspect of grammar—does not reflect the happening order—which is an aspect of reference. This skewing of telling and happening orders is accounted for by a skewing between the grammar and reference. The use of the conjunctions *and* and *but* in (9b) and (9c), and the use of the past perfects in (9a) and (9b), can be related at least in part to the skewing of grammar and reference.

This being a theory paper, it is not the place for any sort of extended analysis. The preceding was only a small example of discourse analysis in a tagmemic framework. (Consult the references in Section 4 for more extensive work.) I shall now adopt a more limited sentence perspective to demonstrate how tagmemics accounts for data that in transformational generative theories are handled via movement rules. For this purpose, I illustrate a tagmemic analysis of active and passive sentences. Consider the sentences in (10).

(10)   a. *The farmer killed the duckling*
           John loves that woman
        b. *The duckling was killed by the farmer*
           That woman is loved by John
        c. *The duckling was killed*

The active sentences in (10a) can be represented by the formula in (11). The direct object in English is represented by "Adjunct-as-Undergoer." The term "adjunct" indicates that the direct object, in contrast to the subject, is out of focus grammatically. (Indirect objects are analyzed as "adjunct-as-scope.") The cohesion rule Subject Number was given in (4) above. The cohesion rule Transitive would be similar in some respects to the rule Intransitive in (5) above.

(11)   Active Transitive Clause = + $\dfrac{\text{Subject} \mid \text{Noun Phrase}}{\text{Actor} \mid \text{Subject Number} >}$

        + $\dfrac{\text{Predicate} \mid \begin{array}{l}\text{Active} \\ \text{Verb Phrase}\end{array}}{\text{Statement} \mid \begin{array}{l}> \text{Transitive} > \\ > \text{Subject Number}\end{array}}$

        + $\dfrac{\text{Adjunct} \mid \text{Noun Phrase}}{\text{Undergoer} \mid}$

The passive counterparts of (10a) are given in (10b). These may be represented by formula (12).

(12)   Passive Transitive Clause = + $\dfrac{\text{Subject} \mid \text{Noun Phrase}}{\text{Undergoer} \mid \text{Subject Number} >}$

        + $\dfrac{\text{Predicate} \mid \begin{array}{l}\text{Passive} \\ \text{Verb Phrase}\end{array}}{\text{Statement} \mid \begin{array}{l}> \text{Transitive} > \\ > \text{Subject Number}\end{array}}$

        ± $\dfrac{\text{Adjunct} \mid \begin{array}{l}\text{Agent} \\ \text{Phrase}\end{array}}{\text{Actor} \mid}$

The notation ± in (12) indicates the optionality of the agent phrase, accounting for the sentences in both (10b) and (10c) in a single formula. (Any restrictions regarding certain verbs that do not permit deletion of the agent phrase in passive would be indicated elsewhere, for example, in the lexicon.)

The formulas (11) and (12) account for the relationship between active and passive chiefly by means of the roles associated with subject. In actives, the role associated with subject is actor, while in passives the role associated with subject is undergoer. (In a sentence like *John was given the axe* (nonidiomatic reading), the role associated with subject is scope.) The obliqueness of the agent phrase in passives is indicated by the slot label ''adjunct'' and the class label ''agent phrase'' (distinct from noun phrase in that it includes the preposition *by*). Formal differences in the active and passive verb phrases are indicated by the different labels in the respective predicate tagmemes.

4. SIGNIFICANCE OF TAGMEMICS

Tagmemics makes significant and distinctive claims regarding the general nature of language. For example, the theory's insistence that language be analyzed as a part of human behavior balances pragmatic, sociolinguistic, and psycholinguistic analyses with more strictly grammatical and phonological analysis. All of these are considered the proper domain of linguistic study, since they all enter into the complex structure of language knowledge and use.

A notable emphasis in tagmemics is on the analysis of WHOLE languages. This is opposed to the fragmented approach of certain theories that center theory formulation around the analysis of a handful of sentences. Tagmemics resists such a preoccupation; it strives to maintain the broad perspective of the whole language as a system even in the analysis of small details of the language.

The articulation of tagmemic postulates (see Section 1.2) provides a strong axiomatic foundation for the theory. There is great benefit from establishing in the theory's foundation the flexibility of the multiple-perspective approach (static, dynamic, and relational). The analyst may adopt a certain perspective and go as far with it as possible, and then switch to one or both of the other two perspectives to fill in gaps. This is similar to the situation in physics where Newtonian physics is the bread-and-butter perspective on most matters (e.g., engineering problems, earth-related matters), but Einsteinian physics is employed for certain purposes (e.g., in dealing with macro-units such as the galaxies). Such switching of perspectives in linguistic analysis holds promise for more closely approaching the great complexity found in language.[8]

I believe that the referential hierarchy posited by Pike has great potential as well for dealing with linguistic complexity, especially by encompassing the diverse areas of pragmatics, speech-act theory, sociolinguistics, philosophical truth and falsity in language, literary studies of plot structure, *etc.*, in a unified treatment. The referential hierarchy itself and its relationship to the other two hierarchies is a new frontier in tagmemics that is very promising.

Analytical techniques have been another important contribution of tagmemics. They have proved to be a useful heuristic in analyzing many unwritten, exotic languages. Taxonomic activity has also been an important contribution. Much recent linguistic feeling has been to disparage taxonomies as uninteresting and trivial. Nevertheless, science cannot function without taxonomies, and linguistic science is not exempt. Thus, carefully constructed taxonomies are important in tagmemics. In fact, taxonomies of sentence, paragraph, and discourse types paved the way for one of tagmemics' most significant contributions to linguistics: discourse analysis.

Pike was one of the first modern heralds of discourse analysis with work dating back to the 1940s. Several papers by Pike (1964a, 1964b) and his book with Evelyn Pike (1977) have forwarded the study of discourse. Longacre has been a leader in discourse studies as well (1968, 1972, 1976a, 1976b, with Levinsohn 1978, and with Woods 1976–1977).

Tagmemic discourse studies have progressed well beyond simply taxonomic analyses. Pike and Pike have analyzed texts in terms of their referential structure. Longacre has studied the effect of discourse types on units both large and small in texts. "In effect once a discourse type is chosen, many decisions as to structure of very small parts of it are already made [1972, p. 133]." Longacre and Levinsohn (1978) have determined various cohesive devices in text, including particles and affixes, tense and/or aspect, anaphora, deictics, lexical ties and paraphrases, conjunctions, introducers, back-reference, and other types of linkage.

Of particular significance, I think has been the focus by various tagmemicists on the discourse FUNCTIONS of various units and constructions. Longacre and his colleagues have found discourse functions for many particles and affixes that had previously been little understood or

---

[8] The tagmemic emphasis on analyzing the data from multiple perspectives, along with its resistance to rigorous formalisms, contribute to the theory being what Longacre (1977, p. 2) calls a "minimal" theory, a "'hang-loose framework' which has much to commend it."

else simply glossed as "emphasis." I (1977) have suggested discourse functions for clefts, pseudo-clefts, and various other constructions in English. Larry Jones and I (1979) have suggested that tense/aspect/mood, many particles, affixes, and some special constructions function in a number of languages to mark different levels of significant information in texts (e.g., to distinguish peak, pivotal events, ordinary events, significant background, and ordinary background). In discourse analysis, as well as other areas just mentioned, tagmemics offers a significant theory of linguistics.

REFERENCES

Botha, R. P. (1973). *The Justification of Linguistic Hypotheses*. The Hague: Mouton.
Jones, L. K. (1977). *Theme in English Expository Discourse*. Lake Bluff, Illinois: Jupiter Press.
Jones, L. B. and Jones, L. K. (1979). Multiple levels of information in discourse. In L. K. Jones (Ed.), *Discourse Studies in Mesoamerican Languages*. Dallas: Summer Institute of Linguistics and University of Texas at Arlington. Pp. 3–27.
Koen, F. M., Becker, A. L., and Young, R. (1968). The psychological reality of the paragraph. In E. M. Zale (Ed.), *Proceedings of the Conference on Language and Language Behavior*. New York: Appleton-Century Crofts. Pp. 1974–1987.
Kuhn, T. S. (1970). *The Structure of Scientific Revolutions*. 2nd ed. Chicago: University of Chicago Press.
Longacre, R. E. (1968). *Discourse, Paragraph and Sentence Structure in Selected Philippine Languages*. 2 vols. Santa Ana, Calif: Summer Institute of Linguistics.
Longacre, R. E. (1972). *Hierarchy and Universality of Discourse Constituents in New Guinea Languages*. 2 vols. Washington, D.C.: Georgetown University Press.
Longacre, R. E. (1976a). *Anatomy of Speech Notions*. Lisse: Peter de Ridder.
Longacre, R. E. (1976b). "Mystery" particles and affixes. In *Papers from the Twelfth Regional Meeting of the Chicago Linguistic Society*. Chicago Linguistic Society. Pp. 468–475.
Longacre, R. E. (1977). Tagmemics as a framework for discourse analysis. In *Second Annual Linguistic Metatheory Conference Proceedings*. East Lansing: Michigan State University Department of Linguistics. Pp. 1–27.
Longacre, R. E. and Levinsohn, S. (1978). Field analysis of discourse. In W. U. Dressler (Ed.), *Current Trends in Textlinguistics*. New York: Walter de Gruyter. Pp. 103–122.
Longacre, R. E. and Woods, F., eds. (1976–1977). *Discourse Grammar: Studies in Indigenous Languages of Colombia, Panama, and Ecuador*. 3 vols. Arlington: Summer Institute of Linguistics and University of Texas at Arlington.
Pike, K. L. (1964a). Beyond the sentence. *College Composition and Communication, 15*, 129–135.
Pike, K. L. (1964b). Discourse analysis and tagmeme matrices. *Oceanic Linguistics, 3*, 5–25.
Pike, K. L. (1967). *Language in Relation to a Unified Theory of the Structure of Human Behavior*. 2nd rev. ed. The Hague: Mouton.
Pike, K. L. (1973). Science fiction as a test of axioms concerning human behavior. *Parma Eldalamberon, 1*(3), 3–4.

Pike, K. L. (1974). Recent developments in tagmemics. In L. Heilman (Ed.), *Proceedings of the Eleventh International Congress of Linguistics*. Bologna: Società editrice il Mulino Bologna. Pp. 163–172.

Pike, K. L. (1976). Toward the development of tagmemic postulates. In R. M. Brend and K. L. Pike (Eds.), *Tagmemics*. Vol. 2. The Hague: Mouton. Pp. 91–127.

Pike, K. L. (1978). Here we stand—creative observers of language. Paper given at the Interdisciplinary Colloquium on Language Development. University of René Descartes, Sorbonne, Paris, December 8, 1978.

Pike, K. L., and Pike, E. G. (1977). *Grammatical Analysis*. Dallas: Summer Institute of Linguistics and University of Texas at Arlington.

COREPRESENTATIONAL GRAMMAR

MICHAEL B. KAC
University of Minnesota

1. GENERAL

Formally, a corepresentational grammar is one that assigns to each
sentence of a natural language one or more structural descriptions consisting of a CATEGORIAL representation (essentially a constituent structure analysis) and a RELATIONAL representation (an unordered conjunction of statements each of which is in the form $X = \rho(Y)$, read "X bears
relation ρ to Y"). Such a grammar is generative in the sense that it consists
of precisely stated principles, applicable to an indefinitely large set of
linguistic objects, governing the pairing of categorial and relational representations. Corepresentational grammar (henceforth CORG) also operates on the assumption that there is only one level of morphosyntactic
structure, namely surface structure; there is no level of "underlying" or
"deep" syntactic structure as in transformational generative grammar
(TGG). Inherent in this position is the denial of a fundamental transfor-
mationalist dogma, the Dogma of the Degeneracy of Surface Structure,
which states that because of such phenomena as variable constituent
order, ellipsis, and discontinuity, surface structure is too impoverished
and chaotic to constitute a level on which to define grammatical relations
by principles of any degree of significant generality and explanatory

97

Syntax and Semantics, Volume 13:
Current Approaches to Syntax

power. If my position is correct, such principles can indeed be given, and a model of syntactic description that is based on this assumption has certain advantages over one that is not. Corepresentational grammar and a provisional treatment of some interesting features of English syntax, are given a detailed presentation in Kac (1978), hereinafter referred to as *CRGS*. For a more general metatheoretical discussion of "abstract" versus "concrete" styles of syntactic description, see Kac (1976).

2. GOALS OF SYNTACTIC THEORY

As one who accepts the legitimacy of the idea of generative grammar in its most basic form, I agree with other generative grammarians that an adequate syntactic description of a language must do two things: define the set of sentences of the language being described, and explicate the manner in which a sentence's form relates to its meaning. However, it is not sufficient on my view merely to recursively enumerate the set of sentences; it is necessary in addition to give some insights into how the structure of a sentence informs the hearer as to the various kinds of meaning relations encoded therein. On this view, the syntactic structure of a language is defnined by giving general principles that state or imply that particular structural patterns can be interpreted only in certain ways. These restrictions may be viewed as constituting a guide to the language user, whose every decision in transducing from the unanalyzed sentence to a complete interpretation thereof must be compatible with them.[1] It might seem at first blush that this is a psychological problem, but it really is not—even though it is definitely RELATED to a psychological problem. From the standpoint of the psychologist, the job is to figure out what processes are employed in making the transduction; the linguist's job is the more basic one of figuring out what regularities inhere in the organization of the linguistic objects themselves that make such processes possible in the first place. This point can be clarified by the following example. Consider the paradigm

(1)   a. *Who does Harry like?*
       b. *Who likes Maxine?*
       c. *Who does Fred think Harry likes?*
       d. *Who does Fred think likes Maxine?*
       e. *Who does George believe Fred thinks Harry likes?*
       f. *Who does George believe Fred thinks likes Maxine?*

In each case, *who* is uniquely associated with *like,* either as Object or as

[1] In one very important sense, the spirit of CORG is closely allied to that of American structuralism, which could be regarded in part as concerned with questions of the form "How do you know an X when you see one?", where X could be interpreted as "noun," "verb," "interrogative clause," "Subject," etc.

Subject; accordingly, there must be some generalization that holds across the paradigm on the basis of which we can account for this fact. Notice that it is begging the question to say that all of the examples in (1) derive from an underlying structure whose most deeply embedded S is of the form *Harry–like–who* or *who–like–Maxine,* since this assumption tells us nothing about how a language user would be able to recover the underlying structure; indeed, unless one is willing to talk in terms of analysis-by-synthesis (which I think could fairly be regarded as begging the question all over again), there is no way within a transformational framework to specify how this recovery might be carried out given the well-known nonreversibility of transformations that chop across essential variables. A popular hypothesis as to the actual processes involved holds that the parsing algorithm for sentences takes the form of an augmented transition network, a device that has the power to forestall the decision about the grammatical function of *who* in sentences like (lc)–(lf) until it encounters a "gap" either immediately before or immediately after *likes,* and that can then evaluate the function of *who* on the basis of the position of the gap. This may or may not be a realistic model of how the actual processing of such sentences is carried out, but even if it were, it would fail to answer the question of most interest to the linguist (as opposed to the psychologist), which is: What is it about the structure of the language that makes it amenable to comprehension via a device of just this kind? To show that the algorithm works, even to show that it is THE algorithm that human language users actually employ, obviously does not answer this question, any more than showing that a particular algorithm for addition or subtraction with Arabic numerals is successful, answers the mathematically interesting question of why the algorithm succeeds. To answer this question, it is necessary to characterize the Arabic numeration system in its essential respects—for example, by noting that it employs a fixed base, that it employs 0 as a placeholder, *etc.* A linguist's description of a language relates to an algorithm for processing it in much the same way a mathematician's description of the Arabic numeration system relates to the familiar algorithms for doing arithmetic.

Let us now consider how, within a corepresentational framework, we would answer the linguistic question posed about the examples in (1). First of all, it is important to note that in each of the examples it is possible to isolate a sequence of the form *who. . .Harry like (s)* or *who. . .likes Maxine.* What is needed, in the case of (lc)–(lf), is some way of guaranteeing that such a sequence can be isolated and analyzed as a predication. Once this is done, the sequence identified will be subject to analysis by the same principles that would be employed in determining the relational representations of (1a) and (1b). In addition, we would like, to the fullest possible extent, to exploit principles that apply also to complex sentences that do not contain discontinuously manifested predications.

In short, we would like to assimilate (1c)–(1f) to simple sentences like (1a) and (1b), on the one hand, and to "normal form" complement constructions (i.e., constructions without any discontinuities) on the other. If this can be done, then the account can fairly be said to have captured the crucial generalizations in which we are interested.

The key to the problem lies in the notion "argument segment" (see CRGS, Section 3.2.1). Let $X = \alpha(P)$, where P is some predicate and α a relation, and let Y be an NP, a predicate, or a predication included (properly or otherwise) in X. Then Y is an α-segment with respect to P. Abbreviatorily, we say $Y = \alpha s_i$, where i indicates that the predicate with respect to which Y is an αs is the ith in the sentence. Note that, because Y need not be properly included in X, Y, and X could be coextensive; in other words, a whole argument can be a segment of itself. Thus any rule which is so formulated as to apply to argument segments applies to whole arguments unless some specific indication to the contrary is given.

We are now ready to state two rules of English, as follows:[2]

(2)   OBJECT RULE (OR): *If P is a transitive active predicate, OBJ(P) must be identified in such a way as to guarantee that as many segments thereof as possible occur to the right of P.*

(3)   OBLIQUE DISTANCE CONDITION (ODC): *If P is an active transitive predicate and has both OBJs and SUBJs to its left (the two being distinct), the elements in question must be in the order OBJs–SUBJs.*

Consider first how a sentence like (1b) would be analyzed. Note that we have not given any rule for picking out Subjects; the reason is that it is unnecessary given the OR and ODC plus a universal principle (the Law of Association), which requires that every predicate be analyzed as having a Subject. This principle could be satisfied for (1b) by taking either *who* or *Maxine* as SUBJ(*like*) but in order to satisfy the OR we must analyze *Maxine* as OBJ(*like*); thus *who* = SUBJ(*like*) by default, as it were.[3] Now consider (1a): Here, there are no elements at all after *like,* and thus the OR will be inapplicable. The ODC applies instead, and it is determined that *who* = OBJ(*like*) and *Harry* = SUBJ(*like*). The complete analysis

---

[2] As stated, these rules apply only to active sentences. In CORG, the terms "Subject" and "Object" are used to refer only to "logical" subject and object; the notion "surface/grammatical subject" is captured via the notion "unmarked argument"; see the Sample Grammar, especially Rules 3.2, 4.1 and 4.5. Any argument of a predicate other than the unmarked argument is marked.

[3] It has occasionally been suggested that this treatment regards Subjects as "redundant" and thus in some sense insignificant. No such interpretation of Subjecthood is either expressed or implied, however; indeed, quite the opposite is true, given that Subjects are treated as obligatory arguments for all precicates, and thus as both essential and fundamental.

may be diagrammed as follows; note that it satisfies all rules presented thus far.

(4)

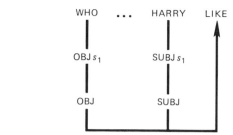

We are now ready to analyze more complex examples. Consider first (1e), whose correct analysis is diagrammed below:[4]

(5)

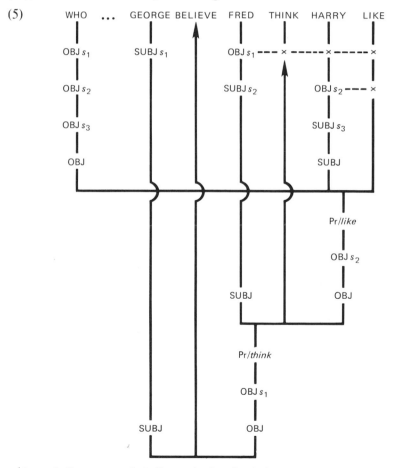

[4] In such diagrams, each "x" on a broken line is intended to represent a copy of the

Notice that all the rules are satisfied for this case as well: Although each of the three verbs has an OBJ*s* to its left, the sentence has been analyzed in such a way that as many OBJ*s* as possible are to the right of each predicate. That there must be one to the left follows simply from the fact that there are not enough elements to the right of either *believe* or *think* for complete predicational Objects to be built for them. Note further that the ODC is satisfied as well as the OR; within each predication, there is an OBJ*s* and a SUBJ*s* to the left of the predicate, but the order maintained is OBJ*s*–SUBJ*s* in each case. Observe finally that no other way of linking up NPs and predicates to form predications will be consistent with both the OR and the ODC. There is, however, one thread still hanging: We have not as yet specified any rule which guarantees that *believe,* which may take both predicational and nonpredicational Objects, may take only the former in this type of construction. This is determined by yet another universal principle, which requires that two predications be on different levels of ordination (i.e., one must be either sub- or super-ordinate to the other) unless certain specific conditions are met, for example, that they may be analyzed as coordinate. (See the Sample Grammar for details.) The conditions in question happen not to be met in the sentence under discussion, and thus all the predications must be on different ordination levels. This in turn requires that both *believe* and *think* be analyzed as taking Object complements rather than nonpredicational Objects since this is the only way to guarantee that a chain or subordination of the required kind obtains.

The analysis of (1f) can be carried out in essentially the same way, the only difference being that the ODC is relevant only to Pr/*believe* and Pr/*think* whereas in (1e) it is relevant to all three predications.

Let us now review exactly what we have done. Our goal was to state some general restrictions that would limit each of the sentences in (1) to a single analysis. We wanted these restrictions to be such that they assimilated the complex sentences in (1) to simple sentences on the one hand, and to complex sentences without discontinuity on the other. We did this by introducing the notion "argument segment," which made it possible for us to state two English–specific rules (the OR and ODC) in such a way that they control the distribution of arguments of predicates both for simple and complex sentences. (Simple sentences are the cases where each argument has only one segment, namely itself.) That is, given the way they are formulated, the OR applies not only to simple sentences like (1b) but also to complex sentences with and without discontinuity,

---

argument segment status label at the beginning of the line. The notation "Pr/P" is read "predication whose predicate is P" or "predication on P."

while the ODC applies to sentences—simple or complex—in which part or all an Object has been "displaced" to the beginning of the sentence. Thus neither rule is motivated solely by the need to handle complex sentences with discontinuity; both apply to other kinds of sentences as well. Finally, we invoked some universal principles, including a requirement that every predicate have a Subject and that all the predications in a sentence be on different levels of ordination unless certain specific conditions are met; again, it is clear that neither of these is ad hoc, designed just to deal with the problem of discontinuity of complements. By making use of the notion "argument segment" we were able to capitalize on an important fact of English syntax, namely that there are certain constraints on the distribution of elements in sentences that apply not only to entire arguments of predicates but also to parts thereof. In the light of this insight, it is possible to see that structures like (1c)–(1f) are not degenerate at all, contrary to what the Dogma of the Degeneracy of Surface Structure implies; though cases like the ones under discussion are often cited as evidence for the dogma, it is clear that they fail to constitute such evidence once the right perspective is adopted.

Before closing this section, I would like to make a final comment on a point that may have occurred to the reader. The rules of a corepresentational grammar are "declarative" rather than "procedural"; that is, they simply state well-formed-ness conditions that corepresentations must meet rather than defining a step-by-step process by which to "crank out" structures. Transformational grammars, by contrast, are primarily (though not exclusively) procedural—they DO define processes for "cranking out" (though of course these are not to be interpreted as modeling the processes of actual sentence production). It is sometimes argued that generative grammars must be procedural, but this is false. All it takes for a grammar to be generative is that it be fully formalized, and all that it takes for a grammar to be fully formalized is that it be constructed in such a way that every one of its rules has a precise interpretation. Whether the rules are declaratively or procedurally stated is irrelevant.[5] Perhaps the clearest way to conceive of the status of a corepresentational description of a language is to think of strings of morphemes constructed at random and assigned structural descriptions (corepresentations) at random as well. The principles of the grammar, then, are axioms from which may be proven as theorems statements to the effect that such-and-such a corepresentation is correct or incorrect for the string to which it has

---

[5] It is thus meaningless to ask "Where do the sentences come from?" All that matters is that the grammar provide a way for deciding about a given string of morphemes what (if any) corepresentations it has.

been assigned. A string of which it can be proven that no corepresentation can be correctly assigned is ungrammatical, and one of which it can be proven that two or more nonequivalent corepresentations can be assigned is ambiguous. In this respect a corepresentational grammar resembles an axiomatization of propositional logic. The axioms make it possible to decide whether an arbitrary sequence of formulas is or is not a proof; if the sequence is a proof, then the last formula of the sequence is valid, and a formula is invalid if it can be shown that it could never be the last formula of a proof. My reason for having adopted this "axiomatic," rather than an "algorithmic," approach is to stay as close as possible to the idea that a grammar of a language is a theory of that language; a theory must be a collection of statements, instructions are not statements, and algorithms are thus not theories. (For additional discussion of this point see Hutchinson, 1980.)

3. DESCRIPTION AND EXPLANATION

A corepresentational grammar is intended both to describe languages and to explain facts about them. In using the terms "description" and "explanation," I have the following definitions in mind: To describe something is to state facts about it, and to explain some fact is to show that it is a logical consequence of some other fact about the object of scrutiny. Now, I am well aware that it is not always easy to determine exactly what constitutes a fact—the line between fact and interpretation is, and always will be, thin and hard to see. One may make of this situation either of two things: On the one hand, one may view it as a rationale for the broadest license in theory construction, or, on the other, one may take it as compelling the most extreme caution. I prefer the latter interpretation—recognizing that one cannot avoid entirely seeing the world through a film of prejudice, one nonetheless does what one can to keep the film as clear as possible.

To illustrate my conception of the relationship between description and explanation, I consider the following example. It is a fact about English that it has relationally equivalent sentence pairs like

(6)   a. *I like beans*
        b. *Beans, I like*
(7)   a. *Harry thinks I like beans*
        b. *Beans, Harry thinks I like*

A fact that has been of interest to syntacticians for some time is that this pattern does not generalize across the full range of construction types in the language; that is, it cannot be asserted that for every sentence of the form X–NP–Y there is a relationally equivalent sentence of the form NP–X–Y. One class of exceptions to the generalization is found in pairs like

(8)   a. *The boy who was eating beans cooked the rice.*
       b.*Beans, the boy who was eating cooked the rice.*
(9)   a. *Harry cooks for his friends who like to eat beans.*
       b. *Beans, Harry cooks for his friends who like to eat.*

The sentence pairs (8)–(9) have in common that their b-members are not relationally equivalent to their a-members, and (8) has the further property that its b-member is ungrammatical. What explanation can be given for these facts? In CRGS, Section 4.3, the following explanation is proposed: The b-members of (8)–(9) differ from those of (6)–(7) in that the former contain complex NPs, and such NPs are characterized as being insular with regard to incoming relational paths; that is, the following restriction obtains:

(10)   No element outside a complex NP may act as an argument of any predicate inside that NP.[6]

Accordingly, *beans* cannot be construed with *eat* in either (8b) or (9b), if it is assumed that *the boy who was eating* and *his friends who like to eat* are complex NPs. (They must indeed be so construed since this is the only way to get the two verbs—neither of which takes a complement in any relation—on different ordination levels, as required by universal principles.) In the case of (8b) there is a further consequence: Since *beans* cannot be construed with *eat* it must be construed with *cook*, and this produces an "overloading" of the main clause.[7] That is, we now have a situation in which three NPs—*beans, the boy who was eating,* and *the rice*—must be construed with a two-place predicate. Note that this interpretation of the facts explains not only why the sentence is ungrammatical but why it is ill-formed in a characteristically severe way. While many ungrammatical sentences are at least intelligible, (8b) is so much spinach; and if we compare it to, say,

(11)   * *Beans, the boy cooked the rice*

---

[6] A modified version of this constraint is given in the sample grammar and accounts also for the ill-formedness of cases like *Bread, a boy came in who was eating.* It is also worth noting that the phenomenon under discussion is more complex than it might appear; for many speakers, sentences like *Bread, I saw the boy who was eating* are more acceptable than cases like the ones discussed here. See *CRGS,* Section 4.4 for a suggested explanation.

[7] A comparable interpretation of the ill-formedness of sentences like (8b) was proposed independently by Cattell (1976).

which is a clear case of ungrammaticality by virtue of overloading, we see ill-formedness of exactly the same degree of severity. We thus have reason to conclude that the ungrammaticality of (8b) and (11) are related phenomena.

Consider now (9b). Here the crucial cases for comparison are

(12)   a. *Harry cooks for his friends*
        b. *Harry cooks beans for his friends*
        c. *Beans, Harry cooks for his friends*

The point here is that *his friends*, by virtue of its status as OBJ(*for*), is not functioning as OBJ(*cook*) but as part of a benefactive construction; in (12a), then, the Object position is empty, but is filled by *beans* in (12b) and (12c). Similarly, in (9b), although *beans* cannot be construed with *eat*, it can be construed with *cook* for exactly the same reason that it can in either (12b) or (12c). Thus (9b) is grammatical, though not relationally equivalent to (9a).

Now, let us return to Principle (10). I would like to say that this statement is both descriptive and explanatory: descriptive because it states a fact about the language, explanatory because it has other facts as consequences. We have shown that it has the nonequivalence of (8a)–(8b) and (9a)–(9b) as a consequence, as well as the severe ungrammaticality of (8b). But does it state a fact? That is, do we have any reasons beyond its usefulness for this particular purpose for believing that the statement is true? The answer is yes; indeed, its original motivation in a corepresentational description of English was unrelated to the particular phenomena just discussed. In a strictly surface–based grammar, it is necessary to solve what in *CRGS* is termed the DOMAIN PROBLEM. (The domain of a predicate *P* is defined as that part of a sentence allowed to contain arguments of *P*.) One manifestation of the problem shows up in cases like

(13)   a. *Harry cooked and ate the fish*
        b. *The boy who cooked ate the fish*

Both sentences are instances of a general structural schema NP. . .P_1. . .P_2. . .NP and yet there is a crucial difference between them: In (13a), *the fish* may be construed either with *eat* alone or with both verbs at once, whereas in (13b) only the first possibility exists. The original reason for adducing (10) was to account for this fact, and also for the ungrammaticality of a sentence like

(14)   * *The boy who liked ate the fish*

Without such a principle, (13b) would erroneously be analyzable as ambiguous in the same way as (13a), and (14) would incorrectly be treated as grammatical under an analysis which would associate *the fish* with both verbs. (Note that such an analysis would satisfy all the other rules we have discussed.) In other words, the grammar without (10), or some such principle, would be too permissive with regard to cases like (13b) and (14). Since the principle is consistent with such cases as these, it may be considered factually true; that it accounts as well for (8) and (9) is what gives it special explanatory force.

It is instructive to compare (10) with the Complex NP Constraint (Ross, 1967), to which it has an obvious kinship. There is, however, also an obvious difference: The CNPC will correctly account for the nonequivalence of (8a)–(8b) and (9a)–(9b) (since derivations consistent with the assumption that they are equivalent will violate the constraint), but it does nothing more; that is, it says "don't move elements out of complex NPs," without saying anything as to why such movements should be impermissible. In the corepresentational account, Principle (10) relates the nonequivalence of the sentences in question to some additional facts about the language, whereas the CNPC is completely irrelevant to the facts cited in connection with (13)–(14).[8]

I want now to return to the question of the relationship between description and explanation. I would like to argue that the two are far more closely related than is commonly supposed; the atmosphere in which linguistic studies are presently carried out has encouraged the mistaken view that there is some kind of radical distinction between description and explanation. Quite the contrary is true: A principle cannot be explanatory unless it is also descriptive. By this, I mean simply that it is not enough to "explain" a fact by showing that it follows from some principle—one must also give compelling reasons for believing the principle to be true. The reason lies in an elementary, if dismal, fact of logic, namely that true statements can follow from false ones; thus facts remain unexplained if

---

[8] The explanatoriness of this account has been questioned by Huddleston (1979) on the following grounds: In a pair of sentences like (i) *I know that Harry ate* and (ii) *I cooked the rice that Harry ate*, no independent support is given for the claim that the sequence *that Harry ate* has different categorial status in the two constructions; accordingly, he claims, the fact that *Harry* could be preposed in (i) but not (ii) remains unexplained. In reply, I would point out first that the assumption that there is a categorial difference between complements and relative clauses could hardly be subject to dispute. But more importantly, what is really significant is not whether or not *that Harry ate* belongs to one or the other category, but rather whether it belongs to a larger expression constituting a term (see Note 13). In (ii) it clearly does, the term in question being the complex NP *the rice that Harry ate*, whereas in (i) it does not. The difference between terms and non-terms appears well motivated (see *CRGS*, Section 4.1); as a result, I see no reason not to accept the claim of explanatoriness advanced here and in *CRGS*.

they are merely shown to follow from statements whose truth is unknown. The point may be put more succinctly still: Facts can be explained only by other facts. Since description consists in the statement of facts, it follows that any genuinely explanatory statement is also a descriptive one.[9] I make an issue of this point partly because I am sometimes challenged with the argument that CORG is uninteresting since its rules are "merely descriptive" and "just state the facts." In the light of the foregoing discussion, the appropriate reply is clear. First of all, it seems to me that any reasonable grammar must state at least SOME facts. What is important is which ones; one wants the facts one chooses to state to be "productive"—that is, such that the things one wishes to explain may be deduced from them. A grammar which has this property must surely count as explanatory in anybody's sense of the term.

4. SYNTACTIC IRREGULARITY IN A COREPRESENTATIONAL FRAMEWORK

In this section, I would like to discuss some phenomena that in TGG are treated under the heading of "rule government." *CRGS* does not discuss lexically based syntactic irregularity, and I am frequently asked what one does in a corepresentational framework to handle lexical exceptions. I will begin by pointing out that that the notion of rule government per se has no place in CORG since the kinds of rules that exist to be governed in a transformational grammar (e.g., Equi-NP Deletion) have no analogues in CORG. For this reason, I will not use the term, preferring the more neutral "lexically based syntactic irregularity."

I will begin by considering the difference between the following verbs with regard to the Subjects of their complements: *want, believe, expect, try, persuade, promise,* and *help.* The first basic distinction to be made is between what we may call argument-sharing and non-argument-sharing verbs. An argument-sharing verb is one which is allowed to share one of

---

[9] I should make it clear nonetheless that I do not deny in principle that it may in some circumstances be possible to determine the truth of particular statements only by very indirect means, as in the case of statements about atomic and molecular structure. It is important to point out, however, that although direct observational tests of theoretical statements are not always possible, this does not mean that they are always impossible; moreover, if one had a choice of theories one of which could be tested only very indirectly while the other could be tested for the most part by observation alone, the latter would have to be considered preferable ceteris paribus. The issue is not whether explanation based on hypothetical constructs is valid in principle, but simply whether such explanation is actually needed in syntactic theory.

its arguments with its complement; if we let the feature [AS] denote this property, then we can mark *believe* as [−AS] and *try* as [+AS]. Verbs which may, but need not, share arguments will not be marked at all. Among the verbs which may share arguments, we must then distinguish between those which share Subjects and those which share non-Subjects. Verbs which share Subjects will be marked [+SS], those which share non-Subjects as [−SS]. Accordingly, we have the following scheme:

want: [+SS]
believe: [−AS]
expect: [+SS]
try: [+AS, +SS]
persuade: [−SS]
promise: [+SS]
help: [+AS, −SS]

If one wants to make a fetish of simplicity, some of these entries can be further cut down. The first four verbs differ from the last three in that the latter take a nonpredicational non-Subject argument as well as a predicational Object;[10] thus the feature [SS] is really relevant only to the latter cases. Accordingly, *want* and *expect* can be left unmarked for both [AS] and [SS]: Thus they are allowed (but not required) to share an argument with the complement, and this could only be the Subject since it is the only argument other than the complement taken by these verbs. In the case of *try*, [+AS] must remain in the entry (since this verb is required to share an argument with its complement) but [+SS] can be dropped as redundant, as in the case of *want* and *expect*. Specific markings for [SS] must remain for *persuade, promise* and *help,* however, since each of these verbs, if it shares, may share only one argument or the other—the choice is not free. (There is one verb I know of that is unspecified for [SS] for some speakers—though not for me—namely *ask.* For these speakers, *He asked me to try on my coat* is ambiguous, meaning either that he requested of me that I try on my coat, or asked of me if he could try it on.) Finally, *help* differs from the other three-place predicates in that it must share, and shares the non-Subject nonpredicational argument: * *He helped the prisoners for Harry to escape* and *He helped the prisoners escape* where only *the prisoners* can be SUBJ (*escape*).

The second phenomenon I would like to consider involves a difference between three-place predicates like *give* and *contribute.* A question was

---

[10] There is a problem is how exactly to treat the two non-Subject arguments of verbs like *persuade* and *promise*: Specifically, it is not clear whether they are of different types (e.g., OBJ, I-OBJ) or of the same type. See *CRGS,* Section 3.2.2.3.

raised in the conference discussion of Dik's paper which could be regarded as addressed to all proponents of nontransformational (or nonderivational) grammatical models. Compare the sentences

(15)   a. *Harry gave $10 to the United Fund*
        b. *Harry gave the United Fund $10.*
        c. *$10 was given by Harry to the United Fund*
        d. *The United Fund was given $10 by Harry*

(16)   a. *Harry contributed $10 to the United Fund*
        b. * *Harry contributed the United Fund $10.00*
        c. *$10 was contributed by Harry to the United Fund*
        d. * *The United Fund was contributed $10 by Harry*

In TGG, the fact that (16d) is ungrammatical while (15d) is grammatical is attributed to the fact that dative passives derive from outputs of Dative Movement; if Dative Movement is impossible, then so are dative passives for a particular verb. The question was how a nonderivational model could handle the parallelism between cases like (16b,d) which apparently requires the notion of "derivation" and, crucially, "intermediate stage of a derivation" (the intermediate stage being the nonpassive output of Dative Movement). The answer is perfectly straightforward: The verbs *give* and *contribute* differ in regard to whether or not they require that their Indirect Objects occur as Objects of the preposition *to*; *give* has no such requirement, but *contribute* does. As long as this difference is marked somehow in the lexicon, then the parallelism between (16b,d) is accounted for. In a corepresentational framework, this would be done by marking *contribute* and similar verbs as [+ * (I-OBJ, + OBJ(*to*))]. (A specification of the form [+ * α] is read "requires an argument of type α." The parentheses indicate that the requirement [+ OBJ(*to*)]—"must occur as OBJ of *to*"—applies only to I-OBJ.) Verbs like *give* need not be marked except as taking I-OBJ as an argument.[11]

5. CONCLUSION

Limitations of length prohibit more extensive or detailed discussion of the many issues raised in this most important symposium. I would like in closing, however, to call attention to one point that I believe to be of special importance. Numerous participants in this conference professed rather similar beliefs about how grammars should be written: For ex-

---

[11] This discussion leaves out of account how to identify Objects of prepositions; see the Sample Grammar, Rule 4.2.

ample, Brame, Dik, Schachter and Cooper, besides myself, have committed themselves now to strictly surface–based approaches. Interestingly, however, we do not all give the same reasons for doing so. In the oral presentations, I cited the metascientific considerations given in Section 2, Brame cited a number of empirical considerations, and Cooper made reference to the preferability of surface–based approaches on psychological grounds. Now, it is possible that all of these reasons are equally valid, but I am not sure. For example, though I am sympathetic to the idea that it is psychologically implausible to assume that human language users operate in terms of the kinds of underlying representations countenanced by TGG, I would question whether considerations of psychological reality (whatever that oft-used term really means) are of any relevance to the grammarian; that is to say, I would question whether we as grammarians are really involved in describing language users rather than languages pure and simple, and I am not entirely sure of how exactly to conceive of the relationship between linguistic description and psychological modeling beyond the observations made in Section 2 above. Thus, I would like to conclude by inviting my fellow nontransformationalists to join me in examining carefully our grounds for believing what we do; without such an examination, I am afraid that the current situation in syntax will become more, rather than less, confused. The organizers of the symposium went to considerable lengths to make us all state our positions clearly and also our reasons for holding them; I urge all of my colleagues to continue in that spirit, which, though it may not produce unity, ought at least to produce understanding and a meaningful dialogue.

6. SAMPLE GRAMMAR

The data provided for the sample grammar contained no ill-formed examples; hence this grammar is written only to fulfill the requirement of assigning correct analyses to well-formed sentences.

1. CATEGORIAL RULES[12]
   1.1. NPs may be of the form (DET)–N or NP–REL.
   1.2. Every REL must contain a P.
2. METACONDITIONS (Universal Constraints on Well-Formedness of Predications)

---

[12] Categorial representations in CORG contain no S-nodes; indeed, it might be unnecessary to recognize any higher-level constituent type other than NP. The notion "predication" does duty for "S"; predications, however, need not be identified via special categorial rules—rather, since a predication by definition consists of a predicate and its arguments, predicational units are read off the relational representation.

2.1. Core Metaconditions

2.1.1. *Law of Correspondence*: Every term[13] in a sentence must be analyzed as an argument of some predicate in the sentence, or as Object of some preposition in the sentence.

2.1.2. *Law of Uniqueness*: (*a*) No single element may bear more than one relation to a single predicate unless conditions are satisfied for the predicate to be construed reflexively; (*b*) no two elements may bear the same relation to a single predicate unless they are coreferential or coordinate, nor may both be unmarked arguments of a single predicate except under the same conditions.

2.1.3. *Law of Association*: Every predicate must have associated with it both a Subject and an unmarked argument. (See Section 4 of Sample Grammar for assignment of markedness values to arguments.)

2.2. Ordination Laws[14]

2.2.1. *First Ordination Law:* Each predication in a complex sentence must bear some ordination relation to another predication in the sentence.

2.2.2. *Second Ordination Law:* Subordination is asymmetric, likewise superordination; coordination is symmetric.

2.2.3. *Third Ordination Law:* Two predications that are not coordinate may be on the same level of ordination only if (*a*) they are members of different arguments of a single predicate, or (*b*) the predicate of one is composite (see Rule 5.3) and the predicate of the other is the superordinate member of that composite.

3. RULES PERTAINING TO VOICE OF PREDICATES

3.1. A predicate is [+PASSIVE] if it occurs in past participial form and the first AUX to its left within its immediate predication is *be*; otherwise it is [−PASSIVE].

3.2. *Markedness Function:* If P is [−PASSIVE], its unmarked argument (U-ARG) is SUBJ(P); if P is [+PASSIVE], U-ARG(P) ≠ SUBJ(P).

---

[13] Terms are NPs and semantically equivalent expressions; in a pair of sentences like (i) *A woman who was wearing a fur coat came in* and (ii) *A woman came in who was wearing a fur coat*, the expression *a woman (. . .) who was wearing a fur coat* is a term in both cases, but an NP only in (i). There is, however, one circumstance under which an NP would not be considered a term, namely if it were employed as a vocative. Vocatives are systematically excluded from the requirement of acting as arguments of predicates.

[14] The idea of incorporating general principles of this type came originally from work by my student Tom Rindflesch.

4. RULES OF COREPRESENTATION (Language–specific rules for determining markedness values and relational status of elements)

    4.1. *Marked Argument Rule:* If P is a transitive predicate, its marked
        argument(s) (M-ARG) Must be identified in such a way that as
        many segments thereof as possible are to the right of P.

    4.2. *Prepositional Object Rule:* An NP to the right of a preposition
        may be analyzed as Object thereof providing no other preposition
        intervenes, and no other rules are violated. If no NP may be found
        to the right of a preposition to act as its Object, the leftmost eli-
        gible NP may be so analyzed. (NB: "eligible" means "capable
        of being so analyzed without violation of any other rule.")

    4.3. *Passive Subject Rule:* If overt, the Subject of a [+PASSIVE]
        predicate must be OBJ (*by*).

    4.4. *Indirect Object Rule:* If overt, I-OBJ(P) must be OBJ(*to*), unless
        it occurs as U-ARG(P) or the first M-ARG to the right of P.

    4.5. *Oblique Distance Condition:* (Given for information only—not
        relevant to the data for this grammar.) If both M-ARGs$_i$ and U-
        ARGs$_i$ occur to the left of P_i and are distinct, they must occur in
        the order M-ARGs–U-ARGs.

5. RULES FOR THE ANALYSIS OF COMPLEMENT CONSTRUCTIONS

    5.1. If the leftmost verbal element (V or AUX) in a predication is
        infinitive, the predication is infinitival.

    5.2. If Pr/P_i = OBJ(P_j) and is infinitival, and if U-ARG(P_i) is not also
        an argu- of P_j, then P_j and P_i together constitute a predicate whose
        Subject is SUBJ(P_j) and whose Object is U-ARG(P_i). (Such pred-
        icates are called "composite"; see Kac, 1976b for a detailed pres-
        entation of the evidence for this rule.)

    5.3. A composite predicate as identified by Rule 5.2 is [α PASSIVE]
        according as P_j is [α PASSIVE].

6. RULES FOR THE ANALYSIS OF TERMS CONTAINING PREDICATIONS
(COMPLEX TERMS)

    6.1. If a REL occurs at the end of a sentence, it need not be directly
        dominated by NP, and forms a term with any NP to its left pro-
        viding that no other rule is violated.

    6.2. The leftmost NP of a complex term is the head of the term.

    6.3. If the head of a complex term is a U-ARGs wrt the main predicate
        of the REL with which it forms this term, the initial element of
        REL must be a subordinator.

    6.4. No element outside a complex term may be an argument of any
        predicate inside that term.

7. RULES FOR THE ANALYSIS OF COORDINATE SENTENCES

    7.1. Two elements are coordinate only if (*a*) a coordinating conjunction occurs between them; or (*b*) Condition (*a*) obtains with regard to both elements and some third element.

7.2. In a sequence of the form *W–X–*CONJ*–Y–Z*, *X* and *Y* are PAR-ALLEL SEGMENTS of the sequence iff (*a*) both contain a predicate; (*b*) at least one argument place of a predicate in each segment can be filled by material within that segment; (*c*) if some argument segment wrt the main predicate of one segment is missing from that segment, a corresponding argument segment wrt the main predicate of the other, having the same markedness value, is missing from that segment.

7.3. If a sentence contains units analyzable as parallel segments, they must be so analyzed unless the conditions are satisfied for construing the main predicate of one of the units as subordinate to the predicate of the other.

7.4. No element in a given segment of a parallel segmentation may act as an argument of a predicate outside that segment.

7.5. In a sequence of the form NP–P–NP–CONJ–NP–NP, the relative order of marked and unmarked arguments to the right of the conjunction must match that found to the left.

7. LEXICON

the: DET	*woman:* N	*walked:* P, [– * OBJ]
every: DET	*farmer:* N	*killed:* P, [+ * (OBJ, [– PREDIC-ATIONAL])]
a: DET	*duckling:* N	*believed:* P, [+ * OBJ]
that: SUBORDINATOR	*John:* N	*loved:* P, [+ * OBJ]
to: SUBORDINATOR	*axe:* N	*gave:* P, [+ * (OBJ, [– PREDICATIONAL])],
and: CONJ	*Bill:* N	[+ * I-OBJ]
to: PREPOSITION	*he:* N	*have:* AUX, infinitive
by: PREPOSITION	*who:* N	*was:* AUX, form of *be*
with: PREPOSITION		

8. DISCUSSION OF SPECIFIC EXAMPLES

The way to check a particular sentence against the grammar is to diagram its correct analysis and determine that it is consistent with the rules; in addition, it should be determined that no incorrect analyses are also consistent with the rules.

Sentence 9

To satisfy the Ordination Laws, Pr/*kill* and Pr/*believe* must be placed on different ordination levels, which can only be done by assuming that the former is an Object complement of the latter. To satisfy Rule 4.1, Pr/*kill* must be built up from the elements to the right of *believe*. By 5.1, Pr/*kill* is infinitival, so *believe–kill* is a composite, by Rule 5.2, whose Subject is *the woman* and whose Object is *John*. Rule 5.2 does the work of "Subject Raising" in the sense that it accounts for the Object-like properties of Subjects of infinitival complements; on this account, however, they are Objects semantically as well as syntactically, which is not true under the Subject-Raising analysis.

Sentence 11

Here, in contradistinction to 9, the composite *believe–kill* is passive (Rule 5.3). As before, however, we must treat Pr/*kill* as subordinate to Pr/*believe*. Pr/*kill* is identified as follows: By Rules 3.2, 4.1, 4.2 and 4.3, *John* = SUBJ(*kill*), and *the woman* = SUBJ(*believe*). Only one other NP is left in the sentence to be analyzed as OBJ(*kill*), namely *the farmer*. This completes Pr/*kill*, which in turn is then analyzed as OBJ(*believe*).

Sentence 15

By Rule 7.5, *Bill* and *the farmer* must be respectively U-ARG/SUBJ and M-ARG/OBJ of *kill*. The complete analysis identifies two Subjects and two Objects for *kill*, which is permissible since the mitigating condition of 2.1.2(*b*) is satisfied (see also Rule 7.1).

Sentence 17

The sentence is subject to the following parallel segmentation:

$$John \underline{\textit{loved the woman}} \text{ and } \underline{\textit{killed the farmer}}$$
$$X \qquad\qquad\qquad Y$$

Accordingly, *the woman* can be construed only with *loved* and *the farmer* only with *killed; John,* however, can be construed with both predicates since it is a member of neither segment.

REFERENCES

Cattell, R. (1976). Constraints on movement rules. *Language, 52,* 18–50.

Huddelston, R. (1979). Review of Kac 1978, *Talanya (Journal of the Australian Linguistic Society).*

Hutchinson, L.G. (1980). Axiom, theorem, and rule. In T.A. Perry (Ed.), *Evidence and Argumentation in Linguistics.* Berlin: W. De Gruyter. Pp. 203–218.

Kac, M. B. (1976a). Hypothetical constructs in syntax. In J. R. Wirth (Ed.), *Assessing Linguistic Arguments.* Washington, D.C.: Hemisphere Press—John Wiley and Sons, Inc. Pp. 49–84.

Kac, M. B. (1976b). On composite predication in English. In M. Shibatani (Ed.), *Syntax and Semantics 6, The Grammar of Causative Constructions* New York: Academic Press. Pp. 229–258.

Kac, M. B. (1978). *Corepresentation of Grammatical Structure.* Minneapolis: University of Minnesota Press, and London: Croom Helm, Ltd.

Ross, J. R. (1967). Constraints on variables in syntax. Unpublished doctoral dissertation, MIT, Cambridge, Massachusetts.

FUNCTIONAL SYNTAX[1]

SUSUMO KUNO
Harvard University

1. INTRODUCTION

FUNCTIONAL LINGUISTICS is an approach to analysis of linguistic structure in which emphasis is placed on the communicative function of the elements, in addition to their structural relations (Garvin, 1963). FUNCTIONAL SYNTAX is a subarea of functional linguistics in which syntactic structures are analyzed with emphasis on their communicative function. Since nothing can be gained in analyzing syntactic structures by ignoring, or being ignorant of, their communicative function, every good syntactician should also be a good functional syntactician.

Functional syntax is, in principle, independent of various current models of grammar such as (standard, extended standard, and revised extended standard) theories of generative grammar, relational grammar, case grammar, tagmemics, and so on. Each theory of grammar must have a place or places where various functional constraints on the well-formedness of sentences or sequences of sentences can be stated, and each theory

[1] This paper is based upon work supported by the National Science Foundation under Grant NSF BNS 76 81732. I am greatly indebted to Linda Shumaker, who has read earlier versions of this paper and has given me numerous invaluable comments.

117

of grammar can benefit from utilizing a functional perspective in analysis of concrete syntactic phenomena. Therefore, in theory, there is no conflict between functional syntax and, say, the revised extended standard theory of generative grammar. Given a linguistic process that is governed purely by syntactic factors, this process will be described in the syntactic component of grammar both by pure syntacticians and by functional syntacticians. On the other hand, given a linguistic process that is governed by both syntactic and, say, discourse factors, the syntactic aspect will be formulated in the syntactic component, while discourse factors that interact with this syntactic characterization will be described in, say, the discourse component of grammar. Pure syntacticians would concentrate on the former characterization, and functional syntacticians, on the latter. There need not be any disagreement between the two.

In actuality, however, there are numerous conflicts between pure and functional syntacticians with respect to how to analyze a given linguistic phenomenon. Disagreements often arise from their respective judgments as to whether a regularity observed for a given linguistic phenomenon should be stated as a syntactic problem or as a nonsyntactic problem. Take, for example, the following set of sentences:

(1)   a. *Did you buy a portrait of Nixon?*
        b. *Who did you buy a portrait of?*

(2)   a. *Did you buy Mary's portrait of Nixon?*
        b. *Who did you buy Mary's portrait of?*

Why is (1b) acceptable and (2b) unacceptable? Pure syntacticians' immediate reaction to this kind of data would be to assume that (2b) is ungrammatical due to a violation of some syntactic constraint. They assume that there is a constraint that says nothing can be moved out of a [NP's N Prep X]$_{NP}$ structure. Some of them relate it to a constraint, independently motivated, though on dubious grounds, that says that no rule can apply, with a trigger upstairs, to a constituent within an NP or S that has a specified subject. More formally stated, this constraint reads as follows (Chomsky, 1973):

(3)   SPECIFIED SUBJECT CONDITION: *No rule can involve X, Y in the structure*

$$\ldots X \ldots [_\alpha \ldots \quad Z \quad \ldots \quad -W \quad Y \quad V \ldots] \ldots$$

where Z is the specified subject of WYV in α, and α is either NP or S.

The same constraint is invoked for explaining the ungrammaticality of the following (b) sentences:

(4)   a. *It is Nixon who I want to buy a portrait of*
      b. **It is Nixon who I want to buy Mary's portrait of*

(5)   a. *Nixon, I don't want to buy a portrait of*
      b. **Nixon, I don't want to buy Mary's portrait of*

(6)   a. *Yesterday, I met the man who I had bought a portrait of*
      b. * *Yesterday, I met the man who I had bought Mary's portrait of*

Some syntacticians believe that the Specified Subject Condition is not a condition that needs to be stated in grammars in individual languages, but is a condition on the construction of grammatical rules, namely a part of the theory of grammar that humans are born with.

Functional syntacticians view this kind of mechanical syntactic formulation with a great deal of suspicion. First, there does not seem to be any obvious reason why such a constraint should exist as a universal constraint. Second, there are clear examples that show that there is something fundamentally wrong with it. For example, observe the following sentences:

(7)   a. *John believes that Mary is fond of this boy*
      b. *Who does John believe (that) Mary is fond of?*
      c. *It is this boy that John believes (that) Mary is fond of*
      d. *This boy, John believes (that) Mary is fond of*
      e. *This is the boy that John believes (that) Mary is fond of*

The string *(that) Mary was fond of* is an S which has *Mary* as a specified subject. Therefore, no rule should apply in such a way as to involve *who*. However, (7b), as well as (7c), (7d), and (7e) are grammatical. This contradiction is circumvented in the pure syntactic approach under discussion by assuming that (7b) is derived not by preposing *who* in one sweep to the sentence-initial position, but by preposing it first to the initial position of the embedded clause, and then, to sentence-initial position:

(8)   [$_s$COMP *John believes* [$_s$COMP *Mary is fond of who*]]
                  2nd cycle   1st cycle

According to this analysis, the preposing of *who* to the COMP position in the first cycle does not violate the Specified Subject Condition because this movement does not involve a higher clause trigger *X*. Similarly, the preposing of *who* from that position to sentence-initial position in the second cycle does not violate the condition, either, because *who*, this time, is not preceded by the specified subject *Mary* of the embedded clause.[2] Functional syntacticians feel that this kind of mechanical explanation is an artifact built on a theoretical artifact, and that it does not have any reality.

Functional syntacticians assume that there must be some other explanation, perhaps a functional one, for the unacceptability of (2b), (4b), (5b), and (6b). They collect many more examples of sentences, either acceptable or unacceptable, that involve movement of *X* out of the [NP's N Prep *X*] pattern. They eventually come across sentences of the following kind:[3]

(9)   *This is the story that I haven't been able to get Mary's version of*

I have not come across any native speakers of English who find anything wrong with this sentence. The sentence does not need any elaborate context to justify it. It is a perfectly normal sentence. Yet, it violates the Specified Subject Condition because Relativization has moved *the story* out of *Mary's version of the story*, where *Mary's* is the specified subject of the entire NP construction. Therefore, the Specified Subject Condition is not even a plausible constraint in English, to say nothing of its implausibility as part of the theory of grammar that humans are born with.

Functional syntacticians do not stop at the above conclusion, but look for an explanation as to why (9) is acceptable while (6b), for example, is unacceptable. The difference in acceptability must be attributable to some difference between *Mary's portrait of the man* and *Mary's version of the story*. What is special about the latter? Functional syntacticians would realize that the semantic content of *version* is such that it can be used only when there is more than one version of something. In other words, the expression *Mary's version of the story*, even without any prior context, implies that there are other people's versions of the story. This expression requires that stress be placed on *Mary's—Mary* is the focus of this expression. On the other hand, there is no such peculiarity with *Mary's portrait of the man*. Out of context, this expression does not imply that there are other people's portraits of the same man. *Mary* ordinarily does not receive a focus stress, and the expression is usually interpreted as

---

[2] According to this analysis, noun phrases do not have COMP in their initial position, and therefore, in sentences such as (2b), *who* has to be moved from its original position into the COMP position of the main clause in violation of the Specified Subject Condition:

[$_S$COMP *you bought* [$_{NP}$ *Mary's portrait of WHO*]]

[3] I am indebted to a participant in my course on functional syntax at the 1977 Linguistic Institute, University of Hawaii at Manoa.

referring to someone who has been talked about in the preceding discourse. Thus, functional syntacticians *tentatively* assume that the acceptability of (9), in isolation, is due to the fact that *Mary* can be readily interpreted as representing contrast in this sentence—that is, as the focus, and not as the topic, of the sentence.

The above observation that the acceptability of (9) should be attributed to the fact that *Mary's* is a focus of the relative clause is further confirmed by the fact that in a context in which *Mary's* of *Mary's version of X* receives a noncontrastive interpretation, sentences of the pattern of (9) are not readily acceptable. Observe, for example, the following sentence:

(10)   ??*This is the story that I haven't been able to get Mary's latest version of*

The expression *Mary's latest version of the story*, out of context, is usually interpreted with *latest* as focus, and not with *Mary's* as focus. For most speakers, (10) is unacceptable.[4] There are speakers who regard (10) as acceptable, but they say that they get only the interpretation in which *Mary's* is contrasted with, say, *Jane's, Martha's,* etc., and not the one in which *latest* is contrasted with *original, second,* etc.[5]

The acceptability of sentences of the pattern of (9) is not limited to cases that involve [NP's *version of X*]. In fact, when the genitive NP of the [NP's N Prep X] pattern in general is stressed, it is rather easy to produce acceptable sentences that involve violations of the Specified Subject Condition. Observe the following sentences:

(11)   a. *This is the term that I don't like Chomsky's definition of*
        b. *This is the event that I liked CBS's reporting of best of all*

These sentences are potentially ambiguous. Sentence (11a), for example, has, theoretically, the following two interpretations.

(12)   a. *Among various terms under discussion, there is one such that I like all the various definitions of it given by various scholars, except for the one given by Chomsky*
        b. *Among the definitions of various terms given by Chomsky, there is one that I don't like—and it is the definition of this term*

In (12a), *Chomsky's* is a focus, while in (12b), *CBS's* is not. The preferred interpretation of (11a) seems to be that of (12a).[6] Similarly, observe the

---

[4] I am indebted to Yukio Otsu for this observation.
[5] I am indebted to Linda Shumaker for this observation.
[6] I will later discuss the (12b) interpretation of (11a).

following example:[7]

(13)   *A politician of this kind, I wouldn't dream of buying even Ave-
         don's portrait of*

Avedon's does not seem to receive a prominent emphatic stress, but it
is still the focus of the sentence. Note that the following sentence, with
his de-stressed, is unacceptable:

(14)   **A politician of this kind, I wouldn't dream of buying even his
         (Avedon's) portrait of*

   Similarly, it is easy to produce counterexamples to the Specified Subject Condition using examples that involve the genitive form of indefinite
noun phrases. Observe the following sentences:

(15)   a. (?)*This morning, I bumped into a man who I had just bought
             a local artist's portrait of*
         b. (?)*A politician of this kind, I wouldn't dream of buying any-
             body's portrait of*

   The acceptability of sentences such as (9), (11), (13), and (15) makes
the pure syntacticians' explanation of the unacceptability of (2b), (4b),
(5b), and (6b) totally unacceptable. It casts a serious doubt as to the
plausibility of a theory of grammar that contains the Specified Subject
Constraint and that heavily depends upon it for explanation of numerous
syntactic phenomena. Functional syntacticians, by having uncovered examples such as (9), (11), (13), and (15), are already ahead of pure syntacticians. However, it still remains to be explained why these sentences
are acceptable, while (2b), (4b), (5b), and (6b) are not. Grosu (1978) attributes the unacceptability of the latter sentences to the fact that they
involve a conflict in topic–comment organization. Kuno (1976a) has
shown previously that only a constituent that qualifies as the theme of
a relative clause can be relativized. Similarly, Kuno has proposed that
interrogative and *it*-clefting constructions also involve a presupposed
topic–comment structure, where the topic is some variable substitutable
for the interrogative pronoun of the focus of the *it*-clefts. Grosu points
out that it has also been shown that certain constructions (both sentences
and noun phrases) have "natural" or "preferred" topic–comment structures, that is, structures that they tend to assume in out-of-the-blue situations (Keenan, 1974). In particular, in a sentence, the subject tends
to be selected as topic, and in a noun phrase of the [NP's N Prep X]
pattern, the genitive NP, and not X, tends to be perceived as a topic.

---

[7] I am indebted to Susan Lhota for this example.

The above observations by Grosu make it possible to explain why some sentences involving extraction of X out of [NP's N Prep X] are acceptable and why others are unacceptable. For example, observe the following sentences:

(16)   a. *Q you bought [a portrait of Nixon]*
        b. *Who did you buy a portrait of?*   (= 1b)

(17)   a. *Q you bought [Mary's portrait of Nixon]*
        b. *Who did you buy Mary's portrait of?*   (= 2b)

(18)   a. *I haven't been able to get [Mary's version of this story]*
        b. *This is the story that I haven't been able to get Mary's version of* (= 9)

In (16a), the noun phrase in square brackets does not involve a genitive noun phrase, and therefore, *Nixon* (or a noun phrase that fills that slot) can readily qualify as the theme of the sentence. Hence, the noun phrase in this position can undergo *wh*-Question Movement. In (17a), on the other hand, in the out-of-the-blue situation, *Mary* qualifies more readily than *Nixon* for themehood, and hence, the unacceptability of (17b). In (18a), on the other hand, *Mary* does not qualify as theme because, due to the semantic nature of *version*, *Mary's* has to be interpreted contrastively. Hence, *this story* can be interpreted as the theme of this clause, and can undergo Relativization.

The above explanation suggests that extraction of X out of the [NP's N Prep X] pattern might be possible even when the genitive NP is not the focus of the phrase just in case X qualifies as a prominent theme, whereas the genitive NP serves as a latent theme (say, a paragraph theme). Such a situation would arise when the genitive NP is semantically transparent, and represents information that is so presupposed that one would not characterize the rest of the sentence as a statement about that genitive NP. For example, observe the following discourse (due to Grosu):

(19)   *I have been collecting one separate picture for each Hollywood actress, and I can show them to you if you like. But I need to tell you in advance, I cannot show you my picture of Marilyn Monroe*

In a sense, the entire discourse can be said to be a statement about the speaker. But the information content that *I/my* represents is so low (that is, it is so presupposed) that it qualifies only as a hyper-theme, and it makes more sense to say that in the last sentence, *Marilyn Monroe*, and not *I/my*, is the prominent theme. Note that the following sentence, which is due to Grosu, can replace the last sentence of (19):

(20)   *But there is one particular actress who I will NEVER show you*
         mỹ picture of Ø.

It is interesting, in this respect, to note that all the counterexamples to
the Specified Subject Condition given in Grosu's paper that do not have
the genitive NP as focus, have either *my* or *you* in the genitive NP position—the two genitive pronouns that are most presupposed, and most
transparent from discourse points of view.[8]

This of course does not mean that only the first and second genitive
pronouns allow extraction of the pattern of (20). Let us return here to
(11a), repeated here for ease of reference:

(21)   *This is the term that I don't like Chomsky's definition of*   (= 11a)

This sentence, as a secondary interpretation, can mean that among the
definitions by Chomsky of various terms, there is one that I do not like,
and that this is the one. In this interpretation, *Chomsky's* is not a focus,
but theme.. Such a sentence can be used only if the preceding discourse
has revolved heavily around Chomsky's definitions of various linguistic
terms. But then, why is it that the sentence that we started out with,
namely, (2b), and the relative clause version of it, are unacceptable?

(22)   a. **Who did you buy Mary's portrait of?*   (= 2b)
         b. **This is the man who I bought Mary's portrait of yesterday*

It seems that the difference between (21) and (22) lies in how easy it is
to come up with a context that would justify the presuppositions that are
involved in these sentences. Sentence (21) presupposes that there are
definitions by Chomsky of various (linguistic) terms. Such a presupposition does not require any special context. Furthermore, (21), in the interpretation intended here, presupposes that the preceding context has
been Chomsky's definitions of various linguistic terms. It is not difficult
at all for the hearer to come up with such a context. On the other hand,
(22b), for example, in the interpretation in which *Mary's* does not receive
a focus stress, presupposes that there is a portrait by Mary of the man
under discussion. Such a presupposition is difficult to justify under the
out-of-the-blue situation. The sentence also presupposes that the preceding discourse has been about Mary's portraits of various people. This
presupposition is necessary in order to interpret *Mary's* not as a prominent
theme, but as a secondary theme. These two presuppositions are unusual,

---

[8] Grosu gives contexts which would make sentences such as (20) acceptable, but does
not explain why such contexts make them acceptable.

and require much more special context than required for (21). It seems
that ordinary speakers of English reject (22b) because they cannot easily
come up with the context of this kind. This explanation is supported by
the fact that (23) is considerably better than (22b) if the hearer knows that
Avedon is a well-known photographer:

(23)   *This is the model who I just bought Avedon's portrait of*

I have exemplified in the above the kind of difference that the pure
syntactic approach and the functional approach give rise to in actual
analysis of concrete linguistic data. Given the unacceptability of (2b),
pure syntacticians tend to assume that it is due to a syntactic constraint,
attribute it to something like the Specified Subject Condition, and have
done with the analysis of this phenomenon. Functional syntacticians try
to find natural explanations for the phenomenon, and resort to a mechanical syntactic conditioning only when they are forced to. In case a
nonsyntactic factor that controls a given phenomenon has a one-to-one
correspondence with some syntactic factor, the two approaches do not
result in any difference in the final analysis. Assume, as I have, that (2b)
is unacceptable due to a violation of the constraint that says that only a
constituent that qualifies as a prominent theme in the sentence can
undergo extraction. Also assume, hypothetically, that the genitive NP of
the [NP's N Prep X] pattern is ALWAYS a prominent theme [see (24a)].
Then, the pure syntactician's analysis of the phenomenon under discussion (based on a syntactic characterization such as the Specified Subject
Condition) would be no different from the functional syntacticians' analysis based on themehood. On the other hand, if themehood sometimes
shows atypical manifestions in the [NP's N Prep X] pattern, and shows
up not in the genitive position, but in the position of X, the pure syntacticians' formulation fails [see (24b)].

(24)   *Monsyntactic*   *Syntactic*   *Syntactic*
            Controlling Factor   *Manifestation*   *Conditioning*

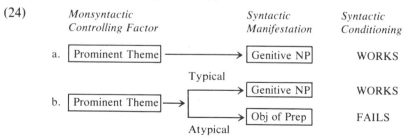

My own experience is that situations of the kind illustrated in (24a) are
rather rare, and that situations such as that shown in (24b) are predom-
inant. The pure syntacticians' analysis of such a phenomenon initially
looks correct because it captures typical cases, but further examination

of the same phenomenon shows that it cannot explain atypical cases, and that it has to be abandoned in its entirety.

It would not be amiss here to compare the attitudes of pure syntacticians and functional syntacticians. Pure syntacticians assume, either explicitly or implicitly, that language is controlled primarily by syntax, and only secondarily by nonsyntactic factors (therefore, given a phenomenon, it is safer to assume that it is controlled by syntactic factors rather than by nonsyntactic factors). They assume that nonsyntactic explanation is a vice that is to be avoided as much as possible. They also seem to assume that having generalizations that are based on concepts—such as "theme"— that cannot be precisely defined or automatically identified are worse than having no generalizations at all. Functional syntacticians, on the other hand, assume that language is controlled primarily by nonsyntactic functional factors, and only secondarily by syntax (therefore, given a phenomenon, it is safer to assume that it is controlled by nonsyntactic factors rather than by syntactic factors). They assume that there is something wrong with syntactic generalizations that do not have obvious nonsyntactic explanation, especially if they are of the language universal type, and that it is better to have generalizations that work, but cannot be formulated and applied rigorously, than to have precise syntactic formulations that do not work. In the rest of this paper, I will illustrate various functional principles that cannot be rigorously formulated, but that can be convincingly shown to be indispensable factors in accounting for major syntactic phenomena in language.

2. FUNCTIONAL SENTENCE PERSPECTIVE

Various concepts that relate to the information content of elements in a sentence in discourse have been shown to play vital roles in stating the conditions for the application of certain syntactic rules. I will give informal definitions of some of these concepts:

(25)   OLD (PREDICTABLE) INFORMATION: An element in a sentence represents old, predictable information if it is recoverable from preceding context.

(26)   NEW (UNPREDICTABLE) INFORMATION: An element in a sentence represents new, unpredictable information if it is not recoverable from preceding discourse.

(27)   THEME: Theme is what the rest of the sentence is about.

(28)   FOCUS: That element in a sentence which represents the newest information is the focus of the sentence.

For example, observe the following exchange:

(29)   a. SPEAKER A: *What does John like?*
         b. SPEAKER B: *He likes fish*

In Speaker B's response to the question, *He likes* represents old, predictable information. Even if that part of the sentence is garbled, it is recoverable from the preceding context. This part of Speaker B's response can be deleted without impairing intelligibility of the answer. On the other hand, *fish* in the answer represents new, unpredictable information, in that, if this part of the response is garbled, there is no way for Speaker A to recover it from the preceding context.

The concept of "old, predictable" information and that of "anaphoric" or "definite" are basically independent from each other. Observe the following exchange:

(30)   a. SPEAKER A: *Which of the two, John or Bill, won the race?*
         b. SPEAKER B: *John did*

In (30a), *John* is anaphoric in that both Speaker A and Speaker B can uniquely determine its referent, namely, the person named John that they both know. In (30a), *John* is anaphoric in the same sense, and also in the sense that it is coreferential with the *John* of (30a). Despite this, the *John* of (30b) represents, not "old, predictable" information, but "new, unpredictable" information. If this part of Speaker B's response were garbled, there would be no way for Speaker A to determine what it was. Similarly, observe the following exchange:

(31)   a. SPEAKER A: *Who has seen a three-legged chicken?*
         b. SPEAKER B: *I have seen one*

In (31b), *one* (=a *three-legged chicken*) is indefinite and nonanaphoric. Despite this, it represents old, predictable information. Speaker B can delete it, and simply say, *I have*. Thus, a nonanaphoric element in a sentence can represent old information given appropriate context.

There are languages, such as Japanese and Korean, that have a formal grammatical device that is used to mark the theme of a sentence. Analysis of these langauges reveals a great deal to us about the characteristics of theme in sentences. For example, they show that there are sentences that do not have themes. Consider the following sentence:

(32)   *Alexander kissed Mary*

This sentence can be interpreted in several different ways, including the following:

(33)   a. *What did Alexander do?—Alexander kissed Mary*
        b. *Did Alexander and Thomas kiss somebody?—Alexander
            kissed Mary, but Thomas didn't*
        c. *Who kissed Mary?—Alexander kissed Mary*
        d. *What do you suppose I saw then? Alexander kissed Mary*

In Japanese, the theme marker *wa* appears after *Alexander* only in (33a)
and (33b). In (33c) and (33d), *Alexander* is followed by the nominative
case marker *ga*, rather than the thematic *wa*. In (33c), *kissed Mary*, although not grammatically marked as theme, clearly represents old information, and in a semantic sense, we can say that this sentence is ABOUT
kissing Mary. On the other hand, (33d) does not contain any old information. It presents the whole event as new. This sentence does not have
a theme either in the grammatical sense, or in the semantic sense. I have
previously (Kuno, 1972) identified the *Alexander* of (32) in the four senses
described in (33) as (*a*) theme, (*b*) contrastive theme, (*c*) subject of exhaustive listing interpretation, and (*d*) subject of neutral description.
These concepts play important roles in English, as well as in many other
languages. Details are found in Kuno (1972).

In the preceding section, I discussed the need for distinguishing between
"prominent theme" and "latent, secondary theme" of a sentence. It is
also necessary to distinguish between "predictable theme" and "unpredictable theme." It is generally held that the theme of a sentence necessarily represents old information. But this is not true. In the exchange
given in (29), *he* in Speaker B's response is the theme of the sentence,
and does represent old information. On the other hand, observe the following exchange.

(34)   a. SPEAKER A: *What do John and Mary like?*
        b. SPEAKER B: *John likes fish, and Mary likes pork*

It is possible to utter (34) without contrastive stress on *John* and *Mary*.
Here, *John* and *Mary* are themes of their respective sentences, but they
also convey new information in that if these two parts are garbled, there
would be no way for Speaker A to guess whether *John* or *Mary* fits into
these slots. Elsewhere (Kuno, 1972), I have distinguished between the
theme representing old information ("predictable theme") and the theme
representing new information ("unpredictable theme"), and have shown
that this distinction interacts with certain syntactic processes.

There is not enough space here to treat in depth any of the above concepts as they are used for explanation of syntactic phenomena. Let me
simply give a few illustrative examples. First, observe the following two

discourse fragments:

(35)   *I have three children: John $_i$, Jane, and Mary. John $_i$ is not terribly bright, but among John $_i$, Jane, and Mary, he $_i$ is the brightest*

(36)   *I have three children: Jane, John $_i$, and Mary. Jane is clearly the brightest. *Between John $_i$ and Mary, he $_i$ is the brighter*

It has been generally believed that forward pronominalization is applicable unconditionally, and that *he* of (35) is the result of application of forward pronominalization with *John* (of *among John, Jane, and Mary*) as trigger. The unacceptability of (36) as a coherent discourse shows that pronominalization into the focus of the sentence that represents the exhaustive listing interpretation is possible only when the pronoun is coreferential with the theme of the discourse. Note that *John* is the discourse theme in (35), but not in (36) (see Kuno, 1975a).

Likewise, observe the following sentences:

(37)   a.   *John persuaded Mary to donate $200, and Jane to donate $300*
       b.   *One alumnus promised Mary to donate $200, and another to donate $300*

It is well known that the latter half of (37a) means (i) [John persuaded] Jane to donate $300, and not (ii) Jane [persuaded Mary] to donate $300. Many scholars have proposed syntactic constraints on the application of Gapping in such a way as to ban the derivation of (37a) in interpretation (ii). If a syntactic constraint were in operation, (37b) should also mean (i) [one alumnus promised] another to donate $300, and not (ii) another [promised Mary] to donate $300. However, (37b) primarily means (ii), and not (i). Therefore, the fact that has been observed in (37a) must be explained not as a syntactic problem, but as a discourse-based phenomenon. It turns out that Gapping leaves behind two constituents that represent new information, and that in a sentence such as *x persuaded y to donate $300*, if both *x* and *y* are anaphoric NPs, it is usually understood that *x* represents older information, and *y*, newer information.[9] Hence, *Jane* of (37a) is taken as the object of *persuade*. On the other hand, if *x* is indefinite, and *y* is anaphoric, it is ordinarily taken for granted that *x* represents the newer information. Hence, it is much easier to interpret *another* of (37b) as corresponding to *x*. It also turns out that if one NP

---

[9] I am assuming here that even languages such as English that are subject to rigid syntactic constraints regarding word order observe the principle of "from old to new." Namely, the closer to the end of the sentence, the newer, the information content. See Kuno (1979) for the interaction of this principle with syntactic word order constraints.

and one VP are left behind after Gapping, the most readily available interpretation is that of the NP as the underlying subject of the VP. Given *x persuaded y to donate $300*, *y* is coreferential with the underlying subject of *to donate $300*. On the other hand, given *x promised y to donate $300*, *x*, and not *y*, is coreferential with the underlying subject of the VP. The above two factors, both functional, conspire to make interpretation (ii) unavailable for (37a), but readily available for (37b). Details of this analysis can be found in Kuno (1976b).

The distinction between thematic adverbs and nonthematic adverbs, which was first systematically examined in Kuno (1975b), has turned out to be a very important one in the framework of functional syntax. Observe the following two sentences:

(38)   a. *John was born in 1960*
        b. *John was still a small boy in 1960*

Sentence (38a) is a sentence that tells us when John was born, whereas (38b) is one that tells us what John was like in 1960. The *in 1960* in (a) is a time-specifying adverb, whereas in (b) it is a scene-setting thematic adverb. Note that only the latter can be preposed to sentence-initial position without changing the meaning:

(39)   a. *In 1960, John was born*
        b. *In 1960, John was still a small boy*

Sentence (39b) is more or less synonymous with (38b), but (39a) means something totally different from (38a). As I have already mentioned, (38a) is a statement with respect to when John was born, whereas (39a) is a statement as to what happened in 1960. The latter clearly sounds as if it had been lifted out of a family chronicle. Kuno (1975b) gives several syntactic tests that distinguish between the thematic and nonthematic adverbs.[10] Reinhart (1976) gives many more. I do not have space to summarize them here.

The distinction between these two types of adverbs manifests itself in the following contrast:

(40)   a. **In John$_i$'s dormitory, he$_i$ smoked pot*
        b. *In John$_i$'s dormitory, only he$_i$ smoked pot*

---

[10] Kuno (1975b) shows that in fact, there is a syntactic difference corresponding to the distinction between thematic and nonthematic adverbs. Namely, nonthematic adverbs are lower adverbs in that they are part of the VP constituency, while thematic adverbs are higher adverbs and are outside the VP constituency.

(40a) is a statement as to where John smoked pot, whereas (40b) is a statement as to what the situation was in John's dormitory. *In John's dormitory* in (40a) is a place-specifying nonthematic adverb, whereas in (40b) it is a thematic adverb. Note the contrast in pronominalizability of the main clause subject in these two sentences. Similarly, note the following contrast:

(41)　　a. **In John's portrait of Mary$_i$, she$_i$ found a scratch*
　　　　b. *In John's portrait of Mary$_i$, she$_i$ looks sick*

We observe here the same contrast recurring. It would be futile to try to explain the above contrast without recourse to the distinction between thematic adverbs (which perhaps originate in sentence-initial position) and nonthematic adverbs.

The above contrast interacts with Verb Phrase Deletion. Note the following contrast:

(42)　　a. *I didn't stay in a hotel in Paris, but I stayed in a hotel in London*
　　　　b. *I didn't stay in a hotel in Paris, but I did Ø in London*

(43)　　a. *I didn't buy this ring in Paris; I bought it in London*
　　　　b. **I didn't buy this ring in Paris; I did Ø in London*

Why is it that (42b) is acceptable, but not (43b)? Here we note that *in Paris* and *in London* are thematic in (42), but not in (43). Note also that these adverbs can appear in sentence-initial position in (42), but not in (43).

Recent work (Kuno, 1978a, 1978b, 1979) on the deletion of non-obligatory constituents has shown that the concept of new and old information has to be further sharpened. Observe the following discourses:

(44)　　a. SPEAKER A: *Did you stay in a hotel in Paris?*
　　　　b. SPEAKER B: *Yes, I stayed in a hotel Ø (because my friend was out of town)*

(45)　　a. SPEAKER A: *Did you buy this perfume in Paris?*
　　　　b. SPEAKER B: **Yes, I bought it Ø*

Why is it that *in Paris* can be deleted in the answer in (44), but not in (45) unless a very unusual reading is intended in which *buy* is used contrastively with, say, *steal*? In the ordinary interpretations of these questions, it is reasonable to assume that *stay in a hotel* is the focus of the question in (44), whereas *in Paris* is the focus of the question in (45). Let us represent this as follows:

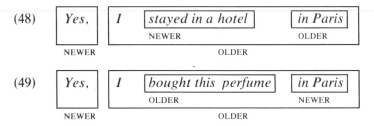

(46)   *Did you* | *stay in a hotel* | | *in Paris* | ?
                        NEWER   OLDER

(47)   *Did you* | *buy this perfume* | | *in Paris* | ?
                        OLDER   NEWER

In the answer, *Yes* represents the new information. The rest of the answer represents old, predictable information. Answering these questions simply with *yes* or *no* would make perfect sense, and there would be no problem in recovering what has been deleted. Despite this, deletion of *in Paris* is allowable in (44), and is not allowable in (45). This must be due to the fact that among the old information that is perfectly predictable from the preceding context, the distinction between old/new is still maintained.

(48) | *Yes,* | | *I* | | *stayed in a hotel* | | *in Paris* |
                                    NEWER   OLDER
        NEWER   OLDER

(49) | *Yes,* | | *I* | | *bought this perfume* | | *in Paris* |
                                    OLDER   NEWER
        NEWER   OLDER

The fact that *in Paris* is deletable in (48), but not in (49) suggests that there is a pecking order for deleting constituents in a sentence:

(50)   PECKING ORDER OF DELETION: Delete order (less important) information first, and newer (more important) information last.

This constraint applies to elements within the old part of a sentence and refers back to the distinction in newness of information that these elements used to have before they became contextually old information. Now, *in Paris* of (48) can be deleted because its deletion does not violate the Pecking Order of Deletion Principle: *stayed in a hotel*, which represents newer information than *in Paris*, has been left behind. On the other hand, *in Paris* of (49) cannot be deleted because it represents newer information than the two constituents that are left behind.[11]

[11] One might suspect that the generalization that is represented in the Pecking Order of Deletion Principle can be captured syntactically by resorting to the fact that *in Paris* in the intended interpretation of (48) is a higher-adverb outside the VP, whereas in (49) it is a lower adverb that is a part of the VP (see Note 10). However, such an analysis would not work for languages that allow deletion of, say, objects of verbs. In such languages, objects can

Note that the Pecking Order of Deletion Principle is perfectly justifiable from the point of view of communicative function of deletion—it says that we should not delete an element that represents important information unless we have deleted all those elements that represent less important information. This suggests that it is a principle that is shared across languages, and my preliminary investigation shows that it is indeed a widely held principle. Where there are apparent counterexamples, there are explanations for the violation of the principle. For example, in (44b), the subject *I* seems to represent information that is clearly older and less important than the deleted element *in Paris*. But, the retention of *I* has been forced by a constraint in English which requires that a tensed verb have a surface subject. In fact, in languages that do not have such a constraint, the retention of the subject would produce a marked answer— in Japanese, which lacks a surface subject constraint, (44b) would be unacceptable unless the subject is interpretable in a contrastive sense, implying that as far as the speaker was concerned, he stayed in a hotel, but others perhaps stayed with their friends. It goes without saying that the contrastive interpretation on the subject assumes that the subject conveys new information, and thus would make the answer one that does not involve violation of the Pecking Order of Deletion Principle.

It is important to note here that the deletion phenomenon that I have observed above is the kind of phenomenon which I believe is part and parcel of the syntax of language, but which pure syntacticians seldom recognize even the existence of. This is because pure syntacticians, since they work in the straight-jackets of a pure and rigid syntax model, tend to become blind to phenomena that do not fit into their framework. There is no reason why they should, but in actuality, they do more often than not. My own evaluation of what has happened in the past 10 years in syntax is that the focus of research interest of pure syntacticians has become narrower and narrower, the data that they deal with have become smaller and smaller, and the generalizations that they come up with, further and further removed from reality.

3. CONCLUSION

In the previous section, I have illustrated the kind of explanation that functional syntacticians come up with, using the area of functional sen-

---

be deleted in case they represent older information than the verbs, but not if otherwise. This is automatically predictable from the Pecking Order of Deletion Principle, but is not attributable to any difference in phrase structure configurations.

tence perspective. The need for many more concepts is already well recognized. For example, Prince (1978) has shown that in order to state the conditions for the use of *wh*-clefts and *it*-clefts, it is necessary to refer to concepts such as (*a*) information that the speaker assumes the hearer knows or can deduce, but is not presumably thinking about, and (*b*) information that the speaker takes to be a known fact, though definitely NOT known to the hearer.

In this paper, I have not had space to cover other areas of functional syntax in which some significant research results have already been obtained, areas such as (*a*) pragmatics, (*b*) factivity, presupposition, opacity and transparency, (*c*) direct discourse perspective, and (*d*) the speaker's point of view or empathy. A brief summary of research results in some of these areas is given in Kuno (1978c). Future research will certainly uncover other promising areas of functional syntax. What is important to point out here again is that pure syntacticians have nothing to gain by ignoring, or by being ignorant of, these functional factors that are known to effect acceptability judgments of sentences. The unacceptability of a given sentence can be due in many cases to the interaction of multitudes of factors—some syntactic and others nonsyntactic—and the more those who work in syntax know about various functional factors that might be responsible for the unacceptability of the sentence, the less likely they are to make mistaken syntactic generalizations of the kind illustrated at the beginning of this paper, and the less likely they are to build a theory upon these mistaken syntactic generalizations.

REFERENCES

Chomsky, N. (1973). Conditions on transformations. In S. R. Anderson and P. Kiparsky (Eds.), *A Festschrift for Morris Halle*. New York: Holt, Rinehart and Winston. Pp. 232–286.

Garvin, P. (1963). Czechoslovakia. In T. A. Sebeok, (Ed.), *Current Trends in Linguistics 1: Soviet and East European Linguistics*. The Hague: Mouton. Pp. 499–522.

Grosu, A. (1978). On unbounded extraction phenomena and the so-called specified subject condition. *CUNY Forum 4*. Flushing, New York: Queens College Press. Pp. 58–115.

Keenan, E. (1974). The functional principle: Generalizing the notion of 'subject of'. *Papers from the Tenth Regional Meeting of the Chicago Linguistic Society*. Chicago: Chicago Linguistic Society. Pp. 298–309.

Kuno, S. (1972). Functional sentence perspective: A case study from Japanese and English. *Linguistic Inquiry, 3*, 269–320.

Kuno, S. (1975a). Three perspectives in the functional approach to syntax. In R. E. Gossman, L. J. San, and T. J. Vance (Eds.), *Functionalism*. Chicago: Chicago Linguistic Society. Pp. 276–336. [Also published in L. Matejka (Ed.), *Sound and Meaning: Quinquagenary of the Prague Linguistic Circle*. Ann Arbor: University of Michigan Press, 1976. Pp. 119–190.]

Kuno, S. (1975b). Conditions for verb phrase deletion. *Foundations of Language, 13,* 161–175.

Kuno, S. (1976a). Subject, theme, and the speaker's empathy—A reexamination of relativization phenomena. In C. Li (Ed.), *Subject and Topic.* New York: Academic Press. Pp. 419–444.

Kuno, S. (1976b). Gapping: A functional analysis. *Linguistic Inquiry, 7,* 300–317.

Kuno, S. (1978a). Two topics on discourse principles. *Descriptive and Applied Linguistics: Bulletin of the ICU Summer Institute in Linguistics 11.* Tokyo: International Christian University. Pp. 1–29.

Kuno, S. (1978b). *Danwa no Bunpoo [Grammar of discourse].* Tokyo: Taishukan Publ. Co.

Kuno, S. (1978c). Generative discourse analysis in America. In W. U. Dressler (Ed.), *Current Trends in Textlinguistics.* Berlin: Walter de Gruyter. Pp. 275–294.

Kuno, S. (1979). On the interaction between syntactic rules and discourse principles. In G. Bedell, E. Kobayashi, and M. Muraki (Eds.), *Explorations in Linguistics: Papers in Honor of Kazuko Inoue.* Tokyo: Kenkyusha Publ. Co. Pp. 279–304.

Prince, E. (1978). A comparison of wh-clefts and it-clefts in discourse. *Langauge, 54(4),* 883–906.

Reinhart, T. (1976). "The syntactic domain of anaphora." Unpublished doctoral dissertation, Massachusetts Institute of Technology, Cambridge, Mass.

TRACE THEORY AND EXPLANATION

DAVID LIGHTFOOT
Rijksuniversiteit te Utrecht

1. GOALS[1]

Scientists are free to formulate the goals of their theories in various ways and there is little scope for dogmatism in this area. The appropriateness of one's goals can be gauged by the fruitfulness of the research program that they support and the consequences for other domains of inquiry; to this extent the appropriateness of goals is a matter for rational discussion. One formulates one's research goals in broad enough fashion to have interesting consequences for other domains of inquiry and narrowly enough to permit useful work, not rendered unattainable by excessively ambitious aims. Characteristically, biologists do not formulate their research in terms of something so broad as a theory of life, nor do physicists seek a theory of matter; such goals are too general, too ambitious to support viable research programs. Rather, they formulate basic questions in terms of a theory of genetically determined hereditability, a theory of electromagnetism, or of yet more limited concepts. So, although the formulation of goals is partly a matter of taste, the success of

[1] I am grateful for comments on an earlier version of this paper from Arnold Evers, Bob Freidin, Riny Huybregts, Henk van Riemsdijk, and Lydia White.

137

a research program and its consequences for other areas of inquiry will depend largely on the skill with which the goals are adumbrated.

Linguists have often engaged in debates about the correct form of a grammar of some language or even of a theory of grammar, without first agreeing on or even discussing the goals of linguistic research in general or of the theory of grammar in particular. The disregard for goals leads to a common predilection for elevating by fiat pretheoretical observations into statements about a theory, entailing a naive descriptivism and a lack of concern for explanation. Perhaps one reason for this pervasive descriptivism has been the tendency to think in terms of a "theory of LANGUAGE" and to assert that a theory of language must "deal with" metaphor, "pragmatics," the interrelationship of language and culture, how a language changes historically, etc. This seems to me to be not a useful concept, and is analogous to the overambitious biologist's "theory of life." Such a "theory of language" is equivalent to "linguistics," that is, a group of related areas of study, and, qua theory, too broad to sustain a coherent research program in the foreseeable future; it will be impossible to formulate interesting and falsifiable hypotheses until more is known about the individual components, subtheories of grammar, historical change, metaphor, etc. This is not to say that data from language acquisition, historical change, etc. is necessarily irrelevant to evaluating claims about the correctness of a theory of GRAMMAR, a point to which I shall return, but one would want a demonstration of how a theory of grammar can be interpreted as making nontrivial claims in these domains. In any case, a theory of language as such bears no relationship to the usual goals of generative grammar. One must judge a theory of generative grammar, like any other theory, either internally with relation to its own stated goals, or externally according to the fruitfulness and significance of the research program; the internal and external evaluations must always be distinct.

Goals may be formulated in various ways, but generative grammarians have customarily set up the most general aim of their work as the characterization of how it is that children can learn their native language in what seems to be a remarkably short time despite a triple deficiency of data:

1. The speech the child hears does not consist uniformly of complete grammatical sentences, but rather of sentences with pauses, slips of the tongue, incomplete thoughts, etc. If only 5% of the sentences the child hears are of this type, there will be a significant problem, because the sentences do not come labeled as ungrammatical (imagine the difficulty in deducing the legitimate rules of chess when exposed to some fabricated

games, even where one knew in advance that exactly 5% of the moves were illegal although not which particular moves these were).[2]

2. The available data are finite but the child comes to be able to deal with an infinite range of new sentences, going far beyond the sentences actually registered in infancy.

3. People attain knowledge of the structure of their language for which no evidence is available in the data to which the child is exposed; crucial evidence for such knowledge consists of judgments concerning complex sentences, paraphrase and ambiguity relations, and ungrammatical sentences, all of which lie outside the primary linguistic data available to the infant.

For the generativist, these are the salient facts of language acquisition, which are compounded by the apparent rapidity of the process and the narrow range of attested errors.

Given these facts, the generativist looks for a priori knowledge available to the organism which permits acquisition to circumvent these environmental deficiencies and thus to take place quickly and not solely by trial and error. If one postulates that much of the child's final ability is determined by genetically encoded principles, which are triggered by environmental stimulus rather than formed by it more or less directly, one has an account of how the child can master a language under the triple deficiency of stimulation. The further fact that children can master *any* human language to which they happen to be exposed in infancy despite significant surface differences, imposes strong limitations on the kinds of principles the scientist can attribute to the genotype. An answer to the problem of acquisition as defined cannot rest content with a mere enunciation of the rules of the specific language that a particular child attains. This would amount to a claim that the specific rules of, say, Dutch are innately specified, which permits no explanation of how, say, Nootka —with a significantly different structure—is acquired. Therefore the genetically encoded principles must be fairly abstract and not language specific. A theory of grammar represents the a priori knowledge making language acquisition possible under the boundary conditions noted (therefore part of the genotype) and delimits the form and functioning of avail-

---

[2] For some experimental evidence, see Braine (1971). He presented adults with simulated languages with and without "ungrammatical" sentences (7% "ungrammatical" sentences, where such sentences were included), and found that they learned the language successfully in both cases, in other words, could detect "funny" sentences without negative evidence. Such results undermine the significance of work purporting to show that children base their language learning on only "motherese," a highly structured set of short, simple, grammatical sentences (Snow, 1972). See the Introduction to Hornstein and Lightfoot (in press) for further discussion.

able descriptions of the linguistic knowledge that is eventually attained, part of the phenotype conventionally called a grammar. I assume therefore that a theory of grammar should be as restrictive as possible.

This is not a necessary approach and there are alternatives. For example, a theory might have sufficient latitude to allow a wider range of grammars than actually occur, but at the same time specify a rich evaluation metric to narrow that range and make the relevant choices. Within this program, the burden of work will lie in the development of an evaluation metric. One cannot show that this is impossible in principle, but, as a matter of historical fact, very little work has been done in this area by proponents of theories permitting a wide range of grammars; there seem to be scant grounds for optimism. Since the mid-fifties fairly straightforward theories have had considerable effect in ranging grammars in complexity, which suggested that the next development should be to restrict the available devices, holding the evaluation metrics more or less constant. Such evaluation metrics are usually based on notions of "simplicity," and simplicity criteria may be able to distinguish the "simplest" of three or four grammars, but it is difficult to imagine them choosing between billions. Again as a matter of historical fact, such simplicity criteria have played a significant role only in resolving more general questions, for example, the choice between a phrase structure and transformational grammar (Chomsky, 1955); on finer questions, as have arisen in the subsequent development of transformational grammar, competing theories usually turn out to be empirically nonequivalent in such a way that it is unnecessary to appeal to an explicit and carefully defined simplicity metric, even if a general notion of simplicity is tacitly assumed. Another approach might seek to develop a set of perceptual mechanisms to restrict possible grammars. Again, one would permit a loose theory of grammar, allowing more grammars than are attested, but here one would claim that the class of actually available grammars is further restricted by general perceptual strategies affecting cognitive domains other than language. No doubt there are further alternatives, but here I pursue an enrichment of the theory of grammar in order to restrict the class of available grammars.

So, a child learning a language constructs a system that will correlate meaning with sound over an infinite domain of sentences. An analyst's grammar is an account of the native speaker's fully developed linguistic capacity, under the usual idealizations. The theory of grammar imposes restrictions on the form a grammar may take and explicit conditions on the way in which grammatical rules may function. Research will be designed to discover the most restrictive principles on the form and function of available grammars. These restrictive principles, when formulated, can be hypothesized to be part of the innate equipment brought by children to the task of acquiring their native language, and making language acquisition possible in a short time, with a narrow range of the logically possible errors, and with only impoverished data. We can view the theory of grammar as

> a common human attribute, genetically determined, one component of the human mind. Through interaction with the environment, this faculty of mind becomes articulated and refined, emerging in the mature person as a system of knowledge of language. To discover the character of this mental faculty, we will try to isolate those properties of attained linguistic competence that hold by necessity rather than as a result of accidental experience, where by "necessity" I of course mean biological rather than logical necessity. We will therefore be particularly interested in properties of attained linguistic competence that are vastly underdetermined by available experience in general, but that nevertheless hold of the linguistic competence attained by any normal speaker of a given language, and in fact by all speakers of all languages (perhaps vacuously in some cases) on the natural assumption of uniformity across the species. The commitment to formulate a restrictive theory of Universal Grammar is nothing other than a commitment to discover the biological endowment that makes language acquisition possible and to determine its particular manifestations. Returning to the matter of "explanatory adequacy", we can explain some property of attained linguistic competence by showing that this necessarily results from the interplay of the genetically-determined language faculty, specified by UG, and the person's (accidental) experience [Chomsky, 1976, p.304].

Such a definition of the theory of grammar assumes that a theory of mind is a wider ranging object encompassing a theory of grammar as one component which intersects with theories of other cognitive domains. Other components will include a theory of perceptual strategies and an account of knowledge of the real world. One may think of this as three intersecting domains.

(1)

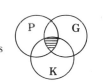

perceptual mechanisms   grammar

real world knowledge

The circles specify well formed objects in each domain. The shaded area encompasses objects that are well-formed from all three viewpoints. These will be sentences, that is, grammatical objects, that accord with perceptual mechanisms and reflect a sensible view of the world. However, some objects are well formed only from two viewpoints. For example, let us assume that a perceptual characterization of short-term memory specifies multiple center-embedding as difficult to interpret, and that center-embedding is usually avoided in domains like natural language, music and arithmetic. Thus some objects may be well formed with respect to grammatical rules and may reflect a coherent world view, but violate restrictions on center-embedding, thereby being perceptually ill formed.

(2)   [[*That* [*that* [*that the moon is bright*] *is obvious*] *disturbs me*] *surprised Harry*]

Other objects may be grammatically and perceptually well formed but convey only nonsense, such as the famous *Colorless green ideas sleep furiously*. One could also have multiply center-embedded nonsense that was grammatically well formed, although perceptually and cognitively deviant. Similarly there are perceptual mechanisms dealing with, say, properties of vision and color differentiation that do not interact at all with the domain of grammar and may or may not have anything to do with one's knowledge of the world. As with distinctions between syntax and semantics, phonology and morphology, etc., analysts have no a priori, principled basis for deciding where a given phenomenon should be located in (1). Whether (2) violates a principle of grammar or a perceptual constraint can be decided only in the light of the success of the theory as a whole; there are no valid discovery procedures here, and what one analyst treats under a grammatical rubric, another might treat perceptually, the choice being made as a function of the OVERALL success of the competing theories.[3]

Given the goal of characterizing the initial state of the mental organ such that it can come to attain mastery of any human language, and given the approach above of seeking the most restrictive possible template on available grammatical hypotheses, the principles postulated can be evaluated according to three criteria:

1. Coverage of empirical data, whereby a class of facts follows from the principles hypothesized
2. Standards of simplicity and elegance, as are normal in scientific theorizing
3. The extent to which the principle sheds light on the essential problem of acquisition

Criterion (3) is of fundamental importance in shaping explanatory prin-

---

[3] Such choices have little importance at this stage of research. As noted in Section 4, one works at the level of abstraction that one can get a handle on, always bearing in mind that the generalizations that one arrives at may hold at a higher level of abstraction, that is, over more domains. As a heuristic, one will assign to the theory of grammar principles that seem to hold only of linguistic objects; linguists might invoke a nongrammatical, perceptual mechanism if their generalization has an apparent analogue in, say, properties of vision.

ciples, due to the way in which our goal has been formulated. One might postulate a simple, elegant principle entailing a significant range of facts, which makes no psychological sense in terms of language acquisition. Lightfoot (in press) discusses typological "explanations" and shows that by being teleological they require postulating that infants have racial memories, knowledge that the language being acquired used to have certain properties no longer present, and even prophetic knowledge that the language will develop certain properties in the future. The implausibility of this psychological assumption means that this is a generalization of no explanatory force, even though it may meet the requirements of (1) and (2).

Criterion (1) is often misconstrued due to a common belief that one can know which facts a theory is responsible to independently of any particular theory. Suppose, for example, that children acquire the use of simple, one-clause structures before compound sentences; there is no reason to assume that this fact must follow from some particular principle of the theory of grammar, as opposed, say, to some property of perceptual maturation or the developing short-term memory capacity. Facts do not come labeled as inherently grammatical or perceptual. One will prefer whichever analysis is compatible with the overall most highly valued theory. Therefore a theory cannot be refuted by showing that some particular fact fails to follow from some particular principle. A principle is responsible only for the RELEVANT facts; since facts do not come labeled, one cannot know which facts are relevant until one has a theory. The relevance of some fact, that is, for treating it as a function of some particular principle, lies in the overall global success of the theory. Thus one justifies a theory in terms of the relevant facts for which it accounts, and one determines the relevance of the facts by the success of the theory that entails them. This kind of circularity is inescapable but is not vicious; the theories remain refutable and subject to rational debate. What is important is the deductive structure of the theory or, to adopt a metaphor, the size of the circles; thus a theory wherein there is a one-to-one relation of facts and abstract principles achieves no depth of explanation and is of no interest.

Under this view, there is no absolute notion of explanatory adequacy. It is not the case that theories either have or do not have explanatory adequacy; rather, they have more or less of it and they can be evaluated for the depth of explanation achieved under the Criteria (1)–(3) above. Given the primacy of Criterion (3), one will prefer a theory illuminating the acquisition process and therefore attaining a greater depth of explanation; one will not prefer a theory simply because it has greater coverage of data.[4] Two theories equivalent under Criterion (3) may be evaluated under (1) and (2), but (3) has primary weight. A single unexplained fact does not constitute a refutation or a reason to abandon a theory. To be a real counterexample, the recalcitrant fact must be shown to be relevant and to follow from another theory equally or more highly valued along Criterion (3). Thus refutation is not a trivial matter to be effected simply by citing some unanalyzed phenomenon (cf. Pullum, 1975) or by elevating a pretheoretical observation by fiat to the status of a claim about a theory, but discussion must be somewhat abstract and theory–bound; this is a recent development for linguistics, although well established in more mature sciences. This does not make refutation impossible. In practice theories are refuted or revised constantly. This is done by offering theories more highly rated along any one of the three weighted criteria. Thus preferred theories may come along any one of the three criteria, showing perhaps greater coverage of data or greater elegance. Chomsky (1957) argued against a theory of finite state grammars on the grounds that they could not attain even minimal success along Criterion (1); quite a different argument was used against a theory of phrase structure grammars when it was shown to be inferior to a transformational grammar theory along Criterion (2). One can also compare grammars of equal coverage and elegance but where one is shown to be compatible with a theory of greater value under (3); for an example, see Lasnik (in press).

This brings us at last to the so-called trace theory of movement rules. Trace theory represents a minor notational revision to the extended standard theory with far-reaching consequences for particular grammars. This

---

[4] Therefore I do not accept a naive falsificationism or, for that matter, a Popperian methodology. To cite a counterexample is to show that a theory is nonoptimal under Criterion (1). That theory, however, may yield greater insight into the nature of acquisition, that is, be more highly valued by Criterion (3), and therefore be of greater empirical force elsewhere and preferable overall [see the Introduction to Hornstein and Lightfoot (in press), which discusses the force of (1)–(3) as criteria for explanatoriness and develops some of these points more fully].

In general, for even the mature sciences, the Popperian view understates the role of idealization and the dismissal of conflicting evidence. If one claimed to refute the law of falling bodies by catching a ball before it hit the ground, the physicist would dismiss this "refutation" on the grounds that he is predicting only for "mechanical systems" and that "human intervention" is not part of such a system (Chomsky, 1975). But why not? He has no real answer, except that he cannot account for human will. Physics works where it works and has no principled basis to exclude counterexamples. Of course much less trivial pseudorefutations have occurred throughout the history of physics. One sticks to a theory if it gives deeper explanation within the range in which it is not falsified by clear and impressive data. Applying Popperian demarcation criteria would wipe out not only linguistics but also the most mature sciences, which is why they are usually ignored by working scientists (see Lightfoot, 1979, Section 1.5 for further discussion).

notational change leads to a theory that is more highly valued along all three criteria and therefore achieves a much greater depth of explanation in relation to the stated goal of the enterprise: to account for how children can attain mastery of a language under the conditions noted at the outset. An internal evaluation of trace theory must be based on the depth of explanation it offers or fails to offer for the central empirical problem, where depth of explanation is defined by Criteria (1)–(3).

2. TRACES

Consider the expressive power of grammars in the literature, insofar as it affects only the structural descriptions of transformations (i.e., disregarding the changes effected by transformations, their obligatory/optional valence, their ordering relations). The terms of a transformational rule may be any combination of variables and constants, where "constants" are single categories or terminal symbols. The rules may include disjunctions, Boolean functions with fixed terms (i.e., dominance relations), quantificational statements (e.g., "directly dominates," clause-mate notions). They may even have access to other stages in the derivation ("derivational constraints"), or to some aspects of the structural description of other sentences ("transderivational constraints"), and, if one lets the imagination roam, to pragmatic information, specifications of illocutionary force, and so on. All of these properties appear in particular grammars, and, if one adopts the orientation of Section 1, are therefore inferred by the language learner. Given our orientation, we shall seek to limit the expressive power of rules as narrowly as possible, eliminating their capacity, for example, to refer to disjunctions and Boolean functions. These will limit the FORM of grammars. One may also limit the way in which rules may FUNCTION, although there is no a priori distinction between what should be handled as a restriction on form and what as a restriction on function, as we shall see later.

A significant step toward tighter restrictions on the form and functioning of grammars was taken with Chomsky's (1973) "Conditions on Transformations," which was the context in which traces were first invoked. Chomsky proposed several restrictions on the functioning of transformational and interpretive rules (which entailed further restrictions on their possible form). In this way he enriched the theory of grammar and thus hypothesized a more elaborate genotype, attributing more structure to the initial state of the mental organ. The expressive power of particular grammars was correspondingly reduced, and thus the burden on the language learner. Given the constraints put forward, the language learner has available a much narrower range of possible grammars, a narrower "space" to search for the correct grammar. Therefore these proposals contributed directly to the explanatory power of the theory, as defined above. In linguistic research there is a constant tension between descriptive and explanatory concerns; any given proposal may be motivated by descriptive concerns, extending the power of grammars beyond what might otherwise be necessary, or by explanatory concerns, narrowing their power while still permitting the formulation of descriptively adequate grammars. The history of generative research can be seen as an interplay of these two forces, but Chomsky (1973) was a contribution to explanatory adequacy.

Chomsky (1973) proposed that in a configuration . . . X . . . $[Z$ . . . Y . . .$]_\alpha$ . . . X . . ., no rule may involve X and Y, where (a) α is a finite clause (the "Tensed S" or "Propositional Island Constraint," henceforth PIC), or (b) Z is the specified subject of α, where a subject is "specified" if it is not controlled by X (the "Specified Subject Constraint," henceforth SSC). These are conditions on the functioning of rules, but they also open up the possibility of simplifying the form of rules. Given these constraints, a very general rule of NP Preposing (3) will move *John* in (4a), but not in (4b) or (4c). In (4b) the rule is blocked by PIC and in (4c) by SSC, and correct predictions emerge without building elaborate conditions into the structural description of the rule, as might be done in other approaches. In (3) lowercase indicates an empty position and uppercase a lexical NP, but this is for exposition only and the rule can be simplified further, as we shall see.

(3)   np X NP$\Rightarrow$3   2

(4) a. *John was expected [⎽⎽⎽ to win]*$_S$

     b. **John was expected [(that) ⎽⎽⎽ would win]*$_S$

     c. **John was expected [Mary to see ⎽⎽⎽]*$_S$

Consider now the semantic rules of Bound Anaphora Interpretation (BAI) and Disjoint Reference (DR). BAI associates reflexives, reciprocal expressions, bound anaphors like *his* in (5c) and the abstract, identity marker *e* in (5d) with a c-commanding NP, marking them [+ anaphoric].[5]

---

[5] To some extent I shall recast earlier discussion in the light of later results. For example, here I do not use the "precede and command" notion of Fiengo (1974) but "c-command" of Reinhart (1976), whereby *a* c-commands *b* if *a* does not contain *b* and *b* is dominated by the first branching category dominating *a*. Also, I use *e* for a nonlexical NP, not *t* and PRO, as discussed below.

Thus the rule associates the two bold italic elements in the structures of (5). Notice that the structures of (6) are also possible surface structures, since *himself, each other, his way, e,* etc. may be generated under any NP in the initial phrase marker. However, they do not meet the structural description of BAI, not being c-commanded by any NP; therefore the bold italic elements will not be interpreted and the derivation will be classed as defective. This illustrates the filtering effect of interpretive rules, eliminating certain surface structures which emerge from the syntactic component (which now "overgenerates" by virtue of its reduced expressive power) but cannot be interpreted.

(5) a. *John washed **himself***
  b. ***The men** wash **each other***
  c. *John lost **his** way*
  d. *John tried **e** to become popular*

(6) a. ***Himself** washed John*
  b. ***Each other** washed the men*
  c. ***His** way was lost by John*
  d. ***e** tried John to become popular*

DR specifies that no two NPs may be interpreted as intersecting in reference, and if they corefer by their very nature (e.g., if they are both first person pronouns), the sentence is classed as ungrammatical. Thus (7) specifies correctly that *they* and *them* in (8a) do not intersect in reference and that (8b) is ungrammatical. In (9a) the two *theys* may corefer and (9b) is grammatical; in (9a) the rule would be blocked by PIC and in (9b) by SSC, which illustrates the generality of those conditions

(7) DISJOINT REFERENCE: *In a configuration* NP_i *X* NP_j, NP_j *is non-anaphoric to* NP_i.

(8) a. *They washed them*
  b. **I washed me*

(9) a. *They voted that they should strike*
  b. *I expected Sam to visit me*

The effects of SSC that we have seen so far [(4c) and (9b)], are each triggered by a lexical subject. Further examples are (10) and (11). Example (11) illustrates the effects in a NP, if one treats *Mary's* as the "subject" of *pictures*. In (11c), presence of *Mary's* allows *they* and *them* to intersect in reference; whereas absence of *Mary's* prohibits such intersection, in accordance with (7).

(10) a. **He wanted [Mary to wash himself]*_S
  b. **They wanted [Mary to wash each other]*_S

(11)   a.   *He bought* [(**Mary's*) *pictures of himself*]$_{NP}$
       b.   *They bought* [(**Mary's*) *pictures of each other*]$_{NP}$
       c.   *They bought* [(*Mary's*) *pictures of them*]$_{NP}$

But an abstract subject has the same effect when controlled by some element other than *X*, the element directly involved in the rule. So in (12) *John* controls *e* and is not involved in the operation of the rules; compare (13), where *e* is controlled by the subject of *promise* and does not trigger SSC.

(12)   a.   **She persuaded John* [*e to wash herself*]
       b.   **They persuaded John* [*e to wash each other*]
       c.   *They persuaded John* [*e to wash them*]   *they = them*

(13)   a.   *She promised John* [*e to wash herself*]
       b.   *They promised John* [*e to wash each other*]
       c.   *They promised John* [*e to wash them*]   *they ≠ them*

Consider now the initial structure (14a). If after application of NP Preposing, the derived structure is (14b), there is no reason not to associate *each other* with *the men*. Extrinsic ordering of *Each*-Interpretation before NP Preposing would entail that SSC would block the interpretive rule, *Susan* being the specified subject. But (*a*) we hope to eliminate extrinsic ordering from expressive power of grammars; (*b*) Each-Interpretation, being an interpetive rule, must apply at surface structure, that is, after application of NP Preposing and the removal of the specified subject (this order is dictated by the organization of grammar and is therefore intrinsic and not "learned"), and (*c*) even if *Each*-Interpretation were reformulated as a syntactic rule, if it were ordered before NP Preposing there would be an ordering paradox (Chomsky, 1973; Lightfoot, 1976a). Therefore we have no account for why in (14b) *each other* cannot be anaphoric to *the men*.[6]

(14)   a.   np *seems to the men* [*Susan to like each other*]
       b.   *Susan seems to the men* [*to like each other*]
       c.   *Susan$_i$ seems to the men* [*e$_i$ to like each other*]

---

[6] The acceptability of *Susan seems to each of the men to like the other(s)* suggests that a semantic or pragmatic account is implausible. The rule relating *each* to *the other(s)* operates across sentence boundaries and is a rule of discourse grammar, not sentence grammar, unlike the rule of *Each*-Interpretation discussed above.

(i)   *Each of them left. The others stayed for coffee*
(ii)   **They left. Each other stayed for coffee*

See Williams (1977) for a distinction between rules of sentence grammar and rules of discourse grammar.

Suppose now that movement rules leave behind a "trace," an abstract, bound anaphoric expression, co-indexed with the moved NP, such that the result of applying NP Preposing to (14a) is (14c). Now *Each*-Interpretation would be blocked by the existing version of SSC and one has an explanation of the facts. This supposition is the emendation known as the "trace theory of movement rules."

This constitutes a minor notational change at the level of the theory of grammar, which in itself neither extends nor reduces the expressive power of grammars; it simply changes grammars such that the structual description of NP Preposing (3) becomes (15), where e is a bound anaphoric expression, which therefore must be interpretable by BAI. This is all prescribed by the theory and therefore does not have to be figured out by the child. The rule of BAI will be (16) and will be subject to all the usual conditions on rules, PIC, SSC, etc; bound anaphoric expressions are e, reflexives, reciprocals, and the possessive pronoun of idioms like *crane x's neck, lose x's way, blow x's cool.*

(15) np X NP $\Rightarrow 3_i$ 2 e_i

(16) A bound anaphoric expression is marked [+anaphoric] to a NP c-commanding it.

The consequences of this notational move are far-reaching and the explanatory power of the theory is enhanced considerably. Three quite independent illustrations of this were invoked in the earliest literature on trace theory (Chomsky, 1975; Fiengo, 1974).

1. It permits a simplification of particular grammars. For example, under trace theory and the independently needed SSC, one can account for the noninterpretability of *Susan seemed to the men to like each other,* without having to invoke extrinsic ordering of rules or deep structure interpretation (I return to this). Moreover, one can contrast this with the acceptable *The men seemed to Susan to like each other,* which would derive from an initial (17a) and have a surface representation (17b), where EITHER *Each*-Interpretation would not be blocked by SSC from associating *each* with *the men* because the intervening e subject is controlled by *the men,* involved in the rule as X, and therefore not counting as a specified subject, OR *Each*-Interpretation may associate *each* with e_i and BAI then associates e_i with *the men,* and therefore *each* is associated with *the men* by transitivity [see (Chomsky, 1980), (Lightfoot, 1977) for a proposal along the latter line, which requires a reinterpretation in certain areas of grammar, including PIC and SSC].

(17)   a.   np *seems to Susan [the men to like each other]*
       b.   *The men$_i$ seemed to Susan [e$_i$ to like each other]*

Examples of such simplification of grammars can be duplicated easily, given only the rules we have described so far in this paper. So, in (18) DR is blocked by SSC interacting with trace theory, so *they–them* may be anaphoric; *e$_i$* is the trace left by *wh*-Movement, but these surface structures omit details of COMP, to which I shall return.

(18)   a.   *Who$_i$ do they want [e$_i$ to wash them]*
       b.   *Who$_i$ do I want [e$_i$ to wash me]*

Similarly for reflexives and reciprocals, it now falls out that in *Who do they want to wash themselves/each other, themselves* and *each other* cannot be anaphoric to *they* because SSC would block BAI from applying in such a fashion. Rather, BAI will associate these elements only with *e$_i$*, which is in turn associated with *who*.

(19)   a.   *Who$_i$ do they want [e$_i$ to wash themselves]*
       b.   *Who$_i$ do they want [e$_i$ to wash each other]*

At all stages there is a specified subject between, say, *they* and *themselves* in (19a); therefore there is no need to require that DR precede *wh*-Movement. A similar logic applies for (18), (19b), etc. Equivalent simplifications have been shown to follow for other areas of grammar, for example, the celebrated contractability of *want to* (Lightfoot, 1976b), quantifier movement in French (Quicoli, 1976), the elimination of extrinsic rule ordering (Jenkins, 1977), and of the optional–obligatory distinction between rules (Fiengo, 1974).

   2.   Trace theory permits a characterization of where a downgrading rule is possible. An asymmetry has often been noted between rules which move elements upwards and to the left, and those which move elements to the right and/or downward. The former are very common, the latter exceedingly rare. Given the trace theory of movement rules, this is to be expected because a downward movement rule will leave a trace which is not c-commanded and therefore not interpretable by BAI. Such rules, however, do occur, notably Extraposition and *There*-Insertion. These rules involve rightward movement, yielding structures like (20), but for each case English has a designated morpheme which occurs in the vacated slot and "covers" the trace.

(20)   a.   *e$_i$ surprised me [that Susan left]$_i$* → **it** *surprised me that Susan left*
       b.   *e$_i$ was [a student]$_i$ arrested* → **there** *was a student arrested*

Therefore, there is nothing to be stipulated and downward movement rules will occur only where the grammar also has a device, a designated morpheme, for covering the uninterpretable trace.[7] This is a strong prediction and a drastic limitation on available grammars; it also suggests an area of research. The literature contains rightward movement rules that do not conform to this pattern and these will turn out either to be based on inferior analyses or to suggest revisions to trace theory. For excellent discussion of this, see Dresher and Hornstein (1979), who invoke the principle that a trace may be covered only by a designated element and propose a reanalysis of Siegel's (1974) rule of Genitive Movement, involving a simpler grammar of English and consistent with a much more restrictive theory.

3. Under the trace theory all semantic interpretation can apparently be done at the level of surface structure. Chomsky (1972) had suggested that semantic interpretation rules have access to initial and surface structures, and Jackendoff (1972) argued that some interpretive rules should apply cyclically, that is, on intermediate structures. Under those views, each interpretation rule will contain some indication of what level it applies at, whether it is a deep, intermediate, or surface structure interpretation rule. Several commentators showed that Jackendoff's arguments for rules applying at intermediate structure were faulty and that these rules should apply at surface structure. His deep structure interpretation rules all dealt with thematic relations, but under trace theory all thematic relations can be determined at surface structure. This results from the fact that thematic relations are defined by the initial structure position of the NP, which is recoverable at surface structure. Following the proposals of Dresher and Hornstein (1979), the deep structure position of a transformationally moved NP will be marked either by the deepest co-indexed

---

[7] Notice that under this view traces will be "covered" *only* by designated morphemes. Following Bresnan (1972) and Hornstein (1977), I assume that there is no rightward movement rule for passives and that agent phrases are base-generated in place. Thus there is no need to invoke a rule $t \rightarrow \emptyset$ for phrases like [*portraits by Rembrandt*] (cf. Fiengo, 1974). Such a rule specifies traces and therefore comes close to rendering the theory vacuous. I also assume that there is no rule of *Each*-Movement (cf. Chomsky, 1973), rather a rule of *Each*-Interpretation; but in any case I know no reason to assume that movement of non-referring categories like quantifier should leave a trace or index.

An a priori preferable analysis would preclude trace covering under any circumstances. Given the proposal of Koster (1978a), Extraposition may be dispensable as a movement rule, allowing the *it* of (20a) to be base-generated; structures such as it_i *has been proven* e_i *that Sam left* suggest that this may be the right approach. Thus covering would play a minimal role, and could perhaps be eliminated altogether. This would eliminate downgrading rules entirely.

trace [e.g., (19)] or by a designated element like *there* or *it* [e.g., (20)].[8]
Under this approach all interpretive rules will apply at surface structure
(enriched with traces) and the language learner will not have to determine
subclasses of interpretive rules. Again, the expressive power of grammars
is reduced significantly.

The fact that traces permit a more homogeneous approach to semantic
interpretation, reducing the burden on the language learner, not only is
consistent with a more restrictive and therefore more desirable theory of
grammar, but at another level it also permits a better description of
"crossover" phenomena involving *wh* constructions in English. Postal
(1971) noted the contrasts of (21)–(23), where * indicates that the bold
italic elements cannot, in Postal's terminology, corefer.

(21) a. ***Who** said Mary kissed **him**?*
      b. **Who** did **he** say Mary kissed?*

(22) a. ***The man who** said Mary kissed **him** was lying*
      b. **The man who he** said Mary kissed was lying*

(23) a. ***Who** fed **his** dog?*
      b. **Who** was **his** dog fed by?*

The correct generalization is that a starred sentence will not arise if the
wh element is fronted from a position to the left of the pronoun. The early
literature offered accounts in terms of either a constraint prohibiting the
crossover of coreferential elements or by ordering a pronominal anaphora
rule before *wh*-Movement. The crossover prohibition is undesirable in
that it forces syntactic rules to be sensitive to semantic information and
entails the curious notion of *wh* words as referring expressions. In an
elegant appendix, Wasow (1972) points out serious difficulties for both
accounts, the latter involving several ordering paradoxes. He offers an
analysis in terms of traces, in which *wh*-Movement leaves a trace and,
for the purposes of anaphora relations, traces behave like names. Thus
the surface structure of (21) will be (21′), analogous to (24).

(21′) a. *Who$_i$ e$_i$ said Mary kissed him*
       b. *Who$_i$ did he say Mary kissed e$_i$*

(24) a. *Bill said Mary kissed him*
      b. *He said Mary kissed Bill*

In (21′a) *him* is preceded and commanded by e_i and therefore may be

---

[8] Therefore we do not need to invoke the claim (attributed to John Goldsmith) that precisely where traces are not recoverable at surface structure there will be an independent
means of recovering thematic relations. Under this view, traces are *always* recoverable.

anaphoric to e_i, which is in turn co-indexed to *who;* therefore *who* and *him* may receive the same index, like *Bill* and *him* in (24a). In (21'b) *he* c-commands e_i and therefore may not be anaphoric to e_i, just as it may not be anaphoric to *Bill* in (24b); since e_i and *who* are co-indexed, *he* and *who* cannot receive the same index. Sentences that yield ordering paradoxes for the earlier accounts have surface structures like (25) and fall into place without difficulty.

(25) a.   [*Which of the women **Bill** had been dating*]$_{NP_i}$ *did **he** marry* e_i
  b.   **He finally married* [*one of the women **Bill** had been dating*]$_{NP}$

In (25a) *he* is preceded by *Bill* and therefore may be anaphoric; e_i is co-indexed with the large NP, and not with *Bill*. In (25b) *he* c-commands *Bill* at all stages of the derivation and therefore may not be anaphoric (see Wasow, 1972 for details of the ordering paradox for the earlier accounts).

This analysis suggests an extremely simple, almost trivial rule of *wh*-Interpretation, whereby the *wh* element is treated as a quantifier operating on a logical variable which is identifiable by the trace. Such a rule would map a surface structure (21'b), where *who* and *e* are co-indexed, into a logical representation (26).

(26)   *(for which person x) (he said Mary kissed x)*

There will be a one-to-one relation between logical variables and the deepest trace co-indexed with the *wh* word, except where it is necessary to unpack the effects of pied-piping. The logical form corresponding to the surface structure (27) will be (28).

(27)   *Whose book$_i$ did you publish e_i*

(28)   *(for which person x) (you published x's book)*

Given such a rule of *wh*-Interpretation, one can say that anaphora relations are determined in a partially developed logical form and that logical variables, not traces, behave like names; we thus gain some empirical insight into the properties of logical representation.

There is a further reason to suppose that rules of anaphora apply to a partially developed logical form and not to surface structures. Consider quantificational statements like (29) and (30).

(29)   *Every soldier has his orders*

(30) a.   *Every soldier is armed, but will he shoot?*
  b.   *Every soldier is armed. I don't think he will shoot*
  c.   *If every soldier is armed, then he'll shoot*

The pronoun is bound in (29), but in (30) refers to somebody whose identity is established elsewhere.[9] This follows from the fact that quantification is clause-bound, such that the rule of Quantifier Interpretation yields the output (29') and (30').

(29')   [$\forall x$, x is a soldier, x has his orders]

(30') a. [$\forall x$, x is a soldier, x is armed] *but will he shoot*
     b. [$\forall x$, x is a soldier, x is armed]. *I don't think he'll shoot*
     c. if [$\forall x$, x is a soldier, x is armed], *then he'll shoot*

Rules of anaphora do not permit a pronoun outside the scope of a quantifier to be assigned an anaphoric relation to a bound variable within this scope. Therefore in (29') the pronoun may be anaphoric to the logical variable, but not in (30').

Since this is a conference on the comparison of syntactic theories, one might note parenthetically that this is a fundamental problem for Montague Grammar. Montague Grammar holds that not only quantified NPs but also NPs consisting of proper names denote sets of properties; it treats the two kinds of NPs as the same semantic type and allows all NPs to be quantified-in over a sentence or VP (see Chomsky, 1976; Cooper, 1977 for discussion). On the contrary, our rule of *wh*-Interpretation seems to reflect the correct approach to anaphora and depends on treating *wh* as a quantifier binding a logical variable; traces permit a straightforward analysis in those terms, whereby the relevant information can be obtained at surface structure with a fairly trivial rule. This in turn illustrates the pleasant consequences of having all interpretive rules apply after all syntactic rules.

In this section I have looked at some of the early motivation for trace theory, sometimes recasting it in the light of later developments in the theory. What emerges is a remarkable convergence of properties, whereby trace theory, itself a minor notational change, permits a greater depth of explanation in three quite independent areas, any one of which would suffice to motivate the proposal: It allows a simplification of particular grammars by extending the range of SSC; it provides a typology of downgrading rules; it permits a homogeneous and otherwise superior approach to the semantic interpretation of syntactic structures. So in three different ways the burden on the language learner is significantly reduced and one has a major step towards a deeper explanation of how acquisition can take place, which is the central problem of this approach.

[9] Some speakers do not share these judgments. Also Henk van Riemsdijk points out a problem for the account given here insofar as the sentences of (30) seem to become acceptable if the second clause is . . . *his officers/the general will tell him when to shoot*. The relevant distinctions are unclear to me and the facts shimmer somewhat.

Trace theory, like any other proposal, is to be evaluated by its explanatory power, which in turn will be a function of one's central empirical problem and the goal of one's theory. This is a fundamental methodological point but it is often not observed; workers formulate and criticize proposals independently of explanatory concerns. This kind of discussion has taken place in the context of trace theory. My own work on the contractability of *want to* (Lightfoot 1976b) has provoked replies by Andrews (1978) and Postal and Pullum (1978), which are worth looking at briefly from this point of view. I argued that in (31a) the indexed trace left by *wh*-Movement would block contraction to *wanna,* whereas the unindexed *e* in (31b) would be invisible to the adjunction rule (32), whose structural description would therefore be met.

(31) a. *Who$_i$ do you want e$_i$ to succeed*

 b. *Who$_i$ do you want e to succeed e$_i$*

(32)   V *to* V $\Rightarrow$ 1 + 2   3

Here I recast the discussion in terms of indexed empty nodes rather than "*t*" and "PRO"; under the earlier version syntactic rules can "see" a *t* but not a PRO, whereas under this version they see lexical NPs, of which an indexed NP is a special instance. The unindexed *e* in (31b) is interpreted as anaphoric to *you* and coindexed with *you* by BAI, which applies after all syntactic rules. Therefore, while the logical form of (31b) is *(for which person i) (you$_j$ want j to succeed i),* the *j* index is not available for syntactic rules. I claimed that this account, depending on traces (or indices), was superior to earlier analyses, avoiding reference to extrinsic rule ordering and eliminating an ordering paradox, and that it shed some light on the proper interpretation of traces, particularly traces left in COMP.

Postal and Pullum are concerned, among other things, that trace theory "add[s] coding devices to preserve information about earlier derivation at stages by the use of phonetically unrealized markers [p.20]." They fail to distinguish between enriching a particular grammar, always a priori an undesirable move and to be motivated by descriptive concerns, and enriching the theory of grammar, always a virtuous move if it entails impoverishing particular grammars; this follows from the way in which explanation is conceived in this approach. The fact that movement rules coindex the position from which a NP is moved is given by universal theoretical convention and therefore does not represent information that has to be inferred by the language learner. In their article, Postal and Pullum echo the confused discussion of globality found in Bach (1977, p.135ff). Traces are "global" in the sense that they preserve deep structure information at the level of surface structure. But this kind of globality is inherent to transformational grammar, wherein relevant deep structure information is carried through to surface structure. So if *the book* is labeled as a NP in deep structure, that information also appears in surface structure; one needs to ensure that the right amount of deep structure information is carried through to surface structure. This is quite different from the global rules of Lakoff (1970), who hypothesized that a particular grammar may contain a rule whose structural description refers to two stages of a derivation, which are therefore specified in the rule and constitute part of what the child has to learn about his language. For the distribution of *wanna*, it is claimed that under trace theory all that children have to learn about English is that there is a rule (33); (33) does not apply to (31a) because at all stages of the derivation something intervenes between *want* and *to*, but it can apply to (31b) because nothing intervenes to which syntactic and phonological rules are sensitive. Children have to learn nothing beyond (33), specifically nothing about where this rule is ordered or about particular conditions on the rule, and certainly nothing about "earlier stages" of derivations. The rest is given by general convention; nothing else has to be stipulated at the level of particular grammar. This seems to be the best conceivable account of the data, because it is hard to imagine a description of English saying less than (33).

(33)   *want to* → *wanna*

Therefore it is entirely beside the point of this claim to speculate whether this rule is idiosyncratic to *want* or part of a more general rule (see Suiko 1978). Compare this to Andrews (1978), who assumes that my argument for invoking traces is vitiated unless either "most verbs have *To* Adjunction forms" or "*use* in [34] and [35] represents the same lexical item [p.264]."

(34)   *Tom usta meet Harry for lunch*

(35)   *Tom used a Nikon to take the picture*

It is beside the point to speculate that *use* in (34) is a kind of modal or a verb followed by a VP complement; that suggests only that *use* provides no evidence one way or the other on the properties of traces. To refute the analysis of Lightfoot (1976b) one will need to show that the grammar of English must be complicated beyond (33) or that under another theory there is a simpler analysis, that is, simpler *at the level of particular grammar.*[10]

[10] See Chomsky and Lasnik (1978) for more on Postal and Pullum (1978). The incoherence stems from failing to distinguish descriptive from explanatory concerns, claims about a particular grammar from claims about the theory.

3. DEVELOPMENTS

Two consequences of Lightfoot (1976b, 1977) were (*a*) that the residue of a movement rule might be relevant for the structural description of a syntactic rule, but that a base-generated nonlexical NP was never so relevant, and (*b*) that a residue of a movement from COMP did not serve to block the *want to* contraction and in general should not be visible to syntactic rules. The latter point involves the assumption that *wh*-Movement applies successive cyclically and that a more complete version of the surface structure of *Who do you wanna succeed* would be (36), where neither the e_i in COMP nor the unindexed *e* serves to block the rule and where *to* is therefore effectively adjacent to *want*.

(36) $[Who_i]_{COMP}$ *do you want* $[[e_i]_{COMP}$ *e to succeed* $e_i]_s$

Lightfoot (1976b) stipulated that an unindexed *e* ("PRO" in the contemporary terminology) and an indexed *e* in COMP would not "count" for the structural descriptions of transformations. This was hardly an elegant solution but the stipulation was an elaboration at the level of grammatical theory, therefore not part of what was attributed to the efforts of the language learner, and therefore not an a priori undesirable elaboration and certainly not a reason to abandon the whole approach, as suggested in the remarks of Bach (1977) and Pullum and Postal (1978). In fact, it suggested a strengthening of SSC and the autonomy thesis (see Lightfoot, 1976b).

As it turned out, there was a solution to this inelegance in the framework of Chomsky and Lasnik (1977). This involved optional deletion of elements in COMP (37), allowing (38) and (39), and the claim that only an unindexed *e* would be invisible to syntactic rules and filters.

(37) $\alpha \rightarrow \emptyset$ / $[---]_{COMP}$

(38)   *I think* $[[(that)]_{COMP}$ *Susan won*]

(39)   *The woman* $[[(who_i)]_{COMP}$ *you met* $e_i]$ *won*

Thus the surface structure of *who do you wanna succeed* might now be (36), where the e_i in COMP would block contraction, or (31a) where the e_i in COMP does not appear, in other words, has been deleted by (37), and contraction is free to occur. Surface structures (38) and (39) suggest the need for such a deletion rule, which would be maximally general. The rule might be given by convention, if it turns out to be universally available; it if is part of English grammar specifically, it could be "learned" or hypothesized by the child (or "triggered") when exposed to just one

sentence like *I think Susan won* or *The woman you met won*. This then
is an elegant solution to the problem of interfering traces in COMP: Either
nothing has to be stipulated at the level of particular grammar or, at worst,
a maximally general rule which is readily "learnable" on the basis of
primary data. Notice that the fact that traces can be deleted does not
render the theory unfalsifiable, ad hoc or whatever; the rule deleting them
is quite general and applies to anything, which happens to include traces;
traces are not mentioned in the rule.

The other inelegance concerned the distinction between *t* and PRO.
Critics of this approach have pointed to the proliferating inventory of
phonetically null elements, "the sounds of silence," claiming that while
trace theory entails a restriction of the expressive power in some areas,
it does so at the cost of setting up several null elements with different
properties (see Lightfoot, 1977 for discussion). Both *t* and PRO represented empty NPs to be coindexed with, that is, interpreted as anaphoric
to, a c-commanding NP; they differed only in how the index was assigned,
either by a movement rule in the case of *t* or a rule of control for PRO.
The terminology adopted here (following Chomsky and Lasnik, 1977) is
perhaps more appropriate and illustrates that the issue is terminological
and, again, does not constitute part of what the child has to "learn" about
his particular language. Therefore the apparent proliferation of dummy
items, at least insofar as it affects *t*, PRO and "△" (the symbol indicating
arbitrary control, as for the understood subject of *attending* in *Attending
the soccer game is a political act)*, is simply a function of terminology:
There are phonetically null NPs which are co-indexed in various ways
(each given by general, therefore "unlearned" convention), and syntactic
rules see only lexical (i.e., indexed) NPs.

Presenting the issue in this way raises the question of whether there
could be just one rule of control, such that "traces" are base-generated
and coindexed with a c-commanding NP by the interpretive rule which
assigns indices to "PRO." This would permit the elimination of movement
rules. As it is, our derivations are much less complex than in earlier versions of generative grammar, and surface structures suitably enriched
with abstract elements permit a drastic reduction in the work done by the
transformational component. This has been a progressive development
since 1965. Having reduced the core of the transformational component
to one rule, Move Category (Chomsky, 1977, 1980), we are close to eliminating such rules altogether.[11] However, it is clear that traces have dif-

---

[11] Transformational rules seem to be still needed for "idiom chunks," for restructuring,
for non-core grammar phenomena and as "root" and "local" transformations (in the sense
of Emonds, 1976). This may not be very extensive; Koster (1978a) has tried to analyze away

ferent properties from other abstract elements [witness the distinction between (31a) and (31b)], and these properties will have to remain distinct even if traces are no longer viewed as the residue of movement rules. One essential property is that movement rules, but apparently not interpretive rules, are sensitive to the Subjacency Condition, which prohibits movement across more than one cyclic node. This condition is crucial for the dramatic simplification of grammar proposed in Chomsky (1977), wherein what had been viewed as many different rules were subsumed under *wh*-Movement. Making the generalized *wh*-Movement subject to Subjacency permits a unified explanation for the island phenomena of Ross (1967). If movement rules are to be eliminated, *wh* elements would be base-generated in COMP and have to be associated with a "gap" or empty NP (or PP, etc.). A new principle doing some of the work of the former Subjacency Condition would now be needed to preserve the explanation of Chomsky (1977). This is no doubt possible (see Lightfoot, 1977, section 3 and Koster, 1978b for proposals along these lines), but it is not clear that there are different empirical consequences.[12]

Other developments which have grown out of the concerns described here involve surface filters and a new model of grammar. Chomsky and Lasnik (1977) put forward a set of surface filters to correct some problems of overgeneration arising from the reduced expressive power of transformations and interpretive rules. For example, while a rule of free deletion in COMP (37) is desirable from several viewpoints, it will also allow the deletion of a *wh* pronoun originating in subject position.

(40)   [*the man* [[who$_i$]$_{COMP}$ e_i *left*]$_{\bar{s}}$]$_{NP}$ *wore black*
         $\Downarrow$
         $\emptyset$

---

the need for some root transformations; and some arguments for restructuring rules do not crucially involve syntactic restructuring as distinct from allowing two (or more) base configurations [e.g., Lightfoot (1978), Weinberg and Hornstein (1980); compare Rizzi (1978b), whose restructuring rule must apply, he claims, after certain transformations]. But it is worth noting that while generativeness is an essential component of transformational generative theory and part of the Lakatosian "hard-core," transformations are an accidental property [Dougherty (1975) illuminates the different status of these terms].

[12] The elimination of movement rules is not only a function of Subjacency. The possibility of eliminating such rules has been entertained frequently since the publication of Emonds' dissertation, which required that the output of cyclic nonlocal rules be generable directly by the phrase structure rules (the structure-preserving hypothesis). But problems arise with idiom chunks and, if one does not employ coding devices like traces, with the surface recovery of thematic relations. For a recent attempt to eliminate certain movement rules, see Bresnan (1978); this approach seems to involve a loss of explanatory adequacy by abandoning the Subjacency Condition, and some internal problems (for insightful discussion see Weinberg and Hornstein, 1980).

Chomsky and Lasnik propose a surface filter that will characterize (40) with *who* deleted as ill formed. They claim in general that many phenomena that might have been handled by extrinsic ordering, by distinguishing obligatory and optional rules, and by building subconditions into the structural descriptions of rules, can be dealt with via appropriate constraints on the COMP node in surface structure. The advantage of this is that while extrinsic ordering, etc. would represent work for the ingenious learner, many of the relevant properties of COMP can be stipulated at the level of theory, therefore not contributing to the language learner's burden. Traces play an important role in facilitating the operation of their filters.

Consider again the rule of free deletion in COMP (37). Presumably *who*$_i$ in (39) will be needed for the correct application of interpretive rules whereby e_i is to be identified with the *woman*. If it is not present in surface structure, it will not be available for the interpretive rules. Such problems led Chomsky and Lasnik to propose a new model of grammar (41), whereby ''surface structures,'' that is, the input to the rules of construal, have undergone no deletion.

(41)

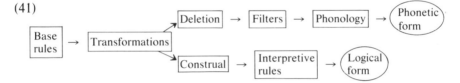

This represents another strong empirical prediction and a further limitation on the expressive power of grammars, since now all deletion rules will have to follow all rules of movement, adjunction and substitution; filters will have no access to the results of interpretive rules, construal rules will be independent of deletion, etc. Again, this is a direct consequence of the research program which I have outlined here.

I turn to one last development of the theory we have been considering. Earlier I distinguished conditions on form from conditions on function and, following Chomsky (1973), presented SSC as a condition on the functioning of rules: A rule would be blocked from applying across a specified subject. Lightfoot (1976b) noted that this entailed that the conditions on rules could conflate syntactic and semantic information and that syntactic rules would be sensitive to properties of control via SSC. I proposed a tightening of the autonomy thesis such that syntactic rules would not have access to information about control and would be blocked by SSC only if a lexical subject intervened. Another way to effect the desired tightening is pursued in Chomsky (1980); this allows syntactic rules to apply freely, again misgenerating wildly, but an analogue of SSC operates on logical form. BAI would be blocked from associating two NPs if a subject intervenes. Thus, given surface structures (42), where *John* has moved from the position marked by e_1, BAI could not associate e_1 with *John* and e_1 would be "free" (i.e., uninterpreted), because there is in each case a specified subject.

(42) a. *John wants [Mary to see e_1]*
      b. *John persuaded Mary [e_2 to see e_1]*
      c. *Mary seemed to John [e_2 to see e_1]*
      d. *John is believed [Mary to have seen e_1]*

Viewing SSC as a well-formedness condition on logical form opens up the chance for a further improvement. SSC and PIC were stated in such a way that COMP constituted an escape hatch and in the derivation (43) *wh*-Movement did not violate SSC or PIC (see Chomsky, 1973 for discussion).

(43)   [*Who [do you think [*COMP [*Bill saw e*]]]]

If one assumes that S is a binding node (see Chomsky, 1977; Rizzi, 1978a), the escape hatch nature of COMP requires an English-specific stipulation and does not follow from the theory. Chomsky (1980) reformulates the conditions such that the escape hatch nature of COMP follows automatically, does not require stipulation, and therefore does not represent an inference on the part of the child learning English. Thus PIC and SSC, now applying as conditions on logical form, are reformulated as an Opacity Condition (44).

(44)   In [. . . *a* . . .]$_b$, where *b* is $\bar{\text{S}}$ or NP and *a* is an anaphor, *a* cannot be free in *b* if
         (i) *a* is c-commanded by the subject of *b* ($\approx$SSC)
         (ii) *a* is c-commanded by the tense of *b* ($\approx$PIC)

(45)

The escape hatch nature of COMP (and of the subject of a nonfinite S) now follows from this formulation. In (45) an anaphor cannot be free in $\bar{\text{S}}$ if dominated by VP because it is c-commanded by Tense and by the subject. However, an anaphor can be free in $\bar{\text{S}}$ (i.e., not bound by any element internal to $\bar{\text{S}}$) if it is in COMP, where it would be c-commanded by neither Tense nor subject, or if it is the subject of a tenseless S. Now the escape hatch proviso need not be stipulated as a language–specific exception. The full empirical consequences of this move remain to be seen, but recasting a putative condition on function as a condition on some level of representation will often have empirical consequences that may be far reaching. For example, Freidin (1978) argues convincingly that under this view the cycle is no longer needed as an independent principle and that Emonds' (1976) structure-preservation principle falls out from the requirement that NPs must appear in "argument position" in logical form; it follows that NP movement will be structure preserving, unless some rule of interpretation converts the surface structure into some appropriate representation in logical form.

4. "EXTERNAL" DATA

Throughout this paper I have looked at grammatical claims from the viewpoint of their explanatory power. This involves a claim about correct descriptions and questions of descriptive adequacy cannot be approached independently of explanatoriness. If the descriptively adequate grammar is defined as the one which the native speaker has actually acquired (Chomsky, 1965), it follows definitionally that the descriptively adequate grammar is the one deduced from the primary linguistic data available to the child, and the theory most highly rated by the criteria for explanatoriness. Under this view it makes no sense to define descriptive adequacy independently of acquisition, for example, through a procedural definition of a "valid generalization."

The theory of grammar makes a claim about the initial state of the mental organ, the innate capacity of the child, and a particular grammar conforming to this theory makes a claim about the final state, the grammar eventually attained. This is a claim about correctness, about truth in the domain of psychology. This has led to much confusion in the literature and is sometimes misconstrued in terms of the misleading concept of "psychological reality." Some workers assume that one can write various grammars that "work" simply and elegantly, and that one can then ask which of these grammars is psychologically real.[13] The question is ap-

[13] The basic explanatory concern serves to resolve one kind of indeterminacy in a specific way: The formulation of the theory of core grammar should err on the side of excessive restrictiveness rather than being compatible with a variety of grammars that "work." This follows from the assumption that children do not have access to negative data, that is, that they are not informed reliably of what is ungrammatical. If the theory of core grammar is too tight to accommodate some fact of, say, Quechua, exposure to the relevant sentence would provoke a "peripheral" rule to accommodate the recalcitrant fact. Conversely, if the theory erred on the side of permissiveness, the formulation of the correct grammar would depend on negative date, which is available to analysts but not to children.

parently to be answered through data of some privileged status, so-called psychological or external data, usually to be drawn from acquisition, pathology, processing times, etc.; allegedly such data thus has special status for establishing claims about psychological reality. To reiterate an earlier point, data does not come labeled pretheoretically in this way; data from morpheme distribution, grammaticality judgments, scope of quantifiers, acquisition, historical change, language pathology, *etc.,* is all relevant for the justification and revision of claims about particular grammars and about the theory of grammar. Perhaps the only significant difference is that so-called linguistic data (i.e., judgments about grammaticality, ambiguity, paraphrase) has been in practice the most commonly and readily used basis for the revision of claims about speakers' linguistic knowledge. In the domains of acquisition, pathology, etc., presumably other cognitive capacities are particularly influential and the explanation of any given fact may lie in the theory of grammar or in the theories of those other cognitive capacities or some interaction of these theories. In the absence of fruitful theories of these capacities, grammatical claims based on such data are difficult to evaluate, although not impossible (see Kean, 1977).

It is sometimes claimed that all explanation must be reductionist and that one has no explanation until grammatical claims correlate with what is known about neurology (Whitaker, 1976). But this misses the point that chemists do not stop doing chemistry because they believe that everything can be explained in terms of quantum mechanics; interesting properties may hold at lower levels of abstraction. Perhaps one day we shall relate linguistic descriptions to neurological networks (then to chemistry, and then to quantum mechanics), but it does not follow that all future work must be conducted in these terms. One attains the level of abstraction that one can reach. At this stage it seems a reasonable strategy to work with fairly concrete levels of abstraction, that one can think about, get a handle on, etc., bearing in mind all the time that the generalizations one arrives at (e.g., PIC, SSC) may hold more generally over more domains, and thus at a higher level of abstraction.

So-called "external" data is not irrelevant but it has no privileged status. ANY claim about the correctness of grammatical hypotheses must have a psychological interpretation (given the nature of our goal) and therefore be a claim about truth in the domain of psychology, hence a contribution to a general theory of mind; thus there is no valid notion of psychological reality independent of a claim of simple correctness. The accessibility and usefulness of data from any given domain will vary according to the development of the various theories. Certain data will be uninterpretable, that is, beyond the range of explanation, at some stage, but come to form the basis for justifying and revising hypotheses as the theories are developed further. Two recent examples are data from language processing and syntactic change, which were more or less unin-terpretable under earlier versions of generative grammar; this data may now become accessible as an arena of argumentation if productive research programs emerge from Frazier's (1978) views on language pro-cessing and Lightfoot's (1979) on syntactic change.

We are now far from the original motivation for trace theory and some of that motivation has been radically recast. This is a normal development, for the justification of a theory lies not in its motivation but in the success of the research program in contributing to the basic explanatory goals. The research program in which trace theory has played a role has yielded significant restrictions on the expressive power of grammars while still allowing sufficient latitude for descriptive adequacy. Here I have tried to convey something of the development of the program and of what it means to do work in this area.

REFERENCES

Andrews, A. (1978). Remarks on *To* Adjunction. *Linguistic Inquiry,* 9, 261–268.

Bach, J.S. (1977). Comments on the Paper by Chomsky. In P. Culicover, T. Wasow and A. Akmajian (eds), *Formal Syntax.* New York: Academic Press. Pp.*133–155.*

Braine, M. (1971). On two types of models of the internalization of grammars. In D. Slobin (Ed.), *The Ontogenesis of Grammar.* New York: Academic Press. Pp.*153–186.*

Bresnan, J.W. (1972). *Theory of Complementation in English Syntax.* Unpublished doctoral dissertation, MIT, Cambridge, Mass.

Bresnan, J.W. (1978). A realistic transformational grammar. In M. Halle, J.W. Bresnan and G. Miller (Eds.), *Linguistic Theory and Psychological Reality.* Cambridge, Mass: MIT Press. Pp.*1–59.*

Chomsky, N. (1955). *Logical Structure of Linguistic Theory.* New York: Plenum [1975]

Chomsky, N. (1957). *Syntactic Structures.* The Hague: Mouton.

Chomsky, N. (1965). *Aspects of the Theory of Syntax.* Cambridge, Mass: MIT Press.

Chomsky, N. (1972). Deep structure, surface structure and semantic interpretation. In *Studies in Semantics in Generative Grammar.* The Hague: Mouton. Pp.*62–119.*

Chomsky, N. (1973). Conditions on transformations. In S. Anderson and P. Kiparsky (Eds.), *A Festschrift for Morris Halle.* New York: Holt, Rinehart and Winston. Pp.232–286.

Chomsky, N. (1975). *Reflections on Language.* New York: Pantheon.

Chomsky, N. (1976). Conditions on rules of grammar. *Linguistic Analysis,* 2, 303–351.

Chomsky, N. (1977). On *wh* Movement. In P. Culicover, T. Wasow and A. Akmajian (Eds.), *Formal Syntax.* New York: Academic Press. Pp.*71–132.*

Chomsky, N. (1980). On binding. *Linguistic Inquiry* 11, 1–46.

Chomsky, N. and Lasnik H. (1977). Filters and control. *Linguistic Inquiry, 8,* 425–504.

Chomsky, N. and Lasnik H. (1978). A remark on contraction. *Linguistic Inquiry, 9,* 268–274.

Cooper, R. (1977). Review of R. Montague, *Formal Philosophy. Language, 53*(4), 895–910.

Dougherty, R. (1975). Harris and Chomsky at the syntax–semantics boundary. In Hockney *et al.* (Eds.), *Contemporary Research in Philosophical Logic and Linguistic Semantics.* Dordrecht: Reidel. Pp.137–193.

Dresher, B. E. and Hornstein N. (1979). Trace theory and NP Movement rules. *Linguistic Inquiry, 10,* 65–82.

Emonds, J. (1976). *A Transformational Approach to English Syntax: Root, Structure-Preserving and Local Transformations*. New York: Academic Press.

Fiengo, R. (1974). *Semantic Conditions on Surface Structures*. Unpublished doctoral dissertation, MIT, Cambridge, Mass.

Frazier, L. (1978). *On Comprehending Sentences: Syntactic Parsing Strategies*. Unpublished doctoral dissertation, University of Connecticut, Storrs, Conn.

Freidin, R. (1978). Cyclicity and the theory of grammar. *Linguistic Inquiry, 9*, 519–549.

Hornstein, N. (1977) S and the X̄ convention. *Linguistic Analysis, 3*, 137–176.

Hornstein, N. and Lightfoot, D. W. (In press). *Explanation in Linguistics*. London: Longman.

Jackendoff, R. S. (1972). *Semantic Interpretation in Generative Grammar*. Cambridge, Mass: MIT Press.

Jenkins, L. (1977). Movement transformations as interpretive rules in the Extended Standard Theory. In C. Rohrer and N. Ruwet (Eds.), *Proceedings of the Colloque Franco-allemand*. Tübingen: Max Niemeyer Verlag. Pp.115–139.

Kean, M-L. (1977). The linguistic interpretation of aphasic syndromes: Agrammatism in Broca's aphasia, an example. *Cognition, 5*, 9–46.

Koster, J. (1978a). Why subject sentences don't exist. In *Recent Transformational Studies in European Languages, Linguistic Inquiry* monograph no.3. Pp.53–64.

Koster, J. (1978b). *Locality Principles in Syntax*. Dordrecht: Foris Publications.

Lakoff, G. (1970). Global rules. *Language, 46*(3), 627–639.

Lasnik, H. (In press). Restricting the theory of transformations: a case study. In N. Hornstein and D. W. Lightfoot (Eds.), *Explanation in Linguistics*. London: Longman.

Lightfoot, D. W. (1976a). The theoretical implications of Subject Raising. *Foundations of Language, 14*(2), 257–286.

Lightfoot, D. W. (1976b). Trace theory and twice-moved NPs. *Linguistic Inquiry, 7*, 559–582.

Lightfoot, D. W. (1977). On traces and conditions on rules. In P. Culicover, T. Wasow and A. Akmajian (Eds.), *Formal Syntax*. New York: Academic Press. Pp.207–238.

Lightfoot, D. W. (in press). Explaining syntactic change. In N. Hornstein and D. W. Lightfoot (Eds.), *Explanation in Linguistics*. London: Longman.

Lightfoot, D. W. (1978) A re-structuring rule. *Linguistic Inquiry 9*, 717–719.

Lightfoot, D. W. (1979). *Principles of Diachronic Syntax*. Cambridge: Cambridge University Press.

Postal, P. M. (1971). *Cross-over Phenomena*. New York: Holt, Rinehart and Winston.

Postal P. M. and Pullum, G. K. (1978). Traces and the description of English complementizer contraction. *Linguistic Inquiry, 9*, 1–29.

Pullum, G. K. (1975). A golden treasury of counterexamples to the Specified Subject Constraint. Mimeo.

Quicoli, C. (1976). Conditions on Quantifier movement in French. *Linguistic Inquiry, 7*, 583–607.

Reinhart, T. (1976). *The Syntactic Domain of Anaphora*. Unpublished doctoral dissertation, MIT, Cambridge, Mass.

Rizzi, L. (1978a). Violations of the *wh* island constraint in Italian and the Subjacency Condition. *Montreal Working Papers in Linguistics* 11, 155–190.

Rizzi, L. (1978b). A re-structuring rule in Italian syntax. In *Recent Transformational Studies in European Languages, Linguistic Inquiry* monograph no.3 Pp.113–158.

Ross, J. R. (1967). *Constraints on Variables in Syntax*. Unpublished doctoral dissertation, MIT, Cambridge, Mass.

Siegel, D. (1974). *Topics in English Morphology*. Unpublished doctoral dissertation, MIT, Cambridge, Mass.

Snow, C. (1972). Mothers speech to children learning language. *Child Development, 43.*

Suiko, M. (1978). A phonological analysis of *wanna* formation. Mimeo.

Wasow, T. (1972). *Anaphoric Relations in English.* Unpublished doctoral dissertation, MIT, Cambridge, Mass.

Weinberg, A. and Hornstein, N. (1980). Case theory and preposition stranding. *Linguistic Inquiry, 11.*

Whitaker, H. (1976). Is the grammar in the brain? In D. Cohen (Ed.), *Explaining linguistic phenomena.* New York: Wiley. Pp.75–90.

Williams, E. (1977). Discourse and logical form. *Linguistic Inquiry 8,* 101–139.

AN UN-SYNTAX[1]

JAMES D. McCAWLEY
University of Chicago

1. CONCERNING THE TITLE OF THIS PAPER

In this paper and in my presentation of the Milwaukee syntax conference I have complied to a large extent with Edith Moravcsik's request
for a presentation on generative semantics, but not with her implicit request that I call what I present "generative semantics." "Generative semantics" is not a technical term, which is just as well: Only historians
of science have any business making a technical term out of a name for
a scientific or scholarly approach, and even they have no business doing
so until they have the benefit of at least several decades of hindsight to
tell them what things technical terms are needed for. In recent years I
have tended not to use the term "generative semantics" at all, not even
on the level of informality with which one would use such terms as "acid
rock" or "nouvelle cuisine," not because of any wish to dissociate myself
from the ideas that are popularly associated with that term (I will in fact
dissociate myself from some of them below, though that has little to do
with my non-use of the term), but because of my realization that there

---

[1] I am grateful to Laurence R. Horn, Judith N. Levi, and Valerie F. Reyna for valuable
comments on earlier versions of this paper.

167

are a huge number of largely independent important issues in grammar and that the use of the small number of popular names for approaches gives the misleading impression that there are far fewer sets of positions on these issues than are actually held by serious scholars, to say nothing of the vast number of potentially viable combinations of positions that, by accident, no one has seriously developed. Like the question "Are you a conservative or a liberal?" the question "Are you a generative or an interpretive semanticist?" both makes the blatantly false assumption that there is basically only a two-way distinction among viewpoints and arrogantly imposes on the addressee the speaker's evaluation of the relative importance of the relevant issues.

In order to encourage discussion in terms of issues rather than in terms of popular labels, I have accordingly chosen to debase the terminological currency through the use of disposable titles, each to be used once and then flushed down the toilet. My presentation at the Milwaukee conference was entitled "Epiphenomenal syntax"; for a presentation of the same material at a seminar at the University of Chicago a couple of days earlier, I used the title "The un-syntax." Both of those titles are unavailable for this paper, having been flushed down toilets in Milwaukee and Chicago respectively.[2] In choosing a new title, I have followed the example of the successive titles that Sadock (1975) applied to his book on speech acts, thus allowing myself the option of calling a later version "Toward an un-syntax." These titles are supposed to suggest an approach in which much of what has been thought of as syntax is largely a reflection of other things, such as morphology, logic, production strategies, and principles of cooperation. I will not be hurt if anyone calls what I present here "generative semantics," provided it is kept in mind that the approach expounded here differs in a number of important respects from what appears in my better-known papers from the early 1970s. I likewise will not be hurt if anyone calls it "epiphenomenal syntax" or "un-syntax"; puzzled, perhaps, but not hurt.

2. MY CONCEPTION OF A GRAMMAR

In this section I will take as reference point "standard transformational grammar," simply because, like Times Square, it is a useful landmark for orientation and direction-giving. Much of the difference between my approach and standard transformational grammar follows from my rejection

---

[2] The astute reader will notice that in this sentence I have not used but only mentioned the two earlier titles.

of an almost universal assumption among transformational grammarians, which I will refer to as COMBINATORIC PLATONISM: the idea that there is a single linguistic level to which all combinatoric restrictions basically relate, both GROSS COMBINATORIC RESTRICTIONS (those that standardly are embodied in phrase structure rules, e.g., the restriction that in English a determiner must precede its noun), and PETTY COMBINATORIC RESTRICTIONS (those that standardly are embodied in selectional and strict subcategorization features, e.g., the restriction that *give* requires two NPs over and above its subject). Combinatoric Platonism is often vulgarized into a view of a grammar as blueprint for a sentence factory, where a sentence is constructed by assembling its deep structure (or its structure on whatever the combinatorically privileged level is) and deriving from that structure its structure on all other linguistic levels. Much common terminology has the effect of reinforcing combinatoric Platonism, especially its vulgarized version: "Base," with its connotations of "foundation," suggests that "base structures" are that on which the whole of syntactic structure is built and without whose support the whole edifice would collapse, and "derivation," by virtue of its morphological relationship to "derive," suggests the deriving of "outputs" from "inputs."

In what follows, I will use the word "derivation," for want of any acceptable substitute, but I hope that the reader will dismiss its relationship to "derive" as merely a curious fact of etymology, of no more significance than the etymological relationship between *remorse* and *morsel*. For the purposes of this paper, a derivation is simply a sequence of linguistic structures, typically a sequence in which the differences between consecutive structures are minimal (relative to some fixed conception of what a minimal difference is), where a grammar is to consist of rules specifying how structures in a sequence may or must differ from one another. Note that acceptance of the notion of derivation does not commit one to combinatoric Platonism: Being completely neutral as to how combinatoric restrictions fit into a grammar, it is consistent, for example, with a conception of grammar in which gross combinatorics is exclusively a matter of surface structure and petty combinatorics exclusively a matter of a level of deep structure, that is, a grammar that specifies those derivations to be well-formed in which the surface structure conforms to a given set of gross combinatoric restrictions, the deep structure conforms to a given set of petty combinatoric restrictions, and the various "stages" of the derivation differ from each other in ways that conform to a given set of "derivational constraints."

Combinatoric Platonism is responsible for the common but preposterous objection to output constraints as being merely devices to remove "garbage" that wouldn't be there if the grammar were doing its job properly.

That objection is intelligible only under assumptions that imply that the "garbage" is "there," that is, that the derivations that are well-formed but for violation of output constraints are real in a way that derivations whose ill-formedness is confined to some other area (e.g., derivations that are well-formed except that some strict subcategorization restrictions are violated) are not real. The vulgarized version of combinatoric Platonism involves just such an assumption: The "base structure" is assembled first and is then transformed into the corresponding surface structure. Rejection of combinatoric Platonism allows one to adopt a conception of language production in which all levels of linguistic structure are assembled in parallel, with combinatoric restrictions on any particular level affecting the speaker's choice among options.[3] The following illustration shows how output constraints could function in a plausible account of a motor activity such as walking, analogous to the role that I have just suggested that they play in speech production. One's knowledge of walking consists (I hypothesize) of several basic motor programs (one for each gait), a number of mechanisms for modifying the execution of those programs (by extending the foot further forward than normal, moving it to one side, etc.), and a set of output constraints such as: *FOOT ON SHARP OBJECT.[4] In walking on terrain that is strewn with sharp objects, one exercises the optional modifications of the motor programs in such a way as to avoid violations of the output constraints. To make use of the output constraints in ambulatory behavior, one need not first mentally construct a series of steps leading from one side of the terrain to the other and then check whether any of those steps leaves one's foot on a piece of broken glass: One generally need choose among the options only a step or two in advance.

The bulk of the better-known arguments for underlying syntactic structures provide evidence that petty combinatoric restrictions (i.e., strict subcategorization and selectional restrictions) relate to underlying rather than surface syntactic structures, but these arguments are neutral as to what level of structure the gross syntactic combinatoric restrictions must be taken as applying to. For example, arguments for transformational treatments of passive clauses on the basis of parallelism in the selectional

---

[3] Combinatoric Platonism has been reinforced by another common policy among transformational grammarians: that of regarding strings as more basic than trees or dependency structures and of formulating rules and principles of rule application in string terms. The conception of "incomplete structure" that is intimately involved in the conception of language production presented in the text is readily available if the structures with which one operates are trees but not if they are strings.

[4] This output constraint is of more general application than merely in the domain of walking.

and strict subcategorization properties of active and passive verbs demand an analysis in which there is a level of structure at which active and passive clauses involve the same configurations of elements; but they are neutral with regard to whether it is that level or some other level (say, surface structure) to which the restrictions that verbs in English follow their subjects and precede their objects apply. The best-known putative example of a gross (or at least, not clearly petty) combinatoric constraint applying to a nonsurface syntactic level, namely Chomsky's formula AUX → Tense (Modal) (*have -en*) (*be -ing*), is spurious: See McCawley (1971) for arguments that the restrictions on the order of English auxiliary verbs follow from details of the semantics and morphology of the individual auxiliary verbs under an analysis in which they are underlying main verbs with sentential subjects, and that thus no combinatoric constraint corresponding to Chomsky's formula need be included in a grammar.

Certain well-known facts provide evidence that gross combinatoric constraints are constraints on surface structure, though they have generally been taken as evidence for other conclusions. I have in mind here Emonds' (1970) observations about the severe language–specific limitations on the configurations that can occur in transformational outputs. Emonds notes that movement and insertion transformations only put items in places where the language otherwise allows items of that category,[5] e.g., the standard formulation (1) of a Passive transformation is not simply an arbitrary deformation of structure, but rather involves creation of a prepositional phrase (*by* + 1) and insertion of it into a position (namely at the end of the VP) where English allows PPs, movement of the NP from after the V to the position before the V where English allows NPs anyway, and insertion of *be* into a position where English allows Vs to occur otherwise (i.e., there are VPs consisting of V followed by VP, as in *try to shut the door*).

(1)   NP   Aux   V   (P) NP   X
         1   2   3   4   5   6
         →5   2   *be* + *-en*   3   4   0   6   *by* + 1

Emonds formulated this generalization in terms of "phrase structure rules," which he took as specifying deep structure gross combinatorics: He defines the notion of "structure-preserving movement transformation" in terms of "moving a constituent labeled X into a position where a node X is already provided for by the phrase structure rules" [Emonds,

---

[5] This exposition relates only to what Emonds calls "structure preserving" transformations; for expository convenience, I will ignore the other two types of transformations that he distinguishes: root and local transformations.

1970, Section II.1.2]. This particular formulation of the notion "structure preserving" forces Emonds to do many things that would be at best pointless under the alternative conception of "phrase structure rules" as specifying surface combinatoric constraints. For example, Emonds takes pains to show that at least some prenominal adjectives are not derived from relative clauses, so that there will be a deep structure prenominal adjective position into which the Adjective Preposing transformation can move things. His approach thus appears to imply that if a language were just like English except for lacking expressions like *main purpose* that (according to Emonds) involve prenominal adjectives in their deep structures, its analogues to *tall man,* etc. could not be derived by Relative Clause Reduction and Adjective Preposing. In the alternative approach developed here, English simply has a surface prenominal adjective position (more accurately, a surface configuration [A N̄]$_{\bar{N}}$), and that position can figure in transformational outputs regardless of whether [A N̄]$_{\bar{N}}$ ever occurs in anything but "late" stages of derivations.

Emonds' approach requires extensive use of "empty nodes" in deep structures, as in his version of Affix Hopping, which operates as in (2):[6]

(2)

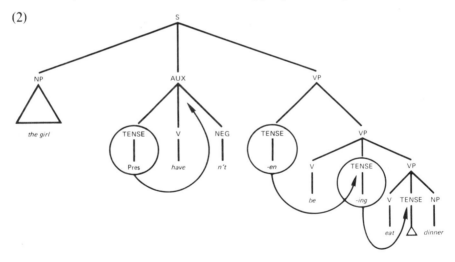

---

[6] This structure is an intermediate stage in Emonds' (1976; p. 222) derivation of *The girl hasn't been eating dinner.* The *have* has undergone application of a rule that moves it from under the topmost VP node to a V position under the AUX node that at that point was occupied by *do.* Note incidentally that in Emonds' version of structure preservation, only the constituent INTO which the item is moved, not the constituent OUT OF which it is moved, need conform to the phrase structure rules in the output of the transformation; for example, replacement of *do* by *have* leaves a [TENSE VP]$_{VP}$ configuration, which Emonds' phrase structure rules do not allow for.

In addition, he is required to have a phrase structure rule specifying that in DEEP structure, Vs are followed by affixes (which he confusingly calls TENSE). But the fact that English verbal affixes are suffixes (when they are separate morphemes at all) is a fact about English morphology having nothing to do with deep structure. Moreover, it is largely by historical accident that English verbal affixes are all suffixes; there are other languages in which some affixes are prefixes and other affixes having exactly the same function are suffixes, for example, Choctaw, in which the first person singular agreement marker is a suffix -*li* and all other agreement markers are prefixes.[7] Affix Hopping puts English verbal affixes in positions where they are allowed to appear, but it is by virtue of English morphology—not its syntax—that they are allowed to appear there. In the alternative presented in this paper, the formulation of transformations gives only a partial specification of the effect of the transformation (e.g., the Passive transformation will specify that *be* is inserted but not where it is inserted), and the transformation will apply in such a way as to yield outputs that conform to the language's gross combinatorics constraints (e.g., *be* will be inserted as a left Chomsky-adjunct to the VP because it is a V and there is no other configuration in which the gross combinatorics of English would allow a V to combine with the remaining constituents).

It is remarkable that there was no serious consideration in the late 1960s of the possibility that gross syntactic combinatorics might be purely a matter of surface structure, in view of the development by Ross (1967) and Perlmutter (1968) of the notion of OUTPUT CONSTRAINT, that is, the notion of surface combinatoric constraint: Given strong arguments that some gross combinatoric constraints relate specifically to surface structure, some doubt ought to have arisen as to whether deep structure gross combinatoric constraints were also needed. I attribute the lack of attention to this now obvious question to the following two factors: None of the

---

[7] In the actual surface structure, the affix and the verb make up a single constituent, for example [*eat-ing*]$_V$. If the structures in (2) were changed so as to correspond to deep structures in which the affix position agreed with surface structure in that detail, a further respect in which Emonds' analysis misrepresents the syntax of English verbal affixes would become apparent: -*ing* would be represented as a deep structure affix OF *be*, which it is not in any stage of the derivation of *be eating dinner*.

I in fact suspect that the level to which SYNTACTIC (as opposed to morphological) output constraints should be taken as applying is a level to which rules positioning bound morphemes have not applied, thus Swedish should be taken as SYNTACTICALLY requiring that determiners precede nouns, even though the definite article, when combined with a one-word noun, is a suffix.

On interactions between syntax and morphology, especially derivational morphology, see Levi (1978), an extensive and insightful study of compounding and derivation done in a framework sharing much with that of this article.

participants in the well-known controversies about syntax and semantics in transformational grammar was at that time yet fully purged of combinatoric Platonism and they thus did not regard "base rules" and "output constraints" as alternatives to one another, and many of the participants (myself among them) failed to distinguish between semantic combinatorics (e.g., the rule that a predicate may combine with one or more arguments) and syntactic combinatorics (e.g., the rule that in English, unlike Malay, a determiner must precede its noun). All assumed that there was only one linguistic level that was the locus of the bulk, if not all, of the combinatoric action, and they argued about what that level was. The character of the disputes was like that of an argument in which one of two persons who agree that there is only one volcano in the world tries to convince the other that Vesuvius is not a volcano by showing him a photograph of Kilauea erupting and the other defends the status of Vesuvius as a volcano by redefining "volcano" so as to exclude Kilauea. Arguments by generative semanticists such as myself for a set of "universal base rules" that coincided with well-formedness rules for logical structures were often perfectly good demonstrations that such rules played a role in what was generally regarded as syntax, but were misinterpreted by their propounders as showing that those rules made up the whole of gross combinatorics.[8]

One other major factor that was responsible for the failure of the disputants to correctly identify the issues in the late 1960s disputes about "base rules" is the consensus that prevailed at that time regarding the nature and role of syntactic categories. In the then universally accepted conception of syntactic categories, the base rules were responsible for all occurrences of all syntactic categories: Any surface occurrence of a syntactic category had to be traceable back to a deep structure occurrence of that same category. In addition, despite occasional mumblings about syntactic categories perhaps being complexes of features, categories were taken to be indivisible wholes. Next to my rejection of combinatoric Platonism in favor of an approach in which gross syntactic combinatorics is formulated in terms of surface structure and petty combinatorics in terms of stages at which lexical items enter derivations, the most important difference between my approach and standard transformational grammar is the adoption of a conception of syntactic categories as merely informal abbreviations for combinations of several kinds of information (lexical category of head, logical category, topological information, dependency information, . . .), with categories "changing" in the course

---

[8] For my current thoughts on logical combinatorics, as well as extensive material on the relationship between logical and syntactic structure, see McCawley (in press).

of the derivation as a result of changes in those factors (e.g., a S becomes a VP when its subject is removed or deleted, or rather, it becomes something that is VP, AP, or "Ñ," depending on the lexical category of the predicate element, and is indeterminate among those three categories prior to insertion of a lexical item in predicate position). My thinking about categories has been considerably influenced by an important article, written in 1966 but not published until 1976, in which Stephen Anderson proposed separating two functions that base rules of transformational grammars conflated: criteria for membership in syntactic categories (such as that anything consisting of a determiner and a noun is a NP), and language-particular combinatoric properties (such as that in English NPs the determiner precedes the noun). Anderson regarded the latter as relating specifically to deep structure but the former as determining category membership at any stage of derivations. Note that in Anderson's scheme, categories can occur in the surface structures of a language that never appear in its deep structures, for example, a constituent resulting from adjunction of a preposition to a NP would be a prepositional phrase because anything consisting of a preposition and a NP is a PP, and thus a language in which all prepositions were transformationally inserted would have surface occurrences but no deep occurrences of the category PP.[9] I find X-bar syntax congenial to the extent that it replaces indivisible category names by complexes of specific types of information—namely, lexical category of the head of the constituent, and depth to which the head is embedded in that constituent. However, I do not regard these as a full list of the factors that play a role in syntax, I regard many of the constituent structures on which determinations of numbers of bars rest

[9] I assume throughout this discussion that the lexical category of any lexical item, even an item that is "transformationally inserted," is part of its dictionary entry, and that the labels N, V, A, P, etc. that appear in representing syntactic structure indicate that part of the dictionary entry of the item rather than constituting separate nodes, so that the former of the following trees is a more accurate representation of syntactic structure than the latter:

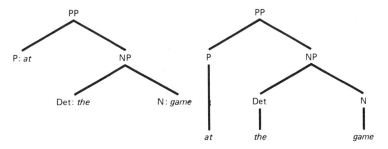

For further remarks on the notion "syntactic category," see McCawley (1977a).

as incorrect, and I reject the X-bar syntacticians' policy of requiring categories to remain constant throughout derivations, on the grounds that the sort of separation of factors that X-bar syntacticians allow eliminates what little rationale that policy had to begin with.

Besides these two most basic differences with standard transformational grammar [(a) gross syntactic combinatorics at surface structure, and (b) syntactic categories as derivative of more basic notions], some additional differences, given in roughly decreasing order of importance, are worth noting: (c) I reject a distinction between transformation and semantic interpretation rule; (d) I am as ready to accept global and extraderivational[10] conditions on rules as to accept any other kind of contextual factor. Differences (c) and (d) go together, in view of the fact that in standard transformational grammar, semantic interpretation rules are global. The principal controversy about global rules has not been whether there are such things but whether a distinction between syntactic and semantic rules can be made in such a way that only semantic rules are ever global. Expressions of horror at the idea of global rules baffle me as much as do expressions of horror at marijuana or pornography. I don't find the idea of global rules particularly remarkable. Look at it this way—the things one does in speaking and understanding speech are global (i.e., one is constructing structures on several linguistic levels in parallel), so would it be surprising if some of the knowledge that one utilizes in speaking and understanding were global too?

A fifth difference (e) is that I admit analyses involving lexical decompositions. On this point, as on most of the controversial matters discussed in this paper, I regard the existing literature as grossly deficient in identifying issues. Since it was abundantly clear by 1970 that sentences involving semantically complex lexical items exhibit some, but far from all, of the characteristics that one could reasonably expect them to have if their semantic structures served as syntactic underlying structures, the parties to the disputes ought to have busied themselves seeking explanations for the facts that did not conform to their fondest hopes, for example, they ought to have diverted their attention from merely finding

---

[10] I have substituted the term "extraderivational" for the better-known but misleading term "transderivational": An extraderivational rule is a derivational constraint that is sensitive to something outside of the given derivation, but that something could perfectly well be, for example, the logical structure of a belief of the speaker rather than a whole derivation. See McCawley (1976a) for discussion of phenomena that require extraderivationally conditioned rules, for example, where underlying structures must be indeterminate as to the number and sex of purported referents and the number and gender of pronouns must be chosen on the basis of extraderivational information.

cases where adverbs can or cannot modify material involved in lexical decompositions (*I opened the door again* and *I simmered the stew slowly* versus **I killed John of heart failure* and **Bill killed Mary on Sunday by stabbing her on Saturday*) to finding what was responsible for whether a given case worked the one way or the other. Attempts in this direction have subsequently been carried out in, for example, Heringer (1976) and McCawley (1977b), where it is argued that Grice's Maxim of Manner gives rise to a division of labor between simple lexical items and their periphrastic counterparts, with the simple lexical item reserved for the core (as opposed to periphery) of the denotation of the complex counterpart. These are the first works in which the appropriate question was raised: Do the differences in use and conveyed meaning between *kill* and *cause to die*, etc. go beyond what follows from the fact that in surface structure the one is simple and the other complex? Of course, to raise that question, one must allow for the possibility that what a sentence conveys might depend on its relationship to things outside of it, such as principles of cooperation, a possibility of which few linguists were even dimly aware before the mid-1970s.

A sixth difference (*f*) is that I restrict the role of left-to-right order in syntax to matters to which it is relevant (e.g., Heavy NP Shift) and accordingly formulate rules in structural terms rather than in terms of formulas that indicate left-to-right order but little or no structure. I regard the proposition that at least some underlying structures in at least some languages involve at least some left-to-right ordering as a weakly supported empirical proposition.[11] A final difference (*g*) is that I reject a level of syntactic deep structure. In view of the preceding points, particularly (*a*) and (*d*), I now regard the question of whether there is a level of deep structure as having far less significance than I once thought it to have. Since there is little reason to believe that the things that were once thought to converge at a single level of deep structure (selectional restrictions, gross combinatorics, semantic interpretation rules, lexical insertion) in fact converge, the main live issue remaining is whether lexical insertion

---

[11] In McCawley (1979b), I discuss the solidest case that I know for an underlying constituent order that differs from surface order, namely Bach's (1970) case for a deep VSO order in Amharic. Bach's arguments have the rare property of not crucially depending on the assumption that there IS a deep constituent order, the way that, for example, the arguments in my mistitled 1970 paper did (it should have been called "English as not an SVO language"). Horn (comments at Milwaukee conference) points out that the analysis of Super-Equi facts in Jacobson and Neubauer (1976) depends on there being a left-to-right order at the stage where Super-Equi gets its chance to apply, where that order may be altered on higher cycles.

can be constrained to all take place at a single linguistic level, which could then be taken as constituting a border between syntactic structure and semantic structure. However, with a global conception of rules, it is harder than ever to establish where in the derivation particular lexical insertions take place or even whether that question is intelligible. To a large extent, to say that a node in an intermediate stage of a derivation bears a morpheme as label is to say that it corresponds to a surface structure node with that label, and to say that it bears a semantic primitive as label is to say that it corresponds to a node of semantic structure with that label. Only occasionally can we find evidence for an intermediate stage involving morphemes that do not appear in surface structure, as in Binnick's (1971) argument for derivation of expressions with *bring* by way of intermediate stages involving corresponding expressions with *come*.

Having listed major differences between my conception of a grammar and that of standard transformational grammar, I should list the more important similarities. These include (*a*) the acceptance of a notion, roughly identifiable with "transformation," of rules specifying how consecutive stages of a derivation may or must differ from each other, where the difference between consecutive stages will generally be minimal, according to some fixed notion of "minimal difference" (e.g., two trees might differ minimally if they differ only in that one contains an extra constituent that the other does not, or a constituent is in one place in the one and a different place in the other, or one has a lexical item where the other has a different constituent); and (*b*) the acceptance of a principle of cyclic rule application, in the sense, say, of a principle to the effect that minimal differences in versions of a lower S will appear earlier in the derivation than do minimal differences in versions of a higher S (or in more popular terminology, rules apply to lower Ss before they apply to higher Ss). Note that (*a*) is only a rough correspondence, since the "transformations" of my approach may be global or extraderivational (i.e., sensitive to details of derivational steps other than the "input" and "output" or to information outside the derivation) and since there can be restrictions other than "transformations" on the relationship between derivational stages.

Coupled with my interpretation of "S" as basically a logical category (i.e., a constituent is a "S" if it corresponds to a proposition in logical structure), (*b*) causes the cyclic principle to predict quite different rule interactions than when it is combined with the more limited set of cyclic domains that correspond to the S of standard transformational grammar. The approach adopted here, for example, provides an explanation not available in standard transformational grammar of why passive *be* follows any other auxiliary verbs. In my approach, the logical structure of (3a) is (3d),[12] and the problem of explaining why (3b)–(3c) are not possible though (3a) is amounts to the problem of explaining why Passive can apply to S_3 but not to S_2 and S_1.

(3) a. *Elsa has been being investigated by the FBI*
     b. **Elsa has been been investigating by the FBI*
     c. **Elsa is had been investigating by the FBI*
     d.

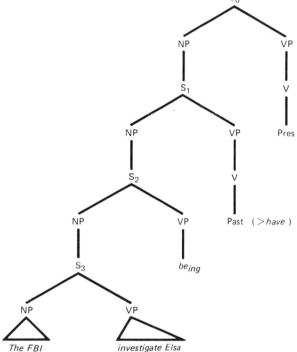

Passive might conceivably apply to any of S_3 through S_0. The question that must be answered is: On which of those Ss are the conditions for Passive met? Under the most simple-minded formulation of Passive, in which it applies to structures in which the VP contains a NP, moving that NP into subject position, adjoining *be* to the VP, and putting the object NP, marked with *by*, at the end of the VP, the conditions for Passive will be met on S_3; if the option of applying Passive is exercised, the result will

[12] For expository convenience, I act here as if Ss in English contained VPs at all stages of derivations. For all I know, they may: I know of no strong reason why logical structures should or should not involve VPs. The argument presented here is in fact neutral on that point: The only significant role played by "VP" in this discussion is that the output of Raising involves a VP, which it does by definition: VP simply means S minus subject.

be (4a), and subsequent applications of Raising on S_2–S_0 will yield (4b) and eventually (3a):

(4)   a.

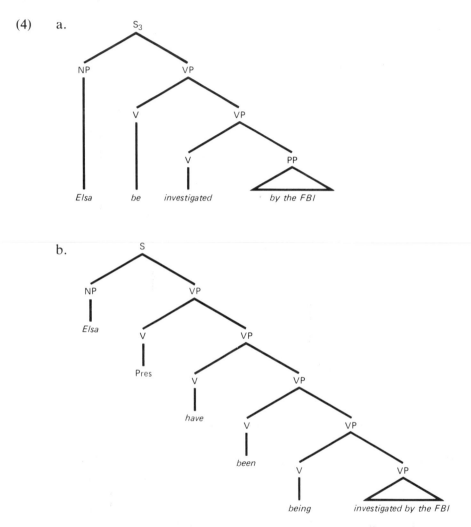

b.

A derivation of (3b) or (3c) would have to involve an application of Passive to S_2 or S_1 respectively, after Raising has applied to it (since before Raising the V of S_2 or S_1 would not have a NP in its VP and there would thus be no possibility of applying Passive). Hence (3b) and (3c) will be impossible if Passive is inapplicable to the structure derived through the application of Raising to a subject complement. But Passive is in fact inapplicable to such structures, for example, one cannot apply Passive to (5c) to yield (5a) [as contrasted with (5b), which results from application of Passive to the embedded S]:

(5) a. *Clara is seemed to admire by Rex
     b. Clara seems to be admired by Rex
     c.

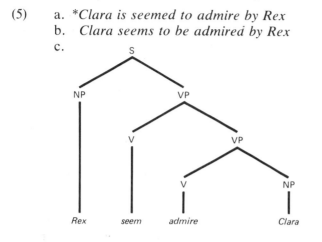

Thus, (3b)–(3c) are impossible for the same reason that (5a) is: Passive cannot make a derived subject out of something in a lower VP but only something in the VP of the main verb.

3. METHODOLOGY

In a course that I teach on linguistics and the philosophy of science, I have introduced a technical sense of the term RED HERRING: A proposition p is a red herring for a scientific community C if p is widely assented to by members of C but is not widely believed by members of C.[13] An alternative and nearly equivalent characterization is: A proposition is a red herring for a scientific community if the members of that community do not believe it but nevertheless teach it to their students.

Three propositions whose status as red herrings for the community of transformational grammarians is fairly obvious are (*a*) that a language is a set of sentences, (*b*) that linguistics is a branch of cognitive psychology, and (*c*) that an adequate theory of language must incorporate a theory of language acquisition. I differ from most transformational grammarians in explicitly denying (*a*) and in accepting (rather than merely assenting to) (*b*) and (*c*). My acceptance of (*b*) and (*c*) is closely related to my rejection of (*a*). Acquisition of a language is not acquisition of a set of sentences,

---

[13] The applicability of this term is not restricted to scientific communities. For example, there are many communities in the ordinary sense for which the proposition that there is a God meets both criteria of being a red herring.

and there is no particular set of sentences that plays a central role in a person's linguistic abilities. I endorse here a remark by Wallis Reid (personal communication): "The relationship between a language and a set of sentences is like the relationship between a car and a set of trips to the supermarket." Allusions by transformational grammarians to a set of sentences are often best interpreted as euphemisms for ideologically suspect notions, for example, when a linguist presents a list of sentences with and without stigmata (*, ?, etc.), he is normally reporting not "grammaticality judgments" (even though he may well say that they are grammaticality judgments) but rather judgments as to the normalness of that sentence as an expression of a given meaning under given contextual conditions. The ability to make "grammaticality judgments" as popularly understood, that is, judgments about the "goodness" of a string of words independently of its syntactic structure or meaning or context, is extremely rare and appears to be a concomitant of virtuosity in constructing puns. In an introductory syntax course there will occasionally be students who possess this unusual and somewhat pathological ability. Their interventions in class, in which they point out that your "ungrammatical" examples are really quite normal in some unsuspected interpretation, can be amusing if they are not too frequent. Such people are often useful informants, though what makes them useful is not their grammaticality judgments (you do not learn anything just from the information that all your examples are "grammatical") but their ability to manipulate variables of meaning and context in the process of doing what other informants are able to do, namely make judgments about the absolute or relative normalness of particular sentences relative to particular meanings and contexts.

My acceptance of (c) leads me to reject a proposition that is related in interesting ways to (a) and (b), namely the proposition that the data of linguistics are linguistic data. "Linguistic data," as usually understood, are propositions of the form "X is/isn't an item of type Y in language/ dialect/. . . Z." I see no reason to suppose that such "data" suffice to determine either what grammar the linguist should hold to be a psychologically correct analysis of the language or what grammar the child develops in the process of acquiring its linguistic knowledge. The data of linguistics are the facts that are relevant to its subject matter, be the data "linguistic" or "nonlinguistic": The fact that certain forms are used in the given linguistic community, that they are judged as normal/abnormal as expressions of such-and-such meanings, that they are replaced by such-and-such forms in speech errors, that they are recalled with such-and-such frequencies in such-and-such memory tasks, . . . No kind of data is "primary," that is, has a privileged kind of factuality or relevance. The prevalence of a limited number of kinds of data in a linguist's argumentation reflects only accidents of history and personal quirks as to what kinds of data he sees the relevance of and/or is comfortable in working with.

I consider it realistic to suppose that the child acquires linguistic rules on the basis of evidence that is both fragmentary and not entirely linguistic and generally retains whatever rules he has learned even if he subsequently encounters facts that could show alternative rules to be superior in some respect. I conjecture that a child will rarely alter already learned rules that work (in the sense of not only specifying a relationship among meanings, contexts, and surface forms that is adequate for his purposes but also allowing him to produce and interpret speech—and writing— rapidly and accurately enough for his purposes) merely in order to shorten his grammar or increase the generality of his rules. I accordingly expect there to be huge amounts of individual variation in speakers' internalized grammars, most of which does not show up in what is normally regarded as "linguistic data." To determine the details of different speakers' linguistic competence, one must do some cognitive psychology and not merely declare by fiat that one's linguistics is to count as cognitive psychology. The relevant cognitive psychology is not exclusively cognitive psychology of language, since there is a division of labor between general purpose facilities and specifically linguistic facilities in both the acquisiton and the use of language. Chomsky's well-known arguments that language acquisition cannot be accomplished purely by general purpose learning faculties should not lead one to the non sequitur of concluding that general purpose learning mechanisms play no role in language acquisition: General purpose learning faculties clearly exist [as shown by the possibility of acquiring the esoteric perceptual skills discussed in Gibson (1969, Chapter 1)], and it is absurd to suppose that they shut off while language is being acquired.

Following Chomsky (1965), transformational grammarians have generally adopted the deplorable terminological practice of applying the term "theory of language acquisition" not to an account of HOW language IS learned but to what is at best an account of WHAT the child HAS learned by the end of his childhood:That is, the "language acquisition device" of Chomsky's language acquisition scheme, is merely a device that selects, on the basis of an "evaluation measure," the "optimal" grammar conforming to a given set of "primary linguistic data." [14] The scheme implies nothing about developmental stages, since the grammar is to be chosen on the basis of a set of data alone, without reference to what the

[14] My reference to a community of transformational grammarians should be understood in sociological terms: Whether one belongs to that community relates not to whether one practices or accepts transformational grammar in any technical sense, but to what meetings one goes to, whose papers one reads, *etc*. In this sociological sense, for example, Michael Brame, who rejects transformations entirely, is a transformational grammarian.

child has already learned on the basis of previously available data. One of the principal virtues that I see in the approach to syntax sketched in Section 2 of this article is that it allows the construction of a plausible scenario for language acquisition. The various factors involved in syntactic category notions can be learned independently of one another (e.g., one can learn that *love* is logically a two-place predicate independently of learning that it is a verb rather than a noun or adjective). Gross combinatorics is learned in terms of surface structure and in terms of these category notions, and thus as soon as the child has learned any category information about any items that he can identify, he is in a position to learn some rules of gross combinatorics by the simple expedient of setting up a rule for each configuration for which he has (albeit partial) knowledge of the categories of the constituents. Rules of gross combinatorics, once learned, are then exploited in the parsing and acquisition of combinations not currently covered by the child's grammar. For example, the configuration $[V\ VP]_{VP}$, once it has been learned through examples such as *wants to eat* and *tried to run,* can be utilized in assigning a surface constituent structure to clauses involving auxiliary verbs, so that *be washing dishes* will be interpreted as a VP, since it consists of a V followed by a VP, as will *has been washing dishes.* Note that under this scenario, the child will acquire a specific analysis of auxiliary verbs without necessarily having yet acquired knowledge of the full set of restrictions on co-occurrence of auxiliary verbs to which adult speech is subject.

As should be clear from my remarks above, I reject entirely the notion of "evaluation measure." The notion has little to recommend it once one rejects the notion of "linguistic data" as the data of linguistics. It originated as a way of avoiding arbitrariness in the choice among analyses whose selection as the candidates for the title of "correct analysis" was itself arbitrary; it served only to replace first-order arbitrariness by second-order arbitrariness (arbitrariness not of the choice but of the criterion on which the choice is made).[15] I further reject the attitude toward notation that has accompanied specific proposals for evaluation measures: the attitude that one can expect to find a notational system whose typographic combinatorics exactly match the combinatorics of the components of rules, *etc.* that it is used to express; see McCawley (1973b) for arguments that such an expectation is unreasonable. I follow a standing policy of creating formalisms ad hoc so as to discourage the reader from attaching significance to details of earlier formalisms that were not put in on purpose. I regard formalization as desirable only as long as the users of the

---

[15] See McCawley (1976c, 1977c, 1979c) for more detailed criticism of Chomsky's notion of "language acquisition device." Chomsky (1975, pp. 120–122) briefly considers ways to revise his notion of language acquisition device so as to accomodate developmental stages, but says nothing concrete.

formalism heed the sagacious advice of H. Dumpty (quoted in Carroll, 1872; p. 214).

Another major methodological point on which I differ with standard transformational grammarians is that I regard variation, both within a speaker and across speakers, as well as across languages, as central to linguistics. Any linguistic analysis carries with it implicit claims as to what the loci of possible variation in language are, for example, Chomsky's analysis of auxiliary verbs suggests that there could in principle be dialects of English in which *have -en* followed *be -ing* and preceded any modal auxiliary, whereas the analysis of McCawley (1971) implies that there could not be such a dialect. Purported explanations of phenomena in a particular language are normally based on hypotheses about language that can and ought to be tested by a cross-linguistic survey. Cole's papers on crossover phenomena (1974a, 1974b) are superb examples of the sort of cross-linguistic testing of claims that ought to be standard procedure; Cole's results are particularly impressive in that the analogical rule that is at the heart of his analysis is in principle untestable in the dialects of English in which it is supposed to apply but gives rise to a cross-linguistic prediction that receives impressive confirmation.

The relationships among the various styles and registers of language that an individual uses (not only in speaking but in comprehending speech and in writing and reading—both women's language and written Japanese are included in the linguistic competence of a male Japanese) have also been scandalously neglected despite obvious cases where linguistic information acquired in one style is transferred to another, as when written forms provide the basis of one's phonological knowledge of a word. A consideration of variation among styles and registers shows a further respect in which a language is not a set of sentences: A set consisting of sentences of all styles lumped together is as irrelevant to the structure of the language as is a set in which the sentences of several historical stages of the language are lumped together; only a person of rare ability could search over the whole gamut of styles and registers in making "grammaticality judgments."

I will conclude this section with some brief remarks on something that is generally regarded as central to discussions of methodology but which I have so far touched on only in passing, namely the testability of the claims made. Obviously, most of the things that I have said above are not empirically falsifiable—you cannot falsify a policy of paying attention to variation in language any more than you can falsify a policy of seeking neurological explanations of psychological facts; the worst that can be said for such a policy is that it has been unproductive, but in that case it is merely discredited, not falsified. The policies do, though, affect my judgments as to what would count as falsification of the claims, or better, as serious problems for the claims: I endorse the critiques by Lakatos (1970), Feyerabend (1975), and Laudan (1976) of "naive falsificationism" and accept instead Laudan's policy of rating the success of alternative approaches in terms of their success in solving problems, discounted by the extent to which they create (and not merely reveal) new problems, with "problems" taken broadly enough as to include not only empirical problems (i.e., conflicts between prediction and observation) but also conceptual problems. Duhem (1954, pp. 183–190) noted that any prediction rests on the conjunction of a large number of explicit and tacit assumptions and that if the prediction turns out false, the blame for its failure cannot definitely be assigned to one particular assumption. Accordingly, one can maintain any proposition to which one is particularly attached, but at a price: by rejecting other conjuncts that, combined with the favored proposition(s), lead to false predictions. A proposition is falsified for a particular scholar when the price of accepting it becomes more than he is willing to pay. This means that different propositions will be falsified for different scholars, since different scholars will not be willing to pay the same prices. With Feyerabend, I regard it as an excellent thing that scholars do not agree as to what is falsified; such disagreement provides insurance against scholarly communities walking en masse down a blind alley.

I thus present the following examples of hypothetical languages as possible falsifications of my claims, in the sense that they would force me to pay disconcertingly high prices in order to continue to maintain those claims.

1. A language just like English except that a modal auxiliary verb was at the end rather than the beginning of a VP (reason: the difference between modals and other verbs does not involve any of the factors that I regard as being the basis of syntactic category notions, and the special behavior of modals in the hypothetical language would not follow from any morphological property of modals).
2. A language just like English except that nonrestrictive relative clauses precede restrictive clauses [reason: restrictive clauses are logically conjuncts to a clause with a predicate noun, e.g., *linguist who owns a cat* corresponds to a constituent (*x* linguist and *x* own a cat) of logical structure, and restrictive clauses are formed by adjoining the other conjunct to the predicate noun, yielding an $[\bar{N}\ S]_{\bar{N}}$ configuration; nonrestrictive clauses, on the other hand, are adjuncts of NPs rather than of $\bar{N}$s; see McCawley (1978a, 1978b) for further details].
3. A language just like English except that passive *be* preceded *have*

and progressive *be* (see discussion in Section 2; this prediction rests on the assumption that each semantically nonempty auxiliary verb corresponds to a different S of logical structure and thus to a different cyclic domain).

4. SAMPLE ANALYSIS

Since I have nothing nonobvious to say about most of the sentences that the conference speakers were asked to analyze, I will confine my remarks to details of three of those sentences First, the passive sentence *The duckling was killed by the farmer.* Ignoring the difference in topic, about which I have nothing cogent to say, I treat this as having the same logical structure as the corresponding active sentence. As I indicated in Section 2, I formulate rules in structural terms except to the limited extent that left-to-right order is relevant, and leave unspecified those details of the effect of the rule that are predictable from surface combinatoric constraints. I thus offer the following tentative Passive rule:[16]

(6)   1(S) directly dominates 2(NP), 3(VP)
        3 dominates 4(NP) with no intervening VP node
        Adjoin *by* to 2 and adjoin result to 3
        Insert *be*
        Make 4 daughter of 1

The result of adjoining *by* to 2 is a PP: *by* is a preposition, 2 is a NP, and anything consisting of a preposition and a NP is a PP; *by* goes at the left of 2 since that is the only place where English gross combinatorics allows prepositions to be in relation to their NPs; the result is adjoined at the right end of the VP since that is the only end at which English allows PPs; and *be* is Chomsky-adjoined to the left of the VP since it is a V and the only admissible surface configuration in which it could combine with the

---

[16] Note that neither the "structural description" (first two lines) nor the structural change (next three lines) of (6) says anything about left-to-right order. One important detail of standard formulations of Passivization that is not built into (6) is a restriction that 4 be the FIRST NP in 3. I have not indicated what determines which NP is to become the derived subject, since I am not sure to what I should attribute the oddity of such examples as *John was given a book to.* I do not reject out of hand an extra condition "4 is the leftmost NP in 3," though I am attracted by Lakoff's (1977) suggestion that that condition has the status of a strategy for extending the applicability of a basically relational Passivization rule (i.e., for Lakoff the rule basically says "Direct Object becomes Subject" and is extended to any NP that is first in its VP, since that position is where a direct object typically occurs). See also Davison (1980) for a promising approach in which an accessibility hierarchy determines priority for becoming derived subject.

other material is [V VP]$_{VP}$. The S to which these operations apply is tenseless and a constituent of a larger S that provides the past tense; the *be* is adjoined to the tense by a rule (McCawley 1971, note 1) that also affects a *have* or a modal auxiliary that is one level below a tense, yielding the familar Tense + Modal/*have*/*be* conbination that acts as a unit throughout English syntax. One qualification to this last remark: In view of Akmajian and Wasow's (1975) demonstration that Affix Hopping for tenses operates under different conditions than the process that attaches -*en* and -*ing* to their verbs, there is no reason to suppose that the "Tense + Modal/*have*/*be* combination" ever has the tense preceding the Modal, *have*, or *be*: The tense could immediately assume its morphologically determined suffixal position as soon as the verb as adjoined to it, without any application of an Affix Hopping rule.

Having nothing to say about instrument subjects that the reader will find any more enlightening than this confession and having no inclination to say anything more about *kill* than to refer the reader to McCawley (1973c, 1977b), I turn to the remaining item of interest in the organizers' Sentence 14, the relative clause. In McCawley (1978a, 1978b), I have argued that the logical structure of a sentence like (7a) is (7b):

(7) a. *The duckling that John loves is fat*
     b. (*the: x duckling and John love x*) (*x fat*)

Restrictive relative clause formation is basically an adjunction of one of two conjuncts to a predicate noun in the other conjunct. The quantifier + S combination is substituted for an occurrence of the bound variable in the matrix S, the subject variable of the N̄ + S combination is deleted, and (with insertion of copula *be* and the usual operations on tense) the surface structure (8) results:

(8)

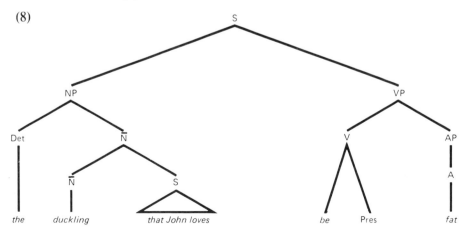

Finally, in (9a), a variant of the organizers' Sentence 11, *a farmer* can be interpreted as logically either inside (9c) or outside (9b) the scope of *believe*:

(9) a. *A farmer is believed to have killed the duckling*
     b. (∃: *farmer x*) (△ *believes* (*x killed the duckling*))
     c. △ *believes* ((∃: *farmer x*) (*x killed the duckling*))

This shows that scope reflects not only surface position but also position prior to application of Raising and Passive (i.e., (9a) has an interpretation corresponding to the role of *a farmer* as subject of the complement of *believe*). Interestingly, an interpretation with *a farmer* in the scope of *believe* and *expect* is not possible in (10a) despite the fact that such an interpretation is possible in (10b):

(10) a. *A farmer is believed to have killed the duckling and is expected to be lynched*
      b. *A farmer is believed to have killed the duckling and a farmer is expected to be lynched*

An explanation for this: Conjunction Reduction requires full identity of the shared items; in the narrow scope interpretation, the two occurrences of *a farmer* in (10b) bind different variables and thus are nonidentical, and thus Conjunction Reduction could not apply to yield (10a);[17] hence, the only derivation of (10a) will be one in which *a farmer* originates outside a structure containing two occurrences of the variable that it binds, as in (11a); after Raising and Passive in both conjuncts, Conjunction Reduction applies to yield the intermediate stage (11b):

(11) a. (*a: x farmer*) (△ *believe* (*x killed the duckling*) *and* △ *expect* (△ *lynch x*))
      b. (*a: x farmer*) (*x* (*be believed to have killed the duckling and be expected to be lynched*))

Thus (10a) can have only a wide scope interpretation for *a farmer*.

5. SELECTED COMPARISONS WITH OTHER APPROACHES

I conclude this article with an evaluation of some real and potential differences between my approach and others represented at the Milwaukee conference. I make no attempt at comprehensiveness here.

---

[17] See Sag (1976) for a more precise statement of the relevant notion of identity.

1. While I have not discussed any phenomena above in terms of grammatical relations, I in fact am reasonably convinced that much syntax works in relational terms. I leave open the possibility that logical structures are relational, for example, that the distinction among the arguments of two- and three-place predicates is basically one of grammatical relation rather than of "abstract" indexing (i.e., first versus second versus third argument). However, even if I adopt a basically relational account of the relationship among stages of a derivation, I still need surface structure gross combinatoric rules, for example, if a change of grammatical relation is marked by adding a preposition to a NP or by adding an auxiliary verb, the resulting PP has to be put in a position where the language allows PPs and the verb must be put in a position where the language allows Vs.
2. While I included "depth to which the head is embedded" (= number of bars in X-bar syntax) as one of the factors that is involved in the conceptual basis of syntactic category notions, I in fact believe that there are fewer category distinctions than that factor allows one to distinguish, that is, that VP and "N̄" can be stacked up ad infinitum, as in the right-branching structure for auxiliary verbs and the structure for restrictive relatives that were discussed above. This reduction in the number of category distinctions allows the first-language learner to exploit already learned syntactic configurations in a way that is not possible in strict x-bar syntax.
3. I have no firm policy as to whether only Ss, or both Ss and NPs, or all constituents are cyclic domains. Any policy on this question would affect whether the approach is compatible with Montague grammar, in which all constituents, in effect, are cyclic domains. Compatibility with Montague grammar also depends on fine details of the interpretation of Montague grammarians' "well-formedness condition," the requirement that all derivational stages be well-formed surface instances of their syntactic category. Well formed as what? A whole utterance? A surface constituent of an utterance? Can a partially specified structure (e.g., a pronoun that is unspecified for person and number, or a tree that is unspecified for linear order of constituents) meet this condition, or are only fully specified structures allowed? If the condition is weakened to a requirement that all cyclic outputs agree with surface constituents in those respects in which they are specified, a high degree of compatibility is possible, otherwise no.[18]

---

[18] See McCawley (1977b, 1979d) for further elaboration of the points raised in this paragraph.

4. Like stratificational grammar, my approach involves "tactic rules" for at least a couple of distinct levels. However, the conceptions of how the different levels are related appear to be considerably different.

5. I share daughter dependency grammarians' willingness to accept more highly structured objects as syntactic structures than transformational grammarians have, for example, objects involving discontinuous structure or multiple mothers for nodes. However, I regard the claim that DDG allows one to dispense with transformations as unsupported, in view of the failure of daughter dependency grammarians so far to provide any account of the relationship of daughter-dependence surface structure to semantic structure. The existing claims of DDG are compatible with a "generative semantic" variant of DDG, in which semantic structure and surface structure are both daughter-dependency structures and are linked by a "derivation," with the rules for the relationships among the stages of that derivation stated in daughter dependency rather than immediate constituent structure terms.

REFERENCES

Akmajian, A., and Wasow, T. (1975). The constituent structure of VP and Aux and the position of the verb *be*. *Linguistic Analysis, 1,* 205–245.

Anderson, S. R. (1976). Concerning the notion 'base component of a transformational grammar.' In J. D. McCawley (Ed.), *Syntax and Semantics, 7: Notes from the Linguistic Underground.* New York: Academic Press. Pp. 113–128.

Bach, E. (1970). Is Amharic an SOV language? *Journal of Ethiopian Studies, 8,* 9–20.

Binnick, R. I. (1971). *Bring* and *come. Linguistic Inquiry, 2,* 260–265.

Carroll, L. (1872). *Through the Looking-glass.* Page reference to reprint in *The complete works of Lewis Carroll.* New York: Modern Library, 1936.

Chomsky, N. A. (1965). *Aspects of the theory of syntax.* Cambridge, Mass: MIT Press.

Chomsky, N. A. (1975). *Reflections on Language.* New York: Pantheon.

Cole, P. (1974a). Backward pronominalization and analogy. *Linguistic Inquiry, 5,* 425–443.

Cole, P. (1974b). Indefiniteness and anaphoricity. *Language, 50,* 665–674.

Davison, A. (1980). Peculiar passives. *Language, 56,* 42–66.

Duhem, P. (1954). *Aim and structure of physical theory.* New York: Atheneum.

Emonds, J. (1970). Root and structure-preserving transformations. Doctoral thesis, MIT, Cambridge, Mass. [Published with substantial revisions as Emonds, 1976.]

Emonds, J. (1976). *A Transformational Approach to English Syntax.* New York: Academic Press.

Feyerabend, P. (1975). *Against Method.* London: New Left Books.

Gibson, E. (1969). *Principles of Perceptual Learning and Development.* Englewood Cliffs, New Jersey: Prentice-Hall, Inc.

Heringer, J. (1976). Idioms and lexicalization in English. In M. Shibatani (Ed.), *Syntax and*

Semantics, 6: The Grammar of Causative Constructions. New York: Academic Press, Pp. 205–216.

Jacobson, P., and Neubauer, P. (1976). Rule cyclicity: Evidence from the intervention constraint. *Linguistic Inquiry, 7,* 429–461.

Lakatos, I. (1970). Falsification and the methodology of scientific research programmes. In I. Lakatos and A. Musgrave (Eds.), *Criticism and the Growth of Knowledge.* Cambridge, England: Cambridge University Press, Pp. 91–196.

Lakoff, G. (1977). Linguistic gestalts. *Papers from the Thirteenth Regional Meeting of the Chicago Linguistic Society.* Chicago: Chicago Linguistic Society. Pp. 236–287.

Laudan, L. (1976). *Progress and its problems.* Berkeley and Los Angeles: University of California Press.

Levi, J. N. (1978). *The Syntax and Semantics of Complex Nominals.* New York: Academic Press.

McCawley, J. D. (1970). English as a VSO language. *Language* 46, 286–299. [Reprinted in McCawley 1973, Pp. 210–228.]

McCawley, J. D. (1971). Tense and time reference in English. In C. J. Fillmore and D. T. Langendoen (Eds.), *Studies in linguistic semantics.* New York: Holt, Rinehart, and Winston. Pp. 96–113. [Reprinted in McCawley, 1973, 257–272.]

McCawley, J. D. (1973a). *Grammar and Meaning.* New York: Academic Press.

McCawley, J. D. (1973b). On the role of notation in generative phonology. In M. Gross *et al.* (Eds.), *The formal analysis of natural languages.* The Hague: Mouton. Pp. 51–62. [Reprinted in McCawley, 1979a, 204–216.]

McCawley, J. D. (1973c). Syntactic and logical arguments for semantic structures. In O. Fujimura (Ed.), *Three dimensions of linguistic theory.* Tokyo: TEC. Pp. 259–376.

McCawley, J. D. (1976a). Morphological indeterminacy in underlying syntactic structure. In F. Ingemann (Ed.), *Proceedings of the 1975 Mid-America Linguistics Conference.* Lawrence, Kansas: University of Kansas. Pp. 317–326. [Reprinted in McCawley 1979a, 113–21.]

McCawley, J. D. (1976b). *Syntax and serantics, 7: Notes from the linguistic underground.* New York: Academic Press.

McCawley, J. D. (1976c). Some ideas not to live by. *Die neueren Sprachen 75,* 151–165. [Reprinted in McCawley, 1979a, 234–246.]

McCawley, J. D. (1977a). The non-existence of syntactic categories. In J. P. Wang (ed.), *Proceedings of the 1977 Michigan State Conference on Linguistic Metatheory.* East Lansing: Michigan State University. Pp. 212–232.

McCawley, J. D. (1977b). Evolutionary parallels between Montague grammar and transformational grammar. *Proceedings of the 7th regional conference, Northeastern Linguistic Society.* Cambridge, Mass: Harvard University. Pp. 219–232. [Reprinted in McCawley 1979a, 122–132.]

McCawley, J. D. (1977c). Acquisition models as models of acquisition. In R. W. Fasold and R. W. Shuy (Eds.), *Studies in language variation.* Washington, D.C.: Georgetown University Press. Pp. 51–64.

McCawley, J. D. (1978a). Conversational implicature and the lexicon. In P. Cole (Ed.), *Syntax and semantics 9: Pragmatics.* New York: Academic Press. Pp. 245–259.

McCawley, J. D. (1978b). Restrictive relatives and surface constituent structure. *Proceedings of the 8th regional conference, Northeastern Linguistic Society.* Amherst: University of Massachusetts, Amherst. Pp. 154–166.

McCawley, J. D. (1978c). Relative and relative-like clauses. *Grammarij, 9,* 149–88.

McCawley, J. D. (1979a). *Adverbs, vowels, and other objects of wonder.* Chicago: University of Chicago Press.

McCawley, J. D. (1979b), Language universals in linguistic argumentation. *Studies in the Linguistic Sciences* 8, no., 2, Pp. 205–219.

McCawley, J. D. (1979c). Towards plausibility in theories of language acquisition. Paper read at Sloan Foundation symposium on criteria of adequacy for theories of natural language, Stanford University, Stanford, Calif.

McCawley, J. D. (1979d). Helpful hints to the ordinary working Montague grammarian. In S. Davis and M. Mithun (Eds.), *Linguistics philosophy and Montague Grammar*. Austin: University of Texas Press. Pp. 103–125.

McCawley, J. D. (In press). *Everything that linguists have always wanted to know about logic (but were ashamed to ask)*. Chicago: University of Chicago Press.

Perlmutter, D. M. (1968). Deep and surface structure constraints. Unpublished doctoral thesis, MIT, Cambridge, Mass.

Ross, J. R. (1967). Constraints on variables in syntax. Unpublished doctoral thesis, MIT, Cambridge, Mass.

Sadock, J. M. (1975). *Toward a linguistic theory of speech acts*. New York: Academic Press.

Sag, I. (1976). Deletion and logical form. Unpublished doctoral thesis, MIT, Cambridge, Mass.

RELATIONAL GRAMMAR[1]

DAVID M. PERLMUTTER
University of California, San Diego

1. ON THE GOALS OF LINGUISTIC THEORY

The basic question of linguistic theory can be stated very simply:

(1)   *In what ways do natural languages differ, and in what ways are they all alike?*

A theory that provides a satisfactory answer to (1) will thereby accomplish the goals of linguistic theory that are stated in different ways in the literature.

First, a theory that provides a satisfactory answer to (1) will thereby provide a satisfactory characterization of the notion "natural language" that makes explicit the class of natural languages.

Second, such a theory will provide explanations for data found in individual languages. This is discussed briefly in Section 2.

Third, the grammars that such a theory makes available for the de-

[1] I am indebted to Judith Aissen, Terry Klokeid, Paul Postal, Geoffrey Pullum, and Carol Rosen for critical comments on an earlier draft of this paper. Errors and shortcomings are mine alone.

This work was supported in part by the National Science Foundation through Grant BNS78-17498 to the University of California, San Diego.

195

scription of individual languages will prove to be adequate and insightful grammars of those languages.

At the present stage of development of grammatical theory, no theory can provide an explicit and adequate answer to (1). Various frameworks have been proposed, many of which include elements of a theory. It is important to distinguish between a FRAMEWORK and elements of a THEORY. A framework offers certain concepts for use in the construction of grammars of individual languages and the statement of universals, and claims that this set of concepts, when appropriately refined, augmented by others, etc. will be adequate for the construction of a theory that can provide an adequate answer to (1). Because of the vagueness of the claims involved, it is probably impossible to falsify a framework. Elements of a theory, on the other hand, make falsifiable empirical claims.

2. ON THE NATURE OF EXPLANATION
   IN LINGUISTICS

A theory's ability to explain data in individual languages is directly linked to its claims concerning the entire class of natural languages. A theory provides an explanation of linguistic data in a language when it gives principled reasons why that language manifests the data that it does rather than other conceivable data. In each such case, the explanation rests on the claim that NO language can manifest data of a kind that would make it fall outside the class of languages characterized by the theory. In order to explain the data in individual languages, a theory must make falsifiable empirical claims about the entire class of natural languages.

3. THE BASIC MOTIVATIONS FOR
   RELATIONAL GRAMMAR

3.1. Motivations for Grammatical Relations

The basic claim of relational grammar (RG) is that grammatical relations such as "subject of," "direct object of," "indirect object of," and others are needed to achieve three goals of linguistic theory:

(2) a. to formulate linguistic universals
     b. to characterize the class of grammatical constructions found in natural languages
     c. to construct adequate and insightful grammars of individual languages

The claim that grammatical relations are needed for these three purposes is basically the defining claim of RG. Various different models have been proposed within a general RG framework incorporating (2)—from the derivational model used in Perlmutter and Postal (1974) and adopted in various works, including Chung (1976), Harris (1976), Kimenyi (1979), and some of the papers in Cole and Sadock (1977), and Perlmutter (in press a), to the uninetwork RG model in some of the papers in Perlmutter (in press a), and the arc pair model in Johnson and Postal (in press). However these models may differ, they share the basic claim that grammatical relations are needed for the three purposes in (2). In many ways, this claim has more the character of a framework than a theory. General though it is, however, it still has an empirical basis and thus is subject to falsification.

3.2. Grammatical Relations as Primitives of Linguistic Theory

Another basic claim of RG, dating back to Perlmutter and Postal (1974), is that grammatical relations cannot be defined in terms of other notions such as word order, phrase structure configurations, or case marking. Rather, they must be taken as primitives of linguistic theory. In Perlmutter (to appear a), various specific proposals to define grammatical relations in terms of other notions are argued to be inadequate. For example, Chomsky's (1965) proposal to define grammatical relations in terms of phrase structure configurations is argued to fail to define the following grammatical relations adequately:

(3) a. the subject relation: for languages without a VP-constituent and languages in which subjects are marked with a preposition or postposition
     b. the direct object relation: for languages without a VP-constituent and languages where direct objects do not differ from indirect objects and/or obliques with respect to prepositional or postpositional marking
     c. other relations, such as the indirect object relation and the chômeur relation,[2] for which Chomsky proposed no definitions in terms of phrase structure configurations

Historically, the RG abandonment of transformational grammar (TG) was a direct consequence of TG's failure to provide cross-linguistically viable notions of grammatical relations for the purposes in (2). Transformations, stated in terms of the linear order of constituents, made it nec-

---

[2] The chômeur relation is discussed briefly in Section 7.

essary to formulate distinct rules for languages with different word orders for what could be characterized in relational terms as the same phenomenon cross-linguistically (see Section 6.2 and Perlmutter and Postal, 1977).

4. ON THE NATURE AND REPRESENTATION OF CLAUSE STRUCTURE

Ignoring questions of semantic and phonological representation, as well as many syntactic issues which limitations of space make it impossible to discuss here, minimally three things must be specified in syntactic representations:

(4) a. which elements bear grammatical relations to which other elements
     b. which grammatical relation(s) each element bears to other elements
     c. the level(s) at which each element bears grammatical relations to other elements

To represent this information, the following types of primitive linguistic elements are introduced:

(5) a. a set of nodes representing linguistic elements
     b. a set of R-signs, which are the names of the grammatical relations that elements bear to other elements
     c. a set of coordinates, which are used to indicate the levels at which elements bear grammatical relations to other elements

As described in Perlmutter and Postal (1977, in press b), the fact that a certain linguistic element bears a certain grammatical relation to some other element at a certain level can be given by formal structures representable by either of the following equivalent notations:

(6)   a. b
              $GR_x \downarrow c_i$
                   a
        b. $[GR_x(a, b) \langle c_i \rangle]$

The object in (6) is called an ARC. The interpretation of (6) is that the primitive linguistic element a bears the relation whose name is GR_x to the primitive linguistic element b at the c_i level. Thus, if GR_x is "2," the name of the direct object relation, and c_i is c_1, then the arc in (7) indicates that a bears the 2-relation to b at the first or c_1 level of b.

(7)   a. b
             $2 \downarrow c_1$
             a
       b. $[2(a, b) \langle c_1 \rangle]$

Since arcs can be represented pictorially as arrows, as in (6a) and (7a),
a in these arcs is called the HEAD of the arc, and b the TAIL. The R-signs
"1," "2," "3," and "Cho" are the names of the subject, direct object,
indirect object, and chômeur relations, respectively. A complete account
of clause structure in these terms will have to specify the class of possible
linguistic elements, the class of primitive grammatical relations, the class
of possible linguistic levels, and constraints on the possible combinations
of these elements in relational networks (RNs).

It is now possible to represent the basic elements of clause structure in
these terms. Consider the Passive clause:

(8)   *Sally was criticized by Marcia*

Ignoring such things as verb tense, auxiliary verbs, prepositions, and the
linear order of elements, the structure of (8) can be represented as:

(9)

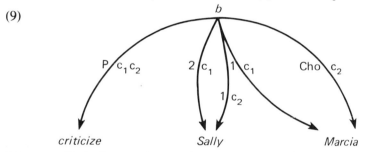

Diagram (9) indicates that (8) has two levels of structure. The fact that
Marcia bears the 1-relation at the first level and the chômeur relation at
the second level is indicated by the fact that *Marcia* heads a 1-arc with
coordinate c_1 and a Cho-arc with coordinate c_2. Similarly, the fact that
Sally bears the 2-relation at the first level and the 1-relation at the second
is indicated by the fact that *Sally* heads a 2-arc with coordinate c_1 and a
1-arc with coordinate c_2. The fact that *criticize* bears the Predicate relation
to b at both the first and second levels is indicated by the fact that *criticize*
heads a P-arc with coordinates $c_1 c_2$.

The notion of linguistic level can now be reconstructed in terms of the
notion of STRATUM. The c_ith or ith stratum of b, where b is a node and
c_i is an arbitrary coordinate, is the set of all arcs with tail b and coordinate
c_i. Thus, the RN in (9) has two strata, the first or c_1 stratum consisting

of the arcs in (10) and the second or c_2 stratum consisting of the arcs in
(11).

(10)

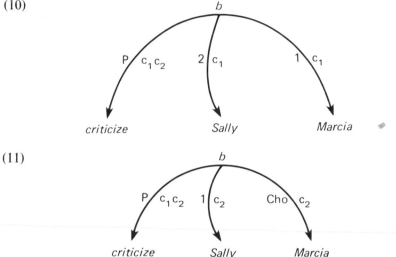

(11)

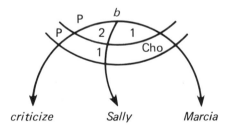

Sometimes it is convenient to represent RNs in the form of *stratal dia-grams* which make the strata stand out more clearly. The stratal diagram
of (9) is given in (12).

(12)

Criticize   Sally   Marcia

In some stratal diagrams, the symbols "$\hat{1}$," "$\hat{2}$," and "$\hat{3}$" are used to
represent the notions "1-chômeur," "2-chômeur," and "3-chômeur,"
respectively. An "n-chômeur" in a stratum c_i is a nominal heading a Cho-arc in the c_i stratum and an n-arc in the stratum immediately before the
first stratum in which it heads a Cho-arc. Thus, in (12) the symbol "Cho"
in the second stratum could be replaced by "$\hat{1}$."

   The representation of clause structure in terms of RNs has an immediate
consequence: Different languages are seen to have the same grammatical
constructions, despite language–particular differences of various kinds.

Thus, as argued in Perlmutter and Postal (1977), RNs of the form of (9)[3] make it possible to capture what is the same in Passive constructions in a variety of different languages, despite language–particular differences in word order, case marking, and verbal morphology. In analogous fashion, it becomes possible to speak in cross-linguistic terms of such constructions as 3–2 Advancement, Benefactive–3 Advancement, Inversion, Antipassive, Clause Union, Possessor Ascension, and other constructions. This approach has two consequences. First, it makes it possible to claim that what at first may appear to be disparate phenomena in various languages are in fact instances of the "same" phenomena, where the sameness can be brought out in terms of grammatical relations. Second, it provides the basis for an eventual characterization of the entire class of grammatical constructions found in natural languages. Work to date has concentrated on the types of constructions found in basic clauses,[4] and even in this domain the class of constructions discovered cannot yet be claimed to be exhaustive, but the bases of an exhaustive characterization of the class of basic clausal constructions have been laid.[5] This is an important step toward achieving (2b).

The representation of clause structure in terms of RNs also brings out an important difference between RG, on the one hand, and both structural grammar and transformational grammar, on the other. The latter two frameworks are alike in taking the syntactic structure of a clause to consist essentially of linear order and dominance relations among elements of the clause. TG differs from structural grammar in positing a level of transformations, with the result that the syntactic structure of a sentence is represented as a sequence of structures called a derivation. Each of the structures in the derivation, however, is a phrase marker representing linear order and dominance relations among elements. In this sense, TG retains structural grammar's conception of the basic nature of clause structure. In positing a rich class of grammatical relations as theoretical primitives and representing clause structure in terms of them, RG proposes a different conception of the nature of clause structure. Despite this different conception of clause structure, it might be thought that the linguistic universals, the characterization of the class of grammatical constructions, and the analyses of particular languages that are proposed in the RG framework can simply be translated into either a structural or a transformational framework. This would be possible only if these frame-

---

[3] More accurately: RNs of the form (14).

[4] On the notion "basic clause," see Perlmutter and Postal (in press b) and Johnson and Postal (in press).

[5] See the brief discussion in Section 6.2.

works possessed the basic relational notions in terms of which these things are stated in RG. But they do not (see Section 3.2). To the extent that RG's basic claim that grammatical relations are needed to achieve the goals in (2) is borne out, the lack of adequate notions of grammatical relations in structural and transformational frameworks is a basic inadequacy of those frameworks.

5. ON THE ORGANIZATION OF SYNTAX

5.1. The Universal Typology of Basic Clausal Constructions and Individual Grammars

Conceiving of grammatical constructions in terms of grammatical relations has led to the discovery that there is a relatively small class of constructions that reappear in languages differing in word order and case marking patterns (see Section 6.2). This has made it possible to conceive of the tasks of linguistic theory and of grammars of individual languages in the following way:

(13) a. Linguistic theory characterizes the set of well-formed RNs for natural languages.
   b. The grammars of individual languages state which subset of the set of RNs characterized by linguistic theory are well-formed in the language in question (see Johnson and Postal, in press).
   c. Rules of grammar are well-formedness conditions on RNs.

Empirical work on a variety of languages provides evidence bearing on the question of which RNs linguistic theory must countenance as possible RNs in natural languages. For example, Perlmutter and Postal (1977, in press c, d) and Perlmutter (1978a, 1978b, to appear d) argue that Passive clauses have subnetworks of the form:

(14)

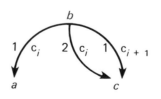

If this characterization of Passive clauses is correct, subnetworks of the form (14) must be characterized as possible RNs for natural languages. Similarly, Harris (1976, in press a, b, c), and Perlmutter (1979, in press b) argue that linguistic theory must countenance subnetworks of the form:

(15)

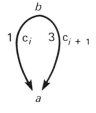

Such subnetworks characterize the Inversion construction, which appears in the following examples:

(16) [Italian]   *A Giorgio piacciono le sinfonie di Beethoven.*
                 'Giorgio likes Beethoven's symphonies.'
(17) [Russian]   *Borisu ne nravjatsja takie ženščiny.*
                 'Boris doesn't like such women.'

In (16)–(17), *Giorgio* and *Borisu* have the markings associated with final 3s (the preposition *a* in Italian and the dative case in Russian) and behave like final 3s in other respects as well, but in other respects they behave like initial 1s. Thus the RNs for these sentences involve subnetworks of the form (15).

In the same way, as work on individual languages verifies the existence of constructions such as Passive, Antipassive, 3–2 Advancement, Inversion, Benefactive–3 Advancement, Possessor Ascension, 2–3 Retreat, and others, and as these constructions are characterized in terms of subnetworks of RNs, more is learned about the class of RNs that linguistic theory must characterize as possible in natural languages. The grammars of individual languages must state which of the various RNs countenanced by linguistic theory are found in the language in question. Thus, grammars must state whether particular languages have Passive, 3–2 Advancement, Inversion, Antipassive, *etc.*

The detailed study of individual languages reveals that a particular construction in a given language may be restricted to a particular mood or aspect, governed by particular predicates or classes of predicates, or possible only in certain syntactic environments. Similarly, a particular construction may be linked in individual languages with semantic, pragmatic, or presuppositional effects, with constraints on definiteness or specificity of reference of nominals, with the organization of the sentence into old and new information, and so on. The general strategy of RG in all such cases is to separate the syntactic nature of a particular construction from the semantic, pragmatic, *etc.*, factors with which it interacts. This goes along with the claim that the syntactic constructions utilized by particular

languages are characterizable in syntactic terms independently of the semantic, pragmatic, discourse, *etc.* conditions under which they will be
used in one language or another. One consequence of this approach is
that it brings out ways that different languages are alike that would not
be apparent otherwise. A particular syntactic construction can be the
same in two languages that use it in very different semantic or pragmatic
contexts.[6] Of course, this does not rule out the possibility that some syntactic constructions (or classes of constructions) may have semantic, pragmatic, discourse, presuppositional, *etc.* correlates not only internal to a
particular language, but even cross-linguistically.

5.2. Types of Terms Figuring in Syntactic Generalizations

Syntactic rules and generalizations refer to notions such as:

(18)   a. the primitive elements in Section 4—constituent nodes, R-
           signs, and coordinates
        b. CLASSES of R-signs, for example, the TERM R-signs ("1,"
           "2," and "3,"), the NUCLEAR TERM R-signs ("1"and "2"),
           the OBJECT R-signs ("2" and "3"), the OBLIQUE R-signs
           ("Inst," "Loc," "Ben," *etc.),* the NONTERM central R-signs
           (all central R-signs other than term R-signs), *etc.* [see Perl-
           mutter and Postal, in press b, especially Figure (13)]
        c. types of elements (e.g., arcs, heads of arcs, tails of arcs) and
           other notions defined in terms of the notions in (18a), e.g.,
           "transitive stratum," "intransitive stratum," (Perlmutter and
           Postal, in press c; Perlmutter, 1978a), the Ergative and Ab-
           solutive relations (Postal, 1977), notions like "initial n," "final
           n" (Perlmutter and Postal, in press b), "working n" (Perlmutter,
           1979), *etc.* (where "n" is a variable over various classes of R-
           signs).[7]

[6] There is thus a sense in which particular syntactic constructions (Passive, Inversion,
etc.) are analogous to phenomena such as reduplication and vowel harmony, which can be
recognized as such cross-linguistically, independently of the uses to which they may be put
in particular languages. Thus, some languages use reduplication to form plurals, some to
form intensives, *etc.,* while vowel harmony may not be correlated with any other phenomena
at all.

[7] For a typology of conditions referring to the 1-relation (i.e., rules and generalizations
stated in terms of the notions "1," "initial 1," "final 1," "acting 1," and "working 1,"
with illustrations from natural languages), see Perlmutter (to appear b). For various rules
and generalizations stated in terms of these notions, see the papers in Perlmutter (in press
a).

Some rules in particular cases (e.g., agreement rules) may have to refer to category membership (e.g., adjective, verb) and to other notions (e.g., animacy, syntactic gender). These are matters for empirical research.

5.3. The Statement of Language-Particular Rules and Generalizations

In addition to stating which of the various basic clausal constructions exist in a particular language (see Section 5.1), grammars must state various language-particular rules and generalizations. In Section 5.3, two examples are used to illustrate how the representation of clause structure in terms of RNs and the notions sketched in Section 5.2 are used for such statements. The relevant phenomena are the necessary condition on antecedents of reflexives in Russian and perfect auxiliary selection in Italian.

Building on Peškovskij (1956) and Klenin (1974), Perlmutter (in press b) formulates a necessary condition on antecedents of reflexives in Russian. It is first shown that nominals heading a 1-arc can serve as antecedents, but nominals heading ONLY a 2-arc or 3-arc are ineligible. Thus, (19) is unambiguous, with the reflexive *sebe* referring only to the 1 (*Boris*) and not to the 3 (*mne*).

(19)   *Boris   mne   rasskazal anekdot o   sebe*
       NOM me/DAT told   joke   about REFL
       'Boris told me a joke about himself/*myself.'

It is also shown that the condition cannot be stated in terms of the linear order of potential antecedents. Further, Passive 1s can antecede reflexives:

(20)   *Rebenok byl otpravlen k svoim   roditeljam.*
       child   was sent   to REFL's parents
       'The child was sent to his parents'.

Passive chômeurs also qualify as antecedents:

(21)   *Èta kniga byla kuplena Borisom dlja sebja.*
       this book was bought INSTR   for REFL
       'This book was bought by Boris for himself'.

Finally, Inversion 3s are possible antecedents:

(22)   *Mne   žal' sebja*
       me/DAT sorry REFL
       'I feel sorry for myself'.

To formulate the necessary condition on antecedents of reflexives in Russian, consider the simplified RNs for these examples:

(23)   [=(19)]

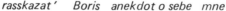

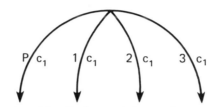

rasskazat'   Boris   anekdot o sebe   mne

(24)   [=(20)]

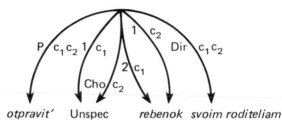

otpravit'   Unspec   rebenok   svoim roditeliam

(25)   [=(21)]

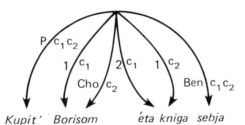

Kupit'   Borisom   éta kniga   sebja

(26)   [=(22)][8]

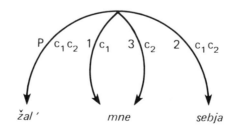

žal'   mne   sebja

---

[8] Diagram (26) is only a PARTIAL RN for (22); portions of it that are not relevant to the present discussion have been omitted. If (26) were the entire RN for (22), it would violate the Final 1 Law (Perlmutter and Postal, in press b).

In each case, the antecedent heads a 1-arc. In (23), it heads *only* a 1-arc. In (24), it heads an initial-stratum 2-arc and a final-stratum 1-arc. In (25), it heads an initial-stratum 1-arc and a final-stratum Cho-arc. In (26), it heads an initial-stratum 1-arc and a final-stratum 3-arc. Thus, the condition can be stated informally as follows:[9]

(27)   *Necessary condition on antecedents of reflexives in Russian:* Only a nominal heading a 1-arc can serve as antecedent of a reflexive.

This condition correctly characterizes the class of nominals that are eligible to serve as antecedents of reflexives in Russian.[10]

The distribution of the perfect auxiliaries *avere* 'have' and *essere* 'be' in Italian also illustrates how RNs, together with hypotheses developed in an RG framework, make it possible to capture a language–particular generalization. This example, given here in much abbreviated and simplified form, is taken from Perlmutter (to appear c).

Some intransitive verbs in Italian use the auxiliary *avere* in perfect tenses, while others use *essere:*

(28)   *Giorgio **ha** lavorato tutta la giornata.*   [*avere*]
          'Giorgio (has) worked all day'.
(29)   *Giorgio **è** arrivato alle cinque.*   [*essere*]
          'Giorgio arrived at five o'clock'.

Transitive clauses use *avere:*

(30)   *Giorgio **ha** comprato un biglietto.*   [*avere*]
          'Giorgio bought a ticket'.
(31)   *Giorgio **ha** ucciso Guido.*   [*avere*]
          'Giorgio killed Guido'.

However, *reflexive* transitive clauses use *essere:*

(32)   *Giorgio si **è** ucciso.*   [*essere*]
          'Giorgio killed himself'.

Essere is also used if the INDIRECT object is reflexive. Thus, (34) contrasts with (30) and (33).

---

[9] Condition (27) is simplified in various ways, including the fact that it makes no reference to the clause membership of either the reflexive or the antecedent. But that is not relevant to the present discussion. The generalization in (27) has important theoretical consequences. These are developed in Perlmutter (1978b, to appear d).

[10] Condition (27) is a necessary but not sufficient condition for successful reflexive–antecedent pairings in Russian (see Perlmutter, in press b for discussion).

(33)   *Giorgio mi **ha** comprato un biglietto.*   [*avere*]
          'Giorgio bought me a ticket'.
(34)   *Giorgio si **è** comprato un biglietto.*   [*essere*]
          'Giorgio bought himself a ticket'.

The distribution of the auxiliaries *avere* and *essere* raises two important questions:

(35)   What determines which intransitives take *avere* and which take *essere?*
(36)   What generalization, if any, unites the distribution of *avere* and *essere* in transitive and intransitive clauses?

Two hypotheses developed in RG provide answers to these questions.

First, according to the Unaccusative Hypothesis (Perlmutter and Postal, in press c; Perlmutter, 1978a), the initial stratum of certain intransitive clauses is "unaccusative," that is, contains a 2-arc but no 1-arc, whereas the initial stratum of other intransitive clauses is "unergative," that is, contains a 1-arc but no 2-arc. In Perlmutter (to appear c), three types of evidence are presented to show that (28) is initially unergative, while (29) is initially unaccusative. Thus, (28) has the simplified RN in (37), while (29) is associated with (38).

(37)

(38)

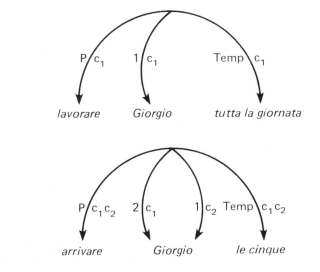

The independent evidence for the contrast between unaccusative and unergative clauses provides an answer to (35).

The second relevant hypothesis is that of multiattachment, that is, that in (at least some) cases of so-called "coreference," there is a nominal heading more than one arc in the initial stratum.[11] Under the Multiattachment Hypothesis, the simplified subnetwork for the initial stratum of (32) is:

(39)

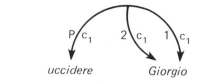

uccidere   Giorgio

Initial stratum (39) contrasts with (40), the initial stratum of (31).

(40)

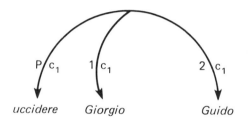

uccidere   Giorgio   Guido

Similarly, the initial stratum[12] of (33), given in (41), contrasts with that of (34), given in (42).

(41)

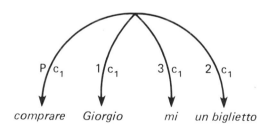

comprare Giorgio   mi un biglietto

---

[11] See the discussion of reflexive impersonal passives in Perlmutter and Postal (in press d), which assumes multiattachment for all cases of so-called "coreference." This assumption is challenged by Rosen (in preparation), who argues that multiattachment is appropriate for only a proper subset of such cases.

[12] The RNs in (41) and (42) make the simplifying assumption that *mi* and *si* in (33) and (34) are reflexes of nominals heading initial-stratum 3-arcs. The other possibility is that they head Ben arcs in the initial stratum and 3-arcs in subsequent strata. Under the second alternative, these sentences would illustrate Benefactive–3 Advancement.

(42)

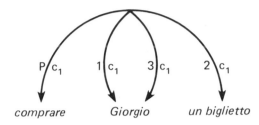

$$P/c_1 \quad 1\,c_1 \quad 3\,c_1 \quad 2\,c_1$$

comprare   Giorgio   un biglietto

Examination of the RNs and subnetworks in (37)–(42) makes it possible to give an informal statement of the condition governing perfect auxiliary selection:[13]

(43)   PERFECT AUXILIARY SELECTION IN ITALIAN: If there is a nominal a heading both a 1-arc with tail b and an object arc (i.e., a 2-arc or 3-arc) with tail b, then clause b requires the auxiliary *essere* in perfect tenses. Otherwise, it requires *avere*.

The Unaccusative Hypothesis, the Multiattachment Hypothesis, and the representation of clause structure in terms of RNs make it possible to state the generalization uniting the distribution of *avere* and *essere* in transitive and intransitive clauses.

5.4. Hierarchy of Grammatical Relations

Since the beginnings of RG as presented in Perlmutter and Postal (1974), the nominal–clausal grammatical relations have been conceived of as organized into the following hierarchy: 1>2>3>Nonterm relations.

5.5. Formalization

In work with David Johnson, Paul Postal undertook to formalize the approach to grammar that he and I had been developing since 1972. The resulting work (Johnson and Postal, in press) contains formalizations of much of what we had developed, but also introduces new notions and goes beyond what we had done in relational grammar in a number of ways. Readers interested in formalization should consult that work.

6. ELEMENTS OF A SUBSTANTIVE THEORY

An approach to syntax is interesting and valuable to the extent that it makes empirical claims about natural language that are validated by em-

[13] See Perlmutter (to appear c) for additional discussion and justification.

pirical research and to the extent that it increases our understanding of the data found in individual languages and of the nature of language in general. The type of structures it posits and the way it conceives of syntactic rules are of no interest unless they lead to significant gains along these dimensions. Since the questionnaire to be followed in preparing papers for this conference stresses the mechanics of each syntactic approach, while the severe length limitation on papers makes it impossible to show in sufficient detail the gains that are achieved, I can do no more here than indicate very briefly what some of these gains are, referring the reader to the relevant literature.

6.1. Laws of Grammar

A number of laws of grammar have been proposed in Perlmutter and Postal (1977, in press a, b, c) which are of interest not only because they make falsifiable claims about language, but also because they are cross-linguistic generalizations stated in terms of grammatical relations. Since many current syntactic frameworks do not possess cross-linguistically viable notions of grammatical relations,[14] the existence of cross-linguistic generalizations stated in terms of these notions provides support for the RG framework over frameworks lacking the necessary concepts.

The basic content of some laws stating such generalizations can be given very informally as follows:[15]

(44)   a. THE 1-ADVANCEMENT EXCLUSIVENESS LAW: A given clause can have at most one advancement to 1.

        b. THE FINAL 1 LAW: Every basic clause must have a 1-arc in the final stratum.

        c. THE NUCLEAR DUMMY LAW: Dummies cannot head arcs with R-signs other than "1" or "2."

        d. THE RELATIONAL SUCCESSION LAW: An ascendee assumes the grammatical relation of the host out of which it ascends.[16]

        e. THE HOST LIMITATION LAW: Only nominals bearing a term relation can serve as hosts of ascensions.

        f. THE STRATAL UNIQUENESS LAW: No more than one nominal can head an arc with a given term R-sign in a given stratum.

---

[14] See the discussion in Section 3 above and in Perlmutter (to appear a).

[15] For statement of the laws and discussion of their empirical predictions, see Perlmutter and Postal (in press a, b, c).

[16] On the notions "ascension," "ascendee," "host," *etc.* see Perlmutter and Postal (in press a).

None of these laws can be stated in frameworks that have not developed cross-linguistically viable notions of grammatical relations. For example, consider the Nuclear Dummy Law, which makes the very strong prediction that dummies will not bear grammatical relations other than 1 or 2 in any language. Frameworks that do not take grammatical relations as primitives have not succeeded in defining them in terms of other notions. They therefore have no cross-linguistically viable notions of 1 and 2 and cannot express the generalization embodied in the Nuclear Dummy Law. Similarly, because of their lack of a cross-linguistically viable 1-relation, such frameworks have no notion of "advancement to 1" and hence cannot state the generalization embodied in the 1–Advancement Exclusiveness Law. The same holds, mutatis mutandis, for the generalizations stated by the other laws in (44).

Some of the laws proposed to date concern the chômeur relation (see Section 7). The Chômeur Law (Perlmutter and Postal, 1977, in press b) stated a condition under which the chômeur relation must hold in all languages, but it now appears to be false (see Section 8 of Perlmutter and Postal, in press b and the Appendix to Perlmutter and Postal, in press c). Two other laws, the Motivated Chômage Law and the Chômeur No-Advancement Law (Perlmutter and Postal, 1977, in press b, d) place strong constraints on the chômeur relation. In so doing they restrict the class of possible grammatical constructions.

Another law is the Oblique Law, which states, in effect, that if a nominal bears a given oblique relation to a clause, it does so in the initial stratum. This restricts the class of revaluations (constructions in which a nominal bears one grammatical relation in one stratum and a distinct grammatical relation in the next) by ruling out revaluations in which the second grammatical relation is an oblique relation.

These laws make falsifiable empirical claims about language, excluding certain otherwise conceivable languages from the class of natural languages. They are essential to explanations of linguistic data, for there is a genuine explanation of why a given language does not manifest certain data only where there is a principle predicting that *no* language will manifest such data. These laws are such principles.

6.2. A Characterization of the Class of Basic Clausal Constructions

One of the basic ideas that launched RG was that conceiving of passivization in terms of grammatical relations (rather than in terms of word order, case marking, or verbal morphology) makes possible a cross-linguistically viable characterization of Passive constructions (see Perlmutter and Postal, 1977). Similarly, it was proposed that 3s in English advance to 2, and then evidence was found supporting 3–2 Advancement in other languages [see Chung (1976) for Indonesian, Allen and Frantz (1978) for Southern Tiwa, and Aissen (in press) for Tzotzil]. In the case of Inversion, Harris (1976, in press a, b, c) and Perlmutter (1979, in press b) have provided evidence for the existence of this construction in Georgian, Italian, Japanese, Kannada, Russian and Udi. It has turned out that when grammatical constructions are conceived of in terms of grammatical relations, the same constructions reappear in language after language, although the languages in question differ with respect to other properties, such as word order and case marking patterns.

This is an interesting empirical result. A priori, any of the following situations would be possible:

(45) a. SITUATION A: Different grammatical constructions are found in different languages. There is no way to conceive of grammatical constructions such that the same constructions reappear in different languages.

   b. SITUATION B: The notion "grammatical construction" is to be identified with the notion "linear arrangement of elements." Languages can be classified typologically according to basic word order type (e.g., SOV, SVO, VSO, VOS). The different grammatical constructions that a given language can have (e.g., Passive) are simply the different deviations from the basic word order that are possible in a given language. Thus, there is one set of possible grammatical constructions in SOV languages, another set in SVO languages, *etc.* Two languages of the same word order type can have the same grammatical constructions, but languages of different word order types cannot.[17]

   c. SITUATION C: The various grammatical constructions in a language are simply the various different patterns it has for marking elements with case, prepositions, or postpositions. There is an important typological division between languages with case desinences and languages without them, and a further typological subdivision among languages of the first type between those with nominative–accusative case systems and

---

[17] An alternative conception of the notion "grammatical construction" in terms of the notion "linear arrangement of elements" would be to consider each order type (SVO, VOS, etc.) a separate construction. This idea, like that in the text, would have to be developed further to take into account constituent types other than V, S, and O. It differs from the proposal in the text in that it would provide a way for languages of different word order types to have the same constructions. Since this is a hypothetical example that has not been developed in any detail, it does not seem relevant to attempt its development here.

those with ergative–absolutive systems. The sets of possible
grammatical constructions in each of these three major linguistic types are disjoint, but the same constructions reappear
in different languages within each type.

d. SITUATION D: The notion "grammatical construction" is to
be conceived of in terms of grammatical relations. There is a
relatively small class of grammatical relations, elements of a
clause can bear different grammatical relations to the clause
node at different linguistic levels, and grammatical constructions can be given universal characterizations in terms of subnetworks of RNs. Thus, the same grammatical constructions
reappear in different languages, despite language–particular
differences in word order patterns, case marking systems, *etc.*

These are only four of the many possible situations that could exist a
priori. Work done to date has yielded evidence in support of the basic
RG claim that Situation D in fact obtains in natural language.[18] This is an
important empirical result.

This result has significant consequences. It makes it possible to characterize in cross-linguistically viable terms the class of basic clausal constructions that are possible in natural languages. With such a characterization, the linguist working on a language has only to discover which of
the universally possible grammatical constructions exist in the language
in question, to find arguments in support of them, and to discover language–particular restrictions concerning the syntactic environments in
which they can occur and the semantic, discourse, pragmatic, or other
conditions associated with them in the language in question.[19]

This makes it possible to achieve the goals of linguistic theory in the
most direct way possible. The class of grammatical constructions characterized by linguistic theory is an essential part of the overall characterization of the notion "natural language" the theory provides. The theory must also specify whatever lawful restrictions there may be on the
combinations of particular constructions in any one language. Any possible combination of the various elements that is not ruled out then constitutes a possible natural language as characterized by the theory.

[18] See the papers in Perlmutter (in press a). Evidence is also available that languages with
ergative case marking systems have the same grammatical constructions as other languages.
For extensive documentation of this claim with respect to the Polynesian languages, see
Chung (1978). For discussions of ergativity, see Dixon (1979), and Klokeid (in press) and
the references cited there.

[19] Of course, work on any language may lead to the discovery of new construction types
not previously known, and hence to revision of the overall typology of grammatical constructions.

The typology of possible grammatical constructions developed to date in an RG framework is sufficiently rich that it is not possible even to give an adequate overview of it here. The reader is referred to the papers in Perlmutter (in press a) for development of some of the main ideas in greater detail. The fact that such a typology becomes possible when grammatical constructions are conceived of in terms of grammatical relations permits a more restrictive overall characterization of the class of natural languages than is possible in frameworks in which the grammatical constructions in different languages are necessarily seen as different. It therefore constitutes support for the overall RG conception of the nature of grammar.

6.3. Substantive Theories of Particular Grammatical Phenomena

There are many grammatical phenomena that have long been noted in traditional grammars but have neither been explained nor even accounted for in a satisfactory and explicit manner. One set of such phenomena is illustrated by the following four sentences of German:

(46)

	Personal	Impersonal
Plain	(47) *Solche Sachen werden nicht oft gesagt.* 'Such things aren't often said'	(49) *Es wurde die ganze Nacht getanzt.* 'It was danced all night'.[20]
Reflexive	(48) *Solche Sachen sagen sich nicht oft.* 'Such things aren't often said'.	(50) *Es tanzt sich gut hier.* 'It is danced well here'.

Sentence (48), with the reflexive pronoun *sich* and the verb in the active voice, illustrates the fact that in many languages, reflexive forms have a "passive use." Sentence (49) illustrates the phenomenon of "impersonal passives," which in many languages can be formed from intransitive verbs. Sentence (50) illustrates the use of reflexive morphology with a verb in the active voice to form a "reflexive impersonal passive." The existence of these four types of passives [arranged in chart form in (46)] raises the question of what each type has in common with each other type and the ways they differ. An adequate theory of grammar must answer this question, making explicit what syntactic structures are associated

---

[20] Since English does not have impersonal passives, I gloss them literally, using the dummy *it,* which is not to be interpreted as referential in the glosses of (49) and (50).

with each type. The basics of such a theory of passives have in fact been worked out in RG. The relevant literature includes Perlmutter and Postal (1977, in press c, d) and Perlmutter (1978a, 1978b, to appear d).

Passive constructions, including impersonal passives and reflexive passives, are only one of the grammatical phenomena for which substantive cross-linguistically valid theories are needed. RG has made strides toward developing substantive theories of a number of phenomena, including causative constructions, ergativity, dummy constructions, so called "pronominal copies," case marking, and verb agreement. Limitations of space preclude further discussion here.

Any syntactic framework with claims to adequacy must develop substantive theories of these phenomena. It is not enough to provide an ad hoc description that works for one language, or for a group of languages with similar word order or case marking patterns, for these phenomena occur in languages that differ along those parameters. Work in RG has shown that substantive cross-linguistically viable theories of these phenomena become possible if they are conceived of in terms of grammatical relations.

7. ONE AREA WHERE RG HAS INCREASED OUR UNDERSTANDING OF NATURAL LANGUAGE

The ultimate test of a linguistic theory is the extent to which it increases our understanding of natural language. This criterion encompasses the answers a theory provides to (1), the substantive claims it makes (such as those sketched in Section 6), and the understanding it provides of the data in individual languages. Limitations of space here make it necessary to restrict discussion to only one concept—that of chômeur—and some ways it has shed light on grammatical phenomena that would otherwise be mysterious. I will cite three examples of a similar nature, the first two drawn from work on Indonesian by Chung (1976), and the third concerning Verb Agreement in Swahili.

Chung shows that direct objects in Indonesian can be relativized in a construction with the complementizer *yang,* as in (52):

(51)   *Ali membawa   surat ini kepada saya.*
        TRANS/bring letter this to   I
        'Ali brought this letter to me'.

(52)   *surat yang Ali bawȧ kepada saya*
        letter that   bring to   I
        'the letter that Ali brought to me'

The general condition is that final 1s and 2s[21] can be relativized in this way in Indonesian. However, there is another grammatical sentence of Indonesian that is synonymous with (51); but in that sentence *surat* cannot be relativized with *yang:*

(53)   *Ali membawakan saya surat ini.*
        'Ali brought me this letter'.
(54)   **surat yang Ali bawakan saya*
        'the letter that Ali brought me'

The contrast between (52) and *(54) needs to be explained.
    Similarly, there are two synonymous passive sentences:

(55)   *Surat ini dibawa   kepada saya oleh Ali.*
        letter this PASS/bring to   I   by
        'This letter was brought to me by Ali'.

(56)   *Saya dibawakan surat ini oleh Ali.*
        I   PASS/bring letter this by
        'I was brought this letter by Ali'.

Again there is a contrast in relativization possibilities; *surat* can be relativized in a *yang*-relative in (57) but not in *(58):

(57)   *surat yang dibawa kepada saya oleh Ali*
        'the letter that was brought to me by Ali'
(58)   **surat yang saya dibawakan oleh Ali*
        'the letter that I was brought by Ali'

These contrasts in relativizability are explained by means of the hypothesis that:

(59)   a. Sentences (53) and (56) involve 3–2 Advancement, with the initial 3 advancing to 2.
        b. In the stratum in which the initial 3 heads a 2-arc, the initial 2 heads a Cho arc.
        c. Only a nominal heading a final-stratum 1-arc or 2-arc can be relativized with *yang* in Indonesian.

Under this hypothesis, (51) is associated with the RN in (60), whereas (53) is associated with the RN given in (61a) and abbreviated as a stratal diagram in (61b).

---

[21] More precisely: nominals heading a final-stratum 1-arc or 2-arc [see (59)].

(60)

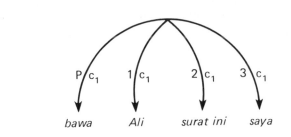

(61)   a.   b.

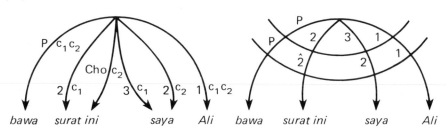

(61) represents the advancement of the 3 to 2 and the chômage of the initial 2 in the final stratum. Since *surat (ini)* does not head a final-stratum 2-arc in (61), the ungrammaticality of *(54) is a consequence of (59c).

Now consider the passives (55) and (56). As Chung shows, these examples would have the RNs that are abbreviated as the following stratal diagrams:[22]

(62)   [= (55)]

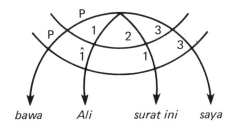

---

[22] Chung presents her results in a derivational framework, but I discuss them here in terms of RNs.

(63)   [=(56)]

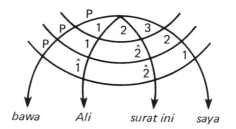

bawa   Ali   surat ini   saya

The crucial difference between them is that in the RN abbreviated as (62), *surat ini* heads a final-stratum 1-arc, while in (63) it heads neither a 1-arc nor a 2-arc in the final stratum. Given (59c), the notion of chômeur explains the contrast in grammaticality between (57) and *(58).

Crucially, as Chung shows, the relevant condition on relativizability cannot be stated in terms of the linear order of elements. A standard transformational approach to problems such as these would be to attempt to reconstruct the notion of "direct object" in terms of linear position, stating the relevant transformations so that they apply to NPs immediately following the verb. While such an approach can account for the nonrelativizability of *surat (ini)* in (53), it cannot account for it in (56), for here *surat (ini)* immediately follows the verb. As Chung argues at length, examples of this type provide strong evidence for handling the relevant phenomena in terms of grammatical relations rather than the linear order of elements.

Indonesian provides a similar argument, both for the notion of chômeur and for treating these phenomena in terms of grammatical relations, based on the fact that the verb of (certain) transitive clauses bears the prefix *meng-*. The arguments are given in Chung (1976), so I will not repeat them here.

A similar argument can be based on the interaction of advancement to 2 and 2–Agreement in data from Swahili cited by Comrie (1976, 286–294). Swahili has the following Verb Agreement rule:[23]

(64)   The verb agrees with the noun class of the nominal heading a final-stratum 2-arc.

---

[23] An adequate statement of the rule would have to be more complex. To account for the fact that it seems to be obligatory in some cases and optional in others, it would be necessary to take into account whether or not the final 2 is in the class designating humans, and perhaps additional factors as well. But that is not relevant to the present argument and so can be ignored here.

The 2-agreement morpheme occupies a slot in the verb complex following the tense morpheme and preceding the stem, as in:

(65)   *Msichana a-li-(u)-fungu-a   mlango.*
        girl   1-PST-2-open-INDC door
        'The girl opened the door'.

Here *-u-* is the 2–agreement marker that agrees with the noun class of *mlango*.

Swahili has sentences in which the initial 3 has advanced to 2:[24]

(66)   *Johni a-li-m-p-a   mkunga zawadi.*
                1-PST-2-give-INDC nurse   present
        'John gave the nurse the present'.

Here the agreement marker *-m-* indicates agreement with *mkunga*, a 2 of the human class. Comrie observes that agreement with the notional 2 is impossible both in (66) and in (67).

(67)   a. *Johni alimpa mkunga.*
                'John gave it to the nurse'.
        b. *Johni alimpa.*
                'John gave it to her'.
        c. *zawadi ambayo Johni alimpa mkunga*
                'the present that John gave to the nurse'

Further, he remarks that *mkunga* passivizes naturally, while *zawadi* does not. Comrie proposes no explanation for examples like (66). In RG, however, the obvious analysis is that (66) has the RN abbreviable as:

(68)

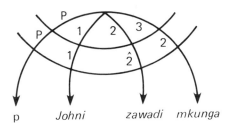

In other words, (66) in Swahili has the same structure as (53) in Indonesian. The reason the verb cannot agree with *zawadi* is that *zawadi* heads a final-stratum Cho-arc, *not* a final-stratum 2-arc, as (64) requires. The

---

[24] As in the discussion of (33–34) in Italian, I make the simplifying assumption that the notional Benefactive is an initial 3.

notion of chômeur thus solves the agreement mystery for these examples from Swahili.

Even more interestingly, Comrie notes that in the passive of (66), NO DIRECT OBJECT AGREEMENT IS POSSIBLE:

(69)   *Mkunga alipewa zawadi na Johni.*
         'The nurse was given the present by John'.

Comrie states that here:

> There is no direct object prefix on the verb, nor any possibility of such a prefix, although our suggested analysis would seem to predict that with the movement of *mkunga* 'nurse' to subject position the original direct object *zawadi* 'present' should take over as closest direct object to the verb. Perhaps one could avoid the dilemma by assuming that a passive verb has no position for object prefixes in its internal structure; or perhaps the analysis suggested here is mistaken [p. 291].

Note that Comrie is basically relying on a notion of direct object which is something like "closest nominal following the verb," or, if his analysis should be interpreted in more relational terms as positing relational notions such as "direct object" in addition to linear position, the relevant notion might be reconstructed as "that one of the several direct objects which follows the verb most closely." Whatever his notion of "direct object," Comrie offers no account of the impossibility of direct object agreement in (69).

The notion Comrie lacks, which is needed to explain the impossibility of 2–Agreement in (69), is that of chômeur. Given (66), (68), and the characterization of Passive clauses proposed in Perlmutter and Postal (1977), (69) has the RN abbreviable as the following stratal diagram:

(70)

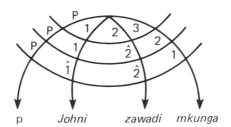

The impossibility of 2-Agreement in (69) now follows from the formulation of 2-Agreement in (64), for in (70) there is no nominal heading a FINAL-STRATUM 2-arc. The crucial notion here is that of chômeur, which provides an explanation of why *zawadi* cannot trigger 2-Agreement in (69).

Thus, the notion of chômeur contributes to an explanation of the impossibility of three phenomena involving the initial 2 of clauses with 3–2

Advancement in Indonesian and Swahili:

(71)   a. Relativization with *yang* in Indonesian
       b. 2-Registration (with *meng-*) in Indonesian
       c. 2-Agreement in Swahili

Further, in all three cases the explanation has the same form: The phenomenon in question is possible for final-stratum 2s, but the initial 2 of 3–2 Advancement clauses is a final-stratum chômeur.

APPENDIX: SAMPLE SENTENCES

In this Appendix, I limit myself to representing those aspects of sentence structure that have been studied in relational terms sufficiently to make it possible to give motivated representations rather than arbitrary ones. The examples for which arbitrary representations would have to be given are discussed briefly at the end.

The RNs below represent basic clause nodes, the elements bearing grammatical relations to those nodes, the relations they bear, and the levels at which they bear those relations (see Section 4 of the paper). In some cases, stratal diagrams are given in addition to simplified RNs. Many aspects of sentence structure that would have to be included in a complete account are ignored below. These include verb tenses, auxiliary verbs, complementizers, the internal structure of nominals, linear precedence, and prepositions.

(1)   *The woman walked*

(3)   *The farmer killed the duckling*

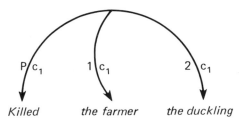

(4)   *The duckling was killed by the farmer*
a.

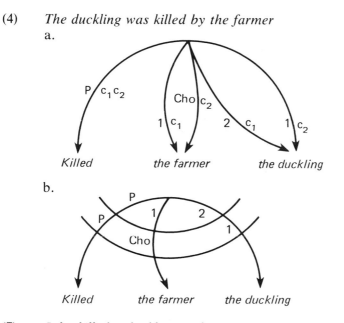

Killed   the farmer   the duckling

b.

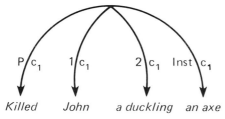

Killed   the farmer   the duckling

(7)   *John killed a duckling with an axe*

Killed   John   a duckling   an axe

(8)   *The woman believed that John killed the farmer*

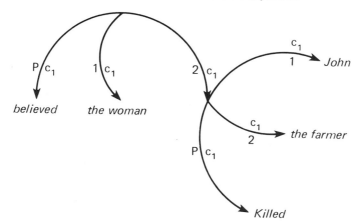

believed   the woman

(9)   *The woman believed John to have killed the farmer*
   a.

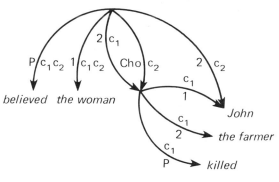

   b.

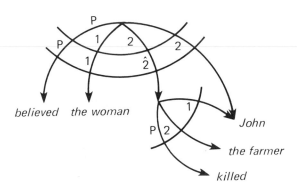

(10)   *The woman believed the farmer to have been killed by John*
   a.

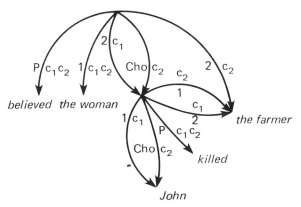

b.

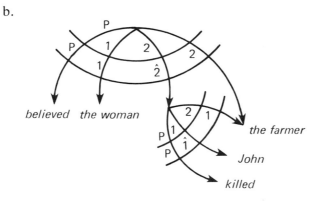

believed   the woman

the farmer

John

killed

(11)   *The farmer was believed by the woman to have been killed by John*

a.

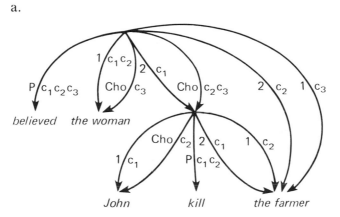

believed   the woman

John   kill   the farmer

b.

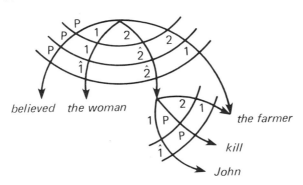

believed   the woman

the farmer

kill

John

(12)   *The farmer gave the axe to John*

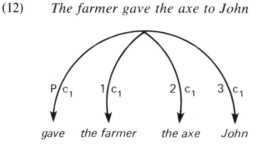

(13)   *The farmer gave John the axe*   [Nonidiomatic reading]
         a.

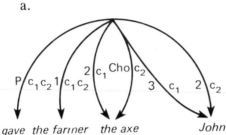

         b.

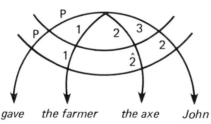

Some comments on the sentences for which RNs are not given above:
Sentence (2) differs from (1) in the presence of the quantifier *every*. I
have nothing nonarbitrary to say about quantifiers at present.

The key point about (5) is the interrogative *who*, which is the final 1
of the clause. If pressed for an analysis of this sentence, I would represent
who as bearing the overlay relation Q' [see Perlmutter and Postal (to
appear b, figure (13)) for a general sketch of the organization of different
types of grammatical relations, including overlay relations]. The issue
that then arises is whether *who* bears the Q' relation to the basic clause
node (call it *b*) to which it bears the 1-relation, or whether it bears the
Q' relation to a distinct node (call it *a*) to which *b* itself would also bear

a relation. The choice between these alternatives could have a bearing on the definitions of other notions such as that of "final stratum."

Sentence (6), like (2), involves a quantifier.

Sentence (14) poses two questions. The first is whether in the initial stratum *the axe* bears the Instrument relation or the 1-relation. If initial grammatical relations are predicted from semantic relations, then *the axe* must bear the Instrument relation in the initial stratum. Since it is a final 1, it is an advancee to 1. Under this analysis, the 1–Advancement Exclusiveness Law (Perlmutter and Postal, to appear c) predicts the impossibility of passivization, and this prediction seems correct: *The duckling that John loved was killed by the axe.*[25] The second issue, linked to the first, is that of whether or not the main clause of (14) has "Unspecified" as initial 1 and final chômeur. Finally, (14) raises the question of how relative clauses are to be represented. This includes a number of distinct issues that it is impossible to shed light on in the space available here.

Examples (15–17) raise the issue of conjunction and some phenomena found in conjoined structures. One can use the relation "Conjunct of" to represent conjoined structures, e.g.,

(14)

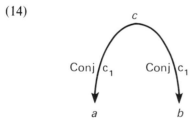

where both a and b are basic clause nodes, and c is consequently a conjoined structure node. Each of these three sentences raises a particular issue about which I have little or nothing to say.

REFERENCES

Aissen, J. (In press). Indirect object advancement in Tzotzil. In D. M. Perlmutter, *Studies in relational grammar*.

Allen, B. J. and Frantz, D. G. (1978). Verb agreement in Southern Tiwa. In *Proceedings of the Fourth Annual Meeting of the Berkeley Linguistics Society*. University of California, Berkeley.

[25] For some speakers this sentence is apparently well-formed. However, it seems that such speakers use the preposition *by* not only to mark Passive chômeurs, but also to mark Instruments, as an alternative to *with* in certain environments.

Chomsky, N. (1965). *Aspects of the theory of syntax*. Cambridge, Mass: MIT Press.

Chung, S. (1976). An object-creating rule in Bahasa Indonesia. *Linguistic Inquiry, 7*, 41–87.

Chung, S. (1978). *Case marking and grammatical relations in Polynesian*. Austin and London: University of Texas Press.

Cole, P. and Sadock, J. (Eds.), (1977). *Syntax and semantics 8: Grammatical relations*. New York: Academic Press.

Comrie, B. (1976). The syntax of causative constructions: Cross-language similarities and divergences. In M. Shibatani (Ed.), *Syntax and semantics 6: The grammar of causative constructions*. New York: Academic Press.

Dixon, R. M. W. (1979). Ergativity. *Language, 55*, 59–138.

Harris, A. C. (1976). Grammatical relations in modern Georgian. Unpublished doctoral dissertation, Harvard University, Cambridge, Mass.

Harris, A. C. (In press a). Case marking, verb agreement, and Inversion in Udi. In D. M. Perlmutter (Ed.), *Studies in relational grammar*.

Harris, A. C. (In press b). Inversion as a rule of universal grammar: Georgian evidence. In D. M. Perlmutter (Ed.), *Studies in relational grammar*.

Harris, A. C. (In press c). *Georgian syntax: A study in relational grammar*. Cambridge: Cambridge University Press.

Johnson, D. E. and Postal, P. M. (In press). *Arc pair grammar*. Princeton: Princeton University Press.

Kimenyi, A. (1979). *A relational grammar of Kinyarwanda*. Berkeley and Los Angeles: University of California Press.

Klenin, E. R. (1974). Russian reflexive pronouns and the semantic roles of noun phrases in sentences. Unpublished doctoral dissertation, Princeton University, Princeton, New Jersey.

Klokeid, T. J. (In press). Revaluation rules and case marking in Pama Nyungan. In D. M. Perlmutter, (Ed.) *Studies in Relational Grammar*.

Perlmutter, D. M. (1978a). Impersonal passives and the unaccusative hypothesis. In *Proceedings of the Fourth Annual Meeting of the Berkeley Linguistics Society*, University of California, Berkeley.

Perlmutter, D. M. (1978b). Empirical evidence distinguishing some current approaches to syntax. Colloquium delivered at the annual meeting of the Linguistic Society of America, Boston.

Perlmutter, D. M. (1979). Working 1s and Inversion in Italian, Japanese, and Quechua. In *Proceedings of the Fifth Annual Meeting of the Berkeley Linguistics Society*, University of California, Berkeley.

Perlmutter, D. M. (Ed.), (In press a). *Studies in relational grammar*.

Perlmutter, D. M. (In press b). Evidence for Inversion in Russian and Kannada. In D. M. Perlmutter, (Ed.), *Studies in relational grammar*.

Perlmutter, D. M. (To appear a). Grammatical relations as primitives of linguistic theory.

Perlmutter, D. M. (To appear b). Syntactic representation, syntactic levels, and the notion of subject. In P. Jacobson and G. Pullum, (Eds.), *The nature of syntactic representation*.

Perlmutter, D. M. (To appear c). Multiattachment and the Unaccusative Hypothesis: Perfect auxiliary selection in Italian.

Perlmutter, D. M. (To appear d). Empirical evidence distinguishing some current approaches to syntax: The subjecthood of passive chômeurs.

Perlmutter, D. M. and Postal, P. M. (1974). Lectures on relational grammar, Summer Linguistic Institute of the LSA, University of Massachusetts, Amherst.

Perlmutter, D. M. and Postal, P. M. (1977). Toward a universal characterization of passivization. In *Proceedings of the Third Annual Meeting of the Berkeley Linguistics Society,* University of California, Berkeley.

Perlmutter, D. M. and Postal, P. M. (In press a). The Relational Succession Law. In D. M. Perlmutter, (Ed.), *Studies in relational grammar.*

Perlmutter, D. M. and Postal P. M. (In press b). Some proposed laws of basic clause structure. In D. M. Perlmutter, (Ed.), *Studies in relational grammar.*

Perlmutter, D. M. and Postal, P. M. (In press c). The 1-Advancement Exclusiveness Law. In D. M. Perlmutter, (Ed.), *Studies in relational grammar.*

Perlmutter, D. M. and Postal, P. M. (In press d). Impersonal passives and some relational laws. In D. M. Perlmutter, (Ed.), *Studies in relational grammar.*

Peškovskij, A. M. (1956). *Russkij sintaksis v naučnom osveščenii.* Gosudarstvennoe Učebno-pedagogičeskoe Izadatel'stvo Ministerstva Prosveščenija RSFSR, Moskva.

Postal, P. M. (1977). Antipassive in French. In *Proceedings of the Seventh Annual Meeting of the North East Linguistics Society,* Harvard University, Cambridge.

Rosen, C. (In preparation). The clause nucleus in Italian: A study in relational grammar. Doctoral dissertation, Harvard University, Cambridge, Mass.

EQUATIONAL RULES AND RULE FUNCTIONS IN SYNTAX[1]

GERALD A. SANDERS
University of Minnesota

1. INTRODUCTION

1.1. Functionality and Functional Analysis in Linguistics

Natural languages are cultural instruments for the systematic association of sounds and meanings for the purpose of effective symbolic communication by the members of human societies. Like other instrumental objects, therefore, languages can be adequately investigated and understood only in terms of their instrumental functions, for it is these that determine the essential properties of instruments and their ranges of possible variation and change. The science of linguistics, which takes natural language as its subject matter, must consequently provide foundations and metalanguages that are adequate for the expression and analysis of facts about the functions of linguistic objects as well as their forms, and about the systematic relationships that hold between the formal structures of languages and their natural functions and functional structures.

The tasks of functional analysis and explanation are exceedingly difficult and complex. Most of our failures in the search for insight and

[1] I am grateful to Ashley Hastings, Edith Moravcsik, and Linda Schwartz for many valuable comments and suggestions.

231

understanding of linguistic phenomena can be directly traced, in fact, either to our frequent oversimplifications of the metatheory and methodology of functional analysis, or to our equally frequent abandonments of the goals and responsibilities of functional analysis altogether. But neither of these evasive courses is legitimately open to us, any more than they would be to the biologist, the anthropologist, the economist, or any other scientific student of physical or cultural instruments. For the problems of functional analysis, difficult though they are, are fundamentally no different in linguistics than in the other biological and social sciences, and certainly no more easily circumvented or ignored. A linguistic theory that failed to take crucial account of the instrumental functions of languages, and of their constituent expressions and constituting rules of grammar, would simply fail to be a real theory about language at all, in fact, in precisely the same sense that a theory referring only to the physical properties of airplanes, or the psychology of airplane users, would fail to be a real theory about airplanes. For it is in the nature of instruments that they are what they are essentially BECAUSE of their functions, and that they have the parts and properties they have largely because of the CONTRIBUTORY functions and functional interactions of these parts and properties relative to the function of the instrument as a whole.

Any potentially adequate framework for productive inquiry and analysis in linguistics must be solidly based, therefore, on an adequate metatheory for functional analysis in general. Such a metatheory must provide an efficient basis for the identification and perspicuous expression of lawlike generalizations about the functions and functional structures of instrumental objects, about the contributory functions of their parts and properties, and about the determining or facilitating relationships that hold between the contextualized functions and functional structures of instruments and their particular forms and formal structures. Any such framework for functional analysis must recognize and take account of a number of crucial conceptual distinctions relating to the central notion of function itself.

In a recent paper, titled "Functional Constraints on Grammars" (1977a), I attempted to isolate some of the most fundamental distinctions of this type, including certain particularly crucial ones that seem to have been most frequently ignored or obscured in past attempts at functional analysis in linguistics. The first of these is the distinction between those characteristics of instruments that are DETERMINED by their functions, those characteristics that are FAVORED, or have positive adaptive values, relative to their functions, and those characteristics that are merely COMPATIBLE with their functions. Form, in fact, is invariably UNDER-determined by function. So, while it is appropriate to SEEK functional explanations for ALL attributes of an instrument, it would be a gross methodological error to expect that every attribute actually HAS such an explanation. Another primary distinction that must be recognized by metatheories for functional analysis is that between the functions of whole instruments and the functions of their constituent parts or properties. Thus, whereas the function of a whole language, or a whole grammar, is to provide an infinite set of socially usable pairings between meanings and expressions, the possible functions of particular constructions or particular rules of grammar will obviously be much more specific than this, and their contributory relationships to the functions of the languages or grammars that include them are frequently quite complex or conspiratorial in nature. Another equally important distinction is that between those characteristics of an instrument that are functionally determined (or functionally favored) for ALL instruments of its type, regardless of any of their other parts or properties, and those characteristics that are determined (or favored) only for certain particular SUBTYPES of the general instrument-type. Thus, for example, while the functional bases for lexical rules or relative clause constructions are the same, and for the same reasons, in all languages, the functional status of passive, or inverse, constructions varies from one type of language to another (Sanders, 1977a), being functionally determined for languages, like Ojibwe, that have both a person-based constraint on clitic ordering and verbal clitics for both subject and nonsubject arguments, while being only functionally favored at most, evidently, for languages, like English, that lack this combination of characteristics.

In addition to such general considerations as these, which are of equal concern to the study of all types of instrumental objects, there are also certain more particular distinctions and methodological prerequisites that are of specific relevance to the investigation and analysis of that particular class of instruments that we call human languages. One of the most fundamental of these is the methodologically crucial distinction between facts about languages and facts about language users. To fail to recognize and observe this distinction is to commit the fallacy of psychologistic reductionism, and to make the more general and even more grossly counterproductive methodological error of confounding FACTS with the particular instruments or means that are used to ESTABLISH them.

Another vital methodological distinction that is of specific relevance to linguistics is the distinction between facts about languages and facts about the GRAMMARS that are used to describe or characterize them. Languages are real things whose existence and particular characteristics are independent of anything that might be said about them. Any factual claim about a language, or about all languages in general, can thus be directly confirmed or disconfirmed on the basis of simple real-world observations alone, independently of the ways in which the claim might be arrived at and the ways in which it might be expressed. Grammars, on the other hand, are HYPOTHETICAL and ARTIFICIAL entities rather than real ones—mere sets of statements, expressible in one way or another according to the conventions of the particular metalanguages employed. Such statements can have no empirical content or significance, moreover, unless they are deductively linked, via explicit principles of inference and interpretation, to explicit, potentially falsifiable observation statements about languages or the linguistic expressions that comprise them.

There is yet another crucial methodological distinction which, though of fundamental importance to all scientific endeavor, is particularly relevant to linguistics. This is the distinction between DESCRIPTIONS and THEORIES on the one hand and METATHEORIES or METALANGUAGES on the other. The importance of these distinctions stems from the fact that each distinct type of scientific instrument has its own distinctive purpose and hence its own distinctive conditions for appropriateness and acceptability. Thus, though there are certain general goals and values shared by all of them—clarity, explicitness, perspicuity, economy of terms, axioms, and axiom-types, *etc.*—the primary and essential desideratum for descriptions is simply accordance with the facts, whereas for theories there is the additional essential requirement that they provide conceptually satisfying answers to some significant set of *why*-questions. Metatheories and metalanguages must meet not only all the conditions for adequacy that are appropriate to the theories and descriptions they generate, but also, in addition, the requirement that they exclude, by principled means, all otherwise possible theories or descriptions that do not meet these conditions. Failure to observe these distinctions, therefore, particularly in all matters concerning the comparison or evaluation of scientific claims and proposals, cannot help but generate counterproductive inquiry and argumentation that could otherwise be avoided.

1.2. The Metalanguage of Equational Grammar: An Overview

The basic hypothesis of equational grammar (Sanders, 1971, 1972) is simply that all nonuniversal, or language-variable, principles of natural language grammar are lawlike assertions of the symbolic equivalence or nonequivalence of two representations of linguistic expressions. Symbolic equivalence is that binary and symmetric relation that holds between the sound and meaning of a word, phrase, clause, or other linguistic expression, as well as between any two representations of its sound or meaning. The hypothesis of equational grammar claims that all of the variable, or functionally underdetermined, characteristics of human languages are due solely to the particular sets of symbolic equivalences that are arbitrarily institutionalized in each such language. It claims, in other words, that the grammars of different languages can differ only in the particular equational rules that they include—that is, in the particular pairs of linguistic representations that are stipulated to be equivalent or nonequivalent—and hence that there can be no differences between languages in the functions or derivational and inferential uses of their rules, or in terms of any other intrinsically nonequational principle or constraint. The equationality hypothesis thus asserts that languages can differ, for example, as to whether "young male human" and *boy* are symbolically equivalent or not, or whether word-final voiced and voiceless obstruents are equivalent or not, but that there can be no differences between languages in the ways in which such generalizations about symbolic equivalence are appropriately used in the derivation of correct consequences or valid proofs of linguistic theorems. The equationality hypothesis thus determines a metalanguage for linguistic description—or, more precisely, a family of related metalanguages—in which all nonuniversal rules or principles of grammar are expressed as simple symmetric statements of equivalence or nonequivalence, and in which all constraints in inference and rule-use are determined by strictly universal principles. The metalanguage of equational grammar thus provides, in a principled and systematic way, a partial differentiation of those characteristics of human languages that are naturally determined by their natural communicative function, and those characteristics that are underdetermined by this function and are thus free to vary arbitrarily, within functionally established limits, from one language to another. The former, according to this metalanguage, includes all principles of inference, function, and functional favorability, and the latter consists wholly of symbolic equivalence relations.

Somewhat more precisely, then, an equational metalanguage for linguistic description and analysis specifies (*a*) that all nonuniversal statements of natural language grammar must be assertions of equivalence or nonequivalence between two linguistic representations; (*b*) that all basic grammatical theorems are assertions of equivalence between a fully interpretable phonetic representation and a fully interpretable semantic representation; and (*c*) that all valid proofs of such theorems are sequences of equations terminating in an identity equation, with all governing principles of inferences being strictly universal. The standard forms and interpretations for all axioms, theorems, and proofs of theorems about natural languages are represented in the following governing schemata of equational grammar:

STATEMENT-TYPES

$A = B$ 'There is a set of one or more linguistic objects, or meaningful expressions, in the given language(s) such that each such object can be appropriately represented both as XAY and as XBY.'

$A \neq B$ 'It is not the case that $A = B$; that is, there is no linguistic object in the language(s) that can be appropriately represented both as XAY and as XBY.'

THEOREM-TYPES

Simple

$A = b$ '(A, B) is well-formed linguistic object; A is a meaning of b; b is a physical expression of A, or the sound of A.'

Compound (sample)

$A = b$; $A = c$ 'b and c are synonymous, or paraphrases.'

$A = b$; $C = b$ 'b is ambiguous.'

(where A and C are terminal (fully interpretable) semantic representations, and b and c are terminal (fully interpretable) phonetic representations, and all distinct variables have nonidentical values.)

PROOF-TYPE

P is a valid proof of the theorem $A = b$ if and only if

1. P is a finite sequence of finite equations such that
2. the first equation is $A = b$;
3. the last equation is either $A = A$ or $b = b$;
4. for each pair of adjacent equations of the form $XAY = Z$, $XBY = Z$, there is a rule, or axiom, either universal or language specific, of the form $A = B$;
5. for any pair of (adjacent or nonadjacent) equations of the forms $XAY = Z$ and $XBY = Z$, there is no rule, or axiom, either universal or language specific, of the form $A \neq B$.

Further explication of this metalanguage, and of its empirical and methodological consequences, will be the primary focus for the remainder of this general study of linguistic metatheory and methodology. The organization of the study follows the standard outline of issues for discussion prepared by the organizers of the Conference on Current Approaches to

Syntax, constituting the Eighth Annual UWM Linguistics Symposium, held at the University of Wisconsin—Milwaukee on March 15–17, 1979. For topics omitted from the present abbreviated version of the paper or only sketchily treated here, see the more extensive preliminary version, distributed prior to the symposium and reprinted also in *Minnesota Papers in Linguistics and Philosophy of Language* 6 (1979).

2. THE GOAL OF SYNTAX

2.1. Data

a. PRIMARY DATA

The primary data for syntactic analysis are facts about the sounds, meanings, and sound–meaning associations of the words, phrases, sentences, and discourses of actual human languages.

These facts, like all other facts about languages, are discovered and verified primarily through direct observation of communicative uses of languages by their native speakers, either actual, via texts and recordings, or hypothetical, via the elicited or self-elicited thought-experiments of skilled informants. It is conceptually and methodologically essential, of course, that all such linguistic facts be sharply distinguished from the various particular facts about texts or about the behavior of language users that serve to establish the linguistic facts themselves. To fail to make this distinction would be like failing to distinguish rocks from the scales or scale-readings used to determine their weight. In fact, languages and the behavior of language users have no properties or principles in common at all, and differ even in their fundamental manners of existence—languages being objects rather than events, and having cultural values and dimensions rather than physical or psychological ones. (For further discussion, see the papers by Dretske and by Sanders in Cohen, 1974.)

b. DOMAIN

The most natural domain for grammatical description and analysis consists of the discourses of all natural languages. In fact, on the basis of general empirical criteria for the identification of productive and conceptually valuable divisions of scientific labor, it has been shown (Sanders, 1970a) that there cannot be any natural, or empirically significant, domains for scientific inquiry comprised only of single languages-types, (like English or Sino-Tibetan or the class of postpositional languages), or of single aspects of linguistic structure (like phonology or syntax), or of single types or sizes of linguistic expressions (like words or phrases or sentences). For purposes of simple description, though, as opposed to analysis or theory-construction, it is often reasonable and of considerable practical convenience to deal with one language at a time, or to treat one mode of linguistic structure, or even one type of expression, independently of all others. What would be methodologically illegitimate, of course, would be to view these artificially limited descriptions of particular languages or language-parts as if they were descriptions of language itself, or, even worse, as if they were explanatory hypotheses or theories about the things that they simply describe or enumerate. To tell why a language has a particular characteristic—for example, to tell why English has agentless passives or extraposed relatives or no gender agreement between subjects and verbs—one cannot appeal to any grammar of English, obviously, or to particular rules of English grammar, since it is precisely the nature of this grammar and its inclusion of these particular rules that are to be explained. There are only two types of explanation that are generally available at all here, in fact: either a HISTORICAL explanation, which would show that the characteristics in question could have been naturally inherited from the language's direct antecedents; or a FUNCTIONAL one, which would show that the given characteristics have necessary or useful contributory functions relative to the natural communicative function of the language as a whole. But to achieve any nontrivial results along either of these lines of analysis, it is clearly necessary to make essential use of at least some true linguistic LAWS, either about language change or about language functioning—that is, empirical generalizations quantified over the set of ALL LANGUAGES. In other words, even if one were concerned with only one language in the universe, significant understanding could nonetheless be achieved only in a domain of inquiry and theory-construction that embraced all languages.

c. VARIABILITY

The range of possible variability in the set of human languages is predictively limited by the equationality hypothesis itself to only such differences as are due solely to differences between possible sets of symbolic equivalences. Languages, dialects, and idiolects are predicted to differ, in other words, only in the particular equational rules of grammar that they have, and not in the ways in which their rules are used, either for making ordinary inferences about linguistic objects, or in the construction or recognition of formal derivations, or proofs of theorems, about them. This contrasts sharply, of course, with the predictions about language variability generated by the standard metalanguages of transformational grammar (Chomsky, 1957, 1965, 1972) and their various nonequational variations, in which grammars can differ not only in the particular representational equivalences they specify, but also in the particular inferential uses of such equivalences that are permitted—that is, in the particular directed substitutions, or derivational transformations, that are allowed, in the optionality or obligatoriness of such substitutions, and in the specified order of application or use of particular substitutions in the construction or recognition of well-formed linguistic derivations or proofs. Since such constraints on the inferential use of grammatical rules cannot possibly be expressed as assertions of either equivalence or nonequivalence between linguistic representations, the hypothesis of equational grammar generates a much more restricted and more homogeneous metalanguage for grammar than that generated by the contrary or contradictory hypothesis of nonequational grammar, thereby predicting that all functions and functional interactions of grammatical rules are determined by strictly universal principles. All relevant observations and tests thus far (see Sanders, 1972, 1976, 1977) indicate that this prediction is correct.

2.2. Empirical Interpretation

With respect to individual languages, there is a simple uniform empirical interpretation for all statements in the metalanguage of equational grammar. Thus every such statement—whether primitive theorem or axiom— is interpreted as asserting with respect to some given pair of linguistic representations A and B either that A and B are possible representations of the same linguistic object (if the statement is of the form $A = B$), or that they are not possible representations of the same linguistic object (if the statement is of the form $A \neq B$). Every statement in an equational grammar of a language thus generates an explicit empirical claim about the actual symbolic equivalence relations that hold in that language.

With respect to linguistics, though, as opposed to the study of individual languages, it is the empirical interpretation of the equationality hypothesis itself, clearly, which is of primary interest and significance, For this hypothesis imposes servere limits not only on the set of possible grammars of human languages but on the set of possible languages themselves. It thereby generates certain direct and directly testable empirical claims about the nature of natural language and its range of potential variation and change.

Every linguistic metatheory or metalanguage imposes some limits on the class of possible grammars. All such limitations have the practical virtue of reducing the number and variety of nonsignificant stylistic variations in grammatical descriptions, with consequent gains in the understandability, explicitness, and comparability of all such descriptions. On such grounds of practical utility, of course, a metalanguage that generates a smaller and more homogeneous class of possible grammars will always be superior to any otherwise equivalent metalanguage that generates a larger or more heterogeneous set. The metalanguage of equational grammar is thus clearly superior on these grounds to any of the various metalanguages of transformational grammar (e.g., Chomsky, 1957, 1965, 1972; Lakoff, 1971), since the latter generate sets of possible grammars that are $2^n \times 2!$ times larger than the set generated by an equational metalanguage, where n is the number of possible distinct pairs of finite linguistic representations (Sanders, 1971, 1979).

But though grammar-delimitation has obvious practical values, it has no EMPIRICAL significance in itself, or course, since it is LANGUAGES and not grammars that constitute the empirical subject matter of linguistics. For a metatheoretical restriction on grammars to have any empirical import at all, in fact, it is necessary that the given limitation on the set of possible grammars have as a deductive consequence some determinable limitation on the set of possible LANGUAGES. Most metatheoretical hypotheses in linguistics fail to meet this necessary condition for empirical significance. For example, the basic metalanguage of transformational grammar (Chomsky, 1965), though it imposes numerous and often quite specific constraints on the forms and even the content of grammars, fails to impose any limits whatever on the class of possible languages that can be generated by the possible grammars that it generates. The same appears to be the case also for all other varieties of transformational grammar, as well as for the metalanguages of tagmemics (Pike, 1967), stratificational grammar (Lamb, 1966), and most other models or types of grammatical analysis that I know of.

The metalanguage of equational grammar, on the other hand, does appear to have at least one set of significant empirical implications concerning the set of all human languages. Thus by restricting all individual grammars to sets of statements asserting the strictly symmetrical relations of equivalence or nonequivalence between representations, the equationality hypothesis necessarily presupposes that, whatever constraints there may be on the appropriate directed use of grammatical rules, these constraints must be determined by strictly universal principles of grammatical inference and function. It follows, therefore, that, since GRAMMARS cannot differ in the directed uses of their rules, there can be no differences between LANGUAGES that can be characterized only by the assumption of such differences in rule application. Thus, for example, since [OBSTRUENT, VOICED, X] \$ $\rightarrow$ [OBSTRUENT, $\varnothing$, X] \$ is the appropriate phonetically directed use of the German rule of grammar [OBSTRUENT, VOICED, X] \$ = [OBSTRUENT, $\varnothing$, X] \$, it follows from the equationality hypothesis that there can be no language that has a grammar for which [OBSTRUENT, Ø, X] \$ → [OBSTRUENT, VOICED, X] \$ is an appropriate phonetically directed use. It follows in turn, then, that since there are natural languages like German in which there is a morphophonemic alternation between voiced obstruents in non-syllable-final position and corresponding voiceless obstruents in syllable-final position, there can be no possible natural language with an alternation between voiceless obstruents in non-syllable-final position and voiced obstruents in syllable-final position. This is a direct consequence of the equationality hypothesis, therefore, that constitutes an explicit and directly testable empirical claim about the set of all natural languages. This claim does not follow, moreover, from either the contrary or the contradictory of this hypothesis. The evident correctness of this claim thus provides FACTUAL support for the equationality hypothesis itself.

Similar empirical claims about natural language—which seem similarly correct thus far—are generated by the equationality hypothesis with respect to all possible cases of potential inverse transformations or directed rule uses and all the potentially inverse processes or alternations they could determine. Thus, for example, the hypothesis predicts that there are no languages that have subject–verb DISagreement under the same circumstances that other languages have agreement. It similarly predicts that since there are languages in which the arguments of semantically subordinate predicates occur as subjects of semantically superordinate predicates (as in the English sentences *John is easy to please* or *Her assertions were believed to be false),* there can be no possible human language in which arguments of superordinate predicates occur as subjects of subordinate ones (as in the hypothetical Counter-English sentence *It is known that the boys drink John* with the meaning "The boys know that John drinks"). It is such predictions as these that constitute the primary empirical interpretation of the hypothesis of equational grammar itself, and, to the extent that they are correct, the primary basis for rejecting all grammatical metatheories or metalanguages that are inconsistent with this hypothesis.

3. THE ORGANIZATION OF SYNTAX

3.1. Levels of Syntactic Representation

In the metalanguage of equational grammar every linguistic expression has a TERMINAL SEMANTIC REPRESENTATION, consisting solely of property elements interpreted into nonnull observation statements about meanings and possible instances of the semantically interpreted relational element for commutative grouping, or co-constituency, and a TERMINAL PHONETIC REPRESENTATION, consisting solely of property elements interpretable into nonnull observation statements about sounds or articulations and instances of the phonetically interpretable relational element for linear ordering, or temporal successivity. In addition to these two empirically interpretable types of representation, every multimorphemic expression will also have a distinct (superficial) SYNTACTIC REPRESENTATION, a string of elements in which all morphemes and multimorphemic constituents are ordered rather than grouped and which is otherwise free of phonetically interpretable elements. These are the only types of linguistic representations that can be defined on the basis of their purely formal or substantive properties alone, independently of any grammars, grammatical rules, or derivational applications of such rules. Given a particular grammar, though, there are certain other distinctions in representation-type that could also be explicitly defined. It would be possible to differentiate, for example, between FULLY SPECIFIED SEMANTIC REPRESENTATIONS and REDUNDANCY-FREE SEMANTIC REPRESENTATIONS, where for every rule of the form $(A) = (A, B)$, where A and B are semantically interpretable elements, a fully specified representation will include (A, B) where its corresponding redundancy-free representation will include only A. A comparable distinction can be similarly drawn between FULLY SPECIFIED PHONETIC REPRESENTATIONS and DISTINCTIVE, or REDUNDANCY-FREE, PHONETIC REPRESENTATIONS. It is also possible to identify a distinct representation-type that could be called (UNDERLYING) PHONOLOGICAL REPRESENTATION, which is that representation of a linguistic object that is derivable by the application of all applicable lexical rules of a grammar to its (superficial) syntactic representation.

Given an adequate equational grammar of a language, every expression in the language can be assigned determinate representations of each of these various types, where each such representation is deductively linked in symbolic equivalence with all of the others, demonstrable by permissible substitutions justified by the rules of that grammar and the principles of inference and grammatical function of its governing equational metatheory. The basic structure of this linkage is illustrated in the following schematic representation of the most standard use of an equational grammar for the construction or identification of well-formed derivations, or proofs of primitive symbolic equivalence theorems.

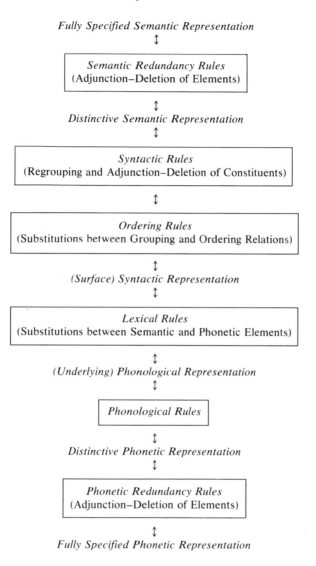

Fully Specified Semantic Representation
↕

Semantic Redundancy Rules
(Adjunction–Deletion of Elements)

↕
Distinctive Semantic Representation
↕

Syntactic Rules
(Regrouping and Adjunction–Deletion of Constituents)

↕

Ordering Rules
(Substitutions between Grouping and Ordering Relations)

↕
(Surface) Syntactic Representation
↕

Lexical Rules
(Substitutions between Semantic and Phonetic Elements)

↕
(Underlying) Phonological Representation
↕

Phonological Rules

↕
Distinctive Phonetic Representation
↕

Phonetic Redundancy Rules
(Adjunction–Deletion of Elements)

↕
Fully Specified Phonetic Representation

3.2. The Nature of Syntactic Statements

a. TERMS

The equationality hypothesis itself imposes no direct constraints on the particular elements, or terms, that constitute the constant vocabulary for linguistic representations or grammatical rules about them, apart from the natural requirement that any such vocabulary must include some subset of semantically interpretable constants and another disjoint subset of phonetically interpretable ones, where such elements and their interpretations are invariant, of course, for the grammars of all possible languages. However, it is clear that any actual, potentially adequate metalanguage of equational grammar will necessarily impose, in addition to the equationality constraint itself, all other motivated constraints on grammatical representation that are consistent with it. One group of such constraints are those determined by the hypothesis of simplex-feature representation (Sanders, 1974). This metalinguistic hypothesis, which is justified on empirical grounds as well as on grounds of appropriateness of expressive power, precludes, among other things, the unrestricted use of uninterpretable or diacritic elements in linguistic representation, as well as any use of such only partially or noninvariantly interpretable complex elements as [-HUMAN], [+NASAL], [mNOMINAL], or [3STRESSED].

The simplex-feature hypothesis, though motivated quite independently of the equationality hypothesis, is highly compatible with it, as well as with all of the other motivated constraints on grammatical analysis that I know of. I thus assume here, as elsewhere, that all potentially adequate metalanguages for grammar, equational and nonequational alike, will be consistent with the hypothesis of simplex-feature representation.

b. RELATIONS

For the representation of linguistic objects, the standard metalanguage of equational grammar provides two and only two relational elements, which are significantly distinct both in their formal properties as relations and in their empirical interpretations. One is the symmetrical relation of GROUPING, constructionhood, or co-constituency, represented standardly by comma between bracketed arguments, and interpreted into observation statements about the (cognitive or conceptual) ASSOCIATION of linguistic constituents. The other is the antisymmetric relation of ORDERING, linear sequencing, or temporal precedence, symbolized by ampersand or simply space between arguments, and interpreted into observation statements about the temporal (or spatial) ORDER, or successivity, of the constituents of linguistic expressions.

Through arguments that are quite independent of the equationality hypothesis (Sanders, 1970b, 1975a, 1975b), it has been shown that all empirically and conceptually appropriate metalanguages for grammar must be consistent with the natural metatheoretical assumptions *(a)* that all terminal semantic representations of linguistic objects are completely free of ordering relations; *(b)* that all terminal phonetic representations are completely free of grouping relations; and *(c)* that all ordering relations are invariant under derivation or alternative representation of any given linguistic object, that is, that if an element *A* is ordered before an element *B* in some representation of expression *E*, then there is no representation of *E* in which *B* is ordered before *A*. The latter assumption, which I have called the Invariant Order Constraint, is the most clearly restrictive of the three, since it effectively precludes the postulation of any rules or rule applications justifying derivational reorderings, or permutations, of grammatical constituents, and thus requires that all specifications of constituent orderings express true generalizations about the actual temporal ordering of their phonetic reflexes.

Though all three constraints on constituent relations can be justified independently of both the equationality hypothesis and the principle of simplex-feature representation, given the latter, the former can be deductively derived from them. Thus, as shown in Sanders (1970), the Invariant Order Constraint follows simply from the equationality hypothesis and the meaning of the notion of ordering itself, which is a relation such that for any (nonidentical) *A* and *B*, *A* & *B* is not equivalent to *B* & *A*. Similarly, the two Completeness constraints follow as consequence of the simplex-feature hypothesis and the fact that the relative ordering of linguistic constituents has no invariant nonnull semantic interpretation and the relative grouping of such constituents has no invariant nonnull phonetic interpretation. But apart from the logical and functional interrelationships among these various principles, it can be reasonably assumed, in any event, that any adequate metalanguage of equational grammar will also be consistent with the Invariant Order and Terminal Completeness constraints.

Since it is the case for any such metalanguage that all individual rules of grammar are simple assertions of equivalence or nonequivalence between two linguistic representations, it follows that, except for their use of variables, grammatical rules cannot make reference to any terms, concepts, or relations other than those that are used in the ordinary variable-free representations of particular linguistic objects. This means, then, that all linguistically significant concepts and relations—like word, agreement, subordination, predicate of, coordinate with—must be treated as derived notions rather than primitive ones, and must be amenable to precise formal definition in terms of the metalinguistically primitive notions of element, grouping, and ordering. This has been done already for a number of such cases, and I know of no reasons to suppose that it will not be possible, in principle at least, for all of them.

c. Effect of Statements

Every statement in an equational grammar asserts either the equivalence or the nonequivalence of two linguistic representations. All nonuniversal principles of grammar are thus expressed in the metalanguage of equational grammar as instances of the statement schemata $(A = B)$, equivalent to $(B = A)$, or $(A \neq B)$, equivalent to $(B \neq A)$, where A and B are linguistic representations, and are empirically interpreted according to the following interpretation schemata for these two statement-types:

$A = B$ 'There is a set of one or more linguistic objects in the language such that for each such object it can be appropriately represented both as XAY and as XBY.'

$A \neq B$ 'It is not the case $A = B$; that is, there is no linguistic object in the language which can be appropriately represented as both XAY and XBY.'

Equivalence statements, instances of the affirmative equation schema $(A = B)$ express ordinary affirmative rules of grammar. Nonequivalence statements, instances of the negative schema $(A \neq B)$, express substantive and relational constraints, or prohibitive rules of grammar. The primary subtypes of equational and nonequational statements, which are distinct both in form and in contributory derivational functions, are indicated and exemplified below.

1. EQUIVALENCE RULES $(A = B)$
   1.1. *Redundancy Rules* ($[A] = [A, B]$, where B is an interpretable constant)
        [HUMAN] = [HUMAN, ANIMATE]
        [NASAL] = [NASAL, VOICED]
   1.2. *Intermodal Rules* ($XAY = XBY$, where A is free of phonetic elements and B is free of semantic ones)
      1.2.1. *Lexical Rules* (where A is the distinctive nonphonological representation of a morpheme, and B is its distinctive phonological representation)
          [YOUNG, MALE, HUMAN] =
          [[LAB, OBST, VCD][VOC, BK][VOC]]
      1.2.2 *Ordering Rules* (where A and B are the relational elements for grouping and ordering)
          [[ADJ], [NOUN]] = [ADJ] & [NOUN]
   1.3. *Idempotency Rules* ($XAYZ = XAYAZ$, where A is variable)
        [X, NP, Y] = [NP, [X, NP, Y]]
        [NASAL] [CONS, X] = [NASAL, X] [CONS, X]
2. NONEQUIVALENCE RULES $(A \neq B)$
   2.1. *Absolute Constraints* (where A is an unrestricted variable)
        $U \neq W[[N, X], [V, TRYING], [[N, \sim X], [V, Y]]] Z$
        $U \neq X[CONS][CONS][CONS] Y$

2.2. *Relational Constraints*
[PRO, CLITIC] & [PRO, CLITIC] $\neq$ [1ST PERS] & [2ND PERS]
. . . $_{NP}$[NP, $_s$[C, X]] . . . $\neq$ . . . [NP, [X]] . . . C . . .

d. CONSTRAINTS

The equationality hypothesis restricts the statements of individual grammars to simple assertions of symbolic equivalence or nonequivalence between representations of linguistic objects. It thereby provides a systematic and principled exclusion of any postulations of language-specific, or nonuniversal, constraints on the inferential use of grammatical rules. In other words, by excluding language-specific statements of nonequational form, the equationality hypothesis automatically excludes any language-specific constraints on the directionality, relative ordering, or optionality or obligatoriness of the derivational substitutions justified by grammatical rules, since there is no such constraint on rule application that can be stipulated by means of a statement of the form $(A = B)$ or $(A \neq B)$ or by any combination of such statements (see Lakoff, 1971; Sanders, 1976). This contrasts sharply, of course, with the much less restrictive metalanguages of nonequational grammar, including the various types of transformational grammar, in which language-particular specifications of directionality, order, and obligatoriness of rule applications are freely expressible by the use of arbitrary rule-labeling diacritics or multirepresentational global constraints on derivations. Given an equational metalanguage, on the other hand, it follows that any and all restrictions on the appropriate uses of grammatical rules for the construction or identification of well-formed derivations or proofs of linguistic theorems must be functionally natural rather than arbitrary restrictions that are determined by strictly universal principles of inference and grammatical function, and are invariant, therefore, across all possible languages and linguistic expressions, and all possible rules or theorems about them.

The equationality hypothesis itself imposes no constraints on such universal principles apart from the constraint of universality. It is reasonable to assume, though, that they will be appropriately expressible in the same metalanguage that is used for the expression of all other lawlike generalizations about human language, whether in ordinary language or some form of predicate calculus, with quantification over the set of all natural languages and linguistic expressions, or all of the grammars, grammatical rules, or theorems that characterize them.

Thus, for example, one such universal principle of linguistic function, which concerns the positive adaptive value, or functional favorability, of right-branching structures relative to self-embedded ones, is expressed by the lawlike generalization that, for any symbolically equivalent linguistic representations of the forms $(X \& C \& Y)$ and $(X \& Y \& C)$, where X and Y are not null and $X \& C \& Y$ is a constituent of the same grammatical type as C, the latter is a closer approximation than the former to a representation of the sound of an optimally useful pairing of sound and meaning for purposes of human communication. It will follow from this law, then, and the natural inferential principles of Maximalization of Terminality and Opposite Use for Opposite Terminality (Sanders, 1972) that for any grammar with the rule $_S[[PRO, S], X] = _S[[[PRO], X], S]$, for example, the transformation, or directed substitution, $[[PRO, S], X] \rightarrow [[[PRO], X], S]$ represents the only appropriate use of this rule in phonetically directed derivations, and $[[[PRO], X], S] \rightarrow [[PRO, S], X]$ represents its only appropriate use in semantically directed derivations.

3.3. The Use of Syntactic Statements

a. DERIVATION

The essential and most fundamental use of grammars is for the purpose of specifying the particular pairings of sounds and meanings that constitute the appropriate linguistic expressions of individual languages. To specify any particular linguistic expression (A, b), where A is the meaning of the expression and b is its sound, is simply to provide a PROOF of the symbolic equivalence theorem $(A' = b')$, where A' is a terminal semantic representation whose interpretation describes A, and b' is a terminal phonetic representation whose interpretation describes b. The essential language-describing function of a grammar can be achieved, therefore, if and only if the grammar provides all of the nonlogical and nonuniversal principles required for the valid proof of a distinct symbolic equivalence theorem of this form for each of the infinitely numerous distinct expressions of the language being described.

A valid proof for any theorem of the form $(A = b)$ can be appropriately defined simply as a finite sequence of equations of the form $(A = b, \ldots, b = b)$ or $(A = b, \ldots, A = A)$, where the equivalence of all equations in the sequence follows deductively from the axioms and rules of inference of some given theory or formal axiomatic system. A theorem is proved, in other words, by the deductive derivation of one of the two given theorematically equated terms from the other, yielding as a final result a tautologically true equation of identities. For grammatical theorems, any proof that terminates in an equation between identical phonetically interpretable representations is called a PHONETICALLY DIRECTED PROOF or PHONETICALLY DIRECTED DERIVATION, and any proof terminating in an identity equation between semantically interpretable representations is called a SEMANTICALLY DIRECTED PROOF or SEMANTICALLY DIRECTED DERIVATION. It has been shown (Sanders, 1972) that validity is decidable for any arbitrary finite sequence of equations and any finite axiomatic system; it has also been shown that if a theorem $(A = b)$ has a valid proof at all, then it will have at least one valid proof that is phonetically directed and at least one that is semantically directed.

All proofs of grammatical theorems have a well-defined instrumental function too, therefore, no less than the languages and linguistic objects that they serve to characterize. Every phonetically directed proof thus has the natural function of establishing a sound–meaning association by deriving a terminal phonetic representation from a terminal semantic one, and every semantically directed proof has the function of establishing such an association by deriving a terminal semantic representation from a terminal phonetic one. And it is for the purpose of making essential contributions to this association function of symbolic equivalence proofs that all empirically justifiable rules and principles of grammar are postulated. Thus, regardless of whatever other possible uses a grammatical statement may have, these will always be derivative and subordinate to its contributory functions with respect to the central grammatical function of determining the validity (or invalidity) of proofs of symbolic equivalence theorems. For it is only on the basis of its contributory functions of this sort that a grammatical statement can be subjected to factual tests for correctness or incorrectness.

b. OPTIONALITY/OBLIGATORINESS

The hypothesis of equational grammar, as we have seen, precludes the postulation of any type of nonuniversal constraint on the application or use of grammatical rules in the construction or identification of well-formed derivations or proofs of linguistic theorems. It thus excludes any language-particular specifications of optionality or obligatoriness of rules or rule-applications. In my paper "On the notions 'optional' and 'obligatory' in linguistics" (1977b), I showed that these notions are neither primitive nor empirically significant, and that the distinction between optional and obligatory rules or rule applications plays no necessary role at all in the description or analysis of linguistic phenomena. It was shown in particular, in fact, that all legitimate cases of free variation, which constitutes the traditional grounds for all stipulations of rule optionality, can evidently be accounted for in very simple and perspicuous ways by metalanguages that permit no reference to the notions "optional" or "obligatory" at all, but which are consistent with certain independent natural metatheoretical hypotheses about the derivational use of ALL grammatical rules.

c. ORDER OF RULE APPLICATION

Like all other nonuniversal constraints on rule use, extrinsic ordering specifications and all such language-specific restrictions on the relative ordering or conjunctivity and disjunctivity of grammatical rule applications in derivations are categorically excluded by the metalanguage of equational grammar. It follows, therefore, as an empirical consequence, that natural languages cannot differ from one another in any ways that can be adequately and most perspicuously described and accounted for only by the postulation of different restrictions for the differing languages on the ordering or applicational interactions of their respective rules. It similarly follows that all actual constraints on the derivational ordering or disjunctivity of rule applications must be natural, rather than arbitrary, restrictions that are determined by strictly universal principles of grammatical inference and function, including both logical or quasi-logical principles like Minimal Application (Iverson, 1976) or Proper Inclusion Precedence (Sanders, 1974), and empirical principles of linguistic function like Kisseberth's (1976) Polarity Principle of functional favorability.

The metatheoretical exclusion of extrinsic-ordering constraints has been thoroughly discussed and justified in the recent literature, and a number of plausible universal principles of rule functions and interactions have been proposed and put to empirical test. See, for example, Iverson (1974), Iverson and Sanders (1978), Hastings (1974), Koutsoudas, Sanders, and Noll (1974), Sanders (1976), and the various references cited therein. Further work remains to be done, of course, on the development, testing, and higher-order explanation of such principles. But it seems clear in any event, from the work that has been carried out thus far, that extrinsic-ordering constraints, and all other such language-variable restrictions on grammatical inference, are not necessary for the adequate description or explanation of any facts about language in general or about the structures of individual languages and their patterns of variation and change. It seems clear, therefore, that the principled exclusion of such constraints by the metalanguage of equational grammar provides an empirically well-supported characterization of the nature and limits of natural language grammar, and thus constitutes direct empirical support for the equationality hypothesis itself.

d. DIRECTION OF APPLICATION

The most obvious and most direct consequence of the equationality hypothesis, of course, is that there can be no language-specific constraints on the direction of application of grammatical rules. Since it is required by this hypothesis that all statements in the grammars of particular languages must be simple assertions of the strictly symmetrical relations of equivalence or nonequivalence between two linguistic representations, it follows that individual grammars cannot possibly express anything at all about the conditions under which it is appropriate or not appropriate for one representation to follow rather than precede, or be substituted for rather than be substituted from, another in well-formed derivations or valid proofs of linguistic theorems. Given an equational metalanguage, in fact, it follows from the nature and function of grammatical proofs in general that every empirically justifiable rule of grammar, whether of the form $(A = B)$ or of the form $(A \neq B)$, will have appropriate derivational uses with respect to BOTH the derivation of A from B AND the derivation of B from A, with the correct choice of directed use being intrinsically determined for each particular proof as a deductive consequence of the particular directional orientation of that proof (whether it is phonetically directed or semantically directed) and the universal principles of inference and grammatical function in general.

Thus, for example, the English lexical rule [YOUNG, MALE HUMAN] = [[LABIAL, OBSTRUENT, VOICED] [VOCALIC, BACK] [VOCALIC]] is appropriately used to justify derivational substitutions of its phonetic member for its semantic member in phonetically directed proofs and of its semantic member for its phonetic member in semantically directed proofs. This pattern of directed use is of course intrinsically determined, moreover, as in the case of all other lexical rules or ordering rules, since these are the only POSSIBLE uses of such rules that can constitute productive contributions to the natural function of grammatical proofs themselves. Any axiomatic STIPULATIONS of directionality in such cases as these would thus be grossly redundant, and would merely serve to obscure the natural functions of the rules in question and the functional structures of the grammars that include them. Similarly, since all redundancy rules of grammars have the inherent contributory functions of assuring maximal specificity in the interpretable terminal representations of linguistic expressions and maximal simplicity and freedom from nondistinctive elements in all their other representations, it follows, for example, that the semantic redundancy rule [HUMAN] = [HUMAN, ANIMATE] can be appropriately used in derivations only to justify substitutions of ANIMATE for null in semantically directed proofs and substitutions of null for ANIMATE in phonetically directed ones. It likewise follows that any phonetic redundancy rule, such as [NASAL] = [NASAL, VOICED], can be appropriately used to justify derivational additions of the redundant phonetically interpretable element VOICED only in phonetically directed derivations and derivational eliminations, or deletions, of that element only in semantically directed derivations. Again, therefore, given the form of a rule and the function of a particular proof, the appropriate directional use (or non-use) of that rule with respect to that proof is deductively determined by strictly universal principles of inference and functionality.

The more interesting cases of directional determination, though, involve principles that are more specifically linguistic in reference, rather than mere principles of inference or scientific methodology alone. Thus, for example, there is a significant fact about natural LANGUAGE—namely, the functional favorability of voiceless obstruents relative to voiced ones in syllable-final positions—that is crucial to the deductive determination of the appropriate directed uses of the rule [OBSTRUENT, VOICED, X] \$ = [OBSTRUENT, $\emptyset$, X] \$ in the proofs of theorems about all languages, like German, that have this rule. Similarly, it is not by logic alone, of course, but also because of the actual functional favorability of linguistic expressions with non-self embedded structures rather than self-embedded ones, that all rules expressing equivalences between structures with interposed clauses and structures with extraposed clauses can be appropriately used to justify the derivational extraposition of clauses only in phonetically directed proofs and their derivational interposition only in semantically directed ones.

All such universal principles of directionality determination are, in fact, only special cases of a single natural law of grammatical rule functionality, which I have called the Principle of Maximalization of Terminality (Sanders, 1972). This principle asserts simply that all (equivalence) rules of grammar are used for the proof of linguistic theorems only to justify those substitutions that yield an increase in approximation to a well-formed and maximally favored terminal representation in the given terminality of the particular proof, where terminal well-formedness and favorability conditions are invariant for all languages and all grammars. Every universal principle that governs the applicational directionality of grammatical rules can thus be expressed as a rule-independent lawlike generalization about natural languages, with standardized formulation, for example, as instances of the following statement schema:

> *For any natural language L, any linguistic object E in L, and any linguistic representations A and B, if A and B are symbolically equivalent representations of E, then A is a closer approximation of the terminal phonetic representation of E than B is, and B is a closer approximation of its terminal semantic representation than A is.*

Every such statement makes a testable empirical claim about human language, which constitutes an appropriate subject, if substantiated, for principled analysis and explanation in terms of the natural communicative function of languages, their cultural bases and concomitants, and the biological, social, and psychological limitations of their natural users. The metalanguage of equational grammar provides principled motivation for the pursuit of such universal principles of linguistic function and a natural basis for their analysis and explanation. It is through this, perhaps, that the metalanguage makes its most important and evidently most distinctive contribution to the study of natural language in general.

4. SIGNIFICANCE

4.1. Universality of Function and Use

The most significant and most distinctive empirical implication of the equationality hypothesis is the claim that human languages differ only in the particular sets of symbolic equivalence relations they institutionalize, and not in the functions or inferential uses of such equivalences. Thus, by restricting the statements of all individual grammars—and hence the class of all language-specific linguistic generalizations—to simple assertions of the symmetric relations of symbolic equivalence or nonequivalence between two possible representations for linguistic expressions, the metalanguage of equational grammar predicts that such generalizations about representational equivalences constitute the only nonuniversal, or linguistically arbitrary, information that is relevant for the effective specification of the linguistic expressions, or sound–meaning associations, of individual languages, or for the correct characterization of all their linguistically significant properties and relations. It also follows, therefore, that the particular contributory functions, or appropriate inferential uses, of all such equivalence generalizations, or individual rules of grammar, are fully determined, with respect to the essential sound–meaning association function of all languages, by the nature of this natural linguistic function itself and the language-invariant natural laws of inference, functionality, and functional favorability that are entailed or presupposed by it. In other words, the equationality hypothesis predicts that no natural language makes essential use of any nonuniversal restriction on the appropriate directionality, order, or optionality or obligatoriness of the inferences or derivational substitutions justified by its individual principles of equivalence or nonequivalence for purposes of establishing the linguistic expressions, or correct sound–meaning associations, of that language. It follows also, therefore, that there can be no pairs of human languages that differ in the manner of application or applicational interaction of their respective generalizations about symbolic equivalence, and that it is only in the possible differences between one such set of equivalence principles and another that one such language can differ from another.

This highly restrictive claim about the nature and possible variability of human language follows as a direct empirical consequence of the hypothesis of equational grammar itself. This claim does not follow, moreover, either from the contrary of this hypothesis (that no grammatical rules are equational) or from its contradictory (that some grammatical rules are nonequational). The evident correctness of the claim thus provides direct empirical support for the equationality hypothesis and direct empirical disconfirmation of all linguistic theories, metatheories, and metalanguages that are inconsistent with it.

4.2. Falsifiability

All principles and constraints of the matalanguage of equational grammar are subject, in principle, to direct empirical testing and potential falsification on the basis of ordinary observable facts about actual human languages. Thus, for example, an equational metalanguage would be definitively falsified simply by the existence of one clear case of a language that can be adequately described only be assuming some language-specific constraint on the directionality, ordering, or optionality of its derivational rule-applications. With respect to the ordering and optionality or obligatoriness of rule-applications, however, it has not yet been shown that there are any differences between the sets of possible languages generated by metalanguages that permit language-specific constraints on application, like the various versions of transformational grammar, and by those that prohibit such language-specific constraints, like the metalanguage of equational grammar. Thus the evidence that has been adduced thus far indicates only that the assumption of such nonuniversal constraints on the ordering or optionality of rule applications is NOT NECESSARY for the adequate description or analysis of linguistic data. With respect to applicational ordering and optionality alone, therefore, there are no clear EMPIRICAL grounds yet for selecting an equational metalanguage over a nonequational one, but only the PRACTICAL and HEURISTIC grounds of greater economy, generality, perspicuity, freedom from vacuous or redundant axioms and concepts, etc.

With respect to the directionality of rule-applications, on the other hand, it has been already established that there are clear and distinctive differences between the universe of possible human languages generated by an equational metalanguage for grammar and any otherwise comparable nonequational metalanguage. There is thus a direct empirical basis here for determining the truth or falsity of the equationality hypothesis, and of the contrary or contradictory hypothesis of all forms of nonequational grammar. It follows from the equationality hypothesis, as we have seen, but not from either its contrary or its contradictory, that all constraints on the directionality of inference or derivational substitution justified by grammatical rules must be determined by strictly universal principles of natural linguistic functionality, and thus that there can be no human languages that make opposite, or inverse, directed uses of the same principle of equivalence or nonequivalence under the same conditions of context and derivational terminality. It follows from this, then, as a distinctive empirical consequence of the equationality hypothesis, that there can be no possible pairs of natural languages with precisely opposite patterns of distribution or alternation—that is, for example, where one language would have A in X_Y and B in W_Z and the other would have B in X_Y and A in W_Z. The nonexistence of such "counterlanguages" would thus constitute direct empirical support for the equationality hypothesis, and the discovery of one clear instance of such a language-pair would definitely establish its falsification.

By excluding all such inversions of relative terminality relations, the equationality hypothesis thus predicts that there are no inversions of distributions or alternation patterns among human languages—that is, that there are no pairs of "counterlanguages" such that, for example, one has agreement (or epenthetic vowels, or promoted arguments) under exactly the same circumstances that the other has disagreement (or syncopated vowels, or demoted arguments). Given any actual language, moreover, the equationality hypothesis predicts the nonexistence—past, present, or future—of all of its logically possible counterlanguages. Thus, for example, given German, whose equivalence rule for syllable-final obstruents, (OBSTRUENT, X, VOICED) \$ = (OBSTRUENT, X, Ø) \$, is appropriately used for the inferential deletion of the interpretable element for voicing in phonetically directed derivations and for its inferential addition in semantically directed ones, it follows from the equationality hypothesis that there can be no possible "Counter-German" language which makes use of this rule to justify phonetically directed additions of the element VOICED and semantically directed deletions, and which would thus have syllable-final neutralization in favor of the voiced member of an opposition rather than the voiceless member.

A similar empirical claim about natural language will be generated by the equationality hypothesis for each rule in every grammar of an actual human language. In an equational grammar, in other words, every generalization about a PARTICULAR language requires an associated generalization about ALL languages. Each statement in an equational grammar is thus subject to empirical falsification in two distinct and logically quite independent ways—through its own implications concerning the particular language it is about, and through the typological implications of the associated lawlike generalization about relative terminality that determines its appropriate directed uses. This double vulnerability—with respect to facts about a single language and facts about all languages—is a necessary consequence of the metalanguage of equational grammar itself, and evidently cannot be achieved in any reasonably natural, principled, or systematic way by any other metalanguage or metatheory for linguistic description and analysis.

4.3. Comparison

The metalanguage of equational grammar has been shown to be superior, on empirical as well as heuristic and conceptual grounds, to all nonequational metalanguages or metatheories for linguistic description and analysis, including, in particular, all of the various forms of transformational grammar, tagmemics, and stratificational grammar that I know of. Thus in comparison with any otherwise equivalent type of nonequational grammar, an equational metalanguage for grammar will

1. Generate a much smaller, more homogeneous, and more redundancy-free set of possible grammars of human languages, thereby better facilitating the tasks of interlanguage comparison and the identification of empirically significant generalizations about both individual languages and language in general

2. Generate a much smaller and more homogeneous set of possible human languages, thereby providing, as an empirical consequence, a much narrower and more precise charactierization of the nature and typological variability of natural language—a characterization, moreover, that is evidently much more thoroughly consistent with the actual facts about natural language, as evidenced thus far by the sample of its known and reasonably well-investigated instances

3. Provide a more precise, more systematic, and evidently much more thoroughly correct differentiation between the natural, universal, and functionally determined characteristics of human languages and those characteristics that are merely arbitrary, language-variable, and underdetermined by the communicative function of language—with the former

including all constraints on the inferential or derivational uses of grammatical rules, and the latter consisting solely of symbolic equivalence principles

4. Provide much more numerous and more direct opportunities for empirical tests and potential falsification, not only of all the particular rules of individual grammars, but also of the universal principles of linguistic function and relative terminality that govern their inferential uses, as well as all the assumptions and constraints of the metalanguage itself.

Given such clear and distinctive advantages and substantiations as these, therefore, it can only be concluded that the general hypothesis of equational grammar expresses a fundamentally correct and heuristically highly valuable lawlike generalization about the nature of human language, and that there can be no potentially adequate linguistic theory, metatheory, or metalanguage that is inconsistent with this hypothesis.

There are, however, many characteristics of languages, grammars, and grammatical statements that remain underdetermined, of course, by the hypothesis of equational grammar, either alone or in conjunction with such other well-supported metatheoretical hypotheses as the principles of invariant ordering and simplex-feature representation. There will thus be many facts, assumptions, and theoretical proposals about natural languages that are neither affirmed nor denied by the metalanguage of equational grammar, but are simply compatible with it. Such compatibility obtains, for example, with respect to the fact that all languages have questions, and with respect to all the essential concepts and principles of case grammar (see Fillmore, 1968). The equationality hypothesis is similarly compatible, as far as I can determine, with the essential features of relational grammar (see Perlmutter, 1979) and role and reference grammar (see Foley and Van Valin, 1979), as well as with all facts and theories about the perlocutionary or pragmatic concomitants of language use. For all such cases as these, however, further tests for mutual consistency and independence are appropriate.

4.4. Future Research

In the metatheoretical framework of equational grammar—as in all other frameworks for linguistic description and analysis, presumably— the primary tasks for future research consist in the identification and empirical substantiation of true lawlike generalizations about the nature and typological variability of human language. This can be achieved only through intensive and extensive studies of the formal and functional structures and structural relationships of individual languages, and though the explicit formulation and careful testing of typological laws about the characteristics of all natural languages in general.

APPENDIX: ILLUSTRATIVE GRAMMAR AND PROOFS

1. Preface

1. The following equational grammar and associated proofs of a symbolic equivalence theorem are based on the given sample of 17 English sentences, and are presented here solely for purposes of illustration. Thus, for example, many of the statements in the grammar are oversimplified and/or insufficiently general relative to the English language as a whole, and there is considerable underanalysis or arbitrary choice among possible alternative analyses throughout.

2. No phonological rules or inferences are presented, and all phonological representations, terminal or otherwise, are symbolized merely by the use of italicized lower-case orthographic representations of English words. Thus, for example, *man* would stand either for the redundancy-free representation ((LABIAL, NASAL) (VOC, FRONT, LOW) (NASAL)) or for any of its symbolically equivalent phonological counterparts, including the fully specified interpretable terminal phonetic representation of this word.

3. For ease of reference alone, all grammatical statements are numbered and grouped roughly into major form-and-function types, and, in some cases, are also named or paraphrased in ordinary language. All such labeling or commentary is strictly redundant, of course, and has no systematic import or significance.

4. To save space here, some rules of the form (XAY = XBY) are abbreviated to (A = B in the context X__Y).

5. Upper-case names (like HUMAN, FARM, PATIENT, AFFIX) and abbreviations for names (like PREP, N, PRED, V) are the mnemonically appropriate symbols either for single constant elements, both interpretable (like HUMAN) and diacritic (like AFFIX), or for some set or grouping of such elements. Thus, for example, when the elementary symbols FARM or KILL are used in the grammar, we intentionally leave open all questions concerning the ultimately appropriate linguistic analyses of the meanings of such particular English words as *farm* or *kill*.

6. Free variables (W, X, Y, Z, *etc.)* stand for any (possibly null) string of elements free of unclosed grouping, or bracketing, elements, with identical variables in a statement having identical values. In general, moreover, any references to representations of the form (. . . A, B . . .) or (. . . A & B . . .) are to be understood as abbreviations for (. . . (A, X), (B, Y) . . .) and (. . . (A, X) & (B, Y) . . .), respectively, where A and B are primary, or generic, constituents of their respective constructions. In lexical rules, on the other hand, all constructions without explicit variables are to be understood as including only the particular elements explicity specified—so that, for example, (A, B, C) = (A, B, C, Ø) ≠ (A, B, C, X) ≠ (A, B, C, D), *etc.*

7. For ease of reference alone, all redundant elements both interpretable semantic elements like ANIMATE or PRED, and uninterpretable syntactic diacritics like PREP, AFFIX, or DET—will he indicated by italicization in the representations of lexical rules.

8. For expository purposes alone, some rules are accompanied by ordinary-language paraphrases or partial descriptions of their derivational or inferential functions.

9. Some of the rules given here are universal rather than language-specific, and others are potentially reducible to universal statements. These do not properly belong in a grammar of English, of course, but are included here for the sake of completeness of the basis for determining validity of proofs.

2. Grammar

2.1. INTERMODAL RULES

a. LEXICAL RULES

    L.1. (*N*, HUMAN, FEM) = *woman*
    L.2. (*N*, ANIMAL, DUCK) = *duck*
    L.3. (*N*, THING, AXE) = *axe*
    L.4. (NAME, MASCULINE, *JOHN*) = *john*
    L.5. (NAME, MASCULINE, *BILL*) = *bill*
    L.6. (*N*, MASCULINE, THAT) = *he*
    L.7. (*N*, HUMAN, THAT, *WH, X*) = *who*
    L.8. (*V*, AGT, WALK) = *walk*
    L.9. (*V*, AGT, PATIENT, KILL) = *kill*
    L.10. (*V*, AGT, FARM) = *farm*
    L.11. (*V*, AGT, PATIENT, BELIEVE) = *believe*
    L.12. (*V*, *HAVE*) = *have*

L.13. ((*V*, TRANSFER, AGT, PATIENT, DAT),
      (*AFFIX*, PAST)) = *gave*
L.14. (*V*, TRANSFER, AGT PATIENT, DAT) = *give*
L.15. (*V*, AGT, PATIENT, LOVE) = *love*
L.16. (*V*, BE, PAST) = *was*
L.17. ((*V*, *BE*), *(AFFIX, PERFECT)*) = *been*
L.18. (*V*, *BE*) = *be*
L.19. (*PREP*, INST) = *with*
L.20. (*PREP*, DAT) = *to*
L.21. (*PREP*, AGT) = *by*
L.22. (*DET*, THAT, *ONE*) = *that* in context (__, (N,
      (V, *X*)))
L.23. (*DET*, THAT, *ONE*) = *the*
L.24. (*DET*, EVERY, *ONE*) = *every*
L.25. (*DET*, ONE) & (CONSONANT) = *a* & (CON-
      SONANT)
L.26. (*DET*, ONE) = *an*
L.27. (*CONJ*, AND) = *and*
L.28. (*PREP*, INF) = *to*
L.29. (*AFFIX*, AGT) = *er*
L.30. (*AFFIX*, DIM) = *ling*
L.31. (*AFFIX*, PAST) = *ed*
L.32. (*AFFIX*, PERFECT) = *ed*

b. ORDERING RULES

0.1. (N, ((V, X), N)) = (N, ((V, X) & N))
     Subordinate nominals are ordered after their verbs.
0.2. ((V), N) = (N & (V))
     Elsewhere (i.e., when superordinate, subjective, topic, head of
     relative, *etc.*), nominals are ordered before their verbs.
0.3. (X, (PREP, Y)) = (X & (PREP, Y))
     Prepositional phrases follow a sister constituent.
0.4. (PREP, Y) = (PREP & Y)
     Prepositions precede a sister constituent.
0.5. (AFFIX, Y) = (Y & AFFIX)
     Affixes follow a sister constituent.
0.6. (DET, X) = (DET & X)
     Determiners precede a sister constituent.
0.7. ((X), CONJ, (Y)) = ((X) & CONJ & (Y))
     Conjunctions occur between the conjuncts of coordinations.
0.8. (V, (V, X)) = (V & (V, X))
     Superordinate verbs precede subordinate ones.

2.2. REDUNDANCY RULES (SAMPLE)

a. SEMANTIC ELEMENTS
    R.1. (HUMAN) = (HUMAN, ANIMAL)
    R.2. (DUCK) = (DUCK, ANIMAL)
    R.3. (FEM) = (FEM, ANIMAL)
    R.4. (MASCULINE) = (MASCULINE, ANIMAL)
    R.5. (NAME) = (NAME, THING)
    R.6. (THING, AGT) = (THING, (AGT, CAUSATIVE))
    R.7. (THING, INST) = (THING, (INST, CAUSATIVE))
    R.8. (THAT) = (THAT, ONE)
    R.9. (EVERY) = (EVERY, ONE)
    R.10. (CAUSATIVE) = (ROLE, (CAUSATIVE))
    R.11. (THING, DAT) = (THING, (ROLE, (DAT)))
    R.12. (THING, PATIENT) = (THING, (ROLE, (PATIENT)))
    R.13. (PAST) = ((PAST), TIME)

b. SYNTACTIC DIACRITIC ELEMENTS
    R.14. (THING) = (THING, N)
    R.15. (PRED) = (PRED, V)
    R.16. (ONE) = (ONE, DET)
    R.17. (AND) = (AND, CONJ)
    R.18. (INF) = (INF, PREP)
    R.19. (HAVE) = (HAVE, V)
    R.20. (BE) = (BE, V)

2.3. OTHER NONPHONOLOGICAL
     EQUIVALENCE RULES

    S.1. *Subjective Grouping*
          (N, V, X) = (N, (V, X))
    S.2. *Objective Grouping*
          (N, (V, N, N)) = (N,) (V, N), N))
    S.3. *Causative Prepositional Grouping*
          (N, (V, X, (N, (CAUSATIVE)))) = (N, (V, X, (N, (PREP,
          (CAUSATIVE)))))
          Nonsubject causative arguments (agents or instrumentals)
          have phonetically proximate grouping of their role features
          in an adpositional sister constituent of the nominal argument
          itself.
    S.4. *Dative Prepositional Grouping*
          (N, ((V, N), (N, DAT))) = (N, ((V, N), ((PREP, DAT), N)))
          Dative arguments that are neither subjective nor objective
          have adpositional grouping of their role features.

S.5. *Nominal Role Nullification*
  (N, (ROLE, *X*), *Y*) = (N, Ø, *Y*)
     Elsewhere—that is, apart from the special cases specified
     in S.3 and S.4—the phonetically proximate reflex of all se-
     mantically interpreted nominal role features is null.
S.6. *Affix Grouping*
  (a) (X, DIM) = ((X), (AFFIX, DIM))
  (b) (X, PAST) = ((X), (AFFIX, PAST))
  (c) (X, PERFECT) = ((X), (AFFIX, PERFECT))
S.7. *Determiner Grouping*
  (N, (DET, X)) = ((N), (DET, X))
S.8. *Objective Clause Grouping*
  (V, (N, (V, X))) = (V, N, (V, X))
S.9. *Infinitude*
  (V, (V, X)) = (V, ((INF, V), X))
S.10. *Perfection*
  (INF, (V, PAST)) = (INF, (HAVE, ((V), (AFFIX, PERFECT))))
S.11. *Passivity*
  ((N, (ROLE,~CAUSATIVE)), ((V, (TIME, X)), Y))
     = ((N, (ROLE,~CAUSATIVE)), ((BE, (TIME, X)), ((V,
  PERFECT), Y)))
S.12. *Relativity*
  (a) *Elliptical:*
  ((N, X), (THAT, (Y, (N, X), Z)))
     = ((N, X), (THAT, (Y, Ø, Z)))
  (b) *Complementary:*
  ((N, X), (THAT, (Y, (N, X), Z)))
     = ((N, X), ((THAT, N, X, WH), (Y, Z)))
S.13. *Interrogation*
  ((IDENTIFY), (SPEAKER, DAT), ((N, ONE,⟨THAT⟩, Ø),
  ((THAT, WH, X), Y)))
     = ((THAT, WH, X), Y)
S.14. *Subordinate Clause Determination*
  (V, X, (V, Y)) = (V, X, (THAT, (V, Y)))
S.15. *Agentive Nominality*
  ((N, ONE, THAT, Ø), ((N, ONE, THAT, Ø, AGT), (V,
  ~TIME)))
     = (N, Ø, (V, ~TIME), (AFFIX, AGT)))
S.16. *Anaphora*
  X = Ø in the context: (W & (N, ⟨HUMAN⟩, ⟨MASC⟩, ⟨FEM⟩,
  ⟨PLURAL⟩, X) & Y & (N, ⟨HUMAN⟩, ⟨MASC⟩, ⟨FEM⟩, ⟨PLU-
  RAL⟩, __) & Z)

S.17. *Coordinative Ellipsis*
((U & (W) & X) & CONJ & (Y & (W) & Z))
= ((U & (W) & X) & CONJ & (Y & Ø & Z))

2.4. Nonequivalence Rules (Sample)

N.1. Y ≠ ((PRED, (ROLE, X)), ~ [(N, (ROLE, X)), Z])
(where the right member is a terminal semantic representation)
Nothing can be equivalent to a semantic representation in
which a predicate is not immediately associated with an appropriately roled argument corresponding to each of the inherent role features of the predicate. In other words, any *n*-
place predicate must be semantically grouped with exactly *n*
arguments of the appropriate types.

N.2. X ≠ ((N, INST), (V, (N, AGT), Y))
No representation can have an instrumental argument of a verb
superordinate to an agentive argument of that verb—that is,
there can be no sentences like *an axe (was) killed the duckling
by John* meaning 'John killed the duckling with an axe'.

N.3. (N, ((N, V), N)) ≠ (N, (((N, INST), V), N))
Instrumentals can never function as objects; that is, there are
no direct objects that have instrumental roles.

3. Proofs of the Symbolic Equivalence Theorem for the Given English Sentence "The duckling was killed by the farmer"

Theorem: the duckling was killed by the farmer = ((ANIMAL, DUCK,
THING, DIM, (ROLE, PATIENT), THAT, ONE),
((HUMAN, ANIMAL, THING, THAT, (ROLE, AGT),
ONE), ((N, ONE, THAT, AGT), (FARM, PRED))), (PRED,
KILL, PAST, AGT, PATIENT))

3.1. Phonetically Directed Proof

1. (*Given by hypothesis*): ((ANIMAL, DUCK, THING, DIM, (ROLE,
PATIENT), THAT, ONE), ((HUMAN, ANIMAL, THING,
THAT,(ROLE, CAUSATIVE, AGT), ONE), ((N, ONE, THAT,
(ROLE, CAUSATIVE, AGT), (FARM, AGT, PRED))), (PRED,
KILL, (PAST, TIME), AGT, PATIENT))

2. (*From 1 by redundancy rules*): ((N, DUCK, DIM, PATIENT,
THAT), (N, HUMAN, THAT, AGT, ((N, THAT, AGT), (V,
FARM, AGT))), (V, KILL, PAST, AGT, PATIENT))

3. (*From 2 by S.1, Subjective Grouping*): ((N, DUCK, . . .), ((N, HUMAN, . . .), (V, KILL, . . .)))
4. (*From 3 by S.11, Passivity*): ((N, DUCK, . . .), ((N, HUMAN, . . .), (BE, (TIME, PAST)), (V, KILL, PERFECT, AGT, PATIENT)))
5. (*From 4 by S.15, Agentive Nominality*): ((N, DUCK, . . .), ((N, (V, FARM), (AFFIX, AGT)), (BE, . . .)))
6. (*From 5 by S.3, S.6, and S.7, Groupings for DET, AFFIX, PREP*): ((DET, THAT), ((N, DUCK), (AFFIX, DIM))), (((DET, THAT), (N, (V, FARM), (AFFIX, AGT)), (PREP, (CAUSATIVE, AGT))), ((V, BE), (AFFIX, (TIME, PAST))), ((V, KILL), (AFFIX, PER-FECT))))
7. (*From 6 by Ordering Rules 0.1, 0.2, 0.3, 0.4, 0.5, 0.8, 0.6*): ((DET, THAT) & ((N, DUCK) & (AFFIX, DIM)) & ((V, BE), (AFFIX, (TIME, PAST))) & ((V, KILL) & (AFFIX, PERFECT)) & ((PREP, (CAUSATIVE, AGT)) & ((DET, THAT) & (N, (V, FARM) & (AFFIX, AGT)))))
8. (*From 7 by lexical rules*): (((*the*) & ((*duck*) & (*ling*)) & ((*was*) & ((((*kill*) & (*ed*)) & ((*by*) & ((*the*) & ((*farm*) & (*er*)))))))
9. (*From 8 by phonological rules*): *the duckling was killed by the farmer*

(Identical to the given phonological member of the theorem)
Q.E.D.

3.2. SEMANTICALLY DIRECTED PROOF

1. (*Given by hypothesis*): *the duckling was killed by the farmer*
2. (*From 1 by phonological rules and lexical rules*): (((DET, THAT) & ((N, DUCK) & (AFFIX, DIM)) & ((V, BE), (AFFIX, (TIME, PAST))) & ((V, KILL) & (AFFIX, PERFECT)) & ((PREP, (CAUSATIVE, AGT)) & ((DET, THAT) & (N, (V, FARM) & (AFFIX, AGT)))))
3. (*From 2 by ordering rules*): (((DET, THAT), ((N, DUCK), (AFFIX, DIM)), ((V, BE), (AFFIX, (TIME, PAST))), ((V, KILL), (AFFIX, PERFECT)), ((PREP, (CAUSATIVE, AGT)), ((DET, THAT), (N, (V, FARM), (AFFIX, AGT)))))
4. (*From 3 by S.3, S.6, and S.7*): ((N, DUCK, DIM, (DET, THAT)), ((V, BE, (TIME, PAST)), ((V, KILL, PERFECT), (N, (V, FARM), (AFFIX, AGT))))
5. (*From 4 by S.15*): ((N, DUCK, . . .), ((V, BE, . . .), (N, HUMAN, THAT, AGT, ((N, THAT, AGT), (V, FARM, AGT)))))
6. (*From 5 by S.11*): ((N, DUCK, . . .), ((V, KILL, PAST), (N, HUMAN, . . .)))))

7. (*From 6 by S.1*): ((N, DUCK, . . .), (V, KILL, PAST), (N, HUMAN, . . .))

8. (*From 7 by Redundancy Rules*): ((ANIMAL, DUCK, THING, DIM, (ROLE, PATIENT), THAT, ONE), (PRED, KILL, (PAST, TIME), AGT, PATIENT), ((HUMAN, ANIMAL, THING, THAT, (ROLE, AGT), ONE), ((N, ONE, THAT, AGT), (FARM, PRED))))

(Identical to the given semantic member of the theorem)

Q.E.D.

REFERENCES

Chomsky, N. (1957). *Syntactic structures*. The Hague: Mouton.

Chomsky, N. (1965). *Aspects of the theory of syntax*. Cambridge, Mass: MIT Press.

Chomsky, N. (1972). *Studies on semantics in generative grammar*. The Hague: Mouton.

Cohen, D. (Ed.), (1974). *Explaining linguistic phenomena*. Washington, D.C.: V.H. Winston.

Fillmore, C. J. (1968). The case for case. In E. Bach and R. Harms (Eds.), *Universals in linguistic theory*. New York: Holt, Rinehart and Winston. Pp.1–88.

Foley, W., and Van Valin, R. (1979). Role and reference grammar. Paper presented at the University of Wisconsin–Milwaukee Conference on Current Approaches to Syntax.

Hastings, A. (1974). Stifling. Indiana University Linguistics Club, Bloomington, Indiana.

Hockett, C. F. (1958). *A course in modern linguistics*. New York: Macmillan.

Iverson, G. K. (1974). Ordering constraints in phonology. Unpublished doctoral dissertation, University of Minnesota.

Iverson, G. K. (1976). A guide to sanguine relationships. In A. Koutsoudas (Ed.), *The application and ordering of grammatical rules*. The Hague: Mouton. Pp.22–40.

Iverson, G. K., and Sanders, G. A. (1978). The functional determination of phonological rule interactions. Indiana University Linguistics Club, Bloomington, Indiana. Revised version to appear in *Studia Linguistica*.

Kisseberth, C. (1976). The interaction of phonological rules and the polarity of language. In A. Koutsoudas (Ed.), *The application and ordering of grammatical rules*. The Hague: Mouton. Pp. 41–54.

Koutsoudas, A. (Ed.), (1976) *The application and ordering of grammatical rules*. The Hague: Mouton.

Koutsoudas, A., Sanders, G., and Noll, C. (1974). The application of phonological rules. *Language, 50*, 1–28.

Lakoff, G. (1971). On generative semantics. In D. Steinberg and L. Jakobovits (Eds.), *Semantics*. Cambridge: Cambridge University Press. Pp. 232–296.

Lamb, S. M. (1966). *Outline of stratificational grammar*. Washington, D.C.: Georgetown University Press.

Perlmutter, D. M. (1979). Relational grammar. Paper presented at the University of Wisconsin–Milwaukee Conference on Current Approaches to Syntax.

Pike, K. L. (1967). *Language in relation to a unified theory of human behavior*. The Hague: Mouton.

Ross, J. R. (1976). Constraints on variables in syntax. Unpublished doctoral dissertation, MIT, Cambridge, Mass.

Sanders, G. A. (1970a). On the natural domain of grammar. *Linguistics, 63,* 51–123.

Sanders, G. A. (1970b). Constraints on constituent ordering. *Papers in Linguistics, 2,* 460–502.

Sanders, G. A. (1971). On the symmetry of grammatical constraints. In *Papers from the Seventh Regional Meeting of the Chicago Linguistic Society.* University of Chicago, Department of Linguistics. Pp. 232–241.

Sanders, G. A. (1972). *Equational grammar.* The Hague: Mouton.

Sanders, G. A. (1974). The simplex-feature hypothesis. *Glossa, 8,* 141–192.

Sanders, G. A. (1975a). On the explanation of constituent-order universals. In C. N. Li (Ed.), *Word order and word order change.* Austin: University of Texas Press. Pp. 389–436.

Sanders, G. A. (1975b). *Invariant Ordering.* The Hague: Mouton.

Sanders, G. A. (1976). On the exclusion of extrinsic-ordering constraints. In A. Koutsoudas (Ed.), *The application and ordering of grammatical rules.* The Hague: Mouton. Pp. 203–258.

Sanders, G. A. (1977a). Functional constraints on grammars. In A. Juilland (Ed.), *Linguistic studies offered to Joseph Greenberg.* Saratoga Cal.: Anma Libri. Pp. 161–178.

Sanders, G. A. (1977b). On the notions 'optional' and 'obligatory' in linguistics. *Linguistics, 195,* 5–47.

Sanders, G. A. (1979). Equational rules and rule functions in phonology. In D. A. Dinnsen (Ed.), *Current approaches to phonological theory.* Bloomington, Ind.: Indiana University Press. Pp. 74–105.

DAUGHTER-DEPENDENCY GRAMMAR

PAUL SCHACHTER

University of California, Los Angeles

In comparison with some of the other theories represented in this volume, the theory of daughter-dependency grammar (DDG) is still somewhat undeveloped. The fullest exposition of the theory to date, Hudson (1976), though arguably of major significance (see Schachter, 1978a), is in large part polemical, aimed at illustrating putative deficiencies of transformational grammar (TG) that are remedied by DDG, and offering only a rather programmatic account of DDG itself. Thus, before DDG can be systematically compared with better established theories, it will be necessary to fill in some of the gaps in existing accounts of the theory, and the present paper is perforce partly devoted to this task.

Under these circumstances, I have not thought it appropriate to try to take up in turn each of the "issues to be discussed" that contributors to this volume were asked to address. Although it is possible at this point to deal seriously with some of these issues in relation to DDG, for others of them there is at present no basis for doing so. For a subset of the latter, moreover, this paper itself seeks to provide the necessary basis for discussion by proposing certain extensions (and in some cases modifications) of Hudson's work. Thus, although I have followed the general outline of "issues to be discussed" to the extent of dividing the paper into three major sections [(1) the goal of syntax, (2) the organization of syntax, (3)

267

Syntax and Semantics, Volume 13:
Current Approaches to Syntax

significance of the approach], within each of these sections I have felt free to concentrate on those issues that seem germane to existing work in DDG or on which I have specific new proposals to offer.

1. THE GOAL OF SYNTAX

Daughter-dependency grammar sets for itself the same basic goal as TG: the achievement of descriptive and explanatory adequacy (cf. Chomsky, 1964). The former of these is relevant primarily to particular-language grammars, the latter to general linguistic theory. A descriptively adequate grammar of a language is one that correctly represents the grammar that has been acquired by a speaker of that language, a grammar that, for example, correctly reflects the speaker's intuitions about grammaticalness, sentential structure and sentential relations. An explanatorily adequate linguistic theory is one that specifies the allowable form of grammars in such a highly constrained way that it constitutes an explanation for speakers' acquiring the particular grammars they do.

As has been noted in the TG literature, there is often a certain tension between considerations of descriptive and of explanatory adequacy. For "to attain explanatory adequacy it is in general necessary to restrict the class of possible grammars, whereas the pursuit of descriptive adequacy often seems to require elaborating the mechanisms available and thus extending the class of possible grammars [Chomsky and Lasnik, 1977, p. 427]." Thus it was considerations of descriptive adequacy that first led Chomsky (1957) to suggest supplementing phrase structure rules with transformational rules—a move which, although it did result in gains in descriptive adequacy, also resulted in an expansion of the set of allowable grammars well beyond the set needed to characterize natural languages (see Peters and Ritchie, 1973). Hence considerations of explanatory adequacy have prompted the search for suitable constraints on transformational rules—in witness whereof see the extensive literature on this subject (e.g., Ross, 1967; Chomsky, 1973). Similarly, the more recent proposal in TG that there is a set of surface filters that determine which surface structures are in fact well formed (see Chomsky, 1965; Perlmutter, 1970; Chomsky and Lasnik, 1977) is, again, an enrichment of TG theory prompted by considerations of descriptive adequacy, an enrichment that entails the development of new constraints in the interest of explanatory adequacy.

Now one basic claim made by DDG is that TG, although correct in recognizing the descriptive deficiencies of its point of departure, phrase structure grammar, has been enriched in the wrong ways. In a DDG there are no transformations and no surface filters. Instead the syntactic rules directly generate all and only the grammatical sentences of the language, assigning to each sentence generated a structure which, from the point of view of TG, can be described as an enriched surface structure. This enriched surface structure may include certain types of information that a TG typically shows only in nonsurface representations of sentences, as well as information that a TG typically does not show at all.

In lieu of transformational rules and surface filters DDG does have certain other descriptive devices that are included in the grammatical model in order to enhance its descriptive adequacy and that in turn require constraining in the interest of explanatory adequacy. It will be argued in this paper, however, that the new devices introduced in DDG are in fact justified by considerations of descriptive adequacy, and that the needed constraints are, in at least certain cases, fairly self-evident and easily formulated.

Let us briefly consider two of the ways in which DDG allows for the specification of structural descriptions that are disallowed in TG, in each case marshaling some empirical support for this increase in descriptive power and noting, in a general way, the types of constraints on the increase in power that appear to be needed. (The actual presentation of proposed constraints is deferred until Section 2, following a general presentation of the DDG model.) The two descriptive enrichments to be considered are: the separation in DDG of the rules that specify constituent ORDER from those that specify constituency per se, and the inclusion in DDG of rules that specify HEAD-DEPENDENT RELATIONS between sister constituents.

First, then, in a DDG there is one set of rules that specifies relations between constituents (such as co-constituency) and another, independent set, the SEQUENCE RULES (see Section 2), that positions constituents in a linear order. This separation of the constituent-relating and constituent-positioning rules allows for certain descriptive possibilities that are not allowed in standard TG. For example, it is possible in a DDG, but not in a TG, to identify two constituents as co-constituents of a particular construction without their ever having been either adjacent to one another or separated from one another only by other constituents of this same construction. Now it is argued in Schachter (1979) that this descriptive enrichment is in fact needed if a grammar is to account satisfactorily for the so-called "adjoined relative" construction, a construction type that is rather widely attested among the languages of the world (see Andrews, 1975). In the adjoined relative construction, a relative clause, instead of

being embedded within the matrix clause in which its head occurs, is
obligatorily adjoined to the matrix clause, as in the Hindi example (1a):

(1)   a.   *Mohan **us-laḍke-ko** dhǔd   rahā hē jo   kal   āyā   thā*
              Mohan the-boy   search Prog be Rel yesterday come be
              'Mohan is looking for the boy who came yesterday'.
         b.   **Mohan **us-laḍke-ko** jo kal āyā thā dhǔd rahā hē*

In (1a) the relative clause meaning 'who came yesterday' follows the
matrix clause, and is separated from its head, 'the boy,' by a verb and
some auxiliaries. That this separation is obligatory is shown by the un-
grammaticalness of (1b). Such facts pose no problem for DDG; for, given
the separation of the constituent-relating and constituent-positioning
rules, the head and the relative clause of sentences like (1a) can be generated as co-constituents without positioning them in relation either to
one another or to other constituents, and the sequence rules can then
assign the attested order. (In a TG, on the other hand, in order to capture
the co-constituency of the head and the relative clause in (1a), one would
presumably postulate an underlying structure in which they are adjacent,
and then have an obligatory transformation extraposing the relative
clause. The postulation of an underlying order that is NEVER attested on
the surface seems questionable from the point of view of correctly capturing the speaker's intuitions, but there is well-established precedent for
it in TG, such as the standard "affix-hopping" analysis of English verbs
and auxiliaries—cf. Chomsky, 1957).

But while there is empirical support for ALLOWING constituent position
to be treated as independent of constituent relations, it is certainly not
the case that the two are in general unrelated. One certainly expects, for
example, that most co-constituents will in fact either be adjacent to one
another or be separated only by other co-constituents. There therefore
seems to be a need in DDG to constrain the independence of the sequence
rules from the rules responsible for constituency per se. One possible
approach to this problem might involve making a distinction between
MARKED constituent orderings, which are wholly specified by language-
particular sequence rules, and UNMARKED orderings, which are partly
specified by the general theory of DDG. Some specific proposals along
these lines are presented in Section 2.

The second descriptive enrichment to be considered is the formal recognition that DDG gives to head–dependent relations between sister constituents. These relations are specified by a set of SISTER-DEPENDENCY
RULES, which have the function of assigning properties to dependent
sisters on the basis of properties of their heads. For example, there is a
sister-dependency rule of English to the effect that a perfective auxiliary

(i.e., a form of *have*) takes as a dependent sister a past participle. (Note that the dependency relations represented by sister-dependency rules have nothing to do with the relative communicative importance of the head and the dependent. A dependent sister is simply one whose occurrence or form depends upon properties of its head.)

I have argued in Schachter (1978a) that the formal recognition of head–dependent relations in DDG, in combination with the previously mentioned separation of the constituency rules and the sequence rules, permits DDG to express otherwise unstated generalizations about the interaction between dependency and word order: specifically, generalizations of the kind first noted in Greenberg (1963). What Greenberg observed was (to simplify somewhat) that there are two regular cross-category ordering patterns that are widely attested in the languages of the world, the patterns summarized in (2):

(2)   *Pattern A*   *Pattern B*
      Verb + Object   Object + Verb
      Auxiliary + Verb   Verb + Auxiliary
      Preposition + Nominal   Nominal + Postposition
      Noun + Adjective   Adjective + Noun
      Noun + Genitive   Genitive + Noun

In a language that conforms to Pattern A, verbs precede objects, auxiliaries precede verbs, there are prepositions rather than postpositions, and nouns precede modifying adjectives and genitives. A language that conforms to Pattern B shows precisely the opposite ordering in each case. Since so many languages conform perfectly to one or the other of these patterns, it is clear that the patterning is not accidental, and it in fact turns out that the patterning of (2) is consistently correlated with head–dependent relations. That is, in Pattern A the head consistently precedes the dependent, while in Pattern B the dependent consistently precedes the head—a generalization that can easily be captured in a DDG (see, for example, Sequence Rule S8 in the sample DDG of English presented as an appendix to this paper), but which could not be captured in the absence of some formal recognition of sister dependencies. (English is a Pattern A language, but not a consistent one, since adjectives and genitives commonly precede nouns. In a full DDG, this would be accounted for by having specific sequence rules for adjective–noun and genitive–noun sequences, which would be given priority over a more general rule like S8; see Section 2 for some discussion of how this type of priority is assigned.)

On the other hand, the recognition of sister dependencies introduces some new descriptive possibilities that require constraining in the interest of explanatory adequacy. As will become clear in Section 2, it is possible in a DDG for a nonhead constituent to be generated in any of three different ways; it may be generated by means of a so-called DAUGHTER-DEPENDENCY RULES (which identify it as a daughter of a dominating node), by means of sister-dependency rules (which, as noted, identify it as a dependent sister of a head), or by means of the interaction of both daughter-dependency and sister-dependency rules. Given these three possibilities, the question arises as to how the theory should be constrained so that, in any specific case of a nonhead constituent, the grammar will provide an empirically correct account. It turns out, I believe, that there is a rather natural answer to this question, an answer that will be proposed in Section 2.

2. THE ORGANIZATION OF SYNTAX

Like a TG, a DDG is a generative grammar that explicitly assigns syntactic structures to grammatical sentences. Instead of the SET of (underlying, surface, and intermediate) structures assigned by a TG, however, a DDG assigns to each syntactically unambiguous sentence a single structure. This structure differs from a typical TG phrase marker in various ways, among them: the representation of all constituents, including clausal and phrasal constituents, as feature complexes; the overt representation of head–dependent relations between constituents; and the assignment to specified constituents of certain functional labels, such as SUBJECT. (For a typical DDG structural representation, see the last figure in the Appendix.)

DDG structures are built up piecemeal, through the interaction of several different types of rules: CLASSIFICATION RULES, DAUGHTER-DEPENDENCY RULES, SISTER-DEPENDENCY RULES, FEATURE-ADDITION RULES, FUNCTION-ASSIGNMENT RULES, and SEQUENCE RULES. (The original model of DDG includes yet another rule type, PERIPHERALITY-ASSIGNMENT RULES, but this rule type seems to me to be superfluous, since the phenomena it is supposed to account for can, in my view, be better accounted for in other ways; I therefore give peripherality-assignment rules no further consideration in this paper.) The function of each type of rule is described in turn below, with examples cited from the sample grammar of English presented in the Appendix. Then there is a discussion of how the various rule types interact in the generation of syntactic structures.

Classification rules have the function of specifying the classes of constituents that occur in the language. (This function is shared, to a limited extent, with the feature-addition rules.) Since all constituents are represented as feature complexes, classification rules take the form of statements about what features may co-occur on the constituent nodes found in syntactic representations. For example, there is a classification rule in the sample grammar (Rule C2) to the effect that a node that is specified as [+ sentence] must also be specified as [+ main] or [− main], that is, that a clause is classified as either main or subordinate.

Daughter-dependency rules state relations between features of mother and daughter nodes; and sister-dependency rules state relations between features of (head and dependent) sister nodes. For examples, a daughter-dependency rule of the sample grammar (DD1) says that a [+ sentence] node has as a daughter a [+ verb, + finite] node, that is, a clause (in this grammar) contains a finite verb. And a sister-dependency rule (SD4) says that a [+ preposition] node has as a dependent sister a [+ nominal], that is, a preposition has an object.

Feature-addition rules are similar to classification rules in that they deal with feature co-occurrences on nodes. But while classification rules say that a node with a given feature specification may be specified in either of two ways (i.e., either positively or negatively) for some other feature(s), feature-addition rules say that a node with a given feature specification must be specified in one particular way for some other feature(s). Some feature-addition rules have the function of "elsewhere" rules, stating feature co-occurrences that hold in the absence of some more specific rule to the contrary. For example, the sample grammar permits sentential nominals, which are specified as [+ nominal, + sentence], to be generated in certain contexts (e.g., as objects of certain verbs), but there is a feature-addition rule (FA2) to the effect that a [+ nominal] node is "normally" [− sentence]: Thus, unless some rule of the grammar (such as the sister-dependency rule that introduces sentential objects) requires that a nominal be sentential, it will necessarily be nonsentential. (The only sentential nominals included in the sample grammar are *that*-clauses, and FA2 correctly prevents such clauses from being generated as, say, prepositional objects.) Other feature-addition rules state co-occurrence constraints on features which, for one reason or another, are inconvenient to build into the classification rules. For example, Classification Rule C1 says that nodes in general may be specified as [+ conjoined] or [− conjoined] (a [+ conjoined] node dominates a set of conjuncts, a [− conjoined] node does not), but FA6 says that in fact certain classes of nodes (e.g., infinitive markers) are necessaily [− conjoined]. Still other feature-addition rules in effect state CONTEXTUAL restrictions on feature co-occurrences— for example, FA5, which specifies that a noun that is the head of a restrictive relative clause must be a common noun.

Function-assignment rules assign certain functional labels to specified constituents of a clause. These functions may be syntactic (e.g., SUB-

JECT) or pragmatic [to borrow the label Dik (1978) uses for discourse-related functions such as TOPIC]. An example of a function-assignment rule is the rule of the sample grammar (F1) that assigns the SUBJECT function to a nominal introduced as a dependent sister of a finite verb.

None of the rule types thus far discussed assigns a sequential order to nodes. This is the province of the sequence rules, which order nodes on the basis of information provided by rules of other types. The sequence rules may refer to features, functions, dependency relations, or some combination of these. For instance, Sequence Rule S4 in the sample grammar says that a node specified as [+determiner] precedes one specified as [+noun] (i.e., determiners precede nouns), S7 says that a subject precedes a finite verb (N.B.: The grammar does not cover "inverted" word order), and S8 says that a dependent sister follows its head. (The sequence rules are hierarchically arranged, in the sense that there is a specification of which of two rules applies in cases of potential conflict. The nature of this specification is discussed below, as part of the general discussion of rule interaction.)

There are also a few sequence rules which, instead of assigning an order to distinct nodes, assign to a single node features that have been introduced into structures on the basis of distinct daughter-dependency or sister-dependency rules. For example, Rule S1 of the sample grammar says that when the head noun of a nominal (head nouns are introduced by DD2) is noncommon, it is assigned the definiteness specification within the nominal (this specification is introduced by DD3). Thus S1 assigns to the node associated with a noncommon noun features which have been initially generated on the basis of two distinct daughter-dependency rules. (Noncommon nouns include proper nouns such as *John*, which are [+definite], and pronouns such as [+definite] *he* or [−definite] *who*. When the head noun of a nominal is a COMMON noun, the definiteness specification within the nominal is assigned not to the noun itself but to a distinct determiner node. Some further observations relevant to this treatment of definiteness are presented toward the end of the present section.)

Before leaving the area of rule typology, mention should be made of one rule that is part of the general theory of DDG, and hence not included in particular-language grammars: the rule of LEXICAL MATCHING. Like a TG, a DDG includes a lexicon in which each lexical item of the language is specified for its syntactic—and, in principle, its phonological and semantic—properties. The function of the lexical-matching rule is to map lexical items onto appropriate parts of the syntactic, phonological, and semantic representations of sentences. (Hudson says almost nothing about how phonological and semantic representations are GENERATED, and I too shall adopt a policy of benign neglect in this regard, except for a few remarks on semantic representations in Section 3.) Ordinarily, the parts of syntactic representations that are appropriate for lexical matching are single (lexical) constituent nodes, and the mapping requires identity between the syntactic features of the lexical item and those of the node. For instance, in the sample grammar, *farmer* is listed in the lexicon with the syntactic features [+ noun, + common, + count, + singular]. Thus, given a node in a syntactic representation with this set of features, it is permissible to map *farmer* onto this node and, simultaneously, onto the appropriate parts of a phonological and of a semantic representation.

Let us turn now to a consideration of how the different types of rules that are found in a DDG interact in the generation of syntactic structures, at the same time summarizing certain related matters having to do with rule ordering and the status of rules as obligatory or optional. (See also, as an example of rule interaction, etc., the derivation of the sentence *The duckling was killed by the farmer* at the end of the sample grammar.) As already noted, the structures of a DDG are generated piecemeal, through the interaction of the various types of rules included in the grammar. One general restriction on rule interaction is that the rules must apply CU-MULATIVELY: that is, that rules can apply only to add to, or further specify, structures, but can never nullify, or alter the effect of, previously applied rules. One implication of this restriction has to do with the order of application of classification rules vis-à-vis feature-assignment rules. Both of these rule types function to add features to nodes with already-specified features. (The reader may wonder how the nodes that initiate derivations—that is, the topmost nodes of syntactic representations—acquire an initial feature specification to be added to by the classification or feature-addition rules. The answer is that, by convention, this node has, to begin with, the one feature specification common to all nodes, the specification [+ item]—a specification that is, incidentally, normally omitted from structural representations because of its redundancy.) The difference between the two rule types is that, whereas the classification rules allow either of two values (+ or −) for a feature to be added to a node, the feature-addition rules require that one particular value be added under the conditions specified in the rule.

Since the feature-addition rules must in fact apply whenever the conditions for them can be met without altering the effects of previous rules, it follows that feature-addition rules always take precedence over classification rules where the conditions for both are satisfied. For example, it was noted above that there is a feature-addition rule in the sample grammar (FA6) that requires that a node that is [+ infinitive marker] be [− conjoined], while there is a classification rule (C1) that allows nodes in general to be [+conjoined]. Since infinitive markers cannot in fact be conjoined (i.e., there are no sentences like *The woman believed John to and to have killed the farmer*), it is clear that FA6, rather than C1, must apply where the conditions for both rules are met. The desired results are achieved by requiring that feature-addition rules apply whenever the conditions for them can be met without altering the effects of previous rules, and by allowing classification rules to add (but of course not change) feature specifications only after any applicable feature-addition rules have applied. [It may be noted that the classification rules—but not the feature-addition rules—are sometimes used to add REDUNDANT features to nodes. This happens when a dependency rule has assigned to a node some feature that presupposes another feature. For example, there is a sister-dependency rule in the sample grammar (SD8) that introduces a node specified as [+perfect]. Since this specification presupposes the specification [+verb] (see Classification Rule C7), this redundant specification is added to the [+perfect] node.]

Apart from the just-mentioned restriction on the classification rules, all rules other than the sequence rules, and perhaps a few daughter-dependency rules that introduce certain types of optional adverbs, may be regarded as obligatory and unordered, applying whenever the conditions for them are met. [Hudson (1976) does have some optional sister-dependency and function-assignment rules, but I believe that such optional rules can, and probably should, be replaced by obligatory rules whose application depends on features specified by the classification rules. For example, Hudson uses an optional sister-dependency rule to introduce an agentive *by*-phrase as a complement of a passive verb. But alternatively he could have allowed passive verbs to be classified for a feature [±agentive complement], with the sister-dependency rule for agentive complements applying obligatorily whenever this feature is positively specified.]

Whether or not all SEQUENCE rules are obligatory depends on how one chooses to account for optional constituent orderings (such as the ordering of the particle and the object nominal in *Take out the trash/Take the trash out*). One reasonable approach seems to be to use language-specific sequence rules only for obligatory constituent orderings, and to handle optional orderings by means of a rule of the general theory, to the effect that constituents not ordered by language-specific sequence rules may be assigned any order (subject to certain general constraints of a kind to be discussed).

The sequence rules are ordered both with respect to rules of other types and with respect to one another. Since sequence rules may be sensitive to various types of information about nodes, including information about features, functions, and sister-dependency relations, it is clear that all relevant information must be specified before the sequence rules apply. Thus, in general, sequence rules are deferred until all applicable rules of other types have applied. (There is a systematic exception to this generalization in the case of those few sequence rules that, instead of assigning an order to distinct nodes, assign to a single node features that have been introduced on the basis of distinct—daughter or sister—dependency rules: for example, Sequence Rules S1—S3 in the sample grammar. Unlike the other sequence rules, rules of this type must evidently be specified as applying as soon as the conditions for them are satisfied.)

As for the ordering WITHIN the set of sequence rules, it was noted above that, in cases of potential conflict between sequence rules (i.e., cases where the conditions for two different sequence rules, with incompatible effects, are satisfied), it is necessary to specify which rule in fact applies. This kind of specification is satisfactorily achieved by assigning to the sequence rules a fixed order of application. (This ordering may be partly determined on a non-language-specific basis—see Hudson, 1976, pp. 114–115, and the discussion later in the present section.) Recall the general constraint requiring that no rule alter the effects of a rule that has already applied. Given this constraint, imposing an order of application on the sequence rules means that, whenever an earlier sequence rule has assigned an order to two constituents, any later rule whose application would change this order is barred from applying. For example, in the sample grammar, Sequence Rule S4 orders determiners before nouns and Sequence Rule S8 orders dependent sisters after their heads. Now determiners happen to be dependent sisters of nouns (see SD13, as well as the discussion later in this section), but S8 does not apply to these constituents because S4 has already assigned them a different sequential order.

Having now concluded the discussion of rule types and rule interaction in DDG, I should like to return to a problem raised in Section 1 of this paper: the problem of imposing suitable constraints on the DDG model in the interest of enhanced explanatory adequacy. To begin with, let me call attention to two constraints that are already built into the model. First, then, there is the above-mentioned constraint to the effect that rule application is always cumulative, a constraint that means that there can be no deletions, substitutions, etc.—that is, no transformation-like operations. (This constraint is to be understood as also barring notational variants of transformations, such as a feature—say [+delete]—that would permit a constituent to have no surface realization.) Now in order for this constraint to be a step in the direction of explanatory adequacy, it must be the case that the analyses that the constraint excludes are descriptively inferior—or at least not descriptively superior—to the analyses it permits. And there is some evidence that this IS in fact the case, that is, instances in which the exclusion of transformations from DDG entails the exclusion of inferior analyses (see the discussion of DDG versus TG analyses of the auxiliary *do* in Schachter, 1978b, pp. 205–211). Although it is certainly too early to say that there are NO cases in which transformations are needed in order for descriptive adequacy to be achieved, this seems, on the basis of present evidence, to be one probably correct result that is predicted by a constraint on DDG.

A second constraint already built into the DDG model has to do with the account the model gives of constructions involving so-called "unbounded movement"—that is, constructions in which a surface constituent of a higher clause appears to have been moved out of a lower clause, and in which any number of clause nodes may, in principle, intervene between the higher and the lower clauses. English examples include *wh*-questions such as:

(3)   *What does John say that Mary thinks that I did?*

in which *what*, although a surface constituent of the topmost clause, is also the object of the most deeply embedded verb, *did*. Now in a DDG such constructions are analyzed as involving double motherhood—that is, the domination of a single node [such as the node associated with *what* in (3)] by each of two different clauses nodes [in (3), the highest and lowest clause nodes]. Double motherhood is a rather restricted phenomenon, which can come about only through the application of certain function-assignment rules, and in which only constituents with functions can be doubly mothered. [I would suggest, in fact, that only constituents with PRAGMATIC functions can be doubly mothered—that is, functions such as the FOCUS function associated with *what* in (3). Hudson (1976) also analyzes as cases of double motherhood certain constructions that involve syntactic rather than pragmatic functions—for example, "subject-raising" constructions like *The woman believed John to have killed the farmer*. But I believe that an analysis that does not involve double motherhood is preferable for such constructions: see the analysis of *believed* in the sample grammar.]

Now if unbounded movement in a DDG always involves double motherhood, and if double motherhood can only characterize constituents with (pragmatic) functions, obviously only a rather restricted set of unbounded movement constructions is compatible with the DDG model. The exact nature of the restrictions depends upon just what claims the model makes about (pragmatic) functions: for example, what functions are recognized, what types of constituents they may be assigned to, what universal positional correlates (if any) each function is claimed to have. Unfortunately, the analysis of functions in a DDG framework is still fairly primitive. In general terms, though, it seems that the functional constraints that a DDG imposes on unbounded-movement constructions correctly predict the properties of such constructions, and hence constitute a further step in the direction of explanatory adequacy (for some additional discussion, see Schachter, 1978a, pp. 360–361).

It is also possible to make use of the recognition of functions in DDG in imposing another kind of constraint on language-specific grammars. As was noted in passing above, Hudson has suggested that the ordering of the sequence rules, which determines which of two rules takes precedence in cases of potential conflict, may be partly specified by the general theory of DDG. One proposal of Hudson's that seems to be a good candidate for a universal constraint is to the effect that sequences rules that refer to FUNCTIONS always take precedence over—and therefore precede— sequence rules that refer to DEPENDENCIES. (For example, the function-based rule of English that places a questioned constituent in clause-initial position takes precedence over the dependency-based rule that places dependent sisters after their heads, as is clear from the fact that a questioned direct object, although a dependent sister of the verb, is clause-initial.) A related universal constraint that might be proposed would be to the effect that sequence rules that refer to PRAGMATIC functions always take precedence over sequence rules that refer to SYNTACTIC functions. (For example, in Breton—see Anderson and Chung, 1977—constituents with the syntactic function of subject normally follow the verb while constituents with the pragmatic function of topic are normally clause-initial. If a constituent is both subject and topic, its status as topic takes precedence, and it is clause-initial.) Again, then, we see that the descriptive framework provided by DDG seems to make it possible to state some nonobvious, but evidently correct, constraints on grammars.

I should like now to turn back to the two descriptive enrichments of DDG (vis-à-vis TG) that were identified, in Section 1, as entailing a need for new constraints: namely, the separation of the rules that specify constituent POSITION (i.e., the sequence rules) from those that specify constituent RELATIONS, and the formal representation (through application of a set of sister-dependency rules) of head–dependent relations. And I should like now to make some specific suggestions about the constraints that are needed.

As was noted in Section 1, although there is empirical support for allowing constituent position to be treated as independent of constituent relations (see the discussion of adjoined relatives), the two are in most cases quite closely related. In particular, in the absence of some language-specific rule to the contrary (such as the rule for positioning adjoined relatives in Hindi) one expects co-constituents to be either adjacent to one another or separated from one another only by other constituents of the same construction. To the extent that a DDG is required to treat what may be regarded as the normal, unmarked positioning of co-constituents (adjacency) in the same way as an unusual, marked positioning (obligatory nonadjacency), the model can be said to lack explanatory adequacy—at least if we make the plausible assumption that marked and unmarked features of language should be clearly distinguished by an explanatorily adequate theory. There is, however, an easily available remedy to this situation: namely, to eliminate from language-specific grammars all sequence rules that assign adjacency to co-constituents, and to replace such rules by a single rule of the general theory, which acts to position constituents whose position is not determined by language-specific rules. The appropriate rule for the general theory seems to be: A dependent sister is placed as close to its head as possible (i.e., as close as is consistent with language-specific sequence rules). In some cases, language-specific rules will require that a dependent sister be separated from its head, either by some other dependent(s) of the same head (e.g., in *The farmer gave John the axe, the axe* is a dependent sister of *gave* but is obligatorily separated from it by another dependent sister, *John*—see Sequence Rule S9 in the sample grammar) or by other constituents (as in the case of the Hindi adjoined-relative construction). But in the absence of any such language-specific rules, application of the proposed rule of the general theory will correctly position dependent sisters next to their heads.

Making a distinction between (marked) language-specific sequence rules and (unmarked) sequence rules of the general theory seems also to be the appropriate way to handle another case in which the sequence-rule component of DDG, as hitherto presented, is in need of constraining. As already noted, it is possible for a sequence rule to assign to a single node features that have been introduced on the basis of two distinct dependency rules (cf. Rules S1–S3 of the sample grammar). But the assignment of separately introduced features to the same node, as compared to the assignment of such features to separate nodes, is clearly a rather restricted phenomenon, and one would wish the theory to reflect this fact. This can be accomplished by adding to the general theory of DDG the following rule: Unless otherwise specified by some rule of a language-specific grammar, features that have been introduced into structures by distinct dependency rules are assigned to distinct nodes. Given this addition, it will, once more, be possible to relieve language-specific DDGs of the responsibility of accounting for unmarked phenomena: That is, there will never be any language-specific rules assigning separately introduced features to distinct nodes—a constraint that seems to be another step in the direction of a more explanatorily adequate theory of DDG.

Let us turn now to the other descriptive enrichment that has been identified as entailing a need for new constraints: the inclusion in DDG of an account of dependency relations between sister nodes, an account that takes the form of a set of sister-dependency rules introducing (features of) dependent sisters into structures on the basis of features of their heads. Since the grammar also includes a set of daughter-dependency rules introducing (features of) daughter nodes into structures on the basis of features of their mothers, it is possible, as was noted in Section 1, for a nonhead node to be introduced into a structure in any of three different ways: by means of a sister-dependency rule, by means of a daughter-dependency rule, or by means of the interaction of these two types of rules. Thus one must be able, in the case of a given nonhead node, to determine which method of introduction is appropriate. (This issue does not arise in the case of head nodes, since these clearly must be introduced by daughter-dependency rules.) Consider, for example, the question of how English determiners should be generated in a DDG. The partial DDG of English presented in Hudson (1976) introduces determiners by means of a daughter-dependency rule, and assigns to a nominal consisting of a determiner and a noun approximately the structure shown in (4a):

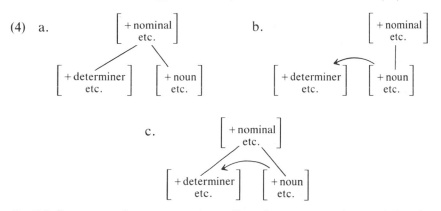

(In DDG structural representations, lines between mother and daughter nodes correspond to daughter-dependency rules, and curved arrows between sister nodes correspond to sister-dependency rules, with the arrowhead pointing to the dependent sister.) Are there clear criteria, however, for selecting this structure over (4b) or (4c)? Certainly no such criteria have thus far been articulated—and this is a serious deficiency from the point of view of both descriptive and explanatory adequacy.

What is required, then, is a principled basis for determining which of the three node-introducing methods made available by DDG is descriptively correct in any given case, and for ensuring that this correct method is in fact chosen. But this requirement turns out, I believe, to be quite easily satisfied. It seems that the desired effects can be achieved by adoption of the following rather natural general principle: Nonhead nodes must be introduced into structures by sister-dependency rules alone whenever their properties depend exclusively on properties of their heads, by daughter-dependency rules alone whenever their properties depend exclusively on properties of the nodes that dominate them, and by the interaction of sister-dependency and daughter-dependency rules whenever their properties depend on properties of both the head and the dominating node.

Let us see how this principle ensures the selection of a unique, correct analysis in some typical cases. First, since the occurrence of a particular type of verb complement in a clause appears to depend entirely on the type of head verb that occurs, and not at all upon the type of clause, verb complements must, according to the proposed principle, be introduced exclusively by means of sister-dependency rules. On the other hand, the occurrence of certain adverbs (some of the so-called sentence adverbs) appears to be dependent on the clause type, rather than the verb type. Thus an adverb like *certainly* can occur in a declarative, but not an interrogative, clause:

(5)   a. *He is certainly being foolish*
        b. **Is he certainly being foolish?*

—a fact which, according to the proposed principle, entails the introduction of the adverb node exclusively by means of a daughter-dependency rule.

Now in the case of determiners, evidence can be cited to show dependency BOTH on properties of the head noun AND on properties of the dominating nominal node—that is, to show that a structure like (4c), rather than one like Hudson's proposed (4a) [or one like (4b)], is actually correct. Thus the classification of the head noun as count or noncount determines the form of a co-occurring indefinite article: for example, *a chair* but not **a furniture* (cf. *some furniture*). But the classification of the dominating nominal node evidently determines whether an article within the nominal is definite or indefinite. Consider, in this connection, the following examples:

(6)   a. *The party is tonight*
        b. **A party is tonight*

In order to permit the grammar to generate (6a) and prevent it from generating (6b), the nominal serving as the subject of a predicate like *is tonight* must be specified as obligatorily [+ definite]. (This is handled in the sister-dependency rules that introduce nominals as sisters of predicates.) Clearly, however, the specification of the nominal as [+ definite] in cases like (6a) entails the specification of a DETERMINER as [+ definite], and this can only be done by a daughter-dependency rule to the effect that, if a definite-nominal node dominates a determiner, this determiner must also be definite. [The relevant daughter-dependency rule in the sample grammar is DD3; the sister-dependency rule that correlates properties of a determiner with those of the head noun is SD13. The interaction of these rules in generating a structure like (4c) is accomplished by Sequence Rule S2.]

Given the aforestated principle, then, determining the way in which a particular nonhead node is introduced is reducible to determining whether its properties depend on those of the dominating node, the head, or both. The principle requires the analyst to find empirical evidence of what the actual dependencies are, and requires that the analysis reflect all and only these actual dependencies, thus narrowing the range of descriptions compatible with the DDG model in an empirically appropriate way, and significantly increasing the model's explanatory adequacy.

3. SIGNIFICANCE OF THE APPROACH

This section briefly addresses itself in turn to the following three general questions:

1. What are the most significant and distinctive claims made by DDG?
2. To what extent, and in what ways, is DDG empirically falsifiable?
3. In what areas is there most need for further research on DDG?

With regard to the first of these questions, I think that the two most significant claims made by DDG both have to do with the nature of the syntactic structures the theory postulates. The first of these claims is that there is only a single level or stratum of syntactic structure, rather than the set of levels or strata postulated in certain other theories (for example, the several syntactic levels—underlying, shallow, surface, *etc*—of TG, or the multiple strata of relational grammar, as presented in Perlmutter and Postal, 1977). This claim, however, while certainly significant, is not necessarily distinctive, since there are certainly various other theories, including some represented in this volume, which agree with DDG in postulating just one level of syntactic structure.

The second significant claim about the nature of syntactic structures is, I think, a claim that does distinguish DDG from other theories, at least those with which I am familiar: namely, the claim that syntactic structures are complex amalgams of several specific kinds of information, and that this amalgam includes, for each constituent of a syntactic structure, the following: the constituent's type (identified as a complex of features that classify it in relation to other constituent types of the language), both its mother–daughter and its head–dependent relations to other constituents of the structure, its pragmatic and/or syntactic function, if any, and its linear position in relation to other constituents. While other theories typically associate some proper subset of these kinds of information with syntactic structures (for example, I would assume that all theories must give an account of the linear arrangement of constituents), I know of none that makes use of exactly this set. Moreover, DDG also claims that it is precisely these kinds of information that underlie both universal and language-specific significant generalizations (for relevant illustrations, see Hudson, 1976; Schachter, 1978a, 1979, and the earlier sections of the present paper).

To turn to the second question to be addressed, the question of the falsifiability of DDG, it is clear that the entire approach would be falsified if it could be shown that, in order to characterize correctly some syntactic construction of some language, it was absolutely necessary to postulate a nonsurface syntactic structure distinct from the surface structure. Suppose, for example, that there is some construction for which there is a descriptively adequate TG analysis that relies crucially on the postulation of an underlying syntactic structure distinct from the surface structure, and suppose further that it is impossible to devise for this construction a DDG analysis of comparable descriptive adequacy. Clearly under these circumstances, the central claim of DDG to the effect that there is only one syntactic structure for each sentence must be false. (It is therefore especially important for DDG to try to come up with descriptively adequate accounts of constructions that are satisfactorily accounted for in other theories through multilevel syntactic analyses.)

It is also possible to falsify various specific claims about universal constraints on grammars that have been, or can be, made in a DDG framework. For example, it was suggested in Section 2 that there is a universal constraint on the interaction of sequence rules that refer to pragmatic functions (such as TOPIC) and those that refer to syntactic functions (such as SUBJECT). The proposed constraint is to the effect that, in the event of potential conflict between rules of these two types, the rule that refers to pragmatic functions always prevails. (Since the resolution of such conflicts is handled in DDG by ordering the rule that prevails before the other rule, the proposed constraint means that no grammar may order a sequence rule that refers to syntactic functions before one that refers to pragmatic functions, at least where the two rules have different consequences for the placement of some constituent.) In order to falsify this claim, it is necessary only to find a language in which there is some instance of a constituent ordering based on syntactic functions prevailing over one based on pragmatic functions: say, a language that, like Breton, normally places subjects after, and topics before, verbs (see Anderson and Chung, 1977), but that, unlike Breton, places a topicalized subject AFTER the verb.

The falsification of specific claims is, of course, not devastating for a theory, since it is always possible to modify such claims in the light of the falsifying evidence. Nonetheless it is clear that much of the interest of any linguistic theory lies in the theory's ability to make correct predictions about what is and is not possible in languages, and it would certainly be worthwhile to try to increase the predictive power—and hence the falsifiability—of DDG by adding to the fairly large set of predictions the theory already makes (see Section 2) such others as seem compatible with known data. For example, it would be both possible and, I think, highly advisable to adapt to a DDG framework certain predictive generalizations originally proposed in other theoretical frameworks, a case in point being the Stratal Uniqueness Law proposed in the framework of relational grammar (see Perlmutter and Postal, 1977). This law is roughly to the effect that only one constituent per clause can have a given syntactic function in a given stratum. Since in DDG there is only one stratum (i.e., surface structure), the DDG equivalent of the Stratal Uniqueness Law would simply say that only one constituent per clause can have a given syntactic function. Building this law, or constraint, into the general theory of DDG would entail a constraint on the function-assignment component of language-specific DDGs, predicting that no DDG will ever assign a given syntactic function to two or more constituents of a clause—a prediction that adds to the falsifiability (and, if correct, also to the explanatory adequacy) of DDG.

The final question to be addressed is that of the areas in which there is most need for further research on DDG. Some answers to this question have already been suggested, both in this section and earlier in the paper. Let me briefly note—in some cases expanding on earlier remarks—four areas in which further research would obviously be useful.

The first area is the development of what at present seems to me to be the least-developed part of DDG syntax: namely, the function-assignment rules. It should, I believe, be possible to incorporate into DDG some of the insights into the interaction of pragmatic functions with syntactic structure that have been developed in other descriptive frameworks, such as that of Dik (1978). It should also be possible to incorporate some of the findings having to do with SYNTACTIC functions that have resulted from work in frameworks such as relational grammar. The aim of research in this area would be to develop a tenable universal inventory of pragmatic and syntactic functions, and a set of claims about the lawful interaction of these functions both with one another and with other aspects of grammar. (A very small amount of preliminary work along these lines has already been done; see, for example, the proposal in Schachter, 1979, that only a questioned constituent can have the focus function in a *wh*-type question.)

The second area is the formulation of appropriate universal constraints on language-specific DDGs in the interest of increasing the explanatory adequacy of the model. While various constraints have already been proposed, both in this paper and in earlier work, it is clear that there is still a tremendous amount to be done before DDG can claim to be a properly restrictive linguistic theory. For example, virtually no attention has thus far been paid by advocates of DDG to the so-called "island constraints" that have received so much attention in the TG literature (see, for instance, Ross, 1967; Chomsky, 1973)—for example, the constraint that prohibits extraction out of an English relative clause. While transformationalists may not be in agreement about how such constraints should be handled, there have certainly been some substantive proposals within a TG framework (as well as certain other frameworks), and it would obviously be a mark against DDG if it could not offer at least a comparably satisfactory account of the facts.

A third area where research is clearly needed is the interaction of syntax and semantics. DDG has thus far had virtually nothing to say about the relation between the form of a sentence and its meaning—a significant gap that I had hoped to start filling in this paper, but given the limited space at my disposal, in fact could not. It is clear that in DDG, as in recent TG, the lexicon has a significant role to play in relating syntax and semantics (see Hudson, 1976, p. 10), but almost nothing specific has been said about how this role is to be performed. My own work in this area to date has involved an attempt to adapt some TG proposals to a DDG framework—specifically, the proposals of Jackendoff (1972, 1975, 1976) concerning the lexical mapping of the syntactic and semantic properties of predicates and the capturing of syntactico-semantic lexical regularities by means of redundancy rules. It can be demonstrated, for example, that the enriched surface structures assigned by DDG provide an adequate basis for mapping onto representations of semantic-argument structures, as well as for capturing certain semantic relations between sentences (namely, those relations which in TG are ordinarily captured with the help of transformations such as Passive, Dative Movement, Raising and Equi-NP Deletion). But this demonstration will have to wait for another forum.

The final area for research, and certainly not the least important, is one that was mentioned earlier in this Section: determining whether descriptively adequate DDG analyses can be devised for all those constructions which, in TG and certain other theories, are commonly accounted for by analyses involving underlying structures that are distinct from surface structures. While generally satisfactory DDG analyses for some of these constructions have already been proposed [e.g., the analysis of *wh*-questions in Hudson (1976), which, while in need of certain refinements and extensions, seems essentially sound], English alone offers enough not-yet-analyzed constructions of the appropriate character to provide useful employment for a host of linguists. It is my hope that the presentation of DDG in this paper has been sufficiently intriguing to attract, if not a host of linguists, at least a few, to this and the other research tasks whose challenges make further work on DDG seem rewarding.

APPENDIX: SAMPLE GRAMMAR

1. Caveat

The assigned corpus to be generated by this grammar includes certain constructions that have not previously been analyzed in a DDG framework, and for which I have improvised analyses that are clearly incomplete. The constructions in question are the relative and conjoined constructions of Sentences 14–17. While the proposed analyses of these constructions appear to offer a reasonable account of the particular examples found in the corpus, these analyses would almost certainly have to be revised—perhaps drastically—if a fuller range of data were taken into consideration.

For practical reasons, I have also chosen to ignore the fact that the corpus includes an interrogative, Sentence 5. While a generally satisfactory DDG analysis of English interrogatives does exist (see Hudson, 1976 and the revisions proposed in Schachter, 1978a, 1978b), incorporating this analysis into the sample grammar would have required rather extensive modifications and additions, in order to account for interrogative word order, etc. Since these modifications and additions happen not to be needed for any of the sentences in the corpus, including Sentence 5, it seemed sensible to exclude them.

Finally, I have also ignored the idiomatic reading of 13: that is, 'The farmer fired John.' It is interesting to note, however, that since, in a DDG, structures like 13 are not tranformationally derived from underlying structures closer to 12, the fact that 13 has an idiomatic reading that 12 may lack poses no problem.

2. Classification Rules

Classification rules have the general form αx: $\pm y$, and are to be interpreted as requiring that a node with the indicated specification for the feature(s) to the left of the colon must also have some specification for the feature(s) to the right of the colon. The notation $\alpha x/\beta y$ indicates a disjunction: that is, one of the indicated feature specifications—either αx or βy—obtains.

C1. + item: ± sentence, ± nominal, ± conjoined, ± conjunct
All nodes (by convention, all nodes are [+ item]) are specified for the features [± sentence] and [± nominal]. Clauses other than nominal clauses are [+ sentence, − nominal], nominal clauses are [+ sentence, + nominal], other nominals are [− sentence, + nominal], and all other nodes are [− sentence, − nominal]. In addition, nodes may or may not dominate conjoined constructions and may or may not be conjuncts.

C2. + sentence: ± main
Clauses are either main or subordinate. (In this grammar the feature combination [+ sentence, − nominal, − main] identifies relative clauses.)

C3. + sentence, + conjoined/ + conjunct: ± gapping
A clause that dominates a conjoined construction or is itself a conjunct is specified as [+ gapping] (for sentences like 15) or [− gapping] (for sentences like 16).

C4. + conjunct: ± initial
Conjuncts are either initial conjuncts or noninitial conjuncts.

C5. + nominal, − sentence: ± definite, ± relative complement
Nonclausal nominals may be definite or indefinite, and may or may not be modified by relative clauses.

C6. − nominal, − sentence: + verb/ + noun/ + determiner/ + preposition/ + complementizer/ + infinitive marker/ + conjunction
A constituent that is neither a nominal nor a clause may be a verb, a noun, a determiner, *etc*.

C7. + verb: ± aux, ± finite/ ± perfect/ + passive
Verbs are auxiliaries or nonauxiliaries. In form they may be finite (e.g., *walked* in Sentence 1), nonfinite (e.g., *have* in 10), perfect (e.g., *been* in 10), or passive (e.g., *killed* in 10).

C8.   + verb, + aux: + perfect complement/ + passive complement
Auxiliary verbs are specified as taking either a perfect or a passive complement.

C9.   + verb, − aux: ± transitive, ± instrumental complement, ± infinitival complement, ± goal complement
Nonauxiliary verbs may be transitive or intransitive, and may or may not take instrumental, infinitival, or goal complements. (For examples of these complements, see Sentences 7, 9, and 12 respectively.)

C10. + verb, + transitive: ± sentential object, ± ditransitive
A transitive verb may take a sentential object—see Sentence 8—or not, and may be ditransitive—see 13—or not.

C11. + noun: ± common, ± singular
Nouns may or may not be common, and may be singular or plural. (All nouns in the corpus are actually singular, but the feature [+ singular] on nouns is useful in accounting for the distribution of *every* and *a(n)* in Sentences 2, 6, and 7—see sister-dependency rule SD13, C14, and the lexical entries for *every* and *a(n)*.)

C12. + noun, + common: ± count
Common nouns may be count or noncount. (All common nouns in the corpus are count nouns, but the feature [+ count] is useful, again, in accounting for *every* and *a(n)*.)

C13. + noun, − common: ± definite
Noncommon nouns may be definite or indefinite. In this grammar the definite nouns are *John, Bill,* and *he,* and the one indefinite noun is *who.*

C14. + determiner: ± definite, ± singular, ± count
Determiners may be definite or indefinite, singular or plural, and count or noncount.

C15. + preposition: + instrumental/ + goal/ + agentive
A preposition is specified as instrumental (*with*), goal (*to*), or agentive (*by*).

3. Daughter-Dependency Rules

Daughter-dependency rules have the general form $\alpha x \underset{\rightarrow}{} \beta y$, and indicate that a node with the feature specification to the left of the lowered arrow must have as a daughter a node with the feature specification to the right of the arrow. By convention, if no value for [± conjoined] is specified to the left of the arrow, as in Rules DD1–DD4, the rule is to be understood as applying when the node is [− conjoined] but not when it is [+ conjoined]. (Nodes that are [+conjoined] dominate conjoined structures. Features of the daughters of such nodes are specified in Rules DD5–DD7.)

DD1.   +sentence$_{\rightarrow}$ +verb, +finite (Condition: +sentence $\neq$ −initial, +gapping)
A clause (other than a noninitial clause in a gapping construction) contains a finite verb.

DD2.   +nominal, −sentence$_{\rightarrow}$ +noun
A nonclausal nominal contains a noun.

DD3.   +nominal, αdefinite$_{\rightarrow}$ αdefinite
A nominal contains a constituent that agrees with it in definiteness. (The (in)definite constituent is in some cases a noun or pronoun—for example, *John* is [+definite], *who* [−definite]—and in other cases a determiner—for example, *the* is [+definite], *a(n)* [−definite]. For the introduction of determiners, see SD13.)

DD4.   +sentence, −main$_{\rightarrow}$ +complementizer
A subordinate clause contains a complementizer.

DD5.   +conjoined, αf$_{\rightarrow}$ +conjunct, +initial, αf (where *f* = the other features of the [+conjoined] node)
A node dominating a conjoined construction has as a daughter an initial conjunct whose feature specifications match those of the mother.

DD6.   +conjoined, αf$_{\rightarrow}$ +conjunct, −initial, αf
A node dominating a conjoined construction has as a daughter a non-initial conjunct whose feature specifications match those of the mother.

DD7.   +conjunct, −initial, +gapping$_{\rightarrow}$ +nominal (Condition: applies twice)
A noninitial clause of a gapping construction consists of two nominals (The only gapping constructions generated are those like Sentence 15, in which the initial clause contains a finite transitive verb and the noninitial clause consists of two nominals. The restriction on the initial clause is specified in Feature-Addition Rule FA9.)

4. Sister-Dependency Rules

Sister-dependency rules have the general form $\alpha x \overset{\rightarrow}{\ } \beta y$, and indicate that a node with the feature specification to the left of the raised arrow must have as a sister a node with the feature specification to the right of the arrow. As noted in the caveat above, it has not been possible to work out a general analysis of conjunction in the time available. In particular, the interaction of conjunction with the sister-dependency rules has not received serious consideration. Only Sentence 17 poses problems concerning this interaction, and the ad hoc conditions on SD1 and SD2 permit this type of sentence to be generated while avoiding the generation of certain ungrammatical strings. These conditions, however, would very likely not be part of a more general account of conjunction.

SD1. $+$ verb, $+$ finite $\longrightarrow$ $+$ nominal (Condition: $+$ verb $\neq$ $+$ conjunct)
A finite verb has a nominal as sister. (This nominal is identified as the SUBJECT by Function Rule F1. In the case of a sentence like 17, the subject nominal introduced by SD1 is the sister of a node specified as [$+$ verb, $+$ finite, $+$ conjoined]. This node has two daughter nodes specified as [$+$ verb, $+$ finite, $+$ conjunct] (see DD5–DD6), and the condition on SD1 prevents these daughter nodes from having their own subjects distinct from the subject of the mother node.)

SD2. $+$ transitive, α sentential object $\longrightarrow$ $+$ nominal, α sentence (Condition: $+$ verb $\neq$ $+$ conjoined)
A transitive verb has a nominal as a sister. If the verb is specified as taking a sentential object, this nominal is sentential; otherwise it is nonsentential. (In the case of a sentence like 17, each of the two [$+$ conjunct] transitive verb nodes has its own object. The condition on SD2 prevents the [$+$ conjoined] verb node that is the mother of the [$+$ conjunct] nodes from having its own object distinct from those of its daughters.)

SD3. $+$ ditransitive $\longrightarrow$ $+$ nominal
A ditransitive verb (such as *gave* in 13) has another nominal as sister.

SD4. $+$ preposition $\longrightarrow$ $+$ nominal
A preposition has a nominal as sister. (Prepositions are themselves introduced by SD5–SD7.)

SD5. $+$ passive $\longrightarrow$ $+$ preposition, $+$ agentive
A passive verb has an agentive preposition (i.e., *by*) as sister. (The corpus does not contain any agentless passives. In a more complete grammar, passive verbs could be classified for a feature [$\pm$ agentive complement], and SD5 could be made contingent on a positive specification of this feature.)

SD6. $+$ instrumental complement $\longrightarrow$ $+$ preposition, $+$ instrumental

A verb specified as [+instrumental complement] has an instrumental preposition (i.e., *with*) as sister.

SD7. +goal complement $\rightarrow$ +preposition, +goal
A verb specified as [+goal complement] has a goal preposition (i.e., *to*) as sister.

SD8. +perfect complement $\rightarrow$ +perfect
A verb specified as [+perfect complement] (e.g., *have* in 10) has a [+perfect] verb form as sister.

SD9. +passive complement $\rightarrow$ +passive
A verb specified as [+passive complement] (e.g., *been* in 10) has a [+passive] verb form as sister.

SD10. +infinitival complement $\rightarrow$ +infinitive marker
A verb specified as [+infinitival complement] (e.g., *believed* in 9) has an infinitive marker (i.e., *to*) as sister.

SD11. +infinitive marker $\rightarrow$ +verb, −finite
An infinitive marker has a nonfinite verb as sister.

SD12. +nominal, +relative complement $\rightarrow$ +sentence, −nominal, −main
A nominal specified as [+relative complement] has a relative clause as sister.

SD13. +noun, +count, +singular $\rightarrow$ +determiner, +count, +singular
A singular count noun has a singular count determiner as sister. (The singular count determiners in this grammar are *every* and *a(n)*; *the* may also be singular and count, but may have other categorizations as well. In a more complete grammar, SD13 would be generalized to account for the determiner co-occurrences of noncount and plural nouns.)

SD14. +conjunct, −initial $\rightarrow$ +conjunction
A noninitial conjunct has a conjunction as sister.

5. Feature-Addition Rules

Feature-addition rules have the general form [αx]: βy and are to be interpreted as requiring that a node with the indicated specification for the feature(s) to the left of the colon must also have the indicated specification for the feature(s) to the right of the colon. (N.B.: Like other rules, feature-addition rules apply cumulatively, and cannot change feature specifications. Therefore, feature-addition rules apply only to nodes which have not been otherwise specified for the feature(s) to the right of the colon by a daughter-dependency or sister-dependency rule.) The notation $[\alpha x \leftarrow \beta y]$ refers to a node with the indicated specification for the feature(s) x which is a daughter of a node with the indicated specification for the feature(s) y.)

FA1. [+item]: +sentence, −nominal, +main
An otherwise unspecified node—that is, the initial node in every derivation—is a main clause.

FA2. [+nominal]: −sentence
Nominals are normally nonsentential. (In this grammar sentential nominals are introduced only by SD2.)

FA3. [+sentence, +nominal]: −main
Sentential nominals are subordinate (and thus contain complementizers—see DD4).

FA4. [+passive]: −aux
A verb that is specified as [+passive] is not an auxiliary.

FA5. [+noun ← +nominal, +relative complement]: +common
The head noun of a relative construction must be a common noun. (N.B.: The grammar generates only RESTRICTIVE relative clauses.)

FA6. [+determiner/+infinitive marker/+complementizer/+conjunction/+preposition]: −conjoined
Determiners, infinitive markers, complementizers, conjunctions, and prepositions (in this grammar) do not conjoin.

FA7. [+item]: −conjunct
If a constituent is not required to be a conjunct (see DD5–DD6), then it is not a conjunct.

FA8. [+sentence, +conjunct]: −gapping
If a sentential conjunct is not required to be [+gapping] (as a result of DD5 or DD6), then it is [−gapping].

FA9. [+verb, +finite ← +sentence, +conjunct, +initial, +gapping]: +transitive
The finite verb of the initial clause of a gapping construction (in this grammar) is transitive (see Sentence 15 and DD7).

6. Function-Assignment Rules

The following function-assignment rules are stated discursively, for the sake of clarity.

F1. Assign SUBJECT to the [+nominal] introduced by SD1.
The subject of a sentence is the nominal that depends on the occurrence of a finite verb.

F2. Assign TOPIC to a [+nominal] constituent of a clause specified as [+sentence, −nominal, −main].

The topic function in a relative clause is assigned to a nominal constituent of the clause. [This nominal is realized as the antecedent of the relative clause—see Sequence Rules S3 and S6. The analysis of the antecedent of a relative clause as its topic is based on Kuno (1976).]

7. Sequence Rules

Some sequence rules are stated discursively for the sake of clarity. In those which are stated formally, $x \rightarrow y$ means 'x precedes y.' As noted in Section 2, some sequence rules are part of the general theory and thus need not be included in language-specific grammars. Among the sequence rules proposed for the general theory are: (*a*) a dependent sister is placed as close to its head as possible (i.e., as close as is consistent with language-specific sequence rules), and (*b*) unless otherwise specified by some rule of a language-specific grammar, features introduced by distinct dependency rules are assigned to distinct nodes. The sequence rules are ordered, with an earlier rule prevailing over a later rule in cases of conflict. (That is, a later rule can never affect a sequence that has already been assigned.)

S1. Within a given [+nominal], if the [+noun] introduced by DD2 is specified as [−common] (see C11), then the [αdefinite] introduced by DD3 is assigned to the same node.

A noncommon noun carries the definiteness specification of the nominal in which it occurs, and there is no other carrier of definiteness within this nominal.

S2. Within a given [+nominal], a [+determiner] introduced by SD13 is assigned to the same node as the [αdefinite] introduced by DD3.

There is (at most) one determiner per nominal, and it carries the definiteness specification of the nominal.

S3. The TOPIC [+nominal] of a [−nominal, −main] clause is combined with (assigned to the same node as) the [+nominal] on which the clause depends.

The topic of a relative clause (see F2) is also its head (see SD12).

S4. [+determiner] $\rightarrow$ [+noun]

Determiners precede nouns.

S5. [+conjunction] $\rightarrow$ [+conjunct, −initial]

A conjunction precedes a non-initial conjunct.

S6. TOPIC $\rightarrow$ [+complementizer] $\rightarrow$ X

Topics precede complementizers; complementizers precede other clause constituents.

S7. SUBJECT → [+verb, +finite]
   Subjects precede finite verbs (in this grammar).
S8. Dependent sisters follow their heads.
S9. The [+nominal] introduced by SD2 precedes other dependent sisters
   of the verb.
   The direct object of a verb (i.e., the [+nominal] that depends upon
   the verb's being [+transitive]—see SD2) precedes any other com-
   plements to the verb.

8. Lexicon

VERBS

The lexical entries for verbs omit most syntactic features not relevant
to the examples in the corpus. (Thus *walked* is not specified as allowing
a goal complement, since the corpus does not include any sentences like
The woman walked to the farmer.) Also omitted are negative specifications for such features as [±sentential object], [±infinitival complement],
[±ditransitive]. It may be assumed that if a verb is not positively specified
for these features, then it is in fact negatively specified. There are three
verbs in the lexicon—*believed, gave,* and *killed*—for which the corpus
attests more than one syntactic classification. For these verbs each distinct classification appears as a separate line in the lexical entry.

been	+verb, +aux, +perfect, +passive complement
believed	+verb, −aux, +finite, +transitive, +sentential object
	+verb, −aux, +finite, +transitive, +infinitival complement
	+verb, −aux, +passive, +infinitival complement
gave	+verb, −aux, +finite, +transitive, +goal complement
	+verb, −aux, +finite, +transitive, +ditransitive
have	+verb, +aux, −finite, +perfect complement
killed	+verb, −aux, +finite, +transitive, ±instrumental complement
	+verb, −aux, +perfect, +transitive
	+verb, −aux, +passive
loved	+verb, −aux, +finite, +transitive
walked	+verb, −aux, +finite, −transitive
was	+verb, +aux, +finite, +passive complement

NOUNS

axe	+noun, +common, +count, +singular
Bill	+noun, −common, +definite

duckling	+ noun, + common, + count, + singular
farmer	+ noun, + common, + count, + singular
he	+ noun, − common, + definite
John	+ noun, − common, + definite
who	+ noun, − common, − definite
woman	+ noun, + common, + count, + singular

OTHER

a(n)	+ determiner, − definite, + count, + singular
and	+ conjunction
by	+ preposition, + agentive
every	+ determiner, + definite, + count, + singular
that	+ complementizer
the	+ determiner, + definite, ± count, ± singular
to	+ infinitive marker
to	+ preposition, + goal
with	+ preposition, + instrumental

9. Derivation of *The duckling was killed by the farmer*

1. The topmost node is specified as [+ sentence, − nominal, + main]
   by FA1. DD1 requires that a [+ sentence] node have a daughter with
   the features [+ verb, + finite]. By adding to this node the features
   [+ aux] and [+ passive complement] (see C7–C8), we derive the
   structure:

$$
\begin{bmatrix} + \text{sentence} \\ - \text{nominal} \\ + \text{main} \end{bmatrix}
$$

$$
\begin{bmatrix} + \text{verb} \\ + \text{aux} \\ + \text{finite} \\ + \text{passive complement} \end{bmatrix}
$$

2. SD1 introduces a [+ nominal] node as a sister of [+ verb, + finite],
   and this node is further specified as [− sentence] by FA2 and
   [+ definite] by C5. Rule SD9 introduces a [+ passive] node, which
   is redundantly [+ verb] by C7, and which is [− aux] by FA4. Our

structure is now:

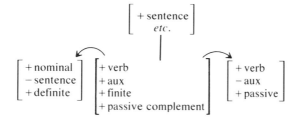

(Actually the sister nodes are unordered at this point, but for expository convenience the nodes are shown in the order that is ultimately assigned to them, in this and in subsequent diagrams.)

3. Rule SD5 introduces a [+ preposition, + agentive] node as a sister of [+ passive] and SD4 introduces a [+ nominal] node as a sister of [+ preposition]. This [+ nominal] is further specified as [− sentence, + definite] as above, yielding the structure:

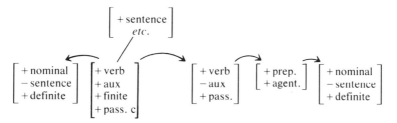

4. Each of the two [+ nominal, − sentence] nodes gets a [+ noun] daughter by DD2, and a [+ definite] daughter by DD3. Each of the [+ noun] nodes is further specified as [+ common, + count, + singular] by C11–C12. Rule SD13 introduces a [+ determiner, + count, + singular] node as a sister of the [+ noun] node. Thus each [+ nominal, − sentence] node is associated with the structure:

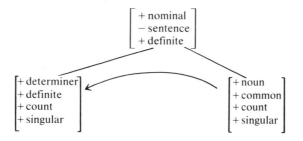

(Actually the [+definite] introduced by DD3 has not yet been assigned to the same node as the [+determiner] introduced by SD13. Rather, this is done later by S2—see Step 5.)

5. Rule F1 assigns the SUBJECT function to the [+nominal] introduced by SD1, and the constituents are assigned a sequential order as follows: Rule S2 assigns the [+definite] specifications introduced by DD3 to the relevant determiner nodes; S4 orders determiners before nouns; S7 places the SUBJECT before the finite verb; S8 orders the [+passive] node after the [+passive complement] node, the [+preposition, +agentive] node after the [+passive] node, and the [+nominal] node introduced by SD4 after the [+preposition] node. Lexical matching now completes the derivation, resulting in the structure:

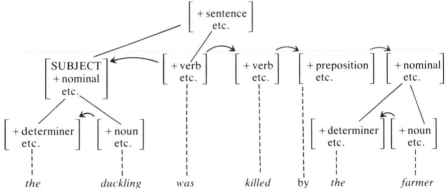

REFERENCES

Anderson, S., and Chung, S. (1977). On grammatical relations and clause structure in verb-initial languages. In P. Cole and J. Sadock (Eds.), *Syntax and Semantics 8: Grammatical Relations*. New York: Academic Press. Pp. 1–25.

Andrews, A. (1975). Studies in the Syntax of Relative and Comparative Clauses. Unpublished doctoral dissertation, MIT, Cambridge, Mass.

Chomsky, N. (1957). *Syntactic Structures*. The Hague: Mouton.

Chomsky, N. (1964). Current issues in linguistic theory. In J. Fodor and J. Katz (Eds.), *The Structure of Language*. Englewood Cliffs, N.J.: Prentice-Hall. Pp. 50–118.

Chomsky, N. (1965). *Aspects of the Theory of Syntax*. Cambridge, Mass: MIT Press.

Chomsky, N. (1973). Conditions on transformations. In S. Anderson and P. Kiparsky (Eds.) *A Festschrift for Morris Halle*. New York: Holt, Rinehart, and Winston.

Chomsky, N., and Lasnik, H. (1977). Filters and control. *Linguistic Inquiry, 8*, 425–504.

Dik, S. (1978). *Functional Grammar*. Amsterdam: North-Holland.

Greenberg, J. (1963). Some universals of grammar with particular reference to the order of meaningful elements. In J. Greenberg (Ed.), *Universals of Language*. Cambridge, Mass: MIT Press. Pp. 58–90.

Hudson, R. (1976). *Arguments for a Non-Transformational Grammar*. Chicago: University of Chicago Press.

Jackendoff, R. (1972). *Semantic Interpretation in Generative Grammar*. Cambridge, Mass: MIT Press.

Jackendoff, R. (1975). Morphological and semantic regularities in the lexicon. *Language, 51*, 639–671.

Jackendoff, R. (1976). Toward an explanatory semantic representation. *Linguistic Inquiry, 7*, 89–150.

Kuno, S. (1976). Subject, theme, and the speaker's empathy—a reexamination of relativization phenomena. In C. Li (Ed.), *Subject and Topic*. New York: Academic Press, Pp. 417–444.

Perlmutter, D. (1970). Surface structure constraints in syntax. *Linguistic Inquiry, 1*, 187–255.

Perlmutter, D., and Postal, P. (1977). Toward a universal characterization of passivization. In K. Whistler *et al.* (Eds.), *Proceedings of the Third Annual Meeting of the Berkeley Linguistics Society*. Berkeley: Berkeley Linguistics Society.

Peters, P. S., and Ritchie, R. W. (1973). On the generative power of transformational grammars. *Information Sciences, 6*, 49–83.

Ross, J. (1967). Constraints on Variables in Syntax. Bloomington, Ind: Indiana University Linguistics Club.

Schachter, P. (1978a). Review article: *Arguments for a Non-Transformational Grammar*, by Richard A. Hudson. *Language, 54*, 348–376.

Schachter, P. (1978b). English Propredicates. *Linguistic Analysis, 4*, 187–224.

Schachter, P. (1979). Further arguments for a nontransformational grammar. In D. Malsch *et al.* (Eds.), *Proceedings of the Eighth Annual Meeting of the Western Conference on Linguistics*, Carbondale and Edmonton: Linguistic Research, Inc. Pp. 131–146.

SYNTAX AND LINGUISTIC SEMANTICS IN STRATIFICATIONAL THEORY

WILLIAM J. SULLIVAN
University of Florida

1. PRELIMINARY REMARKS

Before beginning the main body of this study, I wish to outline in more general terms the immediate and long-term aims of stratificational theory (SG). I follow this with an outline of the stratificational view of language and the basic assumptions of the theory. The study itself describes most of the 17 sentences circulated as the conference data set, in the context of a general description of the surface syntactic structure of the English clause. The study concludes with an explicit set of answers to the questions circulated with the conference data set.

The immediate aim of SG is to account for the production and deciphering of spoken or written texts of arbitrary length. This includes what is produced, how it may be produced, what is understood, and how it may be understood, including the pragmatic and sociocultural purposes of the discourse. If possible, the model used should also give insight into language acquisition and language change. In any case, the model used must be internally consistent in a logical sense and must not contradict anything we know about the structure and operation of the brain. Note that this is a requirement, not a claim that SG is a neurological theory of language.

301

The long-term aim of SG is to account for language and language use as a portion of general cognitive–neurological functions. This includes logical and nonlogical thought, slips of the tongue, troublesome ellipses of all kinds, communicative grunts, *etc*. This suggests to me that linguistics will ultimately have to develop a neurological theory of language.

In making this statement, I şpeak as an individual. No one speaks for all stratificationalists, nor has anyone ever done so. Some stratificationalists would reject most, if not all, of the long-term aims listed above as an unnecessary addition to the aims of linguistics. What stratificationalists have in common is accounting for the first-mentioned immediate aim— encoding and decoding texts of arbitrary length. I would certainly not be dissatisfied with a successful completion of this task for some language. Whatever, plenty of work remains to be done.

The question of compatibility between "theories" emphasized in the literature of this conference may thus be faced on several fronts. However, in light of Edith Moravcsik's excellent introductory paper, I do not dwell on these issues. Moreover, our instructions insist that we must not only focus on what differences there are, but on whether they are incidental. But in keeping with the spirit of mutual study articulated so well during the conference by J. R. Ross, I will omit such discussion. I merely develop a generalized statement of the English clause on the way to describing the conference data set. No such description has ever been supplied in over 20 years of intensive study of English syntax. This may or may not be coincidence; however, a generalized description of the lexotactic relations of the English clause is a necessary result of the application of stratificational methods to the data of English.

2. THE STRATIFICATIONAL ORGANIZATION OF LANGUAGE

2.1. The Definition of Language

Stratificational theory defines language as a complex relational network interconnecting meaning and sound, via which messages are encoded into, and decoded from sound. This definition is purely Hjelmslevian (cf. Fischer-Jorgensen, 1975, Chapter 10), though the insistence on relationships and the need to make them explicit reaches a peak among certain stratificationalists (Lamb, Lockwood, Sullivan). This is not a prerequisite, however; Makkai and Christie are somewhat less oriented toward explicit relational-network diagrams than I, and Griffen tries not to use them at all. Gleason has never insisted on the sufficiency of relations in the descriptive model.

Certain terms in the above definition should be made explicit. Simple RELATIONSHIPS are connections between at least three separate lines or points, defined on some consistent basis. The basis of these definitions could be a verbal statement, an electronic analogue, or a logical or neurological system. A NETWORK is a series of relationships between simple relationships, all defined in the same ways as the simple relationships. COMPLEX here is to be understood in the same sense as Chomsky's "elaborated": a very simple set of basic axioms/assumptions combined indefinitely into a highly elaborated (complex) structure. INTERCONNECTING meaning and sound means that the structure exists between the two. It is not itself directional; it is simply there, and it is used for encoding and decoding. ENCODING has inputs at meaning which follow internally defined paths through the network to outputs at sound. DECODING has inputs at sound which follow internally defined paths through the network to outputs at meaning. MEANING and SOUND are conceptual simplifications referring to the domains of the message(s)/stored knowledge and the medium of communication, respectively.

I speak about a single network between meaning and sound for the sake of simplicity, but this does not rule out other possibilities. That is, linguistic structure might be two parallel one-way networks with extensive interrelations. Moreover, for literates, the written language has its own structure. This overlaps with and must be integrated into the structure of spoken language. And so on.

These informal comments probably should be extended, for the sake of clarity. But I am arbitrarily cutting them off at this point because of space limitations. Anything not made explicit above should probably be considered open to alternative interpretations. No guru has ever preached the way or told which choice must be made. Each choice has its own consequences, which must be determined empirically. This is not to say that all choices are equal; the consequences differ from choice to choice. Further, Gleason has consistently maintained that stratificationalism is a convergence, and he is right. A number of theoreticians whose assumptions began in a radically different fashion are currently adopting a number of features already present in SG. These features have been forced upon them by descriptive considerations. In SG, however, the features are derivable from the assumptions basic to SG which are outlined above, either directly or as a result of their application to language data. I return to this point below.

2.2. The Relationships and Their Patterning

The relationships I see as necessary to the description of linguistic structure are logically specifiable (cf. Sullivan, 1977; Sullivan, in press). There are four logical varieties: the simple AND node, the simple OR node, AND with PRECEDENCE, and OR with PRECEDENCE. The latter two are also called the ORDERED nodes: An ORDERED AND specifies precedence in time; an ORDERED OR specifies precedence in choice.

These nodes are all defined in terms of three logical connectives: and (&), or (∨), and implication (⊃). Each of these nodes has a singular side (one connection) and a plural side (two or more connections). The plural side may be oriented upward, toward meaning, or downward, toward sound. Note that the inventory of nodes and the orientation of their connectivity is a direct consequence of the assumptions made in the preceding paragraph. This is not, however, a claim that they are original descriptive concepts.

The downward AND node represents the relationship called concatenation. The upward version represents portmanteau realization. It also serves as the knot between the realizational and tactic portions of linguistic structure, a consideration to which I shall return. The upward ORDERED AND node seems not to be needed, though permitting it introduces no logical inconsistencies. The downward ORDERED AND node is a syntagm. The simple OR is a paradigm in the downward orientation and a neutralization in the upward orientation. The downward ORDERED OR node indicates markedness in a paradigm. The necessity for an upward ORDERED OR is also open to question, but might be used to indicate a marked interpretation or meaning.

The contribution of stratificational theory (and in particular of Lamb) in this way has been to show exactly how and to what logical extent these various concepts are related. Stratificational descriptions have also used these relationships in more general fashion than was heretofore the case, even among glossematists. Note further that these relationships are the only descriptive primitives in stratificational theory. All linguistic functives found in the model—subject, object, clause, agent, etc.—whatever their importance, are derived from these relationships. A failure to understand this fact leads to a misunderstanding of a number of important consequences of the model. With this caveat, I abandon this topic, in the interest of space considerations.

Now these simple relationships are grouped into larger networks, called STRATA. I emphasize that this patterning is empirical, emerging from descriptive work and not from preconceived notions about how the model should look. Each stratum resolves into a tactic pattern or tactics and a realizational portion. The tactic pattern specifies the permissible combinations of the elements basic to that stratum. The realizational portions interconnect adjacent tactic patterns and, eventually, meaning and sound. There are many questions left unresolved by the structure of the model outlined so far, for example, the number of strata, the evidence necessary and sufficient for defining a stratum, and the locus of knots interconnecting realizational and tactic patterns. These are also empirical issues, which will be resolved in the course of description of substantial amounts of linguistic data.

2.3. The Shape of the Model

What has loosely been called "syntax" is described on the content side of language, as illustrated in Figure 1. The general configuration of the model looks like a conglomeration of suggestions made by many different linguists over the last hundred years or so. It does have that effect. In fact, however, it is what has been established by the empirical means mentioned above: the description of data under stratificational assumptions.

Note that the discipline called semantics in Figure 1 covers both gnostology or general semantics and semology or linguistic semantics. Only semology is a part of language. This distinction requires further discussion. Consider first the sememic role relation (deep case) Agent in Russian. It is a single sememe on the sememic stratum. The agent sememe is realized by the nominative case lexeme if the agentive noun is in subject position of the clause, or by the instrumental case lexeme elsewhere. Agent is, in other words, a single sememe with two lexemic realizations which are in complementary lexotactic distribution. The two lexotactic environments specify the positions of realization as part of their ordering function.

The example can be taken further. The lexemic case "instrumental" is realized as the morphological ending *ami* in the plural or as *om, oj,* or *'ju* in the singular, depending on the morphological stem class. Again, the single lexeme is realized by four morphemes which are in complementary morphotactic distribution.

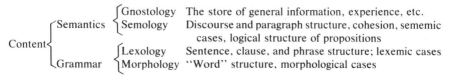

		Gnostology	The store of general information, experience, etc.
Content	Semantics	Semology	Discourse and paragraph structure, cohesion, sememic cases, logical structure of propositions
	Grammar	Lexology	Sentence, clause, and phrase structure; lexemic cases
		Morphology	"Word" structure, morphological cases

Figure 1 The content side of language.

In this fashion, "syntax" is described: some of it as semology, some as lexology, some as morphology. All these levels of language have their contribution to make to what TG has labeled "syntax." Some of the contributions these levels have to make has been forgotten or ignored by the majority of TG syntacticians. Some of it has been painfully rediscovered. Some of it is today remembered only by tagmemicists or stratificationalists.

2.4. Syntax and Nonsyntax

Some of what several TG models have called "syntactic" is not herein considered part of the language at all. Both generative semantics, in assuming that the linguistic remote structure is "the meaning," and interpretive semantics, in assuming it is possible to assign a meaning directly to a single sentence (or lexical item), imply that meaning is a part of or directly attached to language. Gleason's insistence that "language doesn't *have* meaning, it *evokes* meaning," best expresses the stratificational view. The evocative direction of the answer "yes" depends on whether the question is "Should I hand in my homework now?" or "Should I jump out the window now?"

But this is not to claim that gnostology has no real, regular, and directly language-relevant functions. It has many of them, for example, antonymy. This includes the relation between *high* and *low, big* and *little,* but also *buy* and *sell, vanilla* and *chocolate.* But remember that antonymy is outside of language and should be treated as part of general (nonlinguistic) semantics. The linguistic processing of an utterance or text produces sememic outputs which are inputs to the general semantic store. This, in turn processes these inputs to deduce the relevance and greater significance (i.e., immediate and general meaning) of the utterance. This, in short, is SG's view of "meaning."

2.5. Complexity

In sum, stratificationalists believe that the complexity of linguistic structure and of general semantic or cognitive structure is far greater than has been posited before. At the same time, and almost paradoxically, we believe in a very simple axiom set as the basis for our models. To date, these simple but highly elaborated stratificational models have been suddessful. Further research by large numbers of linguists may expose shortcomings, much as the hard work of large numbers of workers in the TG framework did for the Aspects model in the mid- and late sixties. Or further research may demonstrate the basic soundness of the stratificational assumptions. Only time will tell.

3. A STRATIFICATIONAL DESCRIPTION OF A PORTION OF ENGLISH SYNTAX

3.1. Plan of Attack

Below I present a description of certain "syntactic" data. The sentences circulated before this conference form a portion of the data analyzed. But before I describe them, I produce a generalized description of the simple clause in English. The materials circulated are then subjected to scrutiny in light of the structure of the simple clause, and any data not already accounted for are integrated into clause structure. The lexotactic structure involved is fully presented. Certain portions of semotactic structure are also presented, even though the full semotactics is not ready for integrated presentation. The morphological structures, though important, are left out in the interest of simplicity. Sufficient structure is available to demonstrate the stratificational description of "syntax."

In section 5 I answer the questions asked in the preliminary circular explicitly (See Appendix to this volume). Though this order of presentation is not particularly satisfactory from an aesthetic point of view, I leave these answers until last. The questions should be answered in the context of a familiarity with the stratificational mode of description, however minimal the data set may be.

3.2. A Caveat or Two

In Section 2 I discussed both stratificational theory per se and the particular model I use. The distinction is an important one, but one that trips up many observers and would-be critics. To cite one example which appeared in a confused manner in Stockwell's oral comments, the theory is not antineurological; the model used herein is simply logical. Neither the theory nor the model are neurological approaches. But if one cannot see the distinction between "not antineurological" and "neurological," it is perhaps better to leave the issue unbroached.

Stratificationalists all believe in the same theory and may even have the same goals. But with regard to the model, we can differ widely. Perhaps many of us are engineers, whose main interest is in getting the job done as efficiently as possible within the general constraints laid down.

This is my own attitude. Conversely, the "God's Truth" view of descriptive models is not entirely excluded, either. What this means is that criticism of a particular description or model must be very pointed, very well aimed.

3.3. A Fragment of Lexotactics

The lexotactics encompass the generalizations possible at the level of surface syntax. Just what constitutes surface syntax is a question that has traditionally been answered in terms of noun phrases, auxiliaries, verbs, and prepositional phrases. I see these as representing a set of morphological rather than (surface) syntactic structures. Morphology is not incompatible with surface syntax at all; the two must eventually be integrated. But these categories of morphemes and morphemic phrases are not the basic elements of surface syntax, in spite of the fact that they appear as the boundary markers in Chomskyan "deep" structure. In fact, given this bastardized cross between morphological phrase markers and "deep" syntax, I find it difficult to disagree with the criticisms of EST in McCawley (1978).

However, I do not agree with the claim that there is no significant level of description between the logical (sememic) and morphological. My hypothesis is that this intermediate level is the lexemic stratum or "surface" syntax. McCawley and Gleason may be right; the lexotactics may be simply the upper portion of the morphotactics. However, this is a real empirical issue, one that will be resolved in the context of a full description of English syntax and morphology. It can be ignored for the present.

To repeat: My description concentrates on the semotactics and lexotactics. The relations between these tactic patterns are realizational. Realizational relations between strata serve functions during the encoding process parallel to the functions served by transformations which relate deep and surface structure in TG. However, realizational relations differ from transformations in a number of significant ways. First, realizational relations are identical in logical type to tactic relations; transformations differ from phrase structure rules in the areas of context-sensitivity and order of application. Second, realizational relations can be used in both directions, that is, for encoding and decoding; transformations only operate in one direction. Other differences exist, but these two statements focus on the two critical factors. Detailed discussion is found in Lamb (1966) and Sullivan (1977); it is not repeated here.

The realizational relations in the description below are simple, one-to-one relations. They connect the proposition structures in the semotactics, wherein the sememic cases are defined, with the clause structures in the lexotactics, wherein the distributional realizations of the sememic cases across the clause are described.

Because of space limitations, no detailed justification of the sememic cases invoked or of the lexotactic structures is given. The cases used are defined in Table 1 and their application to sample sentences is given in Table 2. The inventory of cases is a preliminary one, a list of everything I could find some need for, and the list should not be considered closed. Moreover, it is possible that some of the cases can be collapsed. A full semotactic investigation is necessary to determine which sememic cases are in complementary distribution. Such considerations are also ignored for the sake of brevity.

Remember that there are numerous questions that must be asked about the inventory and distribution of sememic cases and their interrelations. Although these questions are being ignored for the purposes of this study, they are nonetheless important.

Consider the data in Table 2. They are restricted to sentences consisting of a single clause. That is, one finite verb is permitted. No embedded infinitive phrases or subordinate clauses are included. Modals other than the passive "be" are left out only for the sake of convenience; they fit right in.

Now consider some specific clauses in Table 2. Sentence (e) shows an ambiguity between beneficiary and client, but (f) can only be interpreted with beneficiary. Sentence (l) has a patient in post-verbal complement position. It has been suggested that the complement here is a recipient of the help or hurt, or that it represents beneficiary or maleficiary. But Al's status as beneficiary or maleficiary is deducible directly from the

TABLE 1

SEMEMIC CASES DEFINED[a]

Agent (Ag):	Effector, doer, or performer of the act
Patient (Pa):	Undergoes the act or is in some state
Recipient (Rc):	Receives the patient
Instrument (In):	Means or tool by which the act is performed or effected
Beneficiary (Bn):	Profits from the act
Maleficiary (Ml):	Suffers loss from the act
Identifier (Ir):	Identifies some other case nominally
Range (Ra):	Delimits the act-patient relationship or defines the extent or degree of application of the state
Client (Cl):	For whom the act is performed
Experiencer (Ex):	Experiences the state or act (distinct from both Ag and Pa)

[a]Time and space relations are ignored; cf. Bennett (1975).

TABLE 2

DATA FOR LEXOTACTICS

Surface form of the clause		Realization of sememic cases
John reads	a	Ag V
John read a book	b	Ag V Pa
John read a book to Mary	c	Ag V Pa *to* Rc
John read Mary a book	d	Ag V Rc Pa
Joan bought a gift for Ed	e	Ag V Pa *for* Bn/Cl
Joan bought Ed a gift	f	Ag V Bn Pa
Hal sold a car to Joan for me	g	Ag V Pa *to* Rc *for* Bn/Cl
Hal sold a car to Joan on me	h	Ag V Pa *to* Rc *on* Ml
Bob wrote a letter to Anne with a pencil	i	Ag V Pa *to* Rc *with* In
Bob wrote a letter for me with a pencil	j	Ag V Pa *for* Bn/Cl *with* In
We elected Bob president	k	Ag V Pa Ra
Beth helped/hurt Al	l	Ag V Pa (Bn, Ml implicit)
Sal burned the forest with a fire	m	Ag V Pa *with* In
A fire burned the forest	n	In V Pa
The fire is burning/Fire burns	o	In V
The forest burned	p	Pa V
Jack is the doctor/The doctor is Jack	q	Pa V Ir
Jack is a doctor	r	Pa V Ra
It's cold to me	s	Pa V *to* Ex
I'm cold	t	Pa V
Bert told it to me	u	Ag V Pa *to* Rc
Bert told me that	v	Ag V Rc Pa or Ag V Pa Ra
Mary was given a book by John	w	Rc V Pa *by* Ag
This letter was written for me with a pencil by Bob	x	Pa V *for* Bn/Cl *with* In *by* Ag
This letter was written with a pencil by Bob	y	Pa V *with* In *by* Ag
This letter was written by Bob with a pencil(?)	z	Pa V *by* Ag *with* In
Al was helped/hurt by Beth	aa	Pa V *by* Ag
Bob was elected president by our group	bb	Pa V Ra *by* Ag
The car was sold to Joan for me by Hal	cc	Pa V *to* Rc *for* Bn/Cl *by* Ag
The car was sold to Joan on me by Hal	dd	Pa V *to* Rc *on* Ml *by* Ag
The car was sold to Joan for me	ee	Pa V *to* Rc *for* Bn/Cl
The car was sold for me by Hal	ff	Pa V *for* Bn/Cl *by* Ag
My car was sold on me	gg	Pa V *on* Ml

verb. And whether he actually receives the help or hurt directly is deducible from the greater context. The passive of (l) is found in (aa). This suggests that Al is a patient. Moreover, though this case assignment is vague, its imprecision is a virtue. It allows us to accept the spectrum of possibilities that exist, without the rigidity which would exclude some possible interpretations.

The patient in (s) is expressed by extraphoric deixis, called "ambient *it*" by Bolinger. Though it is a pronoun rather than a noun, I do not consider it an "empty" lexeme or a mere marker of subject position. It has definite semiotic function.

An example of nonunique case assignment is given in (v). This example is included to show that both can be accommodated without difficulty. No resolution of the ambiguity is attempted; it probably should not be resolved.

Sentence (z) is followed by a question mark because I do not like it. It certainly occurs, and I can parse it, but I do not use it myself. Figure 2 below predicts that it will be understood but not produced. Accepting (y) and (z) on the same footing would require an unordered OR node relating In and Ag in the last post-verbal complement position.

Sentences (w)–(gg) give a small sampling of passive types. These neither exhaust the inventory nor show the relationship between an active–passive pair. This relationship is properly a semotactic function, as is the description of the environments in the discourse block that evoke the passive. Sentences (w)–(gg) show only what cases are realized where, and with what prepositional markers in passive sentences. This summarizes the differences in realization of nominal complements between active and passive sentences.

Note also that no asterisked sentences are included in the data set. In general, realizational orders other than the ones included in Table 2 do not occur. That is, (1) is lexotactically ill-formed (cf. c and d). Conversely, (2) can occur, but *Mary* is interpretable only as a patient. The usage is metaphorical, perhaps idiomatic. But whatever is going on, it is clear that *Mary* in (2) cannot be interpreted as a recipient.

(1)   *John read a book Mary*
(2)   *John reads Mary (like a book)*

Much more can be said about these clause realizations, but I close with some comments about the prepositions. They are italicized to indicate that they are determined lexotactic elements or empty lexemes. That is, they are supplied by the lexotactics as a morphological marker of the realization of the sememic case in a particular clause position. This is demonstrably simpler than supplying the preposition everywhere and then erasing it in certain positions. The proof is left to students of simplicity metrics.

Leaving this incomplete discussion, we turn to the possible generalizations. Each clause is related to a subject followed by a predicate. The predicate is related to an obligatory verb and an optional complement. The complement, when present, has up to three positions (C_1, C_2, C_3). These statements are summarized algebraically in (3) and (4), where square brackets indicate optional occurrence.

(3)   Clause∥Subject Predicate
(4)   Predicate∥Verb [C_1 [C_2] [C_3]]

The realizations of three case sememes can fill the lexotactic position of subject of an active voice clause: agent, patient, and instrument. If an agent is present, it is the subject, whether or not the clause complement realizes patient or instrument [for example, see (m)]. If there is no agent in the clause, instrument is realized in subject position [see (n) and (o)]. If there is neither agent nor instrument, patient is realized in subject position [see (p) and (q)]. The lexotactic order of precedence for realization of these case sememes is agent, then instrument, then patient. This is included in (5).

(5)   subject/(Pa^{ψ}, Rc) + Ag + In + Pa

Also included in (5) is the realization of patient and recipient as the subject of a passive clause [see (w) and (x)]. This is a sememically marked realization in which the recipient and patient are preferred over agent. The sememic marking is summarized by the symbol ψ for passive focus. That passive clauses are lexotactically and morphologically marked as well is obvious and is not discussed. Thus (5) includes a sememically marked precedence ordering (for passive) and a set of orderings determined by the lexotactics itself. Note that the precedence ordering is indicated by " + " and that the comma indicates simple choice (OR).

The lexotactics of the English verb is fascinating but far too intricate to be dashed off in a page or two. It is therefore also being slighted.

The first post-verbal complement position (C_1) can realize any case sememe, especially when passives are considered. However, certain facts emerge from a consideration of the data. It is the marked position of realization of recipient and beneficiary in those circumstances known as "dative movement," even though no movement is involved in a stratificational description. It is the normal position of realization of the patient, and is the only position in the clause in which the identifier may be directly realized. These realizations of these four sememic cases take precedence over all other cases.

The order of realization of the other sememic cases is essentially the same as in the combination of the second and third post-verbal complement positions. Recipient and range can occur in first and second complement positions, but not in the third. They therefore take precedence over the other cases in C_2. Beneficiary, client, and maleficiary take precedence over instrument and agent. That is, whenever beneficiary and instrument are realized in the same clause, the beneficiary is realized in a complement position preceding that in which the instrument is realized [see (j) or (x)].

These observations are combined in (6), (7), and (8). Here the parentheses indicate grouping, and the italicized prepositions are lexotactically determined, that is, inserted into the chain.

(6) $C_1/(Rc^\delta,Bn) + (Pa + Ir) + ((to(Rc,Ex)),Ra) + ((for\ (Bn,C1)),(on\ M1)) + ((with\ In) + (by\ Ag))$

(7) $C_2/(Ra + (Pa,(to\ (Rc,Ex)))) + ((for\ (Bn,C1)),(on\ M1)) + ((with\ In) + (by\ Ag))$

(8) $C_3/((for\ (Bn,C1)),(on\ M1)) + ((with\ In) + (by\ Ag))$

These six algebraic formulae, (3)–(8), summarize the surface syntactic structure of the simple clause in English. They cover all direct participants in the clause, excepting only locus phrases. An integrated graphic description of (3)–(8) is presented in Figure 2, for those interested in relational networks.

Figure 2 describes the data of Table 2 in a completely generalized fashion, so far as the surface syntax is concerned. Because of its generalized nature, it also predicts a great deal more. For example, it predicts the order of realization of the various deep cases; it predicts the complement positions that evoke prepositional markers of case; it includes the relative order of preference of realization of deep cases for each complement position.

Figure 2 also has certain built-in limitations. These are explained in Section 3.5. But first, it is necessary to consider the justification and effect of the rightmost ordered OR node in Figure 2.

3.4. An Extension of Lexotactics

One direct extension of the clause structure in the lexotactics is that of including subordinate noun clauses and infinitive phrases (I ignore gerundives). Without discussion, I simply state that *that*-clauses and infinitives are in complementary lexotactic distribution: *That*-clauses have a (surface) subject and infinitive phrases do not. This implies that, ceteris paribus, the lexotactics must prefer a *that*-clause over an infinitive phrase. This is indicated by an ordered OR node—specifically, the right-most such nodes in Figure 2. The *that* and the infinitival *to* are supplied by the lexotactics at that point, just as the prepositions are supplied for certain case realizations in certain clause positions. The *that*-clause is then simply related to "Clause" via an upward OR, and the infinitive phrase is similarly related to "Predicate."

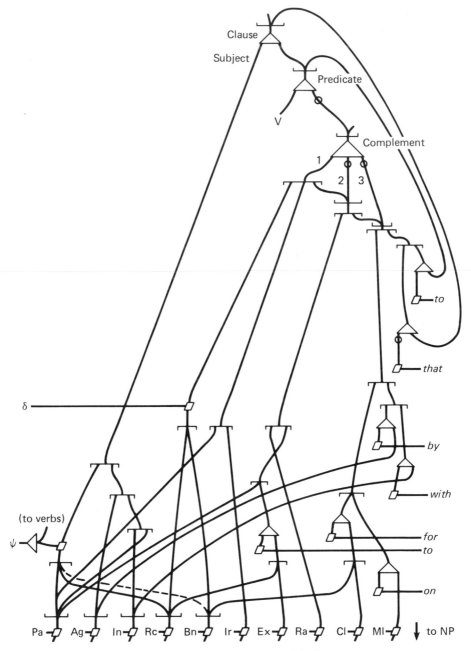

Figure 2 Lexotactics of the English clause.

Note that these relationships predict the possibility of multiply iterative structures, but not of multiply centrally embedded ones. This is a result of these subordinate structures being reached only in final (or only) clause complement position. This treatment, via relationships, avoids the difficulties of TG treatments which refer to sentences and verb phrases as the conditioning factors in transformations. The question of whether they are "under" a noun node or an S-node or . . . does not arise.

Note finally that the *that* inserted in Figure 2 is indicated as optional.[1] In fact, simple optionality does not suffice. Discourse considerations play a large role in determining when *that* occurs. But these are beyond the scope of this study.

3.5. Limitations of Figure 2

Figure 2, as it stands, accounts for the surface syntactic structure of the data of Table 2, including complex sentences with *that*-clauses and infinitive phrases. But the diagram is flexible. No beneficiary passives like (9) are included in Table 2.

(9)   *Ed was bought a gift by Joan*

This is because many native speakers of English, myself among them, have difficulty with this type of passive. However, many native speakers accept this type of passive without hesitation. This may be attributable to dialect or merely to the normal, possibly random differences in the understanding of English observable from speaker to speaker. Beneficiary passives are easily described by a simple modification of Figure 2. Just add a line extending downward from the downward OR under ψ to the upward OR over Bn (the dotted line). Both these nodes are independently justified as part of the lexotactic structure, so the added line is a minimal increase in the surface complexity. Thus (9) is accommodated. Similar comments apply to other sentences that might be added to the data in Table 2. However, the basic structure of the clause lexotactics given in Figure 2 will remain.

Figure 2 also accounts for the lexotactic relations of most of the data in the conference data set (CDS), excepting only the question (CDS-5) and (CDS-14)–(CDS-17). This assumes that the phrases "every woman" in (CDS-2) and "every duckling" in (CDS-6) are lexotactically noun phrases consisting of an adjective followed by a noun.

Of the five sentences not accounted for, I will not be dealing with (CDS-

---

[1] I am indebted to John R. Ross for reminding me of my omission of this fact in the original drawing, and to James McCawley for pointing out certain other of my personal slips.

5) and (CDS-14). Sentence (CDS-14) contains a post-nominal adjective clause. Post-nominal adjectives include prepositional and participial phrases in additional to clauses, and deserve a lengthy treatise by themselves. Space considerations do not permit a full, integrated description of post-nominal adjectivals, even supposing I had one at my fingertips. Therefore, rather than presenting an ad hoc description of a single example, I leave (CDS-14).

Similarly, (CDS-5) is the only question. Any complement of a clause can be questioned. The act or even the whole predication can be questioned. These should be part of an integrated description of questions. Moreover, the relations between questions and relative clauses and the problem of the auxiliaries and *do* belong in a full treatment. Again, this is a treatise (or several) in itself. Rather than accounting for (CDS-5) alone, which would be another ad hoc exercise, I prefer to leave the whole problem aside.[2]

To make up for that, however, Figure 2 also accounts for the surface syntactic structure of so-called equi-sentences like (10), of A-raising sentences like (11), and of even more complex sentences like (12), even though none of these types was included in the original data set considered.

(10)   *I want to go home*
(11)   *John seems to me to be a fool*
(12)   *Harry ordered lunch for Ed to eat*

This demonstrates the strength and predictive power of the generalizations possible on this stratum alone with no more than the absolutely minimal underlying assumptions about description using relationships only.

Now Figure 2 also shows nothing about verbs and verb phrases (in the traditional, pre-Chomskyan sense). It tells nothing about many morphological relations. But more importantly, it does not show how sememic cases are assigned to nouns and how sentence pairs like (13) and (14)—(CDS-3) and (CDS-4)—are related.

(13)   *The farmer killed the duckling*
(14)   *The duckling was killed by the farmer*

The assignment of sememic cases to nominal participants in a predication is a function of the semotactics. Similarly, (13) and (14) constitute

---

[2] My attitude in this is typical of stratificationalists. Given the choice, we prefer to deal with larger fragments rather than smaller, to formulate hypotheses/descriptions on the basis of all possible available data, rather than on an apparently regular subset.

a minimal sememic pair in the semotactics, where their relationship is detailed. I return to this question in Section 4.

Meanwhile, it is necessary to indicate in outline what must be added to Figure 2 to account for (CDS-15), (CDS-16), and (CDS-17), repeated as (15), (16), and (17).

(15)   *John killed the woman and Bill, the farmer*
(16)   *John loved the woman and he killed the farmer*
(17)   *John loved the woman and killed the farmer*

3.6. Some Further Lexotactic Modifications

The relationships necessary to describe the lexotactic realizations of (15), (16), and (17) are added to the relevant portions of Figure 2 in Figure 3. Sentence (17) has a compound predicate, which is described by the

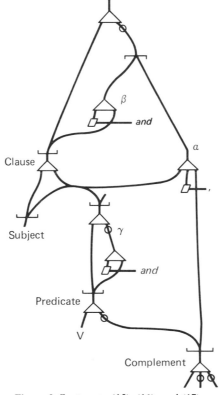

Figure 3 Sentences (15), (16), and (17).

optional relations at γ in Figure 3. Sentences (15) and (16) require similar modifications of the original diagram, but to a different level. Sentence (16) is a compound sentence. It is described at β. Sentence (15) is described via the AND at α.

In fact, none of these descriptions is satisfactory. They all account for the sentences presented. In addition to these simple relations, those at β and γ should be generalized to allow for open-ended series. However, all this is simply scratching the surface. Without an account of the discourse block environments in which sentences of these types are found, no description can be considered adequate.

The lack here is in this researcher, not in SG. The model I am using (or other SG models) could represent the facts and generalize on them, if they were known. But until they are known, until a sufficient amount of research in the discourse block structure of English is performed, the description of these three sentence types and their expansions must remain incomplete.

4. ACTIVE AND PASSIVE

4.1. Some General Considerations

Return to sentences (13) and (14), repeated here for convenience.

(13)   *The farmer killed the duckling*
(14)   *The duckling was killed by the farmer*

A great deal of linguistic writing has been pegged on whether they are "the same" or "different." That question is not at issue here. My own contention is that they are nonidentical but closely related in a formal sense. The critical question is how.

Beyond the co-occurrence of lexemes, there are resemblances between them in three areas. Syntactically, each sentence has a subject, a verb, and a postverbal complement. Sememically, the act is in both cases identical, *the farmer* is the agent of the act, and *the duckling* is the patient. Semantically, both may be used to describe the same event.

There are differences in three areas as well. The (syntactic) order of realization of lexemes is reversed: *the farmer* is subject in (13), object of a preposition in the predicate in (14); *the duckling* is direct object in (13) and subject in (14). Semantically, (13) seems to be a discourse on *the farmer*, (14) on *the duckling*. Morphologically, there is an active voice verb in (13), a passive voice verb in (14).

The job of "syntactic" description, as I see it, is to formulate all possible generalizations as part of an integrated description while preserving the differences that allow us to predict occurrences and to distinguish the marked from the unmarked.

4.2. "Syntax" beyond the Lexotactics

Figure 2 shows how both active and passive constructions are related to the clause. The ordered OR node in subject position indicates that the passive, with patient realized in subject position, is the marked variant. The agent is the unmarked subject. Conversely, the patient is the unmarked complement, and the agent is marked. These statements are justifiable on purely morphological grounds. But the morphological comments are well known. Therefore, though they are important, they are ignored.

On the other hand, the semotactic structures to which a clause is related are necessary to show exactly how active and passive pairs are related. This involves two procedures. First, the semological structure of a single predication must be made explicit; this includes the relations of arguments to acts and to sememic cases. Second, such structures must be integrated into the paragraph and greater discourse block structures to which they are appropriate. The latter is a major task, largely beyond the scope of this study. I therefore limit myself to one suggestive example.

Consider (18) and (19).

(18)   *This is the man filming that novel for TV*
(19)   *This is the novel being filmed for TV by that man*

Sentence (18) must have an active participle, and (19) must have a passive. Of course, they do not subsume the whole spectrum of environments, but there are situations that seem to require a passive verb. A full investigation is required before a formal statement is made. However, if (18) and (19) are characteristic of the general situation, a rule of thumb can be offered:

(20)   If a participant which is thematic in the greater discourse appears as the patient of a particular predication, that predication is realized as a passive construction in the lexotactics; if the predication is realized as a clause, the patient of the predication is realized as the subject of the clause.

This statement is integrated into the semotactic description given in Figures 4–6.

The semological structure of a single predication is easily specifiable. It has several significant characteristics: (*a*) sememic cases are related to certain points in the predication hierarchy; (*b*) hierarchical dominance is specified between the participants and the act; and (*c*) no linear order need be specified between the participants. At the same time, for this particular case, the difference between active and passive is given a unified, minimal semotactic description, however diverse the discourse environments which evoke it.

The semotactic structure describing (13) is given in Figure 4. All AND nodes are unordered, reflecting the lack of underlying linear order. With all linear order specified in the lexotactics, none is necessary in the semotactics. There are several advantages to this approach. First, the relationship between active and passive no longer requires a change in linear order, that is, no movement transformations at all. It simply requires lexotactic encoding according to one or another linear order. Second, it suggests why the continuing search for universal underlying word order has produced indeterminate results. Third, by using both a semotactic and a lexotactic structure for each message encoded or decoded (i.e., by using a portion of two generalized structures), we can dispense with all transformations.

The case relations are provided as a part of the semotactic structure; they are determined semotactic relations with connections downward toward the lexotactics, but without direct connections to "meaning." Hierarchical dominance between the arguments is indicated directly in both Figures 4 and 5. The need for such dominance is clear both intuitively and structurally. The subject of a sentence seems to dominate both the verb and the other complements. Semantic evidence for this is seen in the quantified versions of (13) as given in (21) and (22).

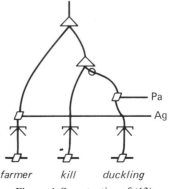

farmer   kill   duckling

Figure 4 Semotactics of (13).

(21)   *Every farmer killed a duckling*
(22)   *The farmer killed every duckling*

Sentence (21) seems to have as many separate acts/events as there are farmers. Conversely, with (22), there is a single act with as many targets as there are ducklings. In a secondary sense it could be argued that there are multiple acts in (22) as well. But this interpretation derives from a recognition of the individual nature of the ducklings involved. Moreover, it can also be argued that (22) communicates a repeated act rather than individual acts. This claim does not apply to (21).

Structural evidence for hierarchical dominance can be found in the interplay between quantifiers and negation. This exercise is left to the logic-minded reader.

For ease of legibility, the quantifiers are left out of the diagrams in Figures 4 and 5. They would simply be stacked hierarchically over the portions of semotactics they dominate in a manner analogous to the stacking of agent in Figure 4. But to suggest that this suffices would be misleading. The system of natural quantifiers is formed from relatively few sememes, though there are many more than the two logical quantifiers (universal and existential) usually cited. Moreover, they have an intricate, highly elaborate system of interrelations. The full story of quantifiers also remains to be told.

The semotactic structure describing (14) is given in Figure 5. It differs from Figure 4 by having the patient argument dominant over the agent in certain discourse block contexts. These conditioning factors are related to the predication via the upward AND node labeled DB.

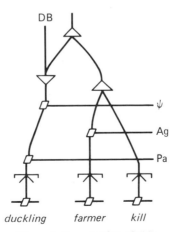

Figure 5 Semotactics of (14).

Figure 6 presents an integrated description of Figures 4 and 5. It accounts for the semotactic relations of a number of active and passive constructions. It identifies the semotactic difference between active and passive as a relative difference in hierarchical dominance between agent and patient evoked by a set of discourse block environments. In those (marked) environments, the patient dominates the agent; in other environments, the unmarked semotactic structure (agent dominating patient) is used to encode the predication.

If the patient dominates the agent, a semolexemic relationship labeled ψ (call it passive focus) is active, indicating the choice of a number of lexotactic alternatives. These choices eventually lead to the passive clause, when combined with Figure 2.

The combination of Figures 2 and 5 presents an integrated description of active and passive and much of the clause lexotactics of English. How they work to encode is explained in Section 4.3.

4.3. Encoding (14) and (13)

The occurrence of (14) presupposes the discourse environment abbreviated DB in Figure 6. The diagram therefore has the activated sememic relations listed in (23). These are listed in arbitrary order, roughly from the top of Figure 6 to the bottom.

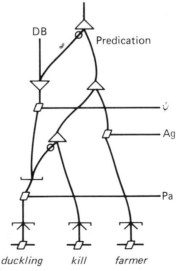

Figure 6 Semotactics of (13) and (14).

(23) $\psi \cdot ((\text{Ag} \cdot \text{farmer}) \cdot (\text{Pa} \cdot \text{duckling}) \cdot \text{kill})$

These relations define the input to the lexotactics during encoding. The lexotactics realizes these sememes as a clause, according to Figure 2. First position in the clause is the subject. Because passive focus (ψ) is present, the left-hand line down from the ordered OR node is taken. This leads to the patient, and *the duckling* is realized as subject. Next, the verb position is processed, and *kill* is realized with the passive auxiliary and participle ending (not shown). Finally, complement position is processed. The agent was, in effect, squeezed out of subject position. But it can be realized in the predicate. *The farmer*, preceded by the preposition *by*, is realized in C_1.

Now consider (13). In the absence of the discourse block environments evoking passive focus, however, a smaller set of sememes is present. These are given in (24).

(24) $((\text{Ag} \cdot \text{farmer}) \cdot (\text{Pa} \cdot \text{duckling}) \cdot \text{kill})$

Now, the patient cannot be realized in subject position. But the right-hand line down from the topmost ordered OR prefers the agent, and *the farmer* is realized as subject. The verb comes next, without passive morphology, followed by the patient, *the duckling*, in C_1 position.

We thus have one syntactic structure permitting two alternative linearizations, only one of which is chosen in a specific instance. One syntactic order is not destroyed as it is being rewritten as another. Since the structure is not destroyed during the application of some transformation, it is available for decoding, as well.

5. COMMENTS ON THE PURPOSE OF THIS CONFERENCE

5.1. The Question Revisited

The primary data for "syntax" includes all domains from word through discourse and speech act, insofar as they are relevant to the content side of language. One might call the diagrams the "competence," and the encoding and decoding according to the diagrams the "performance." Introspection, observation, elicitation, and experimentation are all valid sources of data. My personal caveat would be not to rely solely on introspection—or any single source—to the exclusion of all other sources. Variation and change are represented by differences in part(s) of the diagram. Except for Makkai's work on idioms, I am not sure that any stratificationalist has done work on universal similarities between languages.

I see no reason to suppose they should have any logical features not present in nonuniversal similarities, but I do not consider myself competent to answer questions on universals at the present time.

Stratificational theory is concerned with pragmatic issues; thus the meaning–sound, sound–meaning, meaning–writing, and writing–meaning relations are all of central concern. That is, we are concerned with the production and comprehension of messages. Data must be described as generally as possible, to produce the broadest possible predictions of new data and explanations of observed data. In other words, we try to do the best we can. *I* assign no empirical interpretations to syntactic statements within SG; I leave that to the typologists of possible human language, psychologists, and neurologists among my colleagues (cf. Dell and Reich, 1977). No internally consistent syntactic arguments are excluded a priori by SG. I have no unigue grammar discovery procedures; Bloomfield, Bloch, Jakobson, Halliday, Gleason, and Pike have all had their influence on me. (The list is in chronological order.) As for practical use, Figure 2 could be reduced to a general model of clause/sentence structure in English.

Language description is essentially a black box problem in engineering: You may know what goes in and what comes out, but you cannot know the structure inside uniquely. Again, we do the best we can. Two alternative descriptions are compared for internal consistency, relative completeness, and relative simplicity, in that order (cf. Hjelmslev's empirical principle). For a workable simplicity metric, see Lockwood (1972).

The levels of syntactic representation include the morphemic, lexemic, and sememic strata—at least, others have described as "syntax," considerations that belong on one or the other of these strata. The relationships among terms must be characterizable in terms of the primitive relations mentioned above (AND, OR, PRECEDENCE) and their combinations. I have no things, for example, categories or features, that are not relations. This also constitutes the constraints imposed on syntactic description. SG is a relational, nontransformational approach to language description. The restriction to the three primitive relations is partly motivated by a desire to avoid imposing structures during the description that are artifacts of the descriptive model. This is what happens with transformations. Chomskyan transforms destroy and create structure in the sense that they erase the input structure while writing down the output structure. Relations do no such thing. They simply ARE, connecting points in one way or another. They also define obligatoriness and optionality, order, hierarchy, direction, etc. The relational network diagrams also constitute the formalism I use for description. This is not empirically significant; I do it for my own benefit, lest I leave something out. Finally, the relationship between syntax and semantics is indirect. To repeat Gleason's observation, language does not have meaning; it evokes meaning.

5.2. The Significance of Stratificational Theory

Probably the most significant contribution of SG is in the definition of a model that can encode and decode. The description performed according to this model, moreover, predict that the set of utterances encoded is not isomorphic to the set of utterances decoded. This parallels the observed fact that our "passive" (decoding) knowledge of language is different from our "active" (encoding) knowledge. Thus, SG rules out any approach to language that either cannot account for both encoding and decoding or states that their products must be isomorphic. All the basic postulates about SG are falsifiable, to wit: Evidence for falsifiability would have to demonstrate that the three basic relationships are insufficient or that at least one of them is superfluous. Perhaps moving on to a neurological model would increase the falsifiability of SG; however, I am unsure of my ground in this statement.

Another important contribution of SG is its amenability to the definition of a workable simplicity metric. This is possible because the relationships are all logically comparable. Part of the reason TG has never managed to define a simplicity metric is that different types of transformations, for example, movement and deletion rules, are not obviously logically comparable. Nor is it obvious what value to assign to the lexicon, rule-ordering conventions, phrase structure rules, etc. But in this, TG is no worse off than other theories of language, and is better off than some.

There is another side to simplicity as well. This might be called the metatheoretical simplicity measure, and it concerns the complexity of the basic axiom set of the theory. I give a detailed discussion in Sullivan (1978), and do not repeat it here. So far as I can tell, only SG and glossematics conform to the restrictions of Gödel's theorem, though the basic axiom set of tagmemics and equational grammar may, too. Extended standard theory, whether with or without a trace, does not conform to these restrictions. Of the other theoretical models presented here, it seems to me that some might and others do not. But I am not presently prepared to make more specific statements. In short, however, SG has gone farther in this direction than any other theory.

A third important contribution of SG is in its ability to define concepts like agent, patient, subject, and object directly in logical terms and to make explicit their interrelations. Thus, it might be said that SG uses all of these concepts, but none of them is a primitive in the model.

And so on. Some of the contributions SG has made are those that can be made by any relational network theory of language. Some make sense in almost any theory of language, but cannot be independently justified. Some require a degree of explicitness not yet attained elsewhere. But clearly there is plenty of work to be done, and all workers are welcome.

I know of no "problem areas" for SG. But again, I must remind you that some areas (e.g., universals) have not been extensively researched by stratificationalists. In these areas, problems might arise.

In light of the contributions by SG enumerated earlier, it is easy to list the ways in which I consider SG superior to other theories. It is superior to any theory that cannot encode, cannot decode, or that claims isomorphism between the two; it is superior to any theory without a workable simplicity metric, or to one that is not provably consistent; and it is superior to theories in which linguistic categories (agent, subject, noun phrase) are undefined primitives. It seems compatible with tagmemics and Halliday's version of systemic grammar, though it is not identical to either. McCawley, Lakoff, and Perlmutter, among others, have all reached conclusions which, if adopted, would bring TG closer to SG; at least, the models they are developing are closer to SG than TG. In fact, this demonstrates the convergence Gleason has often pointed out as operating within SG itself. I suspect that the more real-language and language-use description we attempt, the more convergence will occur. But only if we approach the descriptions pragmatically and functionally rather than ideologically.

Finally, I wish to return to the stated aim of this conference: to examine the basic, necessary differences between theories rather than the incidental ones. I am still unsure how one distinguishes between incidental and necessary differences between two theories. Does an "incidental" difference between theories ever become necessary, and how long does it take to be sure? If Chomsky says we must generate sentences alone, who is to be blamed for not looking at discourse? In 22 years of research into English syntax, TG has produced nothing equivalent to Figure 2. I am happy to agree that this is a coincidence, since I see no way of proving that it is a necessary lacuna. But how can anyone justify the lack of a perfectly reasonable set of syntactic generalizations?

In sum, I would like to suggest that, much as I enjoy conferences like this one, we get on with the business of describing natural languages and of accounting for their uses.

REFERENCES

Bennett, D. C. (1975). *Spatial and temporal uses of English prepositions*. London: Longman.
Christie, W. M. (1978). Atemporal logic, temporal logic, and natural language. *Forum Linguisticum, 2*, 247–254.

Dell, G., and Reich, P. A. (1977). A model of slips of the tongue. In R. J. DiPietro and E. L. Blansitt (Eds.), *The Third Lacus Forum*. Columbia, S. C: Hornbeam.

DiPietro, R. J., and Blansitt, E. L. (1977). *The Third LACUS Forum*. Columbia, S. C.: Hornbeam.

Fischer-Jorgensen, E. (1975). *Trends in phonological theory*. Copenhagen: Akademisk Forlag.

Lamb, S. M. (1966). *Outline of stratificational grammar*. Washington, D.C.: Georgetown University Press.

Lockwood, D. G. (1972). *Introduction to stratificational linguistics*. New York: Harcourt Brace Jovanovich.

Makkai, A. (1973). *Idiom structure in English*. The Hague: Mouton.

McCawley, J. D. (1978). The nonexistence of syntactic categories. In J. D. Wang (Ed.), *Second Annual Linguistic Metatheory Conference Proceedings, 1977*. Michigan State University Department of Linguistics. Pp. 212–232.

Sullivan, W. J. (1977). Toward a logical definition of linguistic theory. In R. J. DiPietro and E. L. Blansitt (Eds.), *The Third LACUS Forum*. Columbia, S. C.: Hornbeam. Pp. 393–404.

Sullivan, W. J. (1978). Raising: A stratificational description and some metatheoretical considerations. In J. D. Wang (Ed.), *Second Annual Linguistic Metatheory Conference Proceedings, 1977*. Michigan State University Department of Linguistics. Pp. 47–92.

Sullivan, W. J. (In press). Timing in atemporal logic: A response to Christie. To appear in *Forum Linguisticum*.

Wang, J. D. (1978). *Second Annual Linguistic Metatheory Conference Proceedings, 1977*. Michigan State University Department of Linguistics.

ROLE AND REFERENCE GRAMMAR

ROBERT D. VAN VALIN, JR
Temple University

WILLIAM A. FOLEY
Australian National University

1. INTRODUCTION

This paper presents an approach to syntactic theory and analysis called
ROLE AND REFERENCE GRAMMAR [RRG]. This approach has been developed primarily with regard to the study of Austronesian (especially
Philippine), Australian, and American Indian languages, and the problems
inherent in the analysis of these languages have shaped our thinking and
the resulting theory in much the same way that the major problems of
English syntax have influenced the development of transformational theory. Consequently, the main focus of work in RRG has thus far been on
setting up a universal framework in terms of which these very different
language types may be fruitfully analyzed, rather than on the detailed
analysis of a single language as in transformational grammar. The sketch
of RRG presented in this paper should not be taken as representing a
complete and finished theoretical statement; rather, it should be viewed
as a progress report which reflects the work that has been done on RRG
up to this point and the current state of our thinking. In particular, the
choice of topics to be dealt with is a direct function of previous work
which has been concentrated in certain areas to the temporary exclusion

329

Syntax and Semantics, Volume 13:
Current Approaches to Syntax

of others. A much more extensive and thorough presentation of RRG can be found in Foley and Van Valin (in preparation).

2. BASIC ASSUMPTIONS OF RRG

Role and reference grammar may be characterized in general terms as a FUNCTIONAL approach to syntax and grammatical description. That is, in RRG, grammatical units and constructions are analyzed primarily in terms of their functional role in a linguistic system (parole) and only secondarily in terms of their formal (structural) properties. Since language plays a primary role in human communication, these functions ultimately relate to the exigencies of verbal social interaction (cf. Hymes, 1974; Gumperz and Cook-Gumperz, 1976; Silverstein, 1976a, 1977; Van Valin, 1978). Thus when we speak of "functional considerations," we are concerned with COMMUNICATIVE function. Of course, the formal properties of linguistic elements and constructions are not ignored in a functional approach; indeed, one of the major questions to be investigated is the relationship between (communicative) function and form, in particular, how the same form may have different functions and how the same function may be carried out by different forms. However, in a functionally oriented research strategy, function is viewed as analytically prior to form, and therefore the goal of such a strategy is to describe the latter in terms of the former as much as possible (see Heath, 1978).

Role and reference grammar thus assumes that the use of language in human communication and social interaction is absolutely fundamental to understanding the nature of human language. We therefore take the opposite view from transformational grammar which holds that "investigation of performance will proceed only in so far as understanding of underlying competence permits [Chomsky, 1965, p. 10]," that is, the innate psychological basis of language must be understood before the study of language use can succeed. Our position is that to understand language, one should look FIRST to communication, although we do not take the extreme view that every instance of verbal behavior must be reduced to an instance of communication. Our position is analogous to claiming that one has to take into account the fact that hammers are used for driving nails in order to understand the nature and structure of hammers, even though they may also be used as paperweights or doorstops.

The relationship between syntax and semantics has been a major topic of controversy in generative grammar. Chomsky has steadfastly maintained the autonomy of the syntactic component, whereas generative semanticists attempted to merge the two such that they became indistinguishable. In RRG, syntax is neither autonomous, as in TG, nor identical with semantics, as in generative semantics. Moreover, since RRG seeks to analyze grammatical systems with respect to the communicative function of their elements, pragmatics is crucially involved, and consequently it is not enough to talk only about the relationship of syntax and semantics. We view the interaction of syntax, semantics and pragmatics as being one in which the syntactic patterns of a language are constrained primarily, but not exclusively, by the interaction of semantic and pragmatic factors. In other words, the syntactic structure of an utterance is viewed as the outcome of the interplay between the speaker's intent to communicate propositionally formulable information and the constraints imposed by the social and linguistic context in which the utterance occurs.

There are two very important points that must be made here. First, we are NOT claiming that syntax can be reduced ENTIRELY to semantics and pragmatics. Some aspects of the morphosyntactic structure of a language cannot be described in purely functional terms, for example, why adjectives precede their head nouns in English rather than follow them. Most of these aspects will presumably be attributable to formal typological principles such as those relating to the harmonic word order combinations discussed in Greenberg (1966). Hence morphosyntactic structure constitutes an independent level apart from semantic and pragmatic factors, although we do not posit it as absolutely autonomous as in TG. On the synchronic plane, RRG seeks explanation of the formal properties of language in universal terms, with pragmatic and semantic (i.e., functional) considerations outranking and outweighing formal ones. With respect to language-specific problems, diachronic factors may play an explanatory role in some cases. Thus, for example, the basic clause pattern in modern English [subject + verb + non − oblique object(s) + oblique object(s)] is the result both of the historical development of the language and of certain universal principles of word order, and it is on this structure that semantic and pragmatic functions interact (see, Heath, 1978, p. 88). Second, in RRG, the exact nature of the interaction between syntax, semantics and pragmatics is not decreed universally in advance but rather is an important topic of investigation. Earlier work (e.g., Foley and Van Valin, 1977; Van Valin, 1977b) has shown that this interaction is not the same in all languages, and this is of great typological significance (see Section 3.2.5). Of course, all languages can do the same communicative work, regardless of the way syntactic, semantic and pragmatic factors are treated formally in grammatical systems. The parameters of this interaction will become clearer in our discussion of role structure and pragmatic structure in Section 3.

In a functional analysis, both the grammatically and acceptability of utterances are at issue; the former notion refers to formal properties of utterances and the latter to their semantic and pragmatic properties. This distinction is illustrated in (1)–(5).

(1)   *Revolutionary new ideas appear infrequently*

(2)   *Colorless green ideas sleep furiously*

(3)   **Green furiously ideas colorless sleep*

(4)   a. *The man went to the store*
       b. *He bought two books*

(5)   a. *The man went to the store*
       b. *Two books were bought by him*

The well-known examples in (1)–(3) illustrate the independence of grammaticality, strictly defined formally, from acceptability: despite the fact that both (1) and (2) are grammatical, that is, formally correct, whereas (3) is not, only (1) is an acceptable English sentence, that is, nondeviant semantically. The facts of (1)–(3) must be captured in RRG or any other approach that seeks to attain at least descriptive adequacy. In RRG, however, the notion of acceptability is used not only with reference to sentences such as (2) (i.e., semantic acceptability) but also with respect to contextual appropriateness as in (4) and (5). In these short sequences, (4b) is more natural in the context of (4a) than is (5b), even though both (4b) and (5b) are grammatical. In explaining the appropriateness of (4b) versus (5b), the semantic and formal properties of these utterances must be taken into consideration, and so the explanation of the kind of facts in (1)–(3) is an automatic consequence of the functional account of pragmatic acceptability. Thus the contextual appropriateness (pragmatic acceptability) of utterances, their semantic acceptability, and their purely formal grammaticality are all important in RRG, but in terms of functional analysis, pragmatic and semantic appropriateness play a much larger role than formal grammaticality.

The goals of RRG are twofold: (*a*) the development of an explanatory framework for universal grammar [UG]; and (*b*) the development of a framework for grammatical analysis that relates directly to the study of language in the sociocultural world. These may at first glance appear to be somewhat disparate goals, but they find common ground in the functional orientation of RRG which seeks to describe grammatical elements in terms of their role in communication, that is, in verbal social interaction.

Formal and functional theories of UG differ markedly in terms of their focus of interest. The formal approach is concerned primarily with "formal universals," that is, generalizations about the abstract formal properties of grammars—for example, constraints on the application of syntactic and phonological rules. It has been secondarily concerned with "substantive universals," which are generalizations about the possible formal elements in human language—for example, that all languages make use of the syntactic categories of noun and verb (Chomsky 1965, p. 28). Functional approaches, on the other hand, are interested primarily in substantive universals, and they strive to answer not only the question of what constructions languages have but also that of WHY certain languages have certain constructions whereas others do not (see Van Valin, 1977c). Functional universals will be implicational in nature, expressing co-occurence relationships between functions, for example, maintenance of reference across clause sequences (Heath, 1975), and the formal units carrying out these functions. The relationship between form and function is very complex and problematic since, as was noted, a given function may be effected by different forms and a given form may have different functions in different contexts (see Heath, 1978 for further discussion of functional universals). In addition, an adequate theory of UG must provide a viable framework for the description of individual languages, and RRG attempts to be a flexible framework, one that falls somewhere between the extremes of describing each language in its own terms, thereby making cross-linguistic comparison problematic, and describing each language in purely universal terms, which often results in the glossing over of many of the important grammatical distinctions in the language in favor of those imposed by the theory.

The other major goal of RRG is the development of a framework for grammatical analysis that will yield results directly relevant to sociolinguists and anthropological linguists who study language in the sociocultural world. The study of grammatical systems with reference to communicative function ties in with the sociolinguistic and social anthropological study of language in social interaction, as Silverstein (1976a, 1977) shows. Approaches that limit themselves to the grammatical competence of the ideal speaker–hearer in a perfectly homogeneous speech community have little to offer the sociolinguist or anthropological linguist (see Hymes, 1974; Van Valin, 1978).

3. BASIC CONCEPTS OF RRG

3.1. RRG assumes that the grammatical structure of all languages is organized in terms of hierarchical levels; in this we are following tagmemic theory (Jones, this volume). The standard tagmemic hierarchy includes PARAGRAPH > SENTENCE > CLAUSE > PHRASE > WORD > STEM > MORPHEME. We will be concerned here only with clause- and sentence-level grammar, and so this hierarchy is adequate for the purposes of this paper. (For a discussion of a more complex hierarchy, see Foley and Van Valin, in preparation, Chapter 2.)

3.2. The name "role and reference grammar" derives from our postulation of two major systems in clause-level grammar, one concerned with the semantic (case) role structure of the clause, and the other with the referential or pragmatic properties of the NPs in a clause. These two systems are posited as part of UG, but this does not mean that they are both realized in all languages (see Section 3.2.5). In Section 3.2.1 we will discuss the system that constitutes the semantic role structure of the clause; in the next sections (Sections 3.2.2–3.2.5) we will concentrate on the pragmatically oriented system. (See Foley and Van Valin, in preparation, Chapter 3 for a more extensive discussion of role structure.)

3.2.1. When people talk, they often talk about some action, event or state of affairs in the world around them and the entities involved in or associated with it. These entities may be people, animals, objects, and forces, among other things, and they may play various roles in the different kinds of situations. Language allows people to talk about these things by having means for describing these situations and their participants (i.e., the entities involved in them). Part of these linguistic means constitutes what we term the SEMANTIC ROLE STRUCTURE of the clause, which is concerned with the expression of situations (i.e., actions, events and states), their participants, and the various roles the participants play in them. The most fundamental part of this system is the predicate, which is the primary linguistic device for describing situations. Predicates may be classified along a number of dimensions, the two most important being whether the situation is static or dynamic and whether it is under the control of a participant or not. These two dimensions define four basic predicate-types: stative (static uncontrolled, e.g., *weigh, resemble, tall, sick*), happening (dynamic uncontrolled, e.g., *flash, grow, fall, die*), stance (static controlled, e.g., *sit, stand, lie*), and action (dynamic controlled, e.g., *run, jump, hit, eat*). These four types are of course only the starting point for further analysis aiming toward a universal typology of predicate types; they are adequate for the purposes of this discussion, however.

The participants in situations are rendered linguistically by various types of noun phrases. The characteristic of NPs that is most significant for role structure is what Silverstein (1976b) calls their "inherent lexical content," that is, person, number, humanness, animacy, and concreteness. It is well known that the nature of a participant defines the possible roles it may play in a situation—for example, agents are almost invariably animate, often human, as are perceivers and experiencers of physical and mental states, whereas instrumental and locative participants are virtually always inanimate. Similarly, the semantic relation an NP argument may bear to its predicate is limited by its inherent lexical content—for example, agents and experiencers are typically animate, whereas instruments and locative NPs are not. This parallelism is to be expected, since predicates and NPs are the linguistic devices for expressing and describing situations and their participants.

The third aspect of the role structure of the clause is the expression of the various roles participants may play in situations. These are expressed linguistically by case roles (i.e., thematic relations). In many approaches (including earlier versions of RRG) these case roles are taken to be primitive elements in the underlying syntactic or semantic form of sentences. In RRG, two different systems of case roles are distinguished, one basic and the other derived. The basic system consists of an opposition between participants that perform, effect, instigate or control the situation denoted by the predicate, and participants that do not perform, initiate or control any situation but rather are affected by it in some way. The former type of participant we refer to as an *Actor* [A] and the latter as an *Undergoer* [U] (see Van Valin 1977b, p.25). It must be emphasized that this notion of Actor is NOT equivalent to the case role agent, nor is Undergoer equivalent to the case role of patient. In RRG, case roles such as agent, patient and instrument are part of the derived system to be discussed below. The choice of Actor and Undergoer reflects the PERSPECTIVE (Fillmore, 1977) from which the situation is described, and in many cases the same situation may afford more than one choice of Actor, as in (6) and (7).

(6) a. *John bought the book from Harry*
     b. *Harry sold the book to John*

(7) a. *The landlord rented the students the crummy apartment*
     b. *The students rented the crummy apartment from the landlord*

The two sentences in (6) describe the same commercial event involving the transfer of the book from Harry to John; similarly, the same event is described in both (7a) and (7b). The difference between the sentences in each pair revolves around the choice of the initiating and controlling participant: In (6a) and (7a), the initiating and controlling participants are John and the landlord, respectively, whereas in the (b) versions Harry and the students are viewed as the controllers and the initiators of the action. This difference lies in the choice of Actor. Note that it is not simply a difference in the choice of syntactic subject, as the examples in (8) show.

(8) a. *John was sold the book by Harry*
     b. *The students were rented the crummy apartment by the landlord*

Even though the NP *John* is the subject of both (6a) and (8a), it is the Actor only in (6a); in (8b) the *landlord* is still the Actor, despite its not being syntactic subject. With many predicates (e.g., *kill, hit, eat, make*), there is only one possible Actor.

The opposition of Actor and Undergoer is seen most clearly in simple transitive clauses in which the Actor is the subject and the Undergoer the direct object, for example, *The farmer* (A) *killed the duckling* (U). This opposition is constant under syntactic permutation: *The ducking* (U) *was killed by the farmer* (A). In English, the Undergoer NP is the immediately postverbal nonoblique object.

(9)   a. *Max* (A) *shot the duck* (U)
        b. *Max* (A) *shot at the duck*

(10)   a. *The Feds* (A) *loaded grass* (U) *on the plane*
        b. *The Feds* (A) *loaded the plane* (U) *with grass*

The basic contrast between Undergoer and non-Undergoer object NPs can be seen in these examples. In (9) *the duck* is an Undergoer only in (a), and this relates directly to its interpretation as affected by the action of the verb, in contrast to (9b), which need not be so interpreted. There is an analogous difference in (10a) and (10b); when *the plane* is an Undergoer, as in (10b), it is understood as being fully affected by the action of the verb, whereas it is not so interpreted in (10a). These semantic differences are expressed directly in the derived system of case roles. This discussion of Undergoers has been oriented toward the English examples in (9) and (10), but the phenomenon of oblique/nonoblique alternations with just these semantic differences is found in a wide range of languages, including Tongan, Walbiri, Kabardian and Tagalog (cf. Foley, 1976; Van Valin, 1977a; Foley and Van Valin, in preparation).

Undergoers also occur with certain single-argument predicates, especially stative predicates. Thus the subjects of predicates such as *sick, tall, fat* and *sad* are semantically Undergoers rather than Actors; they are undergoing a physical or mental state rather than performing any sort of action. This distinction is most readily apparent in stative–active languages like Lakhota (Van Valin, 1977b), in which the single argument of an active verb receives Actor inflection, whereas that of a stative verb receives Undergoer inflection.

(11)   a. *wa*kábleche (*I*-break it)   'I break it'
        b. *ma*yákaštake (*me*-you-hit)   'You hit me'
        c. *wa*hí (*I*-arrive)   'I arrive'
        d. *ma*khúže (*me*-sick)   'I am sick'

The Lakhota case marking pattern may be summed up simply by saying that all Actors are inflected one way and all Undergoers another, regardless of whether they are the object of a transitive verb or subject of a stative verb.

The opposition of Actor and Undergoer is the fundamental organizing principle of the case role systems of the role structure of the clause. The traditionally recognized case role system involves case roles of the type originally proposed in Fillmore (1968): agent, patient, instrument, goal, source and locative, to name a few. A major difference between RRG and other approaches employing these notions is that, in RRG, case roles are not treated as primitive underlying concepts, but rather as DERIVED relations. That is, they are viewed as deductive inferences involving four factors: the semantics of the predicate (in particular, whether it is stative, active, stance, etc.), the inherent lexical content of the NP argument, the perspective choices (Actor and Undergoer), and the morphosyntactic status of the non-Actor/Undergoer arguments (i.e., their case marking, in the most general sense). The lexical entry for each verb states the case marking of its arguments. For example, *load* in English would be specified as "load(NP1[Actor], (with) NP2, (on) NP3, . . .)." Here NP1 is marked as Actor and the other two primary arguments are indicated as potentially occurring with certain prepositions; one of them is chosen as Undergoer and therefore occurs without its preposition, while the non-Undergoer NP does occur with its preposition, as the two examples in (10) illustrate. An example of the derivation of a case role is that of agent in a sentence like *The man* (A) *smashed the window* (U) *with a hammer;* here *the man* is the human Actor of an action verb of physical destruction and is therefore an agent. The second NP, *the window*, is an inanimate Undergoer of a verb of physical destruction and is therefore a patient. Furthermore, *hammer* is an inanimate object of the preposition *with*, co-occurring with an action predicate of physical destruction and a human Actor, and hence it can only be interpreted as an instrument. In *The hammer* (A) *smashed the window* (U), on the other hand, it is the Actor of *smash* but must still be interpreted as an instrument because it is inanimate; despite the fact that it does not initiate or control the action of the verb, it does effect it and is therefore the Actor. Examples in which the Undergoer is not a patient include sentences like *Harry* (A) *carved a small statue* (U), in which the Undergoer is created by the action of the verb rather than existing prior to it and being affected by it, and hence is what Fillmore (1968) calls a factitive NP; in *Five dollars* (A) *will buy you* (U) *a steak dinner*, the Undergoer is a recipient or goal NP.

This discussion is not meant to be definitive but is intended to illustrate the way in which Fillmorean case roles may be treated as derived rather than basic. This approach avoids a number of problems which have plagued case grammar formulations from the outset, for example, the number of cases, their motivation, the surface realization of the underlying cases (cf. Fillmore, 1977). We postulate a single fundamental universal semantic opposition of Actor and Undergoer, with the various semantic case roles being language-specific derivatives; that is, the case roles posited in the analysis of any given language will be a function of the factors given above: the semantics of the predicate, the inherent lexical content of the NP arguments, the choice of Actor and Undergoer, and the morphosyntactic status of the other arguments. The derivation of these case roles will be governed by a set of rules specifying the interpretation of the co-occurrence of these factors. Out of the study of the role structures of many languages will come important generalizations about their interaction and about the systems of case roles in human language. It will most likely emerge that there is a set of cases that all languages share, probably including agent, patient, instrument, goal, source, and locative. Regardless of the actual number of case roles found in any given language, we may predict in advance that certain derivations will never occur, in particular, that in no language can an Actor be interpreted as having a patient case role or an Undergoer as having an agent case role.

3.2.2. The second major system in clause-level grammar is concerned with the organization of the clause in terms of the discourse role of its constituents. This pragmatically oriented system we term the PRAGMATIC STRUCTURE of the clause. (In earlier papers it was called "referential structure.") In addition to the universal tendency for elements bearing contextually given information to precede those carrying contextually new information, as discussed by Firbas, Halliday, and others, one nominal constituent in a clause is singled out for special morphosyntactic treatment as the pragmatically most salient NP in the clause. Pragmatic salience is established by two interacting factors, discourse prominence (i.e., definiteness, specificity, and givenness), on the one hand, and what Zubin (1978) calls the speaker's "focus of interest," on the other, that is, that participant which the speaker treats as most salient in the situation under consideration. The pragmatically most salient NP in a clause is called the PRAGMATIC PEAK [PrP].

The factors that determine the choice of the PrP vary somewhat from language to language, but they fall into the two general classes given above. According to Zubin (1978), the speaker's focus of interest plays the primary role in German in determining which NP will occur as the PrP in the nominative case, and this interest relates, as was noted, to the most salient participant in a situation. In general, animate, especially human, participants tend to be more salient than inanimate or abstract ones; this is the same basic point discussed in Section 3.2.1 with respect to the inherent lexical content of NPs. In Tagalog and other Philippine languages (Foley, 1976), as well as in many Bantu languages, for example, Kinyarwanda (Kimenyi, 1976), PrPs must be definite; indefinite PrPs are not possible. By contrast, English and German do allow indefinite PrPs, even though most are definite; "dummy subjects" in these languages (e.g., *it, there* and *es*) are not PrPs. These two sets of pragmatic factors can be characterized as "speaker related" and "hearer related." The speaker-related factors are those discussed by Zubin and reflect the speaker's judgment about the relative importance of the participants in a situation. Note that the notion of most salient participant is not the same as that of Actor, although the two will often coincide. The hearer-related factors, on the other hand, are those of definiteness, specificity and givenness, which are tied up with the speaker's assumptions about the hearer's ability to identify the referents of NPs and about what has been established in the discourse context; these considerations are part of the contextualization of utterances in terms of the situation in which they occur (see Van Valin, 1978).

Pragmatic structure may be realized either by case marking or word order. It is expressed primarily by word order in English, where the PrP is defined in terms of its clause-initial preverbal position. In German, on the other hand, the PrP is signaled by a case inflection on the NP (i.e., the nominative case). Word order is not a factor in the determination of the PrP in German, as any constituent save the finite verb may be clause initial in a declarative utterance. Our use of the term "case marking" should not be construed as referring only to nominal inflection of the type found in German and Latin. Rather, any kind of morphological marking that indicates the grammatical function or pragmatic salience (or both) of an NP in a clause will be considered case marking. In Tagalog, for example, the PrP is marked by a preposition, *ang* (Foley, 1976; cf. Foley and Van Valin, 1977).

Pragmatic structure is thus a second system of clause organization in addition to the system of role structure discussed in Section 3.2.1. We argued there that the choice of Actor is independent of the choice of subject in English, as illustrated in (7b) and (8b); in both sentences *the students* is the PrP, but in (7b) the action of the predicate is attributed to the students, whereas in (8b) it is not. The choice of Actor is thus independent of pragmatic structure, but this does not mean that they do not interact. In active clauses the Actor is the PrP; in passive clauses a non-Actor, usually an Undergoer, is the PrP. We may express the relationship between perspective and pragmatic structure as follows: Actors have primary access to PrP status and accordingly are the unmarked choice; non-Actors are the marked choice, and their marked status is indicated by the resulting passive construction. This may be summarized in the following ''Access-to-PrP Hierarchy'' for English: ACTOR > UNDERGOER > Other. This hierarchy also captures the fact that in English non-Undergoers can become the PrP when there is no Undergoer in the clause; thus one can say *The duck was shot at by Max* but not **The duck was shot an arrow at by Max.*

In Dyirbal, an ergative language spoken in Australia, the unmarked choice for the PrP is the opposite of that in English. The PrP is indicated by the absolutive case (Van Valin, 1977a), and the unmarked choice for it is the Undergoer, which is a patient or goal with most transitive verbs and goal with verbs of giving (data from Dixon, 1972).

(12)   a. *balan dyugumbil baŋgul yaṛaŋgu buṛan*
            woman-ABS(U) man-ERG(A)   see + TNS
            'Man saw woman'
         b. *balan dyugumbil baŋgul yaṛaŋgu baŋgu yuguŋgu wugan*
            woman-ABS(U) man-ERG(A)   stick-INST(Pat) give + TNS
            'Man gave woman stick'

When an Actor occurs as PrP, a marked construction known as an ANTIPASSIVE must be used. Dyirbal has two such constructions, the *ŋay* construction in (13a) and the ''false reflexive'' in (13b).

(13)   a. *bayi yaṛa   balgalŋañu   bagun dyugumbilgu*
            man-ABS(A) hit + *ŋay* + TNS woman-DAT(PAT)
            'Man hit woman'
         b. *bayi yaṛa   balgayiriñu   bagun dyugumbilgu*
            man-ABS(A) hit + REFL + TNS woman-DAT(PAT)
            'Man hit woman'

In these examples the Actor is in the absolutive case, and so the verb is inflected to signal the occurrence of a marked NP type as PrP. There is a third antipassive construction, which allows instrument NPs to be the PrP. Thus the Dyirbal Access-to-PrP Hierarchy is UNDERGOER > ACTOR > Other, which, in its first two terms, is the reverse of the English hierarchy.

We may summarize the situation regarding access to PrP status in English and Dyirbal as follows.

(14)   English   ACTOR > UNDERGOER > Other   (passive)
         Dyirbal   UNDERGOER > ACTOR > Other   (antipassive)

Both of these languages have constructions that allows various NP types to occur as PrP.

The notion of PrP, as we have developed it here, subsumes what has traditionally been called the "grammatical subject" in English, German and French, although "subject" and PrP are not always the same thing in other languages, as we have argued elsewhere (see Foley and Van Valin, 1977; Van Valin, 1977a, b, c; also Section 3.2.5). It is necessary to distinguish PrP from "topic," a term that we will use to designate sentence-level phenomena of the type illustrated in (15).

(15)   a. *As for the World Cup, many people though the refereeing stunk*
        b. *The Yankees, a lot of people love them and a lot hate them*
        c. *Gakkoo wa   boku ga   isogasi-katta* (Japanese)
           school TOP I   PRT busy-PAST
           'As for school, I was busy.'

Sentence (15c) is from Li and Thompson (1976), who suggest a number of criteria for distinguishing subjects from topics which can in general be used to differentiate PrPs from topics in the sense proposed here (see also Van Valin 1977b, p. 66–67).

3.2.3. Given our definition of the PrP as the most salient NP in a clause in terms of discourse prominence and speaker's focus of interest, we might expect to find a heavy functional load for PrPs in forming cohesive discourse. Prominent participants will be referred to frequently, and consequently we might expect devices for linking utterances with previous utterances often to center around PrPs, as they refer to prominent participants and therefore are the central NPs of the utterance.

The nominative case NP is the PrP in a German clause, and so it should play a large role in discourse cohesion; in particular, it should play a much larger role than the dative and accusative cases. Zubin (1978) shows that in sequences of NPs in utterances (what he refers to as "chains"), the frequency of NPs in the nominative referring to the same entity is much greater than that of NPs in either the accusative or dative cases. His results indicate that only a minority of nominative utterances fail to occur in chains (44%), whereas a majority of dative and accusative references fail to occur in chains (66% and 81%, respectively). Furthermore, as chains get longer, the differential of the nominative over the dative and accusative increases: Whereas 19% of the nominative references are found in chains of at least four units (clauses) long, only 8% of dative and 2% of accusative references are found in such chains. Thus, as chains increase in length, the ratio of nominative references to dative and accusative increases. These findings support the claim that the nominative case is the PrP in German and as such is of fundamental importance in discourse cohesion.

Dyirbal, being an ergative language, presents a typologically somewhat different situation from German. However, with regard to the discourse linking function of PrPs, they are remarkably parallel. As pointed out above, the absolutive case signals the PrP in Dyirbal. Dixon (1972) points out the discourse cohesion function of the absolutive case in a phenomenon he calls "topic chaining."

> If a number of consecutive sentences in such a sequence have a common NP, with common referent, then they will form a topic chain: this entails each sentence being transformed into a form in which the common NP is topic NP (i.e. is in [absolutive] case). This NP may only be stated once, at the beginning of the topic chain. . . . Thus it is quite usual to encounter a chain of a dozen sentences all "commenting" on a single topic occurrence [p. 71].

For example, we may add *balan dyugumbil bañiñu* ('woman came') to sentences like those in (12) to form the topic chain given in (16).

(16)　　*balan dyugumbil bañiñu*　　*baŋgul yaṟaŋgu buṟan*
　　　　woman-ABS(A)　come + TNS　man-ERG(A)　　see + TNS
　　　　baŋgu yuguŋgu bagul (yaṟagu)　wugalñañu
　　　　stick-INST(Pat)　man-DAT(Goal)　give + ŋay + TNS
　　　　'Woman came; man saw (her); (she) gave stick to him.'

Here the "topic" (in Dixon's sense) is *balan dyugumbil* ('woman'), which is treated as it if were the PrP in all of the clauses. If the "topic" is an Actor, as in the third clause, then the *ŋay* antipassive construction must be used.

In spite of the typological differences between German and Dyirbal, the function of the PrPs in discourse in the two languages is strikingly parallel. In German the nominative is by far the most common case used to refer to the same participant in chains of utterances in discourse; in Dyirbal the absolutive marks the same central entity through topic chains. This parallelism is strong evidence for our notion of PrP and its function in discourse.

3.2.4. We have provided definitions of the notions of pragmatic structure and PrP and have presented examples of them in several languages. An important practical question which must be answered is how one determines whether a language has pragmatic structure in its clause-level grammar. There are a number of tests that may be used to answer this question, and taken together they yield a reasonably clear picture of the organization of clause-level grammar in a language.

The most significant intraclausal process to be investigated is "subject" selection, since this is the process by which the PrP is determined. The

PrP is defined in terms of pragmatic salience, and so pragmatic factors, such as definiteness or givenness, must play a role in the selection of the PrP. If "subjects" in a language are chosen on a strictly SEMANTIC basis (i.e, Actors are always subjects—and vice versa—in clauses with predicates with more than one argument, and pragmatic factors have no influence), then those "subjects" are NOT PrPs (cf. Section 3.2.5). In general, PrPs tend to be the leftmost NP, the least marked NP morphosyntactically, and very often the indispensable NP (see Foley and Van Valin, 1977; Van Valin, 1977a). We argued in Section 3.2.2 that there are hierarchies of access to PrP status in some languages and that there are constructions that allow NP types lower on the hierarchy to override it and occur as PrP. These are passive and antipassive constructions, and their existence in a language is a clue to the possible existence of pragmatic structure (see Van Valin, 1977c). It must be noted that passives and antipassives may have functions in a language other than allowing NPs ranking lower on such hierarchies to be PrPs, for example, Actor or Undergoer suppression (see Heath, 1976; Sinha, 1978; Silverstein 1978). Indeed, these constructions may exist in a language and not have at all the pragmatic function that has been discussed. Nevertheless, their existence in a language can be viewed as a potentially positive indicator of pragmatic structure which must be evaluated in terms of their function in the grammatical system as a whole. Thus the passive construction in English and German, the various antipassives in Dyirbal, and the focus system in Tagalog (Foley and Van Valin, 1977) are all intimately involved in the pragmatic organization of clause-level grammar in these languages.

We have already discussed the important discourse role of PrPs in German and Dyirbal, and this highlights the fact that PrPs are often singled out for special treatment in interclausal processes. The most important phenomena of this kind involve relativization and "deletions" under coreferentiality in complement constructions and across conjunctions. In some languages, relativization is completely restricted to PrPs (e.g., Tagalog and Dyirbal), and in others there are special strategies for forming relative clauses which apply only to PrPs (e.g., in English and German there are special participial relatives which require that the NP relativized upon be a PrP); in all of these cases, relativization is by "deletion" (see Van Valin, 1977b). Deletion under coreferentiality in complement constructions ("Equi-NP Deletion") is restricted to PrPs in English and German, as is coreferential deletion across conjunctions. (It is not crucial to the argument that these phenomena be analyzed as actual deletions; rather, we are simply using the commonly accepted labels for them.) The existence of restrictions on "deletions" in these kinds of constructions is a strong clue to the existence of pragmatic structure. Evidence from interclausal processes must be evaluated with that from intraclausal processes in order to get a picture of the grammar as a whole.

We have outlined a number of tests for establishing the existence of pragmatic structure in a language. The intraclausal tests, in particular the criteria for "subject" selection, provide strong evidence for pragmatic structure, and this is further supported by the tests relating to interclausal phenomena. Indeed, it is striking that the intraclausal phenomena can be unified with the interclausal in this way, and this lends further support to the notions of pragmatic structure and pragmatic peak.

3.2.5. Implicit in the preceding discussion of tests for pragmatic structure is the premise that there are some languages that "pass" the tests and others that "fail" them. So far we have discussed only languages that "pass," that is, languages with pragmatic structure. In this section we will briefly discuss languages that lack pragmatic structure in clause-level grammar.

If a language lacks pragmatic structure in its clause-level grammar, then it will not have PrPs, and we mentioned in Section 3.2.4 that if "subject" selection in a language is completely determined by semantic criteria, then it lacks PrPs and pragmatic structure. An example of such a language is Choctaw (Heath, 1977). Choctaw has two systems of case marking, one for full NPs and another consisting of bound affixes in the verbal complex; the former signals only a "subject–oblique" distinction, whereas the latter indicates the case roles of agent, patient, dative [Heath's term], instrument and locative. The following examples are from Heath (1977).

(17)   a. *hattak at*   *∅-iya-h*
            man   ART–SUBJ 3Ag–go–PRES
            'The man goes.'
        b. *hattak at*   *oho:yoh (a:)*   *∅-∅-pisa-h*
            man   ART-SUBJ woman   ART–OBJ 3Ag–3Pat–see–PRES
            'The man sees the woman'

(The verbal glosses are Heath's.) In these examples *at* (*a-* 'the' + *-t* 'SUBJECT') signals "subject" and *ã:* (*a-* + *-n* 'OBJECT' = *ã:*), "oblique." The most important fact about this NP case marking system is that it is completely determined by the semantic role functions of the NPs in the clause. Heath (1977, p. 207) formulates a "main subject selection" rule as follows: "Given a descending rank order of Agent > Patient > Dative > other, the highest ranking NP in the clause is marked as subject." The NP which receives *-t* subject marking in a Choctaw clause is determined by its semantic case role; pragmatic factors do not have any influence. Thus subject in Choctaw can be described in ENTIRELY semantic terms, and it cannot therefore be considered a PrP. Hence Choctaw appears to lack pragmatic structure. This conclusion is supported by the results of another intraclausal test. Choctaw lacks a passive construction of the type found in English and German; Heath (1977, p. 207) notes that "there are no productive passivization rules or the like which would affect free [i.e., NP] case marking, though there are the usual intransitive/transitive . . . doublets for verbs meaning 'to be broken/ to break (tr.)', and the like" (see Van Valin 1977c). Further support can be found in the facts regarding relativization. Choctaw relativizes by "deletion," as do Tagalog and Dyirbal, but there appear to be few restrictions on it; in particular, subjects, objects and objects of postpositions may be relativized upon (Van Valin, 1977b). The evidence thus supports the conclusion that Choctaw lacks a system of pragmatic structure in its clause-level grammar.

Choctaw it not unusual in lacking pragmatic structure. Other languages that lack it include Lakhota, Tunica, Barbareño Chumash, Tonkawa, Eastern Pomo, Hopi, Caddo and Iroquoian languages (North America); Walbiri, Walmatjari and Diyari (Australia); Sumerian, Sherpa and Tibetan (Asia); and Enga and Yimas (Papua-New Guinea) (see Van Valin, 1977b, c). Since these languages lack pragmatic structure, the organization of their clause-level grammar is dominated by the systems expressing semantic role structure (see Section 3.2.1). If such a language has a formal passive or antipassive construction, its function will be unrelated to the kinds of pragmatic concerns discussed in Section 3.2.2 and will often center around the suppression of an Actor or Undergoer in a clause. Moreover, many of these languages (e.g., Lakhota, Tunica, Enga and Walbiri) lack formal passives and antipassives altogether. Languages that lack pragmatic structure and have their clause-level grammar organized around the system of role structure are referred to as ROLE-DOMINATED languages. Languages such as English and Dyirbal that have pragmatic structure are called REFERENCE-DOMINATED languages.

In Section 2 we stated the basic assumption of RRG that syntax is to a large extent the result of the interplay of semantics and pragmatics, and in reference-dominated languages the interaction between them is found primarily in the interplay between role and pragmatic structures; in addition, there is of course the influence of the distribution of given and new information on word order in these languages. In a role-dominated language, on the other hand, the influence of pragmatic (discourse) factors is not grammaticalized at the clause level, and so the interaction of semantics and pragmatics in these languages must be different in important respects from that in reference-dominated languages. Such interaction takes place primarily at the SENTENCE level in role-dominated languages. In Lakhota (Van Valin, 1977b), for example, the discourse prominence of an NP is expressed by the system of determiners and through topicalization; NPs may serve as sentence-level topics as in (18).

(18)   a.   *wašíču   hená mathó ki   ktépi   na yugápapi*
             whiteman those bear   the they-kill-it and they-skin-it
             'The whitemen killed the bear and skinned it.'
        b.   *mathó ki wašíču hená ktépi na yugápapi*
             'The bear, the whitemen killed it and skinned it.'

In the second example the Undergoer *mathó* ('bear') has been topicalized and moved into sentence-initial position. Such topicalization is governed by discourse factors and therefore represents pragmatic influence on Lakhota syntax. But *mathó* is clearly a topic, not a PrP, as there are no changes in the structure of the clauses or the morphology of the verbs as there would be if it had occurred in a passive construction in a language like English or German; Lakhota has no such construction. These Lakhota examples illustrate the interaction of semantics and pragmatics in a role-dominated language, an interaction that takes place on a different level than in languages with pragmatic structure (see Van Valin, 1977b).

We discussed the important discourse cohesion function of PrPs in Section 3.2.3, and we will now look briefly at discourse cohesion devices in role-dominated languages. We saw earlier in the Dyirbal topic chain in (16) that the central participant is always in the absolutive case—that is, is the PrP—and that *ŋay* antipassive constructions are used to signal Actor as PrP. Thus in the Dyirbal system the same participant is "tracked" across clauses with the verbal morphology indicating whether it is Undergoer (plain) or Actor (*ŋay* antipassive) (see Silverstein, 1976b). In many role-dominated languages, on the other hand, a different kind of discourse cohesion system is found: A particular semantic function, often the Actor, is tracked across clauses, and there is some morphological device that indicates whether the participant with that function in a clause is the same as, or different from, the participant with that function in the next clause. Such a system has been called *switch-reference* (Jacobsen, 1967), and we can illustrate it with data from Choctaw (Heath, 1975) and Enga (Lang, 1973).

(19)   a.   *∅-∅-pi:sa-ča:*   *∅-iya-tok*   (Choctaw)
             3Ag–3Pat–see–SAME 3Ag–go–PAST
             'He$_i$ saw him$_j$, then he$_i$ left.'
        b.   *∅-∅-pi:sa-na:*
             DIFF *∅-iya-tok*
             'He$_i$ saw him$_j$, then he$_{i/j}$ left.'

(20)   a. *Baa-mé pá-o   kalái p-i-á*   (Enga)
            he–Ag go-SAME work do–PAST–3sg
            'He went and worked (at the same time).'
        b. *Namba p-e-ó-pa   baa-mé kalái p-i-á*
            I   go–PAST–1sg–DIFF he–Ag work do–PAST–3sg
            'I went and he worked.'

The Choctaw switch-reference system monitors the highest ranking NPs
in each clause in terms of the subject selection hierarchy described above
(Heath, 1977, p. 207); if the two are coreferential, -*ča:* is used, and if they
are not, -*na:* is used. Thus the Choctaw system cannot be said to monitor
a particular semantic role but rather to monitor what we may call the
ROLE PEAK of the clause (this term is taken from Olson, 1978). The Enga
system is concerned primarily with signalling same versus different Actor
(Lang, 1973).

If we compare the Dyirbal and Choctaw–Enga systems of clause linkage, we see that the former centers around a main participant with grammatical devices to signal its function in different clauses, whereas the
latter is concerned primarily with a particular grammatical (semantic)
function and whether the participant carrying it out is the same or different
across clauses. Hence we will refer to the Dyirbal-type system as a
SWITCH-FUNCTION system and reserve the term ''switch-reference'' for
the Choctaw-Enga-type system. Both are crucially involved in maintain-
ing discourse cohesion, but they differ from each other in their formal properties. This distinction should not be interpreted as an absolute
dichotomy but as the two end points on a typological continuum of clause-
linkage systems. In general, many role-dominated languages have switch-
reference systems of the kind that has been described. Reference-dominated languages, on the other hand, tend to have switch-function systems,
although there are a few cases of them with switch-reference, including
Eskimo (Woodbury, 1975) and Barai (Olson, 1978). (For a more complete
discussion of pragmatic structure, see Foley and Van Valin, in preparation, Chapter 4.)

3.3. To sum up: We have proposed two major systems of clause-level
grammar—role structure and pragmatic structure. Role structure expresses situations, their participants, and the roles the participants play
in the situations. Pragmatic structure is the organization of the elements
in the clause in terms of their discourse role. Fundamental to pragmatic
structure is the notion of the pragmatic peak, the pragmatically most salient NP in a clause. Not all languages have pragmatic structure in their
clause-level grammar—those that do we call reference-dominated languages; those that do not we term role-dominated languages.

4. CONCLUDING REMARKS

Having outlined the basic concepts of RRG in some detail, we will look at the analysis of a small set of English sentences.

(21) a. *The farmer killed the duckling*
   b. *The duckling was killed by the farmer*
   c. *The woman believed that John killed the farmer*
   d. *The woman believed John to have killed the farmer*

In presenting an RRG analysis of these sentences, the two interacting systems of clause-level grammar in English must be represented: role structure and pragmatic structure. We must therefore represent the fact that in both (21a) and (21b), *the farmer* is the Actor and an agent, and *the duckling* the Undergoer and a patient; the two sentences differ in their choice of the PrP, the Actor being the PrP in (21a) and the Undergoer in (21b). Recognition of these systems obviates the need for a distinction between surface and underlying syntactic structure, and so none is postulated in RRG. This in turn eliminates the need for derivations linking surface and underlying structures. Moreover, no purely grammatical relations independent of these systems (e.g., "subject" or "direct object") are postulated. Although we do not make use of "subject" and "object" as theoretical constructs, we do not deny that languages have subjects and objects—but it should be kept in mind that we are using these terms here as labels for language-specific grammatical categories. Thus for example what we call the subject in English is a particular conflation of role and pragmatic structures not found in many other languages. The subject in Lakhota and Choctaw is a function of role structure alone and is therefore very different from the English subject. Hence cross-linguistic generalizations based on the theoretical construct "subject" which gloss over the substantive differences between English subjects and Choctaw and Lakhota subjects are of highly questionable value (see Foley and Van Valin, 1977; Van Valin, 1977a,b).

In RRG, analytic statements are set forth primarily in the form of hierarchies and constraints. (It must be emphasized here that very little of the work done in RRG to date has been devoted to the development of a symbolic notation for the expression of these hierarchies and constraints and for the representation of analyzed sentences. We have been concerned with developing the substantive aspects of the approach to the neglect of these more formal features. This is an important area for future work in RRG.) We have already presented examples of a hierarchy in (14) in the access-to-PrP hierarchies in English and Dyirbal. The English hierarchy is of course very relevant to the analysis of all of the example sentences, particularly (21a) and (21b). Passive constructions are used in English when, for whatever reason, a non-Actor NP is the PrP. We may therefore propose the following tentative rule.

(22)   PrP ≠ Actor ⊃ PrP – V [+ PASS] – X – (*by* + Actor)

This says simply that when the PrP is not an Actor, a passive construction results. This is not particularly enlightening, since it does not specify the semantic and pragmatic conditions under which non-Actor NPs may be PrPs in English. A complete statement of the "passive rule" in RRG would involve a thorough functional analysis of the construction in order to ascertain the conditions, both semantic and pragmatic, of its occurence, and this in turn presupposes a general functional account of English syntax, something that does not exist at the present time. A more adequate formulation would be stated as a constraint on the occurrence of the passive, specifying the contextual and other conditions on its occurrence. In general, RRG seeks to describe those alternating syntactic patterns that earlier forms of TG analyze in terms of movement transformations with respect to the pragmatic and semantic conditions on their occurrence. This assumes that such alternating patterns do not vary randomly and that there are differences in semantic or pragmatic meaning associated with them.

To return to the analysis of (21a) and (21b), we may represent the relevant grammatical information about (21b) in the format shown in Figure 1. Pragmatic structure and role structure are represented under the Clause node by the PrP and PRED (predicate) nodes. Note that these two nodes dominate the minimally necessary elements in the English clause, namely, the subject and predicate. Perspective is symbolized by the arrows from PRED to the two NPs, with "U" standing for Undergoer and 'A' for Actor. Finally, the semantic case roles themselves are represented by labeled arrows from the verb itself. The relationship of this passive con-

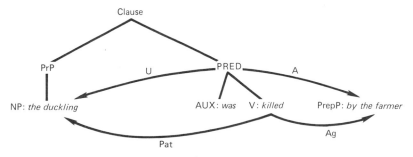

Figure 1

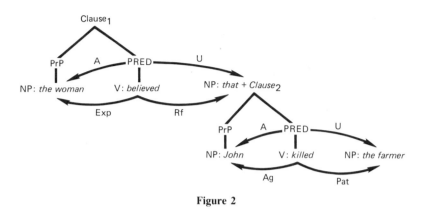

Figure 2

struction to its active counterpart, (21a), is captured in the identity of their perspective choices and case roles; they differ only in their choice of the PrP. The details of the phrase-level grammar of these examples have been omitted.

Work on complement structures of the kind illustrated in (21c) and (21d) has just begun in RRG as part of the development of a general theory of interclausal relations and clause linkage which will deal not only with examples such as these but also with switch-reference and switch-function systems of the type discussed in Section 3.2.5 (see Foley and Van Valin, in preparation, Chapter 7). Nevertheless, we may briefly outline the RRG approach to the analysis of these two sentence-types. In (21c), the complement clause *that John killed the farmer* is both the Undergoer of the main verb *believe* and an argument of it bearing a case role that we will call "referent" (Rf) for the purpose of this discussion; furthermore, *John* is the Actor of *kill* and its agent, while *the farmer* is the Undergoer and a patient. This can be represented as in Figure 2. In (21d), the NP *John* is now the Undergoer of the matrix verb, supplanting the complement clause, and is no longer the Actor of *kill;* however, it is still the agent of *kill,* just as the reduced complement clause is still the referent of *believe.* This is shown in Figure 3. The important thing to note about (21c) and (21d) is that the case roles are the same in both, with the difference between them being whether the whole complement clause or only its subject is the Undergoer of the matrix verb. As with (21a) and (21b), a complete analysis of (21c) and (21d) would specify the semantic and pragmatic conditions on the occurrence of the complement PrP as the Undergoer of the matrix verb. These analyses of the examples in (21) are not intended to be definitive; rather, they are meant to illustrate the way one would approach them in RRG.

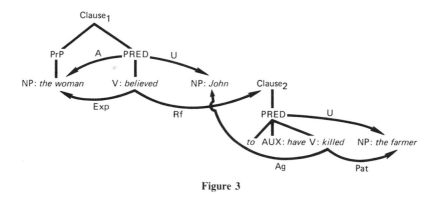

Figure 3

ACKNOWLEDGMENTS

We would like to thank Michael Silverstein, Kenneth Whistler, Johanna Nichols, Henry Thompson and Jerrold Sadock for helpful discussions of many of the topics discussed herein and for comments on an earlier draft. All errors are our own.

REFERENCES

Chomsky, N. (1965). *Aspects of the theory of syntax.* Cambridge, Mass: MIT Press.

Dixon, R. (1972). *The Dyirbal language of North Queensland.* Cambridge: Cambridge University Press.

Fillmore, C. (1968). The case for case. In E. Bach and R. Harms (Eds.), *Universals in linguistic theory.* New York: Holt, Rinehart & Winston. Pp. 1–88.

Fillmore, C. (1977). The case for case reopened. In P. Cole and J. Sadock (Eds.), *Syntax and semantics, 8: Grammatical relations,* New York: Academic Press. Pp. 59–81.

Foley, W. (1976). Comparative syntax in Austronesian. Unpublished doctoral dissertation, University of California, Berkeley.

Foley, W., and Van Valin, R. (1977). On the viability of the notion of 'subject' in universal grammar. In *Proceedings of The Third Annual Meeting of the Berkeley Linguistics Society.* Berkeley: Berkeley Linguistics Society. Pp. 293–320.

Foley, W., and Van Valin, R. (In preparation). Role and reference grammar: A functional approach to grammar.

Greenberg, J. (1966). Some universals of grammar with particular reference to the order of meaningful elements. In J. Greenberg (Ed.), *Universals of language.* Cambridge, Mass: MIT Press. Pp. 73–113.

Gumperz, J., and Cook-Gumperz, J. (1976). Papers on language and context. University of California, Berkeley: *Language Behavior Research Laboratory Working Paper no. 46.*

Heath, J. (1975). Some functional relationships in grammar. *Language, 51,* 89–104.

Heath, J. (1976). Antipassivization: A functional typology. In *Proceedings of the Second Annual Meeting of the Berkeley Linguistics Society.* Berkeley: Berkeley Linguistics Society. Pp. 202–211.

Heath, J. (1977). Choctaw cases. In *Proceedings of the Third Annual Meeting of the Berkeley Linguistics Society*. Berkeley: Berkeley Linguistics Society. Pp. 204–213.

Heath, J. (1978). Functional universals. In *Proceedings of the Fourth Annual Meeting of the Berkeley Linguistics Society*. Berkeley: Berkeley Linguistics Society. Pp. 86–95.

Hymes, D. (1974). *Foundations in sociolinguistics*. Philadelphia: University of Pennsylvania Press.

Jacobsen, W. (1967). Switch-reference in Hokan-Coahuiltecan. In D. Hymes and W. Bittle, (Eds.), *Studies in southwestern ethnolinguistics*. The Hague: Mouton. Pp. 238–263.

Jones, L. (1979). A synopsis of tagmemics. This volume.

Kimenyi, A. (1976). A Relational Grammar of Kinyarwanda. Unpublished doctoral dissertation, University of California, Los Angeles.

Lang, R. (1973). Grammatical sketch. In A. Lang, *Enga Dictionary, Pacific Linguistics Series C*, no. 20. Pp. xviii–lvii.

Li, C., and Thompson, S. (1976). Subject and topic: A new typology of language. In C. Li (Ed.), *Subject and topic*. New York: Academic Press. Pp. 457–490.

Olson, M. (1978). Switch-reference in Barai. In *Proceedings of the Fourth Annual Meeting of the Berkeley Linguistics Society*. Berkeley: Berkeley Linguistics Society. Pp. 140–156.

Silverstein, M. (1976a). Shifters, linguistic categories and cultural description. In K. Basso and H. Selby (Eds.), *Meaning in anthropology*. Albuquerque: University of New Mexico Press. Pp. 11–56.

Silverstein, M. (1976b). Hierarchy of features and ergativity. In R. Dixon (Ed.), *Grammatical categories in Australian languages*. New York: Humanities Press. Pp. 112–171.

Silverstein, M. (1977). Cultural prerequisites to grammatical analysis. In M. Saville-Troike (Ed.), *Linguistics and anthropology*. Washington, D.C.: Georgetown University Press. Pp. 139–152.

Silverstein, M. (1978). Deixis and deducibility in a Wasco-Wishram passive of evidence. In *Proceedings of the Fourth Annual Meeting of the Berkeley Linguistics Society*. Berkeley: Berkeley Linguistics Society. Pp. 238–253.

Sinha, A. (1978). Another look at the universal characterization of the passive voice. In *Papers from the Fourteenth Annual Meeting of the Chicago Linguistic Society*. University of Chicago, Department of Linguistics. Pp. 445–457.

Van Valin, R. (1977a). Ergativity and the universality of subjects. In *Papers from the Thirteenth Annual Meeting of the Chicago Linguistic Society*. University of Chicago, Department of Linguistics. Pp. 689–705.

Van Valin, R. (1977b). Aspects of Lakhota syntax. Unpublished doctoral dissertation, University of California, Berkeley.

Van Valin, R. (1977c). On the distribution of passive and antipassive constructions in universal grammar. Paper presented at 1977 LSA Annual Meeting; to appear in *Lingua*, v. 50.

Van Valin, R. (1978). Meaning and interpretation. To appear in *Journal of Pragmatics*, v. 4.

Woodbury, A. (1975). Ergativity of grammatical processes. Unpublished master's essay, University of Chicago.

Zubin, D. (1978). Discourse function of morphology. In T. Givón (Ed.), *Discourse and syntax*. New York: Academic Press. Pp. 469–504.

SUMMATION AND ASSESSMENT OF THEORIES

ROBERT P. STOCKWELL
University of California, Los Angeles

1. INTRODUCTION

I have tried to single out those differences that seem controversial on substantive grounds and to review the arguments that might lead one to prefer either side of any given controversy. Where the differences seem more notational than substantive in nature, I have tried to lift at least the edges of the blankets of terminology and formalism to peer beneath and determine who is really in bed with whom. In some instances, it turns out to be too dark to tell for sure who is in the same bed, or what they are doing there. My main goal is to isolate genuine irreconcilabilities, though I am not opposed to promoting reconciliations wherever these seem feasible. There is, unfortunately, a degree of incommensurability between some of these presentations such that some decisions about compatability, notational variance, substantive difference, and complementarity are impossible to make yet. I have probably erred in the direction of deciding that compatibilities exist where the theory advocates would believe their theories to be substantively different from the bedmates to whom I have assigned them. I offer here my apology for any misrepresentations of this type that my comparisons have led me into. It is my conviction that a failing of much contemporary syntactic work is that

353

many theorists have insulated themselves against comparison and persist in working within a single tradition, generally comparing their work only with that of their immediate colleagues and students, to such an extent that communication between advocates of different theories has nearly ceased to take place in our profession. If this conference has accomplished anything, it has been to ameliorate that sad state of affairs to some extent.

2. THE OBJECT OF DESCRIPTION

Following Chomsky, Lightfoot (trace theory, conference paper) states[1] that generative grammarians "have customarily set up the most general aim of their work as the characterization of how it is that children can learn their native language" quickly despite nonuniformity of the data they are exposed to; further, how they learn to project from finite observations to an infinite range of novel sentences; and finally, how they figure out structures and rules for which no direct evidence exists in the data. The generativist's solution to these problems is to impute a priori existence in the mind to those theoretical constructs that he finds useful for syntactic description, even though the constructs are the creations of ingenuity applied to extend metaphors from computer technology, formal logic, and the mathematics of axiomatic systems to natural language, without empirical evidence that these metaphors reflect any kind of mental reality. "An analyst's grammar," Lightfoot says, "is an account of the native speaker's fully developed linguistic capacity, under the usual idealizations." The object of description is taken to be a specific mental capacity, not different as an object of investigation from such cognitive skills as memory, perception, musical talent, eye–hand coordination, or facial recognition.

The above is one pole of a scale. At the other pole is the position clearly articulated by Sanders (equational grammar, conference paper) and also by Kac. Sanders views natural languages as "cultural instruments for the systematic association of sounds and meanings for the purpose of effective symbolic communication by the members of human societies" and as "objects rather than events, and [with] cultural values and dimensions rather than physical or psychological ones." Kac (personal communication) claims that "the term 'rule of grammar' refers to a convention or norm shared by the members of a speech community which governs either what is permissible in the language of the community or what is a possible

---

[1] References to the conference papers are based on texts of the pre-conference versions, which may or may not be identical to the papers in this volume.

interpretation of a given sentence." Elsewhere (Kac, 1975, p. 45) he states

> I thus deny . . . the claim that native speakers of languages 'know' theories of these languages. . . . A theory of a language—an axiomatic description of its underlying principles—is not the same thing as an algorithm for manipulating the system. Linguistics is therefore not directly concerned with what a speaker knows, or is able to learn, but only with what makes languages knowable or learnable. . . . I therefore do not define linguistics as a psychological science except in the loosest possible sense—i.e. as a science whose findings may in the future have psychological relevance insofar as they characterize to the student of mental machinery the abstract nature of one kind of system with which the machinery is called upon to deal.

Kac goes on to discuss how distributional–structural observations about [k] and [q] in Arabic and English provide an explanation for the way the difference is perceived: The difference is structurally redundant in English, nonredundant in Arabic, with consequent differences in its perceptual salience for English and Arabic speakers. His point is that the structure exists independently of human perception. As he says, "knowing an algorithm (e.g., for ordinary addition) cannot in any way be identified with knowledge of underlying principles [of structure]—a cardinal, if elementary, principle of mathematics."

These poles may be labeled LANGUAGE AS A PSYCHOLOGICAL OBJECT versus LANGUAGE AS A CULTURAL OBJECT. If I may be permitted a historical footnote, it seems to me that these poles characterize a fundamental aspect of the split between Chomsky's kind of transformational linguistics and that of Zellig Harris. Harris saw transformations as distributional relationships holding "out there" in the cultural norms where, in his view, the structure of the language exists. In such a theory, the "excessive power" of transformations which so exacerbates the current MIT school that they have thrown out all T-rules except "move category"—and even that is likely soon to disappear—is not a defect if transformations provide an elegant kind of axiomatized structure, as distinct from processing-algorithms. There is no question which of these views had the greater social success, however, and even apart from Chomsky's charismatic presence and elegant argumentation, it seems likely that the notion of a linguistic theory which claimed to provide a window on the mind, even if a somewhat cloudy one, was so appealing to psychologists, and so elevating to the self-esteem of linguistics, that its rise to power was a foregone conclusion.

There is a point at which these two poles converge: No theory would defend a kind of structural analysis that is unlearnable. The problem is, what is unlearnable? Consider the learning achievement of a virtuoso violinist. As anyone who has ever seriously undertaken to learn a string instrument knows, the complexity of virtuoso performance is monumental. I cannot imagine that it does not vastly exceed, in complexity of muscle–sense–mind coordination, the achievement of language learning. It has many of the properties of language acquisition: No one ever becomes totally fluent, in the relevant sense, who starts after a critical age—that is, well before puberty. The learning is largely by imitation of a model (called a teacher, but it is clear that modeling is the teacher's main role) and by trial-and-error practicing. Conscious memorization plays almost no role, nor does it in language acquisition. A very high level of skill can be acquired by any normal child in a favorable environment—the word "talent" is the nonmusician's rationalization of why he did not work hard enough to achieve the same result.

In a similar vein, concerning what is humanly unlearnable, consider the fluent mathematician or the fluent reader of an electronic circuit diagram. In both these areas, some people who start young and who are fascinated by the subject acquire a level of skill that is incredibly far beyond the skill that can be acquired after one gets to college. These skills are completely comparable to the skill of the language user. Indeed, the only difference is that every normal child acquires language. But the view that every child acquires language to some level of absolute mastery is simply one of the myths of our profession. There are huge differences between individuals, and they are found in all strata of linguistic structure. There are culturally determined differences as well as individually determined differences. Every normal child learns language to some minimal level of need because it is learnable and one cannot get along without it; but the Gleitmans showed (1970) that we do not all learn it to the same depth. Sheldon (1979) has summarized this position clearly:

> If transformational grammars are not actual speaker grammars then the question of how a child could learn such an abstract formal system of rules is beside the point. . . . Before we postulate . . . a specifically linguistic genetic mechanism [and impute to it our particular preferences of abstract formal systems, whether transformational or other: RPS], we must SHOW that language cannot be learned by general principles of induction and cognition that develop in the normal interaction between children and their environment. . . . The little evidence that we have indicates that language learning may not be as fast, as easy, or as uniform for all learners, or as independent of environmental influence and assistance as we had imagined [pp.15–16].

Not all these papers take a stand on this psychological versus cultural object parameter. As I noted above, Lightfoot is at one extreme, Sanders and Kac at the other. Before classifying the rest, we should perhaps ask: What difference does this make in how the linguist actually formulates his description? The difference it SHOULD make is in the kind of evidence that one takes to be crucial. But, in fact, the evidence on which all the syntactic theories presented here are based is much the same: judgments of grammaticality and judgments of semantic entailment (of which synonymy, paraphrase, and ambiguity are simply special cases). That is, there are few instances in any syntactic description where evidence from how children learn language is cited to support one constituent-structure formulation rather than another. For example, no one argues in favor of formulating rules in terms of linear sequences of category labels rather than in terms of unordered relational labels on the grounds that one or the other is more easily learned by children as demonstrated in such and such an experiment. Lightfoot claims that the linguist who takes the question of how infants come to master language as his goal must indeed look for a priori knowledge, and that to do that he must look at particular areas of grammar where the description is underdetermined by the data—areas where, given the meager data, the child could not possibly figure out the right answer, and therefore must "know" it in advance. Thus the crucial test of a particular formulation is not how well the data fits, as a whole, but rather how much insight the formulation provides for particularly subtle distinctions the child learns to make. Thus an example like *Who do you **wanna**/**want to** succeed?* bears extensive discussion because trace theory reduces the child's learning burden to a simple rule *want to* → *wanna,* assigning all the remainder of the distinction to the syntactic genotype that "knows" that the presence of a trace in *want t to* "blocks" this rule. On the other hand, a theory operating on a set of cultural norms cannot find this argument compelling, since such a theory would assign *wanna* the status of modal (or pseudomodal, like *yusta, hafta*) and show that its distribution shares the properties of other pseudomodals, as well as historical properties of main verbs in transition to modal status (stress reduction; invariant form; loss of tense distinction—there is no corresponding *wanted-to* = PAST + *wanna,* just as there is no *hadda* corresponding to *hafta;* loss of aspectual inflection; loss of nominalization— **his wanna doing it,* like **his can doing it,* etc.) Within a theory of grammar like relational grammar or role and reference grammar, the question that would be evidentially relevant is this: How does this analysis work across a range of significantly different languages (not just, say, English and French, but rather English, French, and Navajo or Papago)? Is there a phenomenon under consideration that is fundamentally the same across all languages, and therefore a characterization of something about the nature of language itself? Modalization is in fact a universal, or nearly so: A description in those terms, rather than in terms of the presence or absence of traces, might well be cross-linguistically (and therefore also in terms of the human linguistic capacity) more informative.

In any case, it is clear that this parameter is not a mere reflection of philosophical speculation about the nature of mind in relation to grammar:

It determines what you look for, and what counts as an answer. It may also determine the form of description: that is, whether you view grammar as an algorithmic set of rules from which true generalizations about well-formedness and entailment can be derived, but in which these generalizations are not actually stated directly—this is the condition of all theories that have derivations of any kind, whether phrase-structure rules, transformations, daughter-dependency rules, or stratificational networks—or, on the other hand, as a set of axioms that directly state the conditions on well-formedness, as in corepresentational grammar (CORG). In some ways, however, this difference is independent of the psychological versus cultural parameter, and I postpone it for further discussion separately.

Taking the other contributors alphabetically now: Brame (presented at the conference, though not published in this volume; his views can be found in Brame, 1978) speaks against "an excess of theoretically elaborate devices, such as traces and empty nodes." He favors "realistic" grammar, that is, direct interpretation of surface strings, and what he provides is a logic that operates directly on surface strings. In this respect, his grammar is quite close to Montague grammar (Cooper's paper) and other logical systems such as that of Keenan and Faltz (1978). None of them make any commitment to either pole of this parameter. Dik claims that a grammar should be psychologically adequate in the sense that the description of the system should be "compatible with what is known about the psychological properties of the human organism," and he asserts that "natural language is not only a social, but also a psychological phenomenon. The psychological correlate to a natural language is COMMUNICATIVE COMPETENCE in the sense of Hymes." From this I infer that Dik would agree that linguistic structure should not be unlearnable, but that the structure exists as a set of social norms which come to be internalized, and that the system itself is distinct from the algorithms by which people use the system. Otherwise I can extract no sense from the phrase "psychological CORRELATE to a natural language." Tagmemics (Jones) clearly views language as a system of norms which can be viewed from various perspectives, not as a set of internalized rules having the sorts of properties Lightfoot attributes to them. Kuno is scornful of the kinds of pure syntactic constraints assigned by Lightfoot to the genotype [e.g., the Specified Subject Condition (SSC)] and asserts that generalizations of this type are "further and further removed from reality." He substitutes "functional factors"—conditions of language use and interpretability in context—and claims that SSC "is not even a plausible constraint in English, to say nothing of its implausibility as part of the theory of grammar that humans are born with." Functional syntacticians, according to Kuno, "assume that there is something wrong with syntactic generalizations that do not have obvious nonsyntactic explanations, especially if they are of the language-universal type." Since his explanations are based largely on pragmatic properties—focus, theme, left–right order, potential ambiguity, etc.—I assume it is safe to place Kuno on the nonpsychologizing end of this parameter, though I can find no explicit statement of his to defend my assumption. As for McCawley, I am unable to determine exactly where he stands on this issue. He asserts that "the individuation of the total grammar into rules . . . implicitly corresponds to individuation of what the learner learns or the speaker uses," and he cites the example of Cena's dissertation as showing that the aw/Λ vowel-shift alternation "is synchronically not a part of vowel shift." Whether this means that a vowel-shift rule is legitimately part of the description of the system even though it may get internalized by some and not by others, I am not sure. If it means that every proposed rule requires empirical testing as to whether people really "know" the rule, then McCawley can go to the head of the class of the psychological-reality group. But for the most part, McCawley's arguments do not sound like this at all, arguing as he does for "cross-linguistic testing of language-particular claims," insisting on judging grammaticalness as acceptability of "given meanings in given classes of contexts," and rejecting the "misconception that [linguists] and their subjects are able to make 'grammaticality judgments,' i.e. decide whether a given string of words is good or bad as a sentence of their language." Certainly he is not at all bothered by whether rules are formally too powerful to be acquired or not, since he asserts that "all God's chillun believe in some sort of global rules, though [for some] . . . the global rules come out being semantic interpretation rules. I don't regard globality as horrifying or even remarkable. . . . The things you do in speaking and understanding speech are global, so would it be surprising if some of the knowledge that you utilize in speaking and understanding were global too?" Given that he allows all kinds of rules— from surface target "filters" to the most abstract derivational conditions, including (though reluctantly) extrinsic rule ordering—I take it that McCawley is looking for a perspicuous characterization of a structure that exists "out there" and that is not limited by the supposed learnability of the processing algorithms of a particular formalism.

Perlmutter (relational grammar) abjures psychological discussion altogether. He is concerned with the cross-linguistic characterization of syntactic phenomena, where "syntactic phenomena" includes a wide range of processes such as Subject-to-Subject Raising, Subject-to-Object Raising, Passivization, and others which are now abhorrent AS RULES to a trace theorist who takes the explanation of language acquisition as a focal goal. I take it that Perlmutter is looking for a characterization of syntactic systems which would have to be learnable but which are not of a form predetermined by putatively innate mechanisms. Though he seeks linguistic universals, he takes no stand on whether these are functionally determined, determined by ultimately uniform linguistic ancestry, determined by general cognitive properties, or determined by special properties of an innate "language organ" (I believe this exhausts the list of explanations for universals that have been proposed, ever).

Ross and Lakoff (conference paper, not included in this volume), aligning themselves with the prototype theory of Eleanor Rosch, place linguistic accomplishments in a category with other cognitive accomplishments. Since they allow network representations of unlimited power, and assert that "you have to relate linguistic structure to the full set of human abilities," it is clear that the psychological aspects of syntax are central to their formalism, though in a way quite different from Lightfoot's. They explicitly assert that a grammar is an on-line, direct-time, real-use device for production and comprehension, a far stronger "psychologizing" position than that taken by Lightfoot. At one point in the discussion, Ross said that Bresnan's "realistic transformational grammar" is the successor to Lakoff's cognitive grammar.

Schachter claims the same goal for daughter-dependency grammar as the goal of TG: a grammar which "correctly represents the grammar that has been acquired by a speaker of that language," and he wishes to specify the form of grammars "in such a highly constrained way that it constitutes an explanation for speakers' acquiring the particular grammars they do." Clearly the descriptive devices of DDG are vastly different from those of TG or trace theory, so that it would appear that both cannot be right about what is pre-wired. That such different theories can with equal fervor claim to explain pre-wiring suggests that both may be, as Sheldon puts it, "METAPHORS for the generalizations that speakers know about sentences." Different metaphors are, of course, only that: Different metaphors are quite compatible, and may throw equally useful light on the object to which they apply. But the specific properties of the metaphor cannot be inherent in the object: ITS properties are independent, and may be metaphorically similar to the properties of theory A in some ways, similar to those of theory B in the same or other ways. The theories, viewed as metaphors, have no direct psychological properties whatever. There is instead a system of regularities that has independent existence and can be explicated by various analogies, some of which are simply more perspicuous than others. Sullivan intends stratificational grammar to be understood in this metaphorical way without direct psychological implications, and he has explicitly disavowed such psychological implications in conversations with me, even though others (including Lamb) have not been so cautious on this score. Van Valin and Foley treat language as a cultural artifact and make no psychological claims other than claims like Kuno's about functional motivations for constructions of different types.

This concludes my survey of the various conceptions of the nature of the object of description as found in these different theories, with respect to the question of the extent to which they impute psychological standing to their formalisms.

3. THE PRIMITIVE ALPHABETS ON WHICH THE "COMBINATORICS" OPERATE

The theories presented at the conference take three positions on this issue:

1. The rules apply to categories, "parts of speech."
2. They apply to semantic roles—"Agent," "Patient," "Benefactor," etc.
3. They apply to syntactic relations—Subject of V, Direct Object of V, etc.

A fourth possible primitive, pointed out by Ken Hale in his comments on Perlmutter's paper, is "formal relations"—word order, surface case-marking, marking in predicate, etc. Since none of the theories take these as the ONLY primitives, and in fact most deal with them as derivative from one or more of the others, I leave this possibility without further discussion.

First a word about why it matters what the primitive alphabet is. There is only one reason: As a function of scientific parsimony, we should never take as primitive any unit that can be derived in a coherent way from the interaction of other units that we have to have anyway. Just as in phonology we distinguish between distinctive and redundant features, in syntax we want to reduce the system to its minimal distinctive units and predict the redundant information by general rules and computations. This does not mean that the output of such computations does not play a role in logically subsequent computations (e.g., in semantic interpretation), only that it is not the prime information. Roles are inferred from the intersection of more primitive bits of semantic information, in particular the semantic properties of verbs, such as Van Valin and Foley's classes—state, process, event, stance, activity, act, perception—which are (as they suggest) intersections of primitive semantic properties such as [±Dynamic], [±Durative], [±Controlled] and the semantic properties of nouns such as [±Anim], [±Hum]. For example:

(1)   a. *Mary received the package*
       b. *Mary received the guests*

To assign to *Mary* the feature "Goal" or "Agent" in (1a) and (1b) respectively is to assert that the speaker/hearer does not MERELY DEDUCE, from his knowledge of what *packages* are, as distinct from what *guests* are, that the relationship between NP₁ and NP₂ is quite different in these two sentences. But this inference is, as far as I can see, exactly like the deductive inferences required by metaphorical language:

(2)   a. *The scholar was **immersed** in his books*
       b. *Rubbish **clogged up** the streets of New York*
       c. *The acid **ate through** the steel plate*

Van Valin and Foley say, "case roles may be given strict definitions in terms of the arguments of certain predicates as set out in the schema 'PRED(NP1, NP2,...NP$_n$)'. Thus for . . . *hit, kill, break* and *smash*, NP1 is Agent, NP2 is Patient and NP3 is Instrument." But in general I claim roles CANNOT be defined strictly in terms of verb features alone. They depend also on noun features. I would not want to say that *crash* was an Agent in

(3)   *The crash smashed the airline's safety record*
       with a single blow

The notion of CONTROL is necessary in an Agent, and that in turn entails consciousness/animacy. Thus inferences about agency depend on the intersection of both verbal and nominal features. From this observation it follows that role labels are not the optimal way of representing semantic inferences that result from the intersection of primitive semantic features that are inherent in the verbs and nouns of a sentence. It is likely, in my opinion, that even a full set of such inherent semantic features is only PART of the basis for role inferences. Knowledge of the world also enters into such inferences. Consider (4):

(4)   *Bill is on Dilantin*

I'm not altogether sure what roles anyone would assign to *Bill* and *Dilantin* here; perhaps

(5)   *Bill* = Patient (he ingests the medicine and presumably is affected
              by it)

       Dilantin   ⎰ Goal?   (it gets ingested, and it is instrumental
                = ⎱ Instrument?   in maintaining his health)

However, to make such decisions (or any other), we have to know that *Dilantin* is some kind of medicine, and that "being on it" entails taking it at regular intervals—something that is not a function of some set of lexical features, but rather of our knowledge of the nature of the medical control of epilepsy.

In a similar vein, I think it is mistaken to assume, as primitive, roles or adverbial categories such as Source or Time, and then assign prepositional (or affixal or postpositional) marking to them (as Dik and Sanders do), because—exactly as inferences about roles depend on the intersection at least of verbal and nominal features—inferences about the meaning of prepositional phrases depend on the intersection of semantic properties of prepositions and nouns, sometimes also intersecting the semantic properties of verbs:

(6) a. *He did it with a hammer*   (Instr)
     b. *He did it with Mary*   (Comitative)
     c. *He did it with ease*   (Man)

(7) a. *He did it in July*   (Tm)
     b. *He did it in Amsterdam*   (Loc)
     c. *He did it in silence*   (Man)
     d. *He did it in a rage*   (Cause)

(8) a. *He writes about aircraft*   (Goal)
     b. *He lingers about the house*   (Loc)
     c. *He had apoplexy about the decision* (Cause)

My general point is that NO DEDUCTIVE SEMANTIC INFERENCE should be given the status of a primitive within a theory of syntax, because syntax provides necessary but not sufficient conditions for the explication of that kind of inference (i.e., function is underdetermined by structure, in general).

So much for semantic roles as elements of the primitive alphabets on which rules operate. The other nonstandard position, that of Perlmutter and Postal in RG, is the focal point of a far-reaching controversy in syntactic theory. I will review first the arguments that support the position that relations are not derivable from categorial or lexical-semantic information that all theories agree must be available to the combining rules. I do not find these unanswerable, and I will review the main lines of a counter-argument, essentially nothing more than the position taken by various forms of semantically interpreted syntax such as Brame's, Montague's, or Keenan and Faltz's.

Unfortunately, various papers by Perlmutter and Postal which are available to me, including the one in this volume, refer to their 1974 Linguistic Institute lectures, which are NOT available to me, as the place where they provided "argumentation of various kinds for taking grammatical relations as primitives." It is therefore likely that I have missed one or more crucial arguments in my summary. The arguments that I am aware of are of two types:

1. Definitions available in the literature that define SUBJECT, OBJECT, etc. in terms of categorial nodes, domination, order, or morphology are vulnerable; and the range even of such definitions is very small, failing to include various oblique relations (benefactive, instrumental, etc.)
2. There are examples in various languages which demonstrate that relations are independent of categories, of formal marking, and of logical and lexical semantic structure—the only bases that have ever been proposed to derive relations from.

The first class of arguments cites VSO languages, where there seems to be no justification for a VP node, as evidence that subject cannot be defined as the highest NP dominated by S, with object being defined as the highest NP dominated by VP. [But in this case, another formal property, word order, can be taken as defining the relations. This would agree with the Keenan (1976) "cluster of properties" approach.]

This takes us to the second class of arguments, in which independence of all categorial and formal information is claimed. Relations are independent of category, as Hale pointed out in his comments on Perlmutter's paper, because a number of different categories can bear the PRED relation (e.g., verbals, adjectivals, nominals, and adpositionals), and also the various term relations, as in these Navajo examples of Hale's:

(9)   *Tsé?áán bii?góne? hóznóní*
       cave   in   SUBJ-ASP-nice
       'In the cave is nice.'
(10)   *Tsé?áán bii?góne? hwiiłtsá*
       cave   in   OBJ-I-saw
       'I saw in the cave.'

In these instances, the case-marking on the verb determines the subject–object relations. As in the VSO examples, there is SOME kind of formal marking. Are there cases where there is no formal marking at all? Hale cites *That he goofed is obvious,* observing that S is subject, but does not have to appear first. While true, it seems to me that something can be made of its dummy replacement *it* that appears in first position. He also cites the Apachean examples of Subject–Object order being determined by a scale of importance (human > animate > inanimate, etc.), where again, however, there is marking in the verb. Finally he cites Papago, where nothing whatever—if I understood him correctly—marks which NP is Subject, which is Object:

(11)   *Wakial ʔat   g   wisilo cepos*   (any order, AUX 2nd)
        cowboy AUX DET calf   branded
        'The cowboy branded the calf.'

There is, however, a possible marking that would be used if there were doubt about who/what was being branded:

(12)   *Wakial ʔat   g   wipsilo ha-cecpos*
        cowboy AUX DET calves them-branded

There is a further example, pointed out by Bernard Comrie, in Bats (NE Caucasian), where the subject of certain verbs may be either absolutive (normally the case form for the subject of intransitive verbs) or ergative (always the case form for the subject of transitive verbs) with a semantic difference. The verbs include *worry, fear, lie, get drunk*. An ergative-marked subject indicates that the subject had at least potential control over the event, but that (as through carelessness) he failed to exercise this control. An absolutive-marked subject indicates that the event was not the subject's fault; he had no control over it:

(13)   a. *Txo   naizdrax   kxitra*
           we [ABS] to-the-ground fell-against
           'We fell to the ground (not our fault).'
        b. *Atxo naizdrax kxitra*
           we [ERG]
           'We fell to the ground (our fault, or deliberately).'

In such examples, it appears that "subject" is not marked by a uniform case-assignment rule, but the verbs that can do this are a small lexically marked class, arguably insufficient to base a whole theory on.

Li and Thompson (1976, p. 472) argue that in Lisu (Lolo-Burmese), "there is no way to identify the notion of subject. . . . If there is more than one noun phrase preceding a verb, then the sentence is normally ambiguous as to which noun phrase represents the agent or the actor and which noun phrase represents the patient. . . . [N N V] sentences may mean either *people bite dogs* or *dogs bite people*." They go on to point out, however, that in Lisu such theoretically possible ambiguity almost never results, because of context and because of selectional restrictions in the semantics of verbs. They also acknowledge that there is a subject-marking morpheme *nya* in sentences of a rare type that lacks any presupposed NPs. I cannot speak for Postal and Perlmutter in respect to how they would handle such a language, but it seems to me a reasonable way would be to assign two structures to the truly ambiguous examples, and to use whatever contextual or selectional information exists to enable a determination to be made in the unambiguous examples.

Anderson and Chung (1977) argue that VSO languages do not provide a solid basis for taking relations as primitives.[2] Their argument, briefly, is this:

1. In Breton, which is VSO, only a SINGLE CONSTITUENT can be topicalized (by a fronting rule).
2. Verbs ALONG WITH VP constituents like DO, IO, DIR, but not "sentence adverbials" like TM, LOC, MAN, can be topicalized, even though there is no other evidence for a basic order distinct from VSO.
3. A verb and its subject, even though adjacent, CANNOT be topicalized.
4. Therefore, AT SOME LEVEL or IN SOME SENSE V + DO/IO/DIR is a constituent.

Possible explanations advanced by Anderson and Chung include:

1. Relations are primitives. They reject this because, though "work in Relational Grammar has uncovered an impressive array of properties associated with the fundamental grammatical relations, . . . the interest of such a theory could only be enhanced by showing that these notions themselves could be reduced to other independently motivated properties such as the internal constituent structure of clauses [p. 25]."
2. Analyze all clauses, as in the generative semantics *do*–performance analysis of English, as having main verb and complements embedded under a matrix verb *ober* 'to do' (thus: "to read a book-do-I every day" with an incorporation rule for those sentences that do not undergo topicalization). Predictably, they reject this analysis as having no independent justification.
3. Allow discontinuous constituents. (No further comment by them.)
4. Allow transformational rules to make reference to "constituents"

---

[2] They also establish that in a VSO language like Samoan, certain rules such as Equi and Raising need to refer to the NP that is SUBJECT, but they acknowledge that semantic conditions may be involved in these constructions, which weakens the force of the argument. They also discuss a rule of clitic placement in Tongan which must apply only to pronoun SUBJECTS, and it is not likely that any sort of semantic conditions would apply to this rule. In this instance, however, it seems likely that trace theory would handle the problem by leaving a trace of a subject removed by Raising, so that in their problematic examples (167) there would be a way of marking the relevant NP for clitic placement. I have therefore cited only that one of their Breton arguments which does not involve movement of a constituent in such a way that its identity as a constituent could be marked by a trace.

that are unitary only in some sort of semantic structure. This alternative is being explored more fully in Keenan–Faltz logical semantics. It and (3) are the ONLY options open to a theory that interprets directly from surface strings which are themselves formed by surface-true syntactic composition rules.

Anderson and Chung conclude that "whether the required relational distinctions can be coded in terms of some notion of hierarchical constituent structure, or should be taken to be unanalyzable primitives, must remain at present an open question [p. 25]."

Perlmutter (conference paper) refers to Chung (1976) as having provided a crucial example in which the conditions on relativizability (of an underlying "Dative" object) cannot be stated in terms of linear order of elements. He claims that similar arguments apply to some observations of Bernard Comrie's about Swahili in which a notion "chômeur" is required to explain the failure of a verb–object agreement rule which would be difficult to block under a traditional category-sequence constituent-structure-based rule formulation, but in this instance it is not unlikely that a trace left by movement of the underlying Direct Object to Subject would suffice to block the object-agreement rule.

These, then, are arguments that I know of which support the RG position that grammatical relations are primitives. The general line of counter-argument to this position goes like this.

Theories that take as their main goal the determination or manipulation of syntactic relations such as "subject of," "object of" may perhaps be engaging in an analytic redundancy. What I am about to say is not true where, as in CORG, such notions as Subject are taken merely as convenient abbreviations for, for example, "that NP which combines with the whole VP to constitute a sentence," or, for example, Object = "that NP which combines with a V_t to form a V_i"—in categorial terms:

(14) $V_i = S/NP$ "V_i is a functional expression which combined with an NP (= SUBJ) yields a sentence."

   $V_t = V_i/NP$ "V_t is a functional expression which combined with an NP (= OBJ) yields a V_i."

This is perfectly sensible, since derivative categories like

(15)   SUBJ DO IO
      $\downarrow$ $\downarrow$ $\downarrow$
   $((S/NP)/NP)/NP)$

      $= V_i$

      $= V_t$

      $= V_{tt}$

[which is the categorial expression for the category "ditransitive verb" (V_{tt})] are quite formidable and therefore better abbreviated by familiar terms.

There is no reason not to introduce notions like "Subject" and "Object" into a syntactic theory as DERIVATIVE categories which merely abbreviate constituency relations, and thereby save a great deal of paper and obfuscation of the type that multiple-categorial labels introduce. The question is whether they are primitives. Do they have syntactic or semantic functions that are independently definable, or that are independently needed for semantics? Currently on the marketplace there are only two model theoretic interpretative systems for relating syntactic constructions to semantic truth-conditions: These are Montague logic and Keenan–Faltz logical types. They use constituency and two primitive categories (plus various logical operators, such as quantifiers), namely Sentence (= Formula) and NP (= Terms = DNP). There does not exist any standard set of translation rules from natural language into standard Fregean logic except by way of Montague grammar, though there is a huge amount of practical experience that enables any skillful logician to make such translations successfully, and people like Jackendoff and Renate Bartsch have formalized such translations for partial grammars of English and German. The whole point of Montague grammar and of Keenan–Faltz logical types is of course precisely to formalize translations from natural language into intensional and extensional logics. And, crucially for the question of relations as primitives, none of these translations require more than constituency relations between categories, the categories themselves being derivative from S and NP. Brame, Kac, and Schachter use labels like SUBJ where they are clearly derivative: For example, Brame's bracketing

(16) $(f(x))((g(x))(j))$
                    $\uparrow$ $\uparrow$
              OBJ SUBJ

is sufficient to distinguish object from subject without the labels. I infer that he introduced the superscript labels in order to make his lexical entries more transparent:

(17)   give; F^v, $\_\_(A^{n[dat]}, A^{n[o]})$ or $\_\_(A^{n[o]}, A^{p[dir]})$

In fact, it is clear that he views syntactic relations as derivative, because he writes, "We must therefore provide for the subject argument and this can be accomplished by providing a rule which will interpret $A^{n[s]}$ [singular] in the appropriate position relative to the interpretation tree." Sanders derives Subject and Direct Object from constituent structure, but takes

Dative (i.e., Indirect Object) as a prime, for reasons which are not clear to me. But since, for Sanders, in general Subject and Object are derivative relations that depend on constituency, as in CORG and Brame, I believe Sanders belongs in the latter group. Dik assigns Subject and Object functions to Goal or Agent in transitive sentences, which in turn determines active or passive verb morphology and the application of his linearization rules. It follows, then, that they are not derivative notions, though they play no other role in the fragment that he presented. Role and reference grammar considers Subject to be a conflation of PrP with Actor or Undergoer in English—their position is unique, since Subject is a derivative notion, but not based on constituency. Since in general they do not find Subject–Object–Indirect Object necessary, relying on roles (Agent, Actor) and on pragmatics instead, I believe it is correct that they do not take relations as primitives. Schachter marks Subject in his diagrams, but it is derivative from the relation "dependent sister of finite verb," assigned redundantly given that relation. The relation "dependent sister" might itself be in question, however: I do not think it is a relation in Perlmutter's terms. It is "dependent" because in the derivational sequence, you have to have the one in order to get the other (i.e., a dependent sister presupposes its head, but not conversely, so the head is "independent" relative to its sister). But since the sister relation obtains between nodes that have quite different kinds of relations in RG—for example, both *you* and ₛ[*what she did*] are sisters of *think* in a DDG analysis of *What do you think she did?*—it appears that sister relations are distinct from functional relations, which are the ones to which RG rules apply.

In short, in the matter of relations as primitives, it comes down to one against all the others, supported to some degree by Dik and by tagmemics (which marks EVERYTHING—categories, functional relations, role relations, dependency relations, and constituency). In stratifications, where the nodes "subject" and "complement" appear as node labels in Sullivan's diagram, it should be noted that these labels are no more than conveniences for explication: As long as the linkages with upward- and downward-ordered and unordered *and*'s and *or*'s are correct, the machine will grind out and interpret sentences without any use of the notions "subject," etc.—subject can be derivatively defined (for English declarative sentences) as the left impulse of a downward-ordered *and*-node of which the right impulse leads to V as its first constituent.

How, then, do we assess the value of taking relations as primitives? It seems most likely that the real virtue of this approach is to make comparisons possible between languages where the relational information, though virtually always signaled by SOME formal device, is the lowest level of abstraction at which comparability exists. That is, though the relational information is derivative in any given language, the basis for that derivation differs from one language to another so considerably that the effort to characterize universal and near-universal processes is frustrated at any lower level. This solution to the problem of describing comparable processes and comparable structures seems to me entirely valid, in principle. The empirical problem of showing that putatively comparable processes are REALLY comparable—and not made so by the choice of relational labels—remains quite far from a satisfactory resolution, in my opinion. For instance, the inversion hypothesis demotes the "1" of sentences like *It seems to me* (= 1) *that John is intelligent* to "3." It is hard to provide independent motivation for this as a rule of English, even though the analysis may then make English appear similar in this process to, say, Dyirbal or Eskimo. Similarly, the unaccusative hypothesis is singularly unattractive as an analysis of English sentences like *John fell,* but it preserves universality for one of the relational laws, and permits the universal semantic characterization of such verbs as having a 2 relation rather than a 1, which gets promoted to 1 as a superficial subject. Indeed, it is hard to see how a relational law might be falsified, since in many instances such laws characterize universal perceptual or semantic relations by, as it were, shoving them down into the syntax. Nonetheless, Perlmutter, Postal, and their colleagues have uncovered rich ore to be mined in accounting for the ways in which languages are alike, and I for one wish to withhold judgment concerning questions like the above ones about empirical falsifiability until we can see more.

4. THE PLACE OF WORD ORDER IN
SYNTACTIC THEORIES

The programmatic goal of all theories of syntactic structure, in relation to meaning, has been and is to lay bare the LOGICAL FORM of sentences. The essence of that program is to establish a notion of "normal syntactic form" that correlates in some one-for-one fashion with a particular logic. When Brame claims that the main argument for transformations is to account for the relation between discontinuous constituents, he is exactly correct, and is saying, in a different way, that there is a set of ORDER relations which correlate one-for-one with CONSTITUENT relations which are directly mappable onto a logic, and that when these order relations are disturbed by some syntactic rule, they have to be restored or given a special interpretation which has the effect of restoring them by assigning to them the semantic interpretation they would have had in their normal syntactic form. This is, as I understand it, also the program of Sanders' equational grammar. Sanders differs from TG very little, in this area: He has rules that assert that some given constituent structure is equivalent to some other constituent structure. Such rules can be understood as transformations, since they are equations between trees except that the trees are linearly ordered. Sanders, DDG, RG, and Dik all have rules that assign linear order to unordered trees or networks. Therefore, where a transformation simultaneously changes order and constituent structure, Sanders changes constituent structure and allows a change in order to follow from the constituent change. I am not sure whether anything of theoretical consequence hinges on this difference, though Sanders' position is the theoretically neater one, since his position makes it absolutely clear that constituent order is a syntactic feature, like affixes or adpositions, whose sole function is to MARK constituency relations, and it is the constituency relations that are semantically relevant. TG has always had a confusing blend of operations which mixed rules of semantic relevance with rules of surface form. Daughter-dependency grammar, like equational grammar, Dik's functional grammar, and relational grammar, assigns order by a set of linearizing rules which in effect substitute order for (in DDG) dependency and functional relationships—and in that respect it is doing the same thing, in the same way, as Bartsch and Vennemann (1972) with their Operator–Operand basis for assigning surface order. Vennemann and Harlow (1977) talk about Specifier and Head as the primitive relationship which determines surface order. The generalizations in all these theories are the same: There is a FUNCTION : ARGUMENT relation between constituents that surfaces as constituent order. Unfortunately it is not always clear that DEPENDENT : HEAD and FUNCTION : ARGUMENT relations would be assigned in a way consistent between theories, and in fact there are conflicting criteria. To illustrate my point:

1. In Montague, VP is viewed as argument and the term phrase (NP) is viewed as function. [The term is a set of properties, and the VP is a particular property; the expression

John´ (^run´)

is translated (Partee) as "the property of running is in the set of properties of (the individual concept of) John."]

2. On the other hand, in Keenan and Faltz (1978), NP (actually "Determined NP") is viewed as argument and VP is viewed as function, with the VP expressing a function from DNP to S—that is, the S is true iff the property assigned by VP to DNP is in fact true of that NP.

3. For Schachter in DDG, V is HEAD of S, and Subject is a dependent

sister. But a standard argument for dependency has always been AGREE-
MENT. The verb agrees with the Subject, whose number is independently
assigned (i.e., inherent to N), just as Adj agrees with N in languages like
Spanish or German. By Keenan and Faltz this is taken as evidence that
VP is a function of DNP subject, a view which is supported by the se-
mantics:

(18)   *John is running* ⎫
         My nose is running ⎬   different interpretation depends on
                              ⎭   Subject (i.e., VP is function on DNP).

   4. In the case of Direct Object, Montague grammar and Keenan–Faltz
agree that TV is a function of the object NP, the evidence being both
syntactic agreement (as in the many languages which have object agreement markers in the verb) and semantic:

(19)   ⎧ *the bread* ⎫
         They cut ⎨ *the class* ⎬   [in which the object determines the
                    ⎩ *the heroin* ⎭   kind of cutting]

For DDG, the TV is head, and the object is dependent sister. Perhaps it
is correct to say that in general, syntactic dependents modify the head,
and that the proper equation of terminology should be

$$\text{Head} = \text{FUNCTIONAL CATEGORY}$$
$$\text{Dependent} = \text{FUNCTIONAL DOMAIN}$$

The equation seems correct, if we confine ourselves to the instances
above, but it reverses the traditional correspondence between the terms
"head" and "dependent," on the one hand, and "argument" and "function," on the other, inside the NP, as below in Vennemann's view.
   5. If we use Vennemann and Harlow's definition of head—"The head
of a [construction] is that constituent which determines the category of
the resulting combination." [The other constituent is either an ATTRIBUTE
or a COMPLEMENT, which jointly count as SPECIFIERS of the HEAD.]—
then Det and Adj are specifiers (dependents) of N, and Subject NP and
Object NP are specifiers (dependents) of V (under the convention that
$S = V^0$—i.e., a predicate with all argument places filled). The trouble
is, we would surely want specifiers in general to bear a consistent semantic
relation to heads (in particular, the relation of function to argument, or
the converse, but not sometimes one, sometimes the other). Thus what
determines agreement of specifiers in the NP is viewed as head; what
determines agreement in the VP is viewed as specifier. Something has
got to be wrong. In Keenan–Faltz, this matter is handled consistently:
That which agrees is the function (= dependent), that which determines

agreement is the domain (= head) of the function. Except for the handling of Subject, Montague grammar is also consistent on this relation.

The preceding discussion about DEPENDENCY is merely an aside: The essential point of agreement among all these theories is that surface order is assigned by rules that take functional relationships as the determinants of order.

There are, of course, theories that do not take order of constituents as derived (i.e., as assigned by rules that apply to unordered hierarchies). The main representative of this group is the standard theory of TG, along with the TG derivatives such as trace theory. Stratificational grammar clearly belongs to the unordered-base group, though it does not provide any principled basis (so far as I can see) for the ordering that occurs as you go down the line to an ordered *and*-node and so does not enter into the discussion above. Stratificational ordering is a device of unlimited power which could with equal ease assign any order to any set of constituents. Direct generation of surface strings, as in Brame and tagmemics, is also a device of unlimited power in respect to any ONE order for a set of constituents, but it is the weakest possible model for the expression of different orders for the SAME constituents—that was, after all, the fundamental argument for transformations. In spite of its weakness in that respect, it is the only device for generating any string whatever in tagmemics, and I think Postal's characterization of tagmemics many years ago, namely that it is a phrase-structure grammar with multiply labeled nodes, is still fully correct and, taken as a criticism, is still unanswered by the version presented at this conference.

No one has vigorously defended the generation of underlying order— the main argument usually given is that you have to specify it at SOME point, and you might as well start out with it from the beginning of the derivation. Emmon Bach's arguments for underlying order, referred to by McCawley in his presentation, go like this:

1. Deep SOV languages gap only right to left (Japanese); but Amharic gaps both SOV SO (left to right, applied BEFORE V-final rule) and SO SOV (right to left, applied AFTER V-final rule).

2. Relative clause is formed by attaching [yə] to the next element to the right, unless there is a verb at the end of the clause, in which case [yə] is attached to the verb. We get a single generalization if Amharic is underlyingly VSO, since V is the next element to which [yə] would be attached before it is moved. To get the same generalization with SOV underlying order, a quantifier must be used in the statement of the variable for [yə]-insertion.

3. Definite determiners (*-u*, *-wa*, m. and f. respectively) are suffixed to nouns that have no adjective, and suffixed to the first adjective if there is one. Thus at least the linearization rules cannot apply after all other syntactic rules, which is problematic for theories that assign total constituency/dependency structure prior to linearization.

My own view is that assigning BOTH constituent structure AND word order at a level close to logical form is clearly redundant, and that therefore any theory that distinguishes between them is better, to the extent that one values the minimization of redundancy. However, a theory that provides for generation of surface order directly, like Brame's, or starts from it, like CORG, if it can adequately handle the problems that motivated transformations in the first place, might be said to have the best of both worlds—namely, correct surface order and interpretability without intermediate abstractions.

5. THE TYPES OF ABSTRACT STRUCTURE, IF ANY

One of the central, frequently repeated claims of all but one or two of these papers is that syntactic rules should hug the surface—reminiscent of Hockett's phrase about the need for phonemic analysis to hug the phonetic ground. Even trace theory has an absolute minimum of transformational content, being reduced to one rule ("move category"). Relational grammar has promotion and demotion rules which can be viewed as equivalent to Sanders' constituent reanalysis rules, though they operate on different primitive elements. What kinds of devices do these theories employ instead, to accomplish what transformations did in a way that most of us thought was pretty neat just a few years ago?

Brame employs "functions" that are quite similar in spirit to λ-extraction operators. Thus his handling of *wh*-questions posits a function whose domain is the rest of the sentence and whose range is the SUBJ-NP, or OBJ-NP, or PREP-NP that would be the moved-constituent in a transformational analysis. Thus

$$F^q(A^{n[x]}) \; (F^v(A^{n[s]}, A^{n[o]}, A^{p[dir]}))$$

is equivalent to

$$\textit{what } \lambda x \; (F^v(A^{n[s]} A^{n[o]}, A^{p[dir]})$$
$$[\text{where } x = \text{any } A]$$

That is, *what* is bound by λ to some logical argument in the domain of the question function. In a similar way, Brame would have topic opera-

theory. The disadvantages of this latter research strategy is of course that typological and universal claims about the nature of language are hopelessly far into the future.

7. THE FORM OF SYNTACTIC GENERALIZATIONS

A major issue, faced in particular by Kac and by Larry Hutchinson as moderator of the final discussion session, is whether syntactic rules should consist of a set of instructional statements for forming sentences, or of a set of axioms and theorems which directly state true generalizations about the syntactic system. An example of an instructional statement is S → NP VP, which on its face is simply false for English and most if not all other languages. An example of an axiomatic generalization for English is "All tags contain an auxiliary verb which is identical to the first auxiliary, if there is one, of the main clause; otherwise the tag contains a *do* auxiliary." The question is, unless the instructional statements either recreate a psychological processing sequence (which no one claims, at least in TG) or provide a special level at which semantic rules operate (which used to claim, but no longer does), then what good is a generative device from which true generalizations about well-formedness can be INferred (by generating the relevant examples and seeing what they have in common) but in which no generalizations are directly stated? Hutchinson provides the following nice analogy—one in which he and I share highest degree of expertise: "One might take as an analogy a model airplane kit in which pictures, blueprints, and descriptive statements have been separated from assembly instructions. Anyone given only the description of the completed model will have his hands full trying to figure out how to assemble it, while anyone given only the assembly instructions will have a difficult time constructing a description of what the completed model would look like. These are utterly distinct enterprises. . . ." It is clear that Kac's CORG is the ONLY theory presented here which states generalizations directly, but Sanders' equational grammar is closely related since he provides not derivations, but proofs of equivalence relations, each of which is in effect a Kac-type axiom: For example, X (PREP & Y) says, "Prepositions precede a sister constituent. (N, V), N)) ≠ (N, (((N, INST), V), N)) says, "Instrumentals don't function as objects; that is, there are no direct objects that have instrumental roles."

The gain in the direct statement of generalizations is the well-known one that the linguist is not forced, as he is by a generative procedure, to decide borderline eventualities. He can, as traditional grammar did, leave

tors, relative operators, and corresponding operators for any "gapped" NP constituent. It is not clear how he would handle *yes/no* interrogatives, since they leave no gap (unless *whether* is viewed as being gapped; cf. *I don't know whether he is leaving* versus *Is he leaving?*). Nor is it clear how he would handle movement rules that leave neither gaps nor copies, such as REL-EXTRAPOSE. The fact that some movement rules leave different kinds of traces might constitute a problem:

(20)   a. *There was a boy that got lost*
          b. *It was a boy that got lost*

Whether these are to be handled by different lexical features assigned to *there* and *it,* I do not know.

But what is most important, in this context, is not whether there are technical problems still to be overcome in Brame's kind of functional-operator theory of moved constituents; no doubt we all have still insuperable problems in any theory. The important question is whether in principle such a theory has significant advantages. My own view is that there are significant advantages if and only if the syntactic rules are matched by rules that translate the syntactic constructions directly or indirectly into a corresponding logic. Otherwise, we merely have a much enriched base component and a sizeable number of uninterpreted functions that correspond, one-for-one, to some erstwhile transformation. I am not clear whether Brame succeeds in mapping fully into a logic, but that is clearly his intent.

It should be remembered that base rules—generally speaking, context-sensitive phrase-structure rules, or else context-free phrase-structure rules with context-sensitive lexical-insertion rules—are simply economical summaries of lists of construction types. To merely lengthen the list of possible construction types is not in itself meritorious. Arguments that transformational rules are "too powerful" really miss the point if what we replace transformations with is a lexicon of indeterminate power and interpretive rules of equally indeterminate power. Transformational rules may be powerful, but they are elegant in a perfectly normal use of the word "elegant" in science. They express generalizations simply. The huge common vocabulary we all use in talking about construction types— such notions as verb gapping, Equi, Raising-to-Object, Raising-to-Subject, Topicalization, Extraposition—are all intelligible and well-defined in terms meaningful only within a movement-rule (i.e., transformational) frame of reference.

Consider the status of the one theory we have that does not generate anything, namely CORG. I do not know where the strings on which Kac's rules operate come from—I suppose they are randomly generated by throwing out labeled dice or pulling words out of a hat—but given a string, what CORG does is attempt to parse it with the goals (a) of determining whether it is grammatical (and if not, why not), and (b) of assigning relational labels which ultimately correspond to constituent grouping for the purpose of translation into a logic. These are, indeed, the two minimum goals that all theories of syntax must share, in my opinion, though some (like DDG) have not gotten to the second goal, being still preoccupied with the first. [As an aside, I think it is extremely unlikely to turn out that a syntax which is assembled with only the first goal in mind will be optimal for purposes of meeting the second goal effectively; therefore I think that the very earliest work on TG was correct in associating these two goals closely—and no matter what claims are made about autonomous syntax, it seems clear to me that the early work DID associate these two goals and that Ross (1974) was right when he claimed that Harris' transformations, and Chomsky's early ones, amounted to saying both (a) and (b): (a) Big sentences are syntactically made up of little sentences; (b) Meanings of big sentences are semantically made up of meanings of little sentences.] Now what is it that CORG accomplishes? It in effect extracts precisely that information from surface strings that is necessary as input to a logic, using whatever clues the language user might reasonably be assumed to have available to rely on, discounting context, probability, real-world knowledge, etc. It sets up no relations that are not semantically motivated, and by implication all semantic relations are analyzed as functions from category to category—which corresponds exactly to the interpretive functions seen in Montague grammar and (more perspicuously, I think) in Keenan-Faltz logical types. I therefore see CORG as belonging in a different category of surface-structure hugging from the type that we see in Brame, because it tries to show how the information might be extractable from the surface string that leads to a particular propositional segmentation, whereas Brame builds that information into his generative rules. Brame replaces movement rules with operators across sentential domains and various binding conditions for interpretation. Hopefully, Brame's operators will have a uniform logic, though that conclusion has not been demonstrated and I personally think there are grave difficulties in the way of it. The fact that Kac is able to attack the interpretive question directly, however, stems from the fact that, unlike Brame or Schachter or various others, he takes no responsibility for generating "all and only" the well-formed sentences of L. By throwing dice, he dodges a host of problems. The question is, are they pseudoproblems? What would a reasonable processing model look like, given only Kac's parsing rules and some properly associated interpretive device (which

Kac of course does not claim to have provided, but one can imagine tying his output into Fregean logic, at least if Kac also has something to say about quantifiers and tense/aspect systems)? I suggest that Hockett' notions of syntactic analogy, blending, and editing would be sufficient regularize the process of assembling words into strings, and that par' the editing function would closely resemble Kac's rules. Perhaps the p lems of all generating devices—phrase-structure rules or networ whatever—would fall away under the assumption that surface stri not formatively rule governed, only interpretively rule governe would also be compatible with Sanders' equational grammar, the equivalence rules amount to a test applied at the editin determine proper correspondence between sound and meani have already seen that Sanders' constituent-structure equi are transformations without order features. It should follo Kac's parsing procedures are also isomorphic to transfor extent that they reconstruct predicate–argument relatior present in the deep structure to which transformatio sense, Kac's parsing rules may be viewed as invers given the same qualification that applies to Sanders, n nothing about "underlying order" (whatever that is' functions are, as he has said, equivalent in effec mations.

6. A QUESTION OF RESEARCH STRATEG'

Theories like RG, DDG, equational gra' RRG, and earlier versions of TG start w terms of which any syntactic structure o be stated, in principle, and they try to sh this theory. Given the broad sweep of to bring up apparent counter-example such, indeed, has been the history of RG. One of the weaknesses of suc with which they have been patche such problems. At the other extr explicit formal characterizations of a single language without about how far or how generall successfully either to the rest languages: thus Montague,

all kinds of things to the imagination of the reader and overlook problem areas because his generalizations are not mechanically testable except by constructing rules that generate in accord with his generalizations and then checking the output against them. Probably more new observations have been made about syntactic problems in the last 20 years than in the last 2000 because of the generative ethic. But this is a procedural virtue, not one which justifies a format for the description of the regularities in a system. The direct statement of regularities has the enormous virtue of local falsifiability. In derivation by rules, a later rule can contravene the orders of an earlier rule, so that only a global falsification is possible. A system like DDG, in which no later rule can contravene an earlier rule, perhaps provides a compromise that has both the virtues of explicit derivation and of local falsifiability, except that I am not sure DDG cannot create ad hoc features to serve as governors of some dependency rule: To the extent that it can, it is as weakly constrained as any other derivational theory.

8. THE DERIVATIONAL MODEL OF GRAMMAR

Relational grammar rejects the derivational model in favor of "well-formedness conditions on relational networks." Perlmutter and Postal claim that RG syntactic statements are distinct from transformations because they do not appeal to linear order and dominance relations, they do not convert one structure into another, there are no derivations, no rule ordering, etc. But RG retains the notion linguistic level/stratum, which reconstructs the notion of successive structures in a derivation, and Perlmutter acknowledges that "the empirical import of derivational vs. nonderivational conceptions of linguistic structure must await . . . future research."

9. RELATION OF SYNTACTIC STRUCTURE
   TO DISCOURSE

As Perlmutter remarks, "A particular construction may be linked in particular languages with semantic or pragmatic effects, . . . with the organization of the sentence into new and old information, and so on." Different theories lay different stress on such facts, but in fact they all— except Kuno—end up separating the syntactic nature of constructions from the nonsyntactic factors with which the syntax interacts. This is the explicit strategy of RG, as Perlmutter says: ". . . the syntactic constructions utilized by particular languages are characterizable in syntactic terms independently of the semantic, pragmatic, discourse, etc. conditions under which they will be used in one language or another." Mc-Cawley also claims that all ill-formed discourse can be viewed as having a sentence or sentences that are ill-formed relative to the particular discourse context, thus reducing the question of discourse well-formedness back to sentential well-formedness. Whether this strategy succeeds or not, at least in these papers there is nothing substantive or new said about the structure of discourse.

10. GENERAL CONCLUSIONS, IF ANY

If these papers are representative, the direction of current syntactic research is unarguably toward nonabstract syntax, direct generation of surface strings, and interpretive semantics. The conspicuous exception is RG, which is more abstract than any of its predecessors or contemporaries. At the same time, there is considerable resistance to syntactic formalism as explanation of constraints: Witness Kuno's, Dik's, and Van Valin and Foley's eloquent defenses of functional and pragmatic considerations in syntax. I am not willing to conclude that syntax is healthy, but it is at least alive and struggling.

REFERENCES

Anderson, S. R., and Chung, S. (1977). On grammatical relations and clause structure in verb-initial languages. In P. Cole and J. M. Sadock (Eds.), *Syntax and semantics, 8: Grammatical relations*. New York: Academic Press. Pp. 1–25.

Bartsch, R., and Vennemann, T. (1972). *Semantic structures: A study in the relation between semantics and syntax*. Frankfurt: Athenäum.

Brame, M. K. (1978). *Base generated syntax*. Seattle: Noit Amrofer.

Chung, S. (1976). An object-creating rule in Bahasa Indonesia. *Linguistic Inquiry, 7*, 41–87.

Gleitman, L. R., and Gleitman, H. (1970). *Phrase and paraphrase: Some innovative uses of language*. New York: Norton.

Kac, M. B. (1975). Autonomous linguistics and psycholinguistics. *Minnesota Working Papers in Linguistics and Philosophy of Language, 2*, 42–47.

Keenan, E. L. (1976). Towards a universal definition of 'subject'. In C. Li (Ed.), *Subject and Topic*. New York: Academic Press. Pp. 303–333.

Keenan, E., and Faltz, L. M. (1978). Logical types for natural language. *UCLA Occasional Papers in Linguistics,* No. 3.

Li, C., and Thompson, S. A. (1976). Subject and topic: A new typology of language. In C. Li (Ed.), *Subject and topic*. New York: Academic Press. Pp. 457–489.

Ross, J. R. (1974). Three batons for cognitive psychology. In W. B. Weimer and D. S.

Palermo (Eds.), *Cognition and the symbolic processes*. Hillsdale, N.J.: Lawrence Erlbaum. Pp. 63–124.

Sheldon, A. (1979). Assumptions, methods, and goals in language acquisition research. In F. R. Eckman and A. J. Hustings (Eds.), *Studies in first and second language acquisition*. Rowley, Mass.: Newbury House Publishers. Pp. 1–16.

Vennemann, T., and Harlow, R. (1977). Categorial grammar and consistent basic VX serialization. *Theoretical Linguistics*, 4, 227–254.

EPILOGUE: AN ASSESSMENT

JESSICA R. WIRTH

University of Wisconsin—Milwaukee

The conference seemed to be quite successful as a meeting. It is none-theless worth reflecting on the intended goal and whether it was in fact achieved, and if not, what was learned from the conference and what should be done in the future.

The ideal result of a conference like this would be that its participants, and the readers of the subsequent volume, would come away able to say, point by point, exactly how each approach differs from the other in respect to the goals pursued, the facts to be investigated, and the particular claims implied by the descriptive mechanisms utilized, and would thus know which approaches are genuinely competing theories, and which are not. For example, in the ideal case it would be possible for us to say with certainty that Kuno's functional grammar and Montague grammar are in general agreement about what constitutes a linguistic fact to be dealt with, but that the descriptive mechanisms they use are incompatible because they embody contradictory claims about the types of languages to be found in the world: that Montague grammar, by virtue of having no de-scriptive apparatus to describe "focus" and "topic" phenomena, em-bodies a claim that no languages have syntactically realized pragmatic structure, that is, that no languages require for sentences to be well formed and meaningful that the sentences exhibit any overt realizations (through

383

Syntax and Semantics, Volume 13:
Current Approaches to Syntax

word order preference, morphological marking, etc.) of topic–focus structure; and that Kuno's model, by virtue of having such descriptive terms, embodies the contradictory claim that there are languages that have syntactically realized pragmatic structure (i.e., where a necessary condition for well-formedness and meaningfulness of sentences is an overt realization of topic–focus structure). Or, it would be an ideal result if we could say with certainty, for example, that their descriptive mechanisms are in a contrary relation (not both true, but both possibly false) on this point: that Montague grammar implies that no languages have syntactically realized pragmatic structure, whereas Kuno's functional grammar claims that all languages have syntactically realized pragmatic structure. If we could be certain that the two approaches were in fact incompatible on this point we would be in a much better position to evaluate each and accept one or reject one or both. Or, if we could say, with certainty, that Montague grammar IS consistent with the claim that there are languages with syntactically realized pragmatic structure, then some kind of collaboration could take place between practitioners of both approaches in an effort to identify just the right categories of units that would simultaneously allow characterization of the well-formedness of sentences as well as the semantic (truth-conditional) and pragmatic (topic-focus) properties of sentences. The guidelines that we sent to the authors (Appendix, pp. 387–392) constituted our attempt to ensure that the conference would achieve the ideal result.

What did the conference in fact achieve? As often happens, the actual result does not match the ideal, but it is fair to say that it moved us a step toward the ideal result, by provoking thought about what can constitute substantive similarities and differences between approaches, as well as giving us a glimpse at the apparent similarities and differences between currently practiced approaches.

The conference, and this volume, have not yielded the desired point-by-point understanding of the differences among all the approaches viewed, for a variety of reasons having to do with practical problems, human nature, and the state of the art. The practical problems are the limitations on time of presentation and discussion in the conference and the much more severe limitations on space in the book which prevent the authors from going into detail on every point raised in the set of issues. Human nature comes in because people's own creativity will not, apparently, be suppressed: For some, to be given a framework in advance and to be asked to follow it is perhaps equivalent to being shackled in chains and is thus to be resisted at all costs; or perhaps we organizers were not as tyrannical as we should have been. However, the most important reason for the lack of the point-by-point comparison with respect to compatibility is, I believe, due to the state of the field. The distinction made by Perlmutter (this volume, p. 196) between theories and frameworks is useful here: Whereas theories are falsifiable, frameworks are probably not, for they simply offer concepts that may prove useful in a theory, and they are characteristically rather vague. This could be elaborated further to say that frameworks do not constrain the set of actual claims to be made by the theory but rather only suggest some aspects of a language in which at least some claims of a theory may profitably be couched. So for example, Montague grammar as a framework suggests that if a theory contains statements that make use of syntactic categories that are drawn up from a look at the semantics (truth-conditions) of a language, then that theory will likely help to provide us with a description of language that will suit our purposes; but it suggests nothing about whether such a theory should consist exclusively of such types of statements, or could also contain statements which make use of categories drawn from a look at other (e.g., pragmatic) aspects of language. It consequently does not imply that there is no language with syntactic reflexes of pragmatic structure, nor does it imply that there are such languages; thus Montague grammar cannot be determined to be incompatible with Kuno's functional grammar on this point. Similar considerations explain our uncertainty about whether functional grammar says that all or only some languages have syntactic reflexes of pragmatic structure. Probably most of the approaches represented at the conference and in this volume are primarily frameworks in this sense and contain only partially articulated theories. Hence the difficulty in identifying whether they make empirically distinct claims about language.

The conference, and this volume, have yielded some progress toward the ideal result, however. The atmosphere of the conference was generally one of willingness to share thoughts and offer criticism in a friendly manner, conducive to communication between proponents of different approaches and in striking contrast to the hostilities of the late 1960s and early 1970s. Thus the conference helped to establish some lines of communication between parties who otherwise may not have listened to one another, although at times the goodwill diverted attention from attempting genuine evaluation of different approaches. In addition, the very existence of a collection that explicitly concerns itself with how approaches might differ and offers a set of brief outlines of a number of selected approaches provides an initial impetus for undertaking extended serious comparison and evaluation. Moreover, Stockwell's summary paper brings us a step closer by offering comparisons on a number of parameters, mostly parameters along which the descriptive mechanisms differ. The bringing together of the points of comparison of the mechanisms provides us with a basis for assessing whether the different approaches make compatible, contradictory, or contrary claims about language. For example, Stockwell points out that whereas in relational grammar grammatical relations, particularly the notion "subject of," are primitives, in role and reference grammar the subject is derived, the result of the interaction of several factors. This provides the basis for the next question, which is, does this difference between derived subject and primitive subject mean that relational grammar and role and reference grammar are empirically incompatible, that relational grammar implies that there exist some language types that role and reference grammar says do not exist? An answer to this question will be one of the types of results we have sought.

However, it is apparent that the answer to questions like this will not be immediately forthcoming. It is entirely possible that both systems of grammar could describe the same set of language types despite the difference in derived versus primitive status of subject; and it is equally possible that the primitive versus derived status of subjects countenanced by the two approaches imply, together with the other statements in the theories, contradictory or contrary claims about languages. Returning again to the distinction between theory and framework, what is necessary in addition to systematic comparisons of the overt points of difference and similarity between approaches is fuller, more complete articulation of the theories suggested by the frameworks. Only then will it be possible to identify the boundaries that each theory places on the set of languages or language types that it countenances, and only then will it be possible to ascertain whether two theories are compatible or not with respect to the empirical statements they make.

What conclusions can be drawn from the conference to abet future research? Continued work on more complete articulation of each theory is clearly in order, to facilitate substantive comparisons and fruitful evaluation of the theories. And this is best done not in isolation from one another, but through continuing communication with one another.

We urge that the lines of communication indeed continue to remain open between proponents of the various approaches, and we hope that the conference and this book have provided an initial basis and some stimulus for continued, useful comparison and evaluation of the numerous approaches to syntax, including not only the approaches represented in this volume, but other approaches to syntax as well.

APPENDIX: BASIC ISSUES AND SAMPLE SENTENCES

Several of the papers included in this volume make reference to the "set of basic issues" and "sample sentences" that were provided by the organizers of the conference for contributors to follow in order to make the various approaches easily comparable. These guidelines were included in a letter which was sent to speakers of the conference a few months before the event was to take place and which read as follows.

1. INTRODUCTION

In order to ensure comparability among presentations at the Conference on Current Approaches to Syntax, we have attempted to systematically enumerate a set of basic questions which we would like to ask you to discuss in your paper. We hope each question is significant in that each defines a logically possible parameter along which syntactic approaches can differ from each other (whether substantively or formally), and that the list is comprehensive in that there is in fact no way for syntactic approaches to differ that would not in some form be touched upon. Should you, however, find that there are dimensions of variability for

Syntax and Semantics, Volume 13:
Current Approaches to Syntax

syntactic approaches that have escaped us, we would appreciate hearing about them.

In discussing most of the questions on the list, we feel it would be important for you to distinguish between accidental and essential characteristics of the approach you will be presenting. For example, the standard theory of transformational generative grammar can be characterized by saying that it is a sentence grammar where transformations do not change meaning. There is, however, an important difference in status between these two characteristics. Whereas the constraint that transformations do not change meaning is an explicitly claimed essential property which follows from other features of the theory, the fact that most actual grammars written according to this theory have been sentence grammars appears to be an accident—nothing in the theory seems to require this choice of domain, and phrase or discourse grammars could also be constructed within the framework of this approach without requiring major changes in other aspects of the theory. The reason why drawing such a distinction between accidental and essential properties seems important is that only by keeping this distinction in view can one decide if two theories are contradictory or compatible, the establishment of which is one of the goals of the conference. Thus, for instance, there would be no point in concluding that standard theory and tagmemics are "competing theories" because the former provides for sentence grammars and the latter provides for discourse grammars—rather, this difference is only an accidental one and thus, were this the only distinction between the two approaches, they would be combinable. On the other hand, standard theory and extended standard theory are true competitors, at least in a formal sense, since they differ in the essential feature of transformations being meaning-preserving or meaning-changing.

In addition to the list of issues, we are also enclosing a short set of English sentences. We would like to ask you to append to your paper a grammar for these data constructed in terms of your approach, as well as a demonstration of how the grammar can be used (e.g., a "sentence derivation") for Sentence 4, *The duckling was killed by the farmer.* The purpose of this little grammar is intended to be twofold. First, it should give the reader an idea of what grammars and sentence derivations "look like" in each approach—that is, give him a feel for the basic mechanics of the approach. Second, we also hope that it will be possible for you to highlight at least one of the important features of your approach in writing these grammars. We tried to construct the sentence list so as to include a couple of the "crucial" construction types for each approach where this seemed applicable; but if you feel the list is unfair to your theory, please add one or two other sentences to the basic corpus.

2. THE GOAL OF SYNTAX

2.1. Data

2.1.1. What are your PRIMARY DATA for syntax? Do you make a distinction between syntactic competence and syntactic performance (e.g., between grammaticality and acceptability)? Are your data obtained by (*a*) introspection, (*b*) elicitation, (*c*) experimentation? Are all of these equally legitimate sources of data as you see it? If not, how do they differ?

2.1.2. In what DOMAIN(S) does your syntax operate (i.e., word, phrase, clause, sentence, discourse, or speech act)?

2.1.3. How are CONSTANCY and VARIABILITY within and across languages represented by your approach? For example, how does your approach handle (*a*) idiolectal variation; (*b*) variation according to styles, registers, sociolects, age groups and dialects; (*c*) historical change; (*d*) universal and non-universal similarities among different languages.

2.2. Accounts

2.2.1. To what extent and in what way should SYNTACTIC ACCOUNTS involve (a) describing data (e.g., abbreviating, classifying); (b) predicting data; (c) explaining data?

2.2.2. Is your approach centrally concerned with MEANING–SOUND RELATIONS?

2.2.3. What EMPIRICAL INTERPRETATIONS do you assign to syntactic statements? For example, do you view them as (*a*) serving to delimit the class of ACTUAL HUMAN LANGUAGES within the class of logically possible ones; (*b*) serving to delimit the class of ACTUAL HUMAN PSYCHO-LOGICAL–PHYSIOLOGICAL MECHANISMS within the class of logically possible ones (e.g., modeling speech production, speech comprehension, language acquisition, language deficiencies).

2.2.4. To what PRACTICAL USE, if any, can your type of syntax be put?

2.2.5. What types of SYNTACTIC ARGUMENTS are legitimate within your approach?

2.2.6. Does your approach involve the formulation of GRAMMAR DIS-COVERY PROCEDURES?

2.3. Evaluation

2.3.1. Is it possible to construct within your approach more than one grammar for a set of data? Do you assume that there is only one CORRECT GRAMMAR for each set of data and if so, what goals and criteria are used to evaluate competing grammars?

2.3.2. Do you assume that there is only one CORRECT APPROACH to syntax? If so, what goals and criteria would you use to select this optimal approach from among a set of alternative approaches?

3. THE ORGANIZATION OF SYNTAX

3.1. Levels of Syntactic Representation

Is there more than one level of syntactic representation assumed in your approach (e.g., "surface structure," "deep structure," "semantic representation," "shallow structure")? If so, do they differ in significance and exactly how?

3.2. The Nature of Syntactic Statements

3.2.1. What types of TERMS figure in syntactic generalizations according to your approach? (e.g., categories (Noun), features (+Animate); constants (particular lexical items), variables (X); semantic terms (Animate), syntactic terms (Neuter))

3.2.2. What types of RELATIONS among terms figure in your syntactic generalizations? (e.g., "member of," "part of," "sister of," "daughter of," "head of," "modifier of," "dependent on," "interdependent with," "subject of," "object of," "temporally adjacent to," "temporally precedent to," "simultaneous with," "syntagmatically related to," "paradigmatically related to," "semantically associated with")

3.2.3. What is the EFFECT of your syntactic statements? Are they positively or negatively stated? Would you describe them as any of the following:

1. "Rules" [such as "formation rules" (e.g., phrase structure rules), or "transformational rules" (additions, deletions, substitutions)]
2. "Constraints on individual syntactic representations" (or "filters," "output constraints," "well-formedness conditions")
3. "Constraints on syntactic derivations" (or "global/derivational constraints")
4. "Constraints on sets of syntactic derivations" (or "transderivational constraints")
5. "Principles"
6. "Strategies"
7. "Hierarchies"
8. (Other)

Please define the designations that you have chosen. For example, if you say that your approach is a transformational one, in what sense are your syntactic statements transformations? And if you say it is not a transformational one, then exactly how do your statements differ from transformations?

3.2.4. Are there any explicit CONSTRAINTS imposed upon the nature of syntactic statements? If so, what are they? For example, if the approach is a transformational one in that there are processes of change taking place in the course of a syntactic derivation, which aspects, if any, of syntactic representations are allowed to be subject to such derivational changes and which aspects are stipulated to remain invariant (e.g., some terms, or some relations such as grammatical relations or order of constituents)?

3.3. How Is Syntax Used?

3.3.1. Is the concept SYNTACTIC DERIVATION applicable in some sense of this term?

3.3.2. Is there a distinction made between OBLIGATORY AND OPTIONAL rules? If so, in what sense; and is there any general way of predicting the obligatory–optional status of a rule?

3.3.3. Is the ORDER in which rules are applied crucial? If so, in what sense; and is there any general way of determining the proper order of the use of rules?

3.3.4. If your approach involves process-statements, what determines the DIRECTIONALITY of these (e.g., whether a phrase structure rule is used to analyse or to synthesize; or whether a transformational rule is used to map A into B or B into A)?

3.4. The Place of Syntax within the Total Grammar

3.4.1. What is the relationship between SYNTAX AND SEMANTICS? In particular, how do you envisage the meanings of sentences to be represented in a grammar?

3.4.2. What is the relationship between SYNTAX AND OTHER ASPECTS of a grammar, such as (*a*) pragmatic/speech act theory, (*b*) lexicon, (*c*) morphology, (*d*) phonology–phonetics?

3.5. The Form of Syntax

Does your approach involve statements cast in some formal language distinct from everyday discourse style? If so, is the formalism empirically significant? If not, is your syntax formalizable in principle and is it considered desirable that it be formalized?

4. THE SIGNIFICANCE OF YOUR APPROACH

4.1. Of the various claims that are made by your approach, which ones do you consider the MOST SIGNIFICANT AND MOST DISTINCTIVE (whether pertaining to particular syntactic constructions or to the general nature of language)?

4.2. Which aspects of your approach are EMPIRICALLY FALSIFIABLE and which are not? Exactly what evidence would falsify your approach? Is it possible to cite an example of a logically conceivable human language (or a logically conceivable human psychological–physiological mechanism) that your approach correctly excludes as not actually occurrent? What would it take to further increase the falsifiability of your approach?

4.3. Exactly how would you characterize the relationship of your syntactic approach to OTHER ONES that you are familiar with? Are there any aspects of your approach that render it (*a*) competitive, (*b*) superior, (*c*) inferior, (*d*) combinable with other approaches? Exactly what are these aspects?

4.4. What are PROBLEM AREAS for your approach—areas where future research appears necessary?

5. DATA FOR THE SAMPLE GRAMMAR

1. *The woman walked.*
2. *Every woman walked.*
3. *The farmer killed the duckling.*
4. *The duckling was killed by the farmer.*
5. *Who killed the duckling?*
6. *A farmer killed every duckling.*
7. *John killed a duckling with an axe.*
8. *The woman believed that John killed the farmer.*
9. *The woman believed John to have killed the farmer.*
10. *The woman believed the farmer to have been killed by John.*
11. *The farmer was believed by the woman to have been killed by John.*
12. *The farmer gave the axe to John.*
13. *The farmer gave John the axe.*
14. *The axe killed the duckling that John loved.*
15. *John killed the woman and Bill, the farmer.*
16. *John loved the woman and he killed the farmer.*
17. *John loved the woman and killed the farmer.*

INDEX OF LANGUAGES*

* Indexes prepared by Cynthia Plaumann, University Wisconsin–Milwaukee.

INDEX OF NAMES

INDEX OF TERMS

399

CONTENTS OF PREVIOUS VOLUMES

Contents of Previous Volumes